MANCHESTER MEDIEVAL LITERATURE AND CULTURE

Bestsellers and masterpieces

Manchester University Press

Series editors: Anke Bernau, David Matthews and James Paz

Series founded by: J. J. Anderson and Gail Ashton

Advisory board: Ruth Evans, Patricia C. Ingham, Andrew James Johnston, Chris Jones, Catherine Karkov, Nicola McDonald, Haruko Momma, Susan Phillips, Sarah Salih, Larry Scanlon, Stephanie Trigg and Matthew Vernon

MANCHESTER MEDIEVAL LITERATURE AND CULTURE

Manchester Medieval Literature and Culture publishes monographs and essay collections comprising new research informed by current critical methodologies on the literary cultures of the global Middle Ages. We are interested in all periods, from the early Middle Ages through to the late, and we include post-medieval engagements with and representations of the medieval period (or 'medievalism'). 'Literature' is taken in a broad sense, to include the many different medieval genres: imaginative, historical, political, scientific and religious.

Titles available in the series

35. *Harley manuscript geographies: Literary history and the medieval miscellany*
    Daniel Birkholz
36. *Play time: Gender, anti-Semitism and temporality in medieval biblical drama*
    Daisy Black
37. *Transfiguring medievalism: Poetry, attention and the mysteries of the body*
    Cary Howie
38. *Objects of affection: The book and the household in late medieval England*
    Myra Seaman
39. *The gift of narrative in medieval England*
    Nicholas Perkins
40. *Sleep and its spaces in Middle English literature: Emotions, ethics, dreams*
    Megan G. Leitch
41. *Encountering The Book of Margery Kempe*
    Laura Kalas and Laura Varnam (eds)
42. *The narrative grotesque in medieval Scottish poetry*
    Caitlin Flynn
43. *Painful pleasures: Sadomasochism in medieval cultures*
    Christopher Vaccaro (ed.)

Bestsellers and masterpieces

The changing medieval canon

Edited by Heather Blurton and
Dwight F. Reynolds

Manchester University Press

Published by Manchester University Press
Oxford Road, Manchester M13 9PL

www.manchesteruniversitypress.co.uk

British Library Cataloguing-in-Publication Data
A catalogue record for this book is available from the British Library

ISBN 978 1 5261 4748 6 hardback
ISBN 978 1 5261 7877 0 paperback

First published 2022

Typeset
by New Best-set Typesetters Ltd

Contents

List of contributors *page* vii
Acknowledgements xi

Introduction – Heather Blurton and Dwight F. Reynolds 1

Part I: Hanging by a thread: unique manuscripts and their place in the 'modern' medieval canon

1. Contemplating books with Usāma ibn Munqidh's *Book of Contemplation* – Paul M. Cobb 23
2. Dons and dragons: *Beowulf* and 'popular reading' – Daniel C. Remein and Erica Weaver 49
3. Ibn Ḥazm's *Ṭawq al-ḥamāma* (*The Neck-Ring of the Dove*) – Boris Liebrenz 79
4. 'Thirty pieces of silver': interpreting anti-Jewish imagery in the *Poema de mio Cid* manuscript – Ryan D. Giles 113
5. 'Let no bad song be sung of us': fame, memory and transmission in/and the *Chanson de Roland* – Sharon Kinoshita 140

Part II: Medieval bestsellers: reading the 'medieval canon'?

6. World literature and its discontents: reading the Life of Aḥīqar – Daniel L. Selden 169

7. The Alexander Romance in the age of scribal reproduction: the aesthetics and precariousness of a popular text – Shamma Boyarin 199
8. Wisdom literature and medieval bestsellers – Karla Mallette 215
9. Lost worlds: encyclopaedism and riddles in the tale of Tawaddud/Theodor – Christine Chism 234

Index 262

Contributors

Heather Blurton is Professor of English at the University of California, Santa Barbara. Among her publications are *Cannibalism in High Medieval English Literature* (2007), *The Critics and the Prioress: Antisemitism, Criticism, and Chaucer's* Prioress's Tale (with Hannah R. Johnson, 2017) and *Inventing William of Norwich: Thomas of Monmouth, Antisemitism, and Literary Culture, 1150–1200* (forthcoming).

Shamma Boyarin is an Assistant Professor in the English Department at the University of Victoria. He is also appointed to the Religion, Culture and Society Program. His research and teaching interests span medieval Hebrew and Arabic literature and the intersection of religion, and pop culture – with a special focus on heavy metal. His most recent publication is 'The New Metal Medievalism: Alexander the Great, Islamic Historiography and Nile's "Iskander Dhul Kharnon"', in Ruth Barratt-Peacock and Ross Hagen (eds), *Medievalism and Metal Music Studies: Throwing Down the Gauntlet* (2019).

Christine Chism joined the faculty of UCLA in 2009. Her research and teaching situate England amid Mediterranean, Asian and African circuits of encounter, violence and transmission. Since completing her first book, *Alliterative Revivals* (2002), she has edited the second volume of the five-volume Wiley Blackwell *Companion to*

World Literature, CE 600–1500 (2019), and is revising a book on medieval friendship. Other current projects include Arabic and European travel narratives, and the Middle English and Arabic Alexander romances.

Paul M. Cobb is the Edmund J. and Louise W. Kahn Term Professor of Near Eastern Languages and Civilizations at the University of Pennsylvania. He is the author of *Usama ibn Munqidh: Warrior-Poet of the Age of Crusades* (2005) and the translator of Usama's *Book of Contemplation* (2008). His most recent book is *The Race for Paradise: An Islamic History of the Crusades* (2014).

Ryan D. Giles is Professor in the Department of Spanish and Portuguese at Indiana University, Bloomington. He is the author of *The Laughter of the Saints: Parodies of Holiness in Late Medieval and Renaissance Spain* (2009) and *Inscribed Power: Amulets and Magic in Early Spanish Literature* (2017). He is the co-editor of four volumes, most recently with E. Michael Gerli, *The Routledge Hispanic Studies Companion to Medieval Iberia: Unity in Diversity* (2021), and with José Manuel Hidalgo, *A New Companion to the 'Libro de buen amor'* (2021).

Sharon Kinoshita is Professor of Literature at the University of California, Santa Cruz, specialising in medieval French literature, Mediterranean studies and the Global Middle Ages. Among her publications are *Medieval Boundaries: Rethinking Difference in Old French Literature* (2006), co-authored books on Chrétien de Troyes (2011) and Marie de France (2012), and two co-edited volumes: the Wiley-Blackwell *Companion to Mediterranean History* (with Peregrine Horden, 2014) and *Can We Talk Mediterranean?* (with Brian Catlos, 2017). She has translated Marco Polo's *Description of the World* (2016) and is currently completing a volume on Marco Polo for the Reaktion Press series Medieval Lives.

Boris Liebrenz studied history and Arabic philology at Leipzig University and is a research fellow at the Bibliotheca Arabica project at the Saxon Academy of Sciences and Humanities. His publications explore documentary and manuscript sources from several eras, from early Arabic papyri to eighteenth-century merchant letters.

His second book, *Die Rifā'īya aus Damaskus* (2016), was awarded the *Annemarie Schimmel Research Prize* in 2017. Recent projects include *The* Waqf *of a Physician in Late Mamluk Damascus* (2019) and *The Notebook of Kamāl al-Dīn the Weaver: Aleppine Notes from the End of the 16th Century* (with Kristina Richardson, 2021).

Karla Mallette is Professor of Italian in the Department of Romance Languages and Literatures and Professor of Mediterranean Studies in the Department of Middle East Studies at the University of Michigan. She is the author of *The Kingdom of Sicily, 1100–1250: A Literary History* (2005), *European Modernity and the Arab Mediterranean* (2010) and *Lives of the Great Languages: Latin and Arabic in the Medieval Mediterranean* (2021), and co-editor of *A Sea of Languages: Rethinking the Arabic Role in Medieval Literary History* (2013). She has written numerous articles on medieval literature and Mediterranean studies.

Daniel C. Remein is Associate Professor of English at the University of Massachusetts Boston where he teaches medieval literature and poetics. He is currently completing a book, *The Heat of Beowulf*, exploring an alternative trajectory for the study of *Beowulf*'s aesthetics that emerges from the encounters of twentieth-century poets Robin Blaser and Jack Spicer with that poem and the genealogies of its study at mid-century. He is also the co-editor, with Erica Weaver, of *Dating Beowulf: Studies in Intimacy* (2020), and the author of a collection of poems, *A Treatise on the marvelous for prestigious museums* (2018).

Dwight F. Reynolds is Professor of Arabic Language and Literature at the University of California, Santa Barbara. He is author of *Heroic Poets, Poetic Heroes: The Ethnography of Performance in an Arabic Oral Epic Tradition* (1995), *Arab Folklore* (2007), *The Musical Heritage of al-Andalus* (2021) and *Medieval Arab Music and Musicians* (2022), as well as editor and co-author of *Interpreting the Self: Autobiography in the Arabic Literary Tradition* (2001), *The Cambridge Companion to Modern Arab Culture* (2005), and co-editor of *The Garland Encyclopedia of World Music, Volume 6: The Middle East* (2002) with Virginia Danielson and Scott Marcus.

Daniel L. Selden is Research Professor of Literature at the University of California, Santa Cruz. He holds a doctoral degree in comparative literature from Yale and taught at Columbia University and Stanford before joining the Literature Faculty at Santa Cruz. A former Getty Scholar and Fellow of St John's College, Cambridge, he is currently completing a book on the Alexander Romance.

Erica Weaver is Assistant Professor of English at the University of California, Los Angeles, where she is currently finishing a book about the role of distraction in the development of early medieval literature and literary theory, particularly during the tenth-century monastic 'correction' movement traditionally known as the English Benedictine Reform. She is also co-editor, with A. Joseph McMullen, of *The Legacy of Boethius in Medieval England: The Consolation and its Afterlives* (2018) and, with Daniel C. Remein, of *Dating Beowulf: Studies in Intimacy* (2020).

Acknowledgements

The earliest conversations on the topic of *Bestsellers and masterpieces: The changing medieval canon* took place during a National Endowment for the Humanities Summer Institute in 2015, 'Negotiating Identities: Expression and Representation in the Christian-Jewish-Muslim Mediterranean', led by Brian Catlos and Sharon Kinoshita. Our first thanks are due to them and the other participants in that seminar (although any views, findings, conclusions or recommendations expressed in this book do not necessarily reflect those of the National Endowment for the Humanities). We are grateful for our conversations with Shamma Boyarin, Christine Chism, Paul Cobb, Matthew Fisher, Sharon Kinoshita, Elias Muhanna and Daniel Selden. Thanks are also due to the UC Santa Barbara Interdisciplinary Humanities Center, College of Letters and Science, Center for Middle Eastern Studies, Medieval Studies Program and Department of English for their support of this project. Finally, heartfelt thanks are due to Meredith Carroll of Manchester University Press for her patience and guidance, as well as to the external reader who provided such helpful critiques of the early draft of the manuscript.

Introduction

Heather Blurton and Dwight F. Reynolds

Bestsellers and masterpieces: The changing medieval canon takes as its starting point a paradox in the modern study of medieval European and Arabic literature: On the one hand, many of what are now the most widely studied and highly appreciated works of medieval literature have survived in a single copy, a *unicum* manuscript; while on the other hand, many texts that are attested in numerous manuscripts and were translated into multiple languages are rarely studied, taught or even mentioned in modern scholarship and are almost entirely absent from anthologies of medieval literature. Although the number of surviving manuscripts is not a precise measure of popularity or readership, texts that survive in a single copy, in the absence of other evidence, presumably circulated less widely and were less commonly read than texts that have survived in dozens of manuscripts and that were translated into diverse languages. How is it that texts that appear *not* to have been widely read or owned in the Middle Ages have become so central to the modern study of medieval literature, while other texts that circulated widely are now all but ignored? The two terms that we use in the title of this volume to describe this phenomenon – 'bestsellers' and 'masterpieces' – are admittedly anachronistic, and they take on meaning only in hindsight. They do not account for indexes of popularity beyond manuscript survival and, importantly, they do not account for oral circulation. We intend the terms 'bestseller' and 'masterpiece', therefore, as a provocation, rather than a description, and one that motivates us to re-evaluate this shared paradoxical situation in the history of the fields of medieval European and Arabic literature.

The most dramatic demonstration of this disparity can be found in the surprising number of medieval texts now regarded as 'masterpieces' that have survived in but one exemplum. On the European side this list includes *Beowulf*, *Sir Gawain and the Green Knight*, *The Book of Margery Kempe*, the Oxford *Song of Roland*, *Hildebrandslied*, *El Poema de mio Cid*, Sir Thomas Malory's *Le Morte d'Arthur*, *Pearl* and others, a list that could function almost on its own as a standard undergraduate survey of European medieval literature. On the Arabic side notable examples include Ibn Ḥazm's *Ṭawq al-ḥamāma* [*The Neck-Ring of the Dove*], Usāma ibn Munqidh's *Kitāb al-I'tibār* [the 'memoirs' of Usāma ibn Munqidh] and 'Abd Allāh Ibn Buluggīn's *Kitāb al-Tibyān* [*The Autobiography of Ibn Buluggīn*], works that possess a status in the study of Arabic literature comparable to that of the European examples cited above.

In contrast, many of the texts that circulated most widely and were most frequently read, copied and appreciated in the Middle Ages are not central to the modern canons of medieval literature. Consider, for example, the case of Middle English literature: *The Prick of Conscience*, an early fourteenth-century work, is by far the best-attested Middle English poem, surviving in over 120 manuscripts, almost twice as many as *The Canterbury Tales*. Its popularity is further attested by the famous stained-glass window in the parish church of All Saints North Street in York, which illustrates apocalyptic scenes captioned with lines from the poem. As its most recent editor notes, 'This fact is cited as evidence of the poem's popularity, and *The Prick of Conscience* makes a cameo appearance in most histories of Middle English literature. Even so, one looks in vain even for extracts from it in the major anthologies of Middle English.'[1] A similarly popular medieval English work is the Middle English *Brut*, a legendary history of Britain, which exists in so many recensions that our understanding of its textual history is still evolving. If *The Prick of Conscience* wins the contest for the most popular Middle English poem, the prose *Brut* edges it out with over 180 extant manuscript witnesses, making it second only to the Wycliffite Bible.[2] In the case of *The Prick of Conscience*, its fall from favour may be due to changes in taste, as a result of which the devotional literature that has left such a huge mark on the Western European medieval manuscript record simply no longer appeals to contemporary – or even post-Reformation – readers. It is more difficult, however, to understand why the *Brut* should have fallen into anonymity, since it includes the stories of King Arthur as well as King Lear and embodies that unique intersection of history and romance that made *Game of Thrones* a global cultural phenomenon.

Indeed, romance is perhaps the most prolific and enduring of medieval genres – and the trajectory of how the stories of King Arthur and the knights of the round table came over the course of the nineteenth century to be thought of primarily as children's literature is one we should keep in mind. The group of romances that take as their hero Alexander the Great, for example, were, as Daniel Selden has noted, 'the single most popular narrative for roughly a millennium and a half, in effect a protean network of interrelated texts disseminated over massive tracts of Asia, Africa and Europe'.[3] Although its reach is certainly exceptional, the Alexander Romance is not alone – the romance of Bevis of Hampton, originally composed in the twelfth century in Anglo-Norman, the dialect of French peculiar to England, was translated into English, French, Dutch, Venetian, Romanian, Russian, Polish, Serbo-Croat, Irish, Welsh, Old Norse and Yiddish. As with Alexander, the geographical distribution of translations of Bevis's adventures nearly map the itinerary of the hero. Bevis's escapades feature dragons, lions, giants and pirates as well as true love, and yet, like the Alexander Romance and any number of similar – and popular – medieval romances, it is rarely taught to undergraduates today. Instead, a typical undergraduate survey of Western medieval literature is more likely to feature texts that are extant in only one copy and that seem not to have been popular in their own day. This is not exclusively the case, of course, and Geoffrey Chaucer is, as ever, the exception that proves the rule, along with William Langland and John Gower.[4] Bracketing these three, however, the typical syllabus might include texts such as *Beowulf*, *Sir Gawain and the Green Knight*, *Pearl* and *The Book of Margery Kempe* – all of which survive in a single manuscript exemplar. No doubt some of this has to do with the exigencies of manuscript survival, but tellingly, these texts do not seem to have been widely read at the time. *Beowulf*, for example, mentions other heroes of the Germanic story-world, such as Siegfried and Ingeld, but no other texts return the favour: no other epic mentions a great hero and dragon-slayer called Beowulf. *Beowulf*'s survival may actually be due to the fact that the eleventh-century manuscript in which it is extant also contains a version of the Alexander material – the Old English *Letter of Alexander to Aristotle.* Instead of Alexander, however, the most common representative of romance on our syllabuses is *Sir Gawain and the Green Knight*, a poem that exists only in Middle English and whose hero traces a still-recognisable path through the geography of Wales. Gawain fights no battles, slays no dragons. Instead, he lies in bed, wrestles with his conscience, and tries not to have sex.

In Arabic literature we find a similar pattern of *unica* manuscripts achieving canonical status among modern scholars and readers. The 'memoirs' of Usāma ibn Munqidh (more properly, *The Book of Contemplation*) were only discovered in the late nineteenth century in a single incomplete manuscript in the Escorial Library in Spain, and yet it is now one of the most widely read works of Arabic literature. The sole copy of Ibn Ḥazm's manual on love, *The Neck-Ring of the Dove*, another of the most widely read Arabic works, sat ignored on a shelf in the library of Leiden for two and a half centuries before suddenly attracting the attention of a scholar who was not even an Arabist by training. The unique manuscript of the autobiography of the last Zirid emir of Granada (d. after 1094) was discovered by chance by Évariste Lévi-Provençal in the library of the al-Qarawiyyin mosque in Fez in the 1930s, and the single copy of the collected poems of Ibn Zamrak (d. 1393), the poet whose verses grace the walls of the Alhambra, recently materialised in a private collection in Tunisia after having been lost for nearly half a millennium.[5]

The role that Western scholars have played in selecting which medieval Arabic texts have been edited, published, translated and hailed as 'masterpieces' is nowhere more evident than in the astonishing history of *The Thousand and One Nights.* The French scholar Antoine Galland spent over fifteen years in Istanbul and neighbouring regions in the seventeenth century. During that time, however, he appears never to have heard of the *Nights* or encountered a copy. After his return to France, he somehow became aware of its existence and obtained a manuscript that contained 282 nights and broke off in the middle of the tale of Qamar al-Zaman. The French fairy tales (*contes de fées*) of Madame D'Aulnoy, Charles

Perrault and others were all the rage in Paris at this time, so Galland decided to translate the Arabic manuscript of the *Nights*, freehandedly reorganising the tales and inserting additional materials. The *Nights* grew so popular that his publisher pressured him to add to the collection, which he did, though he rather dishonestly passed off these new tales as being part of the Arabic manuscript. The work became an immediate bestseller in the West and was translated into multiple languages from Galland's French translation. During the nineteenth and twentieth centuries scholars searched feverishly for a 'complete' Arabic manuscript, which was of course never to be found, since Galland's text had surreptitiously incorporated materials from other sources.

The fame of the *Nights* as a masterpiece of Arabic literature in the West led to its 're-translation' back into Arabic, including the materials that had never formed part of the medieval Arabic text. Eventually, several other Arabic and Turkish manuscripts were discovered, so the *Nights* does not fall strictly into the category of a *unicum* manuscript. However, a collection of medieval Arabic tales was plucked from near obscurity by a single Western scholar, Antoine Galland, and catapulted into global fame, not only influencing the path of Western literature but also generating a myriad of stereotypes about the Middle East.[6] Similar to Galland's role in turning *The Thousand and One Nights* into a global phenomenon, several of the texts examined in this volume were rocketed to fame through the efforts of individual scholars.

In contrast, the work of Arabic fiction that was most widely read, copied, owned, memorised and illustrated in the Middle Ages was almost certainly the *Maqāmāt* of al-Ḥarīrī (d. 1122): the author himself claimed to have authorised 700 copies![7] The genre appears to have been invented by al-Hamadhānī (d. 1008) and consisted of a new 'frame' into which old or new anecdotes could be adapted: a naïve and rather gullible narrator travels to different locations or social settings where he invariably encounters the central figure, an unscrupulous but extraordinarily clever con man. The centrepiece of the story is usually an astonishingly eloquent speech of some sort delivered by the scoundrel-hero, after which the long-suffering narrator realises that he has yet again been duped by his nemesis. A century later al-Ḥarīrī adopted this form and imbued it with pyrotechnical displays of erudition, using rare vocabulary and remarkable rhetorical *tours de force*, including a poem in which every verse is a palindrome, a letter that can be read backwards and forwards, riddles and their answers in verse, answers to ninety difficult legal questions, answers to one hundred thorny grammatical problems, poems in which the letters of alternate words do or do not have dots in the Arabic script, etc.[8]

Al-Ḥarīrī's work spawned dozens of imitations during the Middle Ages by other authors not only in Arabic, but also in Hebrew, Persian and Turkish. The very qualities that were most appreciated by its medieval readers, however, have given these remarkable works a reputation for being all but untranslatable, and extremely challenging for students and scholars alike.[9] Though perhaps for different reasons than the Middle English examples cited above, the contrasting cases of *The Thousand and One Nights* and the *Maqāmāt* of al-Ḥarīrī demonstrate a similar pattern of an obscure work transformed and hailed as a 'masterpiece' and a work that was extraordinarily popular in the Middle Ages that has been marginalised in modern scholarship.

Why, then, are texts that survive in dozens of manuscripts such as *The Prick of Conscience* and texts that circulated in multiple languages such as the Alexander Romance, the Arabic-Castilian-Mayan-Tagalog tale of Tawaddud/Teodor, the ancient Hebrew-Syriac-Greek-Armenian *Book of Aseneth*, the Syriac-Armenian-Arabic-Georgian-Turkic-Ethiopic Life of Aḥiqār, the Sanskrit-Arabic-Greek-Georgian-Latin-Catalan-Provençal-German-English *Barlaam and Josaphat*, the Sanskrit-Arabic-Persian-Greek-Latin-French-German-Spanish *Seven Sages*, and other works that commanded impressive readerships in the pre-modern era not accorded a place in the literary canon? And why is it that so many of the texts that have *not* found a place in modern literary canons of medieval literature are precisely those that link the Middle Eastern and European story-worlds? These are not simple questions, but their implications for the study of medieval literature and culture are profound. Those texts that have been rescued from near oblivion and raised to the status of masterpieces of medieval literature clearly possess characteristics that appeal to modern readers and modern literary tastes; but in many cases, they cannot, or at least should not, be presented as *characteristic* of their times. We can obviously study and teach such works for the joy of the texts themselves, but a great deal will be lost if we do not couple that approach with accounts of how these 'orphan texts' become so famous in our own era. Our students should be made aware of the decisive roles that individual scholars and nationalist ideologies have played in creating the reading lists they study. As the chapters by Paul Cobb, Boris Liebrenz, Ryan Giles, Sharon Kinoshita, Daniel Remein and Erica Weaver in this volume show, it would be naïve to assume that those solitary manuscripts that have achieved canonical status in modern times have done so based solely on their literary merits.

On the other hand, one of the conclusions that emerges most clearly from this collection is that there exists a large body of medieval texts that were remarkably popular over centuries and generated multiple versions and translations into other languages, but are not typically included in surveys or anthologies of medieval literature. It seems apparent that one of the reasons for this neglect is that these wandering texts are not perceived as belonging to a national literature, and for all of the advances made in the study of literature in recent decades, and all of the attempts to promulgate more inclusive approaches such as the increasingly popular field of 'world literature' and appeals to the global Middle Ages, the imagined boundaries of national literatures – and the academic departments that house them – still determine to a great extent how and why literature is studied and taught. Perhaps it is time to imagine what a 'counter-canon' composed of medieval texts that circulated widely would look like. We could then challenge our students and ourselves to read comparatively and ask, for example, whether the Oxford Roland is truly so much better than the hundred or so other medieval French *chansons de geste* that it deserves to stand as the sole representative of the genre in the public imagination, while all others languish in near total obscurity? Is the *Chanson de Roland* really a better read, a more compelling text, and/or artistically superior to *Le Charroi de Nîmes*, *La Prise d'Orange* or *Raoul de Cambrai*?

In addition, as Shamma Boyarin, drawing upon Walter Benjamin, argues in this volume, there may be a deep-rooted appeal to *unica* manuscripts as embodiments of *the* authoritative and authentic text – after all, what could be more authoritative than a single extant copy? For eighteenth- and nineteenth-century scholars who devoted their lives to creating manuscript *stemma*, a *unicum* represented a text of almost unassailable purity. Texts such as those studied here by Shamma Boyarin, Christine Chism, Karla Mallette and Daniel

Selden, however, represented for traditional scholars a dizzying kaleidoscope in which no one version can be deemed authoritative and no specific textual incarnation can be imagined to mirror the soul of a single nation or people; their fluidity challenges many modern critical approaches to the study of literature.

The chapters in this collection, by scholars from Western and Middle Eastern medieval studies, examine the processes through which some of the most and least canonical of medieval texts in modern times have achieved that status. Each of the texts studied here has its own complex history and its own intricate story to tell. In some cases, medieval texts have been raised to the status of 'masterpieces' primarily through the intervention of a single scholar who has championed their cause. In other cases, texts have been hailed as masterpieces or completely marginalised based on the judgement of scholars who sought to project the modern concept of 'national literatures' backwards into the Middle Ages: those texts that fitted nationalist agendas have been lionised and incorporated into standard curricula, while those that did not support nationalist claims have been sidelined and ignored. Moreover, although the indebtedness of the early consolidation of a canon of medieval literature in the eighteenth and nineteenth centuries to the ideologies of Romantic nationalism, and the patriotic quest for national epics that might rank alongside those of antiquity, is well known, the implications of this indebtedness for the canon of medieval literature has not greatly affected our scholarly and pedagogical practices. Indeed, it seems highly significant that *Beowulf*, the *Chanson de Roland* and the *Poema de mio Cid* – the 'national epics' of England, France and Spain respectively – each survive in a single copy. As is demonstrated in several of the chapters in this volume, modern scholarship has all but ignored texts that do not have a clear 'national' origin, as well as works of which no one single version can be deemed authoritative. Modern scholarship seems to be intensely uneasy with the fluidity of medieval literature, and yet that very fluidity appears to have been one of the primary characteristics of literary production and consumption during the Middle Ages. Perhaps the modern focus on the individual as a social entity and on individual agency makes it difficult for scholars and readers to engage with texts that are anonymous, not composed by a single known author, and which are transformed, unnervingly, over time, space and across languages. As the second half of this volume shows, these were characteristics shared by a large body of medieval literature.

In several recent publications, however, a number of scholars have begun to explore new approaches to texts that travelled widely and were translated into multiple languages. As Marilyn Booth has argued,

> Whatever terms one chooses to label such circulations and reworkings, and however one highlights parallels and similarities, the point is to historicise translation processes and to situate translation products by looking closely at how works and concepts moved across space and time, in multiple directions, how their producers labelled and justified them, and how translation redefined text.[10]

Viewing translation as a manifold process that embraced many different techniques and aims, each avatar of these texts can be studied as an act of purposeful transformation aimed at a new audience within a new cultural context, rather than as a 'derivative' phenomenon to be judged on how accurately or inaccurately it carried the meaning of the 'original' into a new language.[11]

A set of related issues has to do with literary aesthetics and the themes and genres that appealed to medieval readers versus those that appeal to modern readers. Have modern scholars, consciously or unconsciously, chosen to study and teach only those texts that speak to the modern fascination with novel-like portrayals of individuals and reject those that are imbued with a more religious worldview or narratives that deploy elements of magic and the fantastic? In the medieval English tradition, at least, the texts that we now consider canonical have in common a single hero/protagonist and a strong predilection towards biography and, to a somewhat lesser extent, introspection. They are vernacular and monoglot. Those texts that have not entered the canon, on the other hand, tend to be multilingual, and to have complicated textual transmission histories. They also tend to be relatively longer, not structured around a single narrative arc, and not to adhere to Aristotelian ideals of closure. How have certain genres, such as 'wisdom literature', dropped off the map entirely after having maintained widespread popularity for centuries and even millennia? If the modern canon of medieval literature reflects *modern* literary tastes, are scholars and students in fact rejecting the values and reading practices of the period we purport to study?

This volume provides intriguing insights into the literary tastes of the medieval period as they intersect with the literary and political forces behind the creation of the 'modern canons' of medieval Arabic and European literature. Indeed, a remarkable aspect of this project is that the processes that have shaped the modern canon of medieval literature have taken place in the study of both European and Arabic literature, revealing some of the ways in which the pre-modern world has been constructed by contemporary ideologies that cross linguistic, religious and national boundaries. Although scholars of European and Arabic literatures have long been interested in the histories of their disciplines, they have rarely been studied together, as emerging out of the same cultural moment in the late eighteenth and early nineteenth centuries, in concert with the European imperial project. Yet it is difficult not to see similarities in the scholarly interventions that led to the elevation of these European and Arabic texts to their currently canonical status.

The terms 'medieval' and 'Middle Ages' are grounded in European history and scholarship and do not correspond to the periodisation used in the study of the Middle East. With apologies to our colleagues in Middle Eastern studies, however, we have opted for this terminology because it is broadly understood, whereas the dynastic terminology commonly used for Middle Eastern history (Umayyad, 'Abbasid, Mamluk, Seljuk, Ottoman, etc.) is familiar only to specialists. In addition to the distinct periodisations used for European and Middle Eastern history, the production of literature in these two regions was remarkably different during the period that falls roughly between the seventh and fourteenth centuries CE. For Arabic literature, this is a period that witnessed an explosive growth in literacy, authorship and the circulation of written texts. The arrival of paper-making from China in the mid-eighth century transformed the world of texts and quickly replaced the costly and bulky use of parchment, as well as the use of the more delicate papyrus. Chinese paper, however, was manufactured from plant materials that were unavailable in other regions, so it was only with the technological advances in paper-making in the Islamic Empire that substituted flax, cotton and other fibres that the full impact of the paper revolution was felt in other parts of the globe.[12]

Already by the early tenth century, tens of thousands of literary works were in circulation, produced by thousands of authors, as attested in the remarkable catalogue of the Baghdadi bookseller Ibn al-Nadīm.[13] In addition to the impact of less expensive writing materials, Islamic society developed remarkable new methods of 'publishing' books. A scholar would often read one of his works publicly in a mosque at set times, during which students, scholars and even intellectually active craftsmen would listen and take the work down in dictation. One such 'reading' might take place at certain times on certain days over several weeks or even months, and result in multiple new copies. These, however, were copies for private use and were not 'authorised' copies. In order to transform a dictated copy into an authorised copy, one had to read the text aloud back to the author, who might then correct errors and question the copyist to make sure that he had fully understood the contents. At the end of this second reading or 'proof reading', the author would award a certificate of authority (Arabic *ijāza*) that allowed the copyist to give out new copies and to teach the work in question. One 'reading' might therefore result in two dozen new copies of a work, a handful of which would become authorised texts, which could then be taught elsewhere, producing a similar number of new copies. For several centuries this oral–written interface was common practice.[14]

Eventually, however, Islamic society became more and more literate and more and more oriented towards written-to-written transmission of knowledge. The marketplace of the booksellers, copyists and paper-makers (Arabic *sūq al-warrāqīn*) became an important part of every major city in the Middle East, and, along with authors, a whole class of copyists, booksellers, compilers and editors began to be employed in the book trade. Private and caliphal libraries containing tens of thousands of volumes emerged at a time when Europe's greatest libraries boasted only a few hundred works (in 1443, for example, the Vatican library contained just 350 volumes). A sort of proto-university, the *madrasa*, emerged in which religious and legal knowledge was given pride of place, but which also included the study of poetry, rhetoric, philosophy and the sciences.[15]

The spread of literacy also created a readership that desired works not only of 'high literature', but also of entertainment, along with religious and scholarly works. A class of what we moderns might term 'popular' literature came into being, usually written in a language that more closely resembled everyday speech than the more erudite language of scholars.[16] The emergence of this less formal register of Arabic, sometimes termed 'Middle Arabic', was similar to the emergence of the European vernaculars, but never evolved so far as to produce independent written languages. Romances, tales of adventures, books of wonders, reworked versions of ancient love stories, joke books, tales of magic and anthologies of poems and anecdotes that explored nearly every imaginable topic, works on hunting, archery, chess and other leisure pastimes, all emerged and began to circulate widely. These popular literary works were often frowned upon or even outright condemned by religious authorities and serious scholars, but this did little to halt their production.

The study of medieval Arabic literature is therefore shaped by a rather remarkable fact: an enormous number of texts exist in manuscript that have never been edited, published or translated. Rather than being faced with a limited corpus, scholars of medieval Arabic literature are confronted by a large body of texts, many of which have not been examined by modern scholars, and their choices of which texts to study, edit and publish at times have a profound influence on our understanding of medieval Arabic literary activity. It is a field that is constantly being reshaped by the discovery of works thought lost and the sudden appearance of texts previously unknown. As such, when a medieval Arabic text is said to survive in but a single manuscript copy, that claim can only be provisional, and might change at any moment. The boundaries of medieval Arabic literature are in constant flux, and the publication of new editions and translations regularly changes our perception of the field.

In western Europe, a comparable explosion of availability of literature did not occur until the advent of the movable-type printing press in the fifteenth century, although the expansion of manuscript production out of monastic scriptoria and into urban bookshops in the thirteenth century had the effect of increasing the availability of manuscripts. The question of how to think of the relationship between production and reception, however, is a tricky one. The most 'popular' literature may have always been oral.[17] Moreover, the distinction we are drawing between a 'bestseller' and a *unicum* text is not hard and fast. Indeed, many of the 'unique' texts we discuss here depend upon the intertextuality of their literary tradition. The reader of *Sir Gawain and the Green Knight*, for example, is expected to come to the romance knowing of Gawain's reputation as a ladies' man. The *Chanson de Roland* is extant in versions other than the one that has been elevated into the canon. Nevertheless, while the creation of a modern 'canon' of medieval Arabic literature has been a much more recent and more partial development than the sense of the canonical works of medieval European literature, it is clear that both are rooted in Western scholarship of the nineteenth and early twentieth centuries. The strangely parallel situation that has led to the elevation of particular works found in a single copy to the status of 'masterpieces' of medieval literature offers us the opportunity to reassess how the ideas of that period of scholarship have shaped our concepts of medieval literature both in the Arabic-speaking world and in Europe.

The first section of this volume examines the remarkable histories of five *unica* manuscripts that are now deemed literary masterpieces: Ibn Ḥazm's *The Neck-Ring of the Dove*, the *Chanson de Roland*, Usāma ibn Munqidh's *Book of Contemplation*, *Beowulf* and the *Poema de mio Cid*. Paul M. Cobb's 'Contemplating books with Usāma ibn Munqidh's *Book of Contemplation*' recounts the discovery of a few loose folios in the Escorial Library by the French Arabist Hartwig Derenbourg, who, noting several mentions of the *Ifranj* or 'Franks' (the medieval Arabic term for Europeans), followed by curses, realised that he had found fragments of a text that dealt with the Crusades. He eventually assembled a large portion of the text and identified the author as Usāma ibn Munqidh (d. 1188), about whom he proceeded to publish a lengthy biography, lauding him as the personification of Muslim chivalry, before translating the text itself. Quickly incorporated into French scholarship on the Crusades, the work's appearance in English and its subsequent extraordinary popularity are the result of the chance encounter between a Princeton professor and a young Lebanese scholar who accompanied the professor on his tour of Crusader castles. The work has survived 'the vicissitudes of fate' not only due to the remarkable coincidences that punctuate its history, but also, as Cobb notes, because of the sheer force of the image that Usāma crafted of himself in the original Arabic text.

In 'Dons and dragons: *Beowulf* and "popular reading"', Daniel Remein and Erica Weaver present the fascinating history of how the single, singed manuscript of *Beowulf* edged out other works such as *Bede's Death Song* and Wulfstan Cantor's *Narratio metrica* to become nearly synonymous with Old English literature in both the scholarly and popular imagination. Along the way, they debunk the oft-repeated myth that a lecture delivered by J. R. R. Tolkien single-handedly wrested *Beowulf* from the pedantic philologists and resurrected it as a work of literature, and elucidate the less known racial and misogynistic dimensions of its rise to the status of a national 'masterpiece'.

Perhaps the single most widely read and translated work of medieval Arabic literature other than *The Thousand and One Nights* is *The Neck-Ring of the Dove* by the Andalusian writer Ibn Ḥazm (d. 1064), a treatise on love and lovers which was not widely known in the Middle Ages. As Boris Liebrenz demonstrates in his chapter, it might well have remained in obscurity had the sole manuscript, preserved in Leiden, not attracted the attention of the Russian scholar Dimitri Konstantinovic Pétrov, who otherwise wrote on Spanish poets and Russian socialists. This unique manuscript, however, has a remarkable tale to tell, including indications about what the *original* work, of which this is a later copy and abridgement, might have been like. On its publication in 1914, however, it was almost immediately recognised as a stylistically accessible guide to the concept and theory of love in the Islamic Middle Ages and appears to have achieved its popularity to a great degree on its own merits.

Ryan Giles begins with the famous philologist Ramón Menéndez Pidal's elevation of the *Poema de mio Cid* to the status of the national epic of Spain in the wake of the country's loss of its overseas empire at the end of the nineteenth century. The price of this elevation was, in part, turning a blind eye to the poem's anti-Judaism, which Pidal attempted to explain away. It is to the episode of the Cid's cheating of two Jewish bankers that Giles turns our attention in 'Thirty pieces of silver: interpreting anti-Jewish imagery in the *Poema de mio Cid* manuscript', embedding it in a broader textual network obscured by our understanding of the manuscript of the *Poema* as a *unicum*.

In '"Let no bad song be sung of us": fame, memory and transmission in/and the *Chanson de Roland*', Sharon Kinoshita notes in her analysis of the *Chanson de Roland* that survival in a single manuscript does not preclude being a well-known and popular tale, for while the text known today exists in only one copy, the story of Roland is echoed, referred to and portrayed in various different medieval media, literary and visual. Since the nineteenth century it has been intimately linked to the very idea of French literature and to French national identity, and yet it is only one of about a hundred medieval French *chansons de geste*, the rest of which have been relegated to obscurity by the canonisation of *Roland*, producing 'a highly distorted view of medieval "epic"'. Championed by the influential medievalist Joseph Bédier as the work of a consummate and learned author, the *Chanson de Roland* has been reassessed in more recent scholarship as a work rooted in oral tradition.

Complementing these case studies of 'orphan texts' that are now considered masterpieces, the second half of this volume examines 'bestselling' medieval texts that are now often ignored: the Life of Aḥīqar, the Alexander Romance, the story of Tawaddud/Teodor, the Seven Sages of Rome, the Book of Secundus, Kalilah and Dimnah and Barlaam and Josaphat. Each of these works is found not only in multiple manuscripts, but in multiple languages and recensions. They offer testimony to a vast medieval network of narratives that connected the Mediterranean, European and Islamic worlds, and they challenge many widely held notions about the relationship among those cultural zones. Several of these narratives are legendary in nature, others are more commonly classified as 'wisdom literature', but they all resist any attempts to subsume them within categories of 'national literature'. The authors in this section offer not only descriptions of these texts but also new approaches to this little studied, but highly significant, body of literature.

Daniel L. Selden's chapter builds on the concept of 'distributed authorship' as a means of addressing a widespread phenomenon that has existed since early antiquity, indeed since the compilation of Gilgamesh, the Torah and the Homeric poems: 'it is a writing practice that informs world literature from its inception'. Although the Life of Aḥīqar is not, in its origin, a medieval text, the story of its circulation and reception is nevertheless paradigmatic of many of the texts that were popular in the medieval world. Moreover, it offers a useful reminder that most, if not all, of the texts that were most popular in the medieval world were not native to it, but rather had antique antecedents. Such works, for which no single 'author' can be identified, but are instead the product of a series of 'participants', challenge not only attempts to establish histories of national literatures, but also the foundations of the fields of comparative and world literature. Using the Life of Aḥīqar as a focal point,

Selden ultimately questions how and why such significant texts are 'almost entirely absent both from theoretical discussions of world literature' and from the numerous anthologies that have become one of the mainstays of the field. Shamma Boyarin considers perhaps the most popular of all these traditions, the collection of stories that recount the exploits of Alexander the Great, now known to scholars as the Alexander Romance. Boyarin turns to the Hebrew translations of the Alexander Romance, focusing on the aesthetic appeal of the narrative. But here he also finds evidence for the way in which the very popularity of the romance became reason enough for its translation, a motivation that is worth considering in relation to the other texts in this section as well.

Taking a comparative approach to the Seven Sages of Rome and other texts of the ancient genre known as 'wisdom literature', that is, texts that seek to provide guidance for ethical living, Karla Mallette compares four narrative traditions that were wildly popular in the pre-modern world, but which have not been adopted as canonical texts (even though their traditions continued in some cases until the nineteenth century): the Seven Sages of Rome, the Book of Secundus, Kalilah and Dimnah and Barlaam and Josaphat. Mallette notes striking similarities among these texts: they all depend on a frame-tale structure to provide flexibility, each tradition encompasses significant variation within its textual tradition, and each tradition is emphatically multilingual. A provocative comparison with the canonical works of Dante and Boccaccio further underlines those elements that enable a text to transition to modern popularity: in Mallette's estimation, a fine balance between didacticism and entertainment, as well as attitudes towards women that steer clear of misogyny. Finally, Christine Chism provides an analysis of the tale of Tawaddud, the brilliant slave girl who bests the most respected scholars of Abbasid Baghdad both in encyclopaedic knowledge and in riddling, and thereby saves her master. Chism argues in part that the very characteristics that made this an appealing text in the Middle Ages, and led to translations into Castilian, Mayan and Tagalog, have impeded the text's ability to draw a broader audience more recently.

Ultimately, the goal of this collection is not to advocate for any particular group of texts or to suggest that the imitation of medieval reading tastes might enable us to reconstruct more authentic canons of medieval literature, but rather to heighten our overall awareness of the nature of the texts we study and teach, and how our academic fields took shape; in other words, to make us mindful of how our modern 'canons' came into being. By reflecting on our own disciplinary histories, we hope to open up new disciplinary horizons. Our exploration of these issues, however, also opens up new horizons in medieval literature by taking a non-Eurocentric approach and questioning why such similar modern views of medieval literature have been promoted about both European and Arabic literature, while at the same time recognising the differences between medieval literary production in the Arabic-speaking world and in Europe. A reconsideration of our scholarly and pedagogical imperatives invites a rethinking of the ways in which we represent our own imaginary pasts to ourselves, and to our students, and how we create the past that underwrites our present.

Notes

1 James H. Morey, 'Introduction', in *The Prik of Conscience*, ed. James H. Morey, TEAMS (Kalamazoo, MI: Medieval Institute Publications, 2012), p. 1.
2 Michael G. Sargent, 'What Do the Numbers Mean? A Textual Critic's Observations on Some Patterns of Middle English Manuscript Transmission', in Margaret Connolly and Linne R. Mooney (eds), *Design and Distribution of Manuscripts in Late Medieval England* (Woodbridge: Boydell and Brewer, 2008), p. 206.
3 Daniel L. Selden, 'Mapping the Alexander Romance', in Richard Stoneman, Kyle Erickson and Ian Netton (eds), *The Alexander Romance in Persia and the East* (Eelde, Netherlands: Barkhuis, 2012), pp. 32–3.
4 Christopher Cannon offers an interesting argument about how the relationship of these authors to forms of education, 'schoolroom practice', animates their particular style of literary production in *From Literacy to Literature* (Oxford: Oxford University Press, 2016), p. 12.
5 Muḥammad Tawfīq al-Nayfar, *al-Baqiyya wa-l-mudrak min shi'r Ibn Zamrak* (Beirut: Dār al-Gharb al-Islāmī, 1997).
6 For a history of the *Nights*, see Mia Gerhardt, *The Art of Storytelling: A Literary Study of the Thousand and One Nights* (Leiden: Brill, 1963) and Dwight F. Reynolds, '*A Thousand and One Nights*: A History of the Text and its Reception', in Roger Allen and D. S. Richards (eds),

The Cambridge History of Arabic Literature: The Post-Classical Period (Cambridge: Cambridge University Press, 2006), pp. 270–91. For an account of the various manuscripts, see Aboubakr Chraibi, *Arabic Manuscripts of the Thousand and One Nights* (Paris: Espaces et signes, 2016).

7 Wolfhart Heinrichs, 'Prosimetrical Genres in Classical Arabic Literature', in Joseph Harris and Karl Reichl (eds), *Prosimetrum: Cross-Cultural Perspectives on Narrative in Prose and Verse* (Woodbridge: D. S. Brewer, 1997), p. 262.

8 Devin Stewart, 'The Maqāma', in Allen and Richards (eds), *The Cambridge History of Arabic Literature: The Post-Classical Period*, pp. 145–58.

9 For a history of the various translations of this purported untranslatable text, see al-Ḥarīrī, *Impostures: Fifty Rogue's Tales Translated Fifty Ways*, trans. Michael Cooperson (New York: New York University Press, 2020), pp. xxix–xlix.

10 Marilyn Booth (ed.), *Migrating Texts: Circulating Translations around the Ottoman Mediterranean* (Edinburgh: Edinburgh University Press, 2020), p. 7.

11 See Sif Ríkharðsdóttir, *Medieval Translations and Cultural Discourse: The Movement of Texts in England, France and Scandinavia* (Cambridge: D. S. Brewer, 2012), and Carolina Cupane and Bettina Krönung (eds), *Fictional Storytelling in the Medieval Eastern Mediterranean and Beyond* (Leiden: Brill, 2016).

12 Jonathan M. Bloom, *Paper before Print: The History and Impact of Paper in the Islamic World* (New Haven, CT: Yale University Press, 2001).

13 *The* Fihrist *of Ibn al-Nadim: A Tenth-Century Survey of Muslim Culture*, trans. Bayard Dodge (New York: Columbia University Press, 1980).

14 Johannes Pedersen, *The Arabic Book* (Princeton, NJ: Princeton University Press, 1984); Gregor Schoeler, *The Genesis of Literature in Islam: From the Aural to the Read* (Edinburgh: Edinburgh University Press, 2009).

15 George Makdisi, *The Rise of Colleges: Institutions of Learning in Islam and the West* (Edinburgh: Edinburgh University Press, 1981).

16 Dwight F. Reynolds, 'Popular Prose in the Post-Classical Period', in Allen and Richards (eds), *The Cambridge History of Arabic Literature: The Post-Classical Period*, pp. 245–69.

17 Sargent, 'What Do the Numbers Mean?', p. 207; K. Reichl (ed.), *Medieval Oral Literature* (Berlin: De Gruyter, 2016)

Works cited

Bloom, Jonathan M., *Paper before Print: The History and Impact of Paper in the Islamic World* (New Haven, CT: Yale University Press, 2001).

Booth, Marilyn (ed.), *Migrating Texts: Circulating Translations around the Ottoman Mediterranean* (Edinburgh: Edinburgh University Press, 2020).

Chraibi, Aboubakr, *Arabic Manuscripts of the Thousand and One Nights* (Paris: Espaces et signes, 2016).

Cupane, Carolina, and Bettina Krönung (eds), *Fictional Storytelling in the Medieval Eastern Mediterranean and Beyond* (Leiden: Brill, 2016).

Gerhardt, Mia, *The Art of Storytelling: A Literary Study of the Thousand and One Nights* (Leiden: Brill, 1963).

al-Ḥarīrī, *Impostures: Fifty Rogue's Tales Translated Fifty Ways*, trans. Michael Cooperson (New York: New York University Press, 2020).

Heinrichs, Wolfhart, 'Prosimetrical Genres in Classical Arabic Literature', in Joseph Harris and Karl Reichl (eds), *Prosimetrum: Cross-Cultural Perspectives on Narrative in Prose and Verse* (Woodbridge: D. S. Brewer, 1997), pp. 249–76.

The Fihrist *of Ibn al-Nadim: A Tenth-Century Survey of Muslim Culture*, trans. Bayard Dodge (New York: Columbia University Press, 1980).

Makdisi, George, *The Rise of Colleges: Institutions of Learning in Islam and the West* (Edinburgh: Edinburgh University Press, 1981).

Morey, James H., 'Introduction', in James H. Morey (ed.), *The Prik of Conscience*, TEAMS (Kalamazoo, MI: Medieval Institute Publications, 2012).

al-Nayfar, Muḥammad Tawfīq, *al-Baqiyya wa-l-mudrak min shi'r Ibn Zamrak* (Beirut: Dār al-Gharb al-Islāmī, 1997).

Pedersen, Johannes, *The Arabic Book* (Princeton, NJ: Princeton University Press, 1984).

Reichl, K. (ed.), *Medieval Oral Culture* (Berlin: De Gruyter, 2016).

Reynolds, Dwight F., '*A Thousand and One Nights*: A History of the Text and its Reception', in Roger Allen and D. S. Richards (eds), *The Cambridge History of Arabic Literature: The Post-Classical Period* (Cambridge: Cambridge University Press, 2006), pp. 270–91.

— 'Popular Prose in the Post-Classical Period', in Roger Allen and D. S. Richards (eds), *The Cambridge History of Arabic Literature: The Post-Classical Period* (Cambridge: Cambridge University Press, 2006), pp. 245–69.

Ríkharðsdóttir, Sif, *Medieval Translations and Cultural Discourse: The Movement of Texts in England, France and Scandinavia* (Cambridge: D. S. Brewer, 2012).

Sargent, Michael G., 'What Do the Numbers Mean? A Textual Critic's Observations on Some Patterns of Middle English Manuscript Transmission', in

Margaret Connelly and Linne R. Mooney (eds), *Design and Distribution of Manuscripts in Late Medieval England* (Woodbridge: Boydell and Brewer, 2008), pp. 205–44.
Schoeler, Gregor, *The Genesis of Literature in Islam: From the Aural to the Read* (Edinburgh: Edinburgh University Press, 2009).
Selden, Daniel L., 'Mapping the Alexander Romance', in Richard Stoneman, Kyle Erickson and Ian Netton (eds), *The Alexander Romance in Persia and the East* (Eelde, Netherlands: Barkhuis, 2012), pp. 17–58.
Stewart, Devin, '*The Maqāma*', in Roger Allen and D. S. Richards (eds), *The Cambridge History of Arabic Literature: The Post-Classical Period* (Cambridge: Cambridge University Press, 2006), pp. 145–58.

Part I

Hanging by a thread: unique manuscripts and their place in the 'modern' medieval canon

1

Contemplating books with Usāma ibn Munqidh's *Book of Contemplation*

Paul M. Cobb

Hartwig Derenbourg's hot summer

In the summer of 1880 it was murderously hot in Madrid. It was particularly stifling in the monastery of San Lorenzo where, at the end of the sixteenth century, King Philip II had spent his last years in isolation slowly dying of cancer. There, in the Escorial Library, a French Arabist named Hartwig Derenbourg (d. 1908) was sweating nearly to death over heaps of Arabic manuscripts. Derenbourg later wrote that the heat in the monastery that summer was so intense that it 'drained my energies and subjected those of my wife, my inseparable companion, to a cruel test'.[1] Thankfully for us, it also forced him to look at some manuscripts that he might otherwise have ignored.

Derenbourg was visiting the Escorial that summer to prepare an annotated catalogue of the library's Arabic manuscripts. But the working situation was so unhealthy that he was obliged to skip various manuscripts in genres that were either already well-catalogued, such as medical and theological works, or others, such as works devoted to mathematics, which Derenbourg very sensibly called 'terra incognita; a realm into which I dare not adventure'.[2] But this did mean that he suddenly had the time to look into a box of uncatalogued manuscripts, the library's grab-bag of as-yet-unidentified manuscripts, fragments and mouldy odds and ends. Derenbourg sorted through the loose sheets he found there and eventually noticed that a group of loose folios, nine in number, seemed to be from the same work, which contained scattered references to Europeans, called generically in Arabic *Ifranj* (Franks), and which invariably cursed them when their name appeared: a sure sign that an Arabic work from the era of the Crusades had been discovered. 'The last days of our studious captivity at the monastery of San Lorenzo had arrived,' Derenbourg later recalled, 'and we only hoped not to die there sadly and melancholically like Philip II.'[3]

Derenbourg had no cause to be melancholic. Eventually, he located fifty-six additional folios of this one unique manuscript, and arranged them in order as best he could, the first twenty-one folios having been lost. Thanks to the codicological work of Qāsim al-Sāmarrāʾī, who produced the most recent edition of the Arabic text, we can say more accurately that the manuscript is missing its first two fascicles and the first folio of its third, or, put another way, that it originally was comprised of eighty-eight folios, of which only sixty-seven have come down to us, about 82 per cent of the original work.[4] On the basis of this incomplete manuscript, Derenbourg was able to identify it as a heretofore lost work, the *Kitāb al-Iʿtibār* or *Book of Contemplation* by a medieval Syrian poet, warrior and diplomat named Usāma ibn Munqidh, who died in 1188.[5]

This book, popularly, though I think inaccurately, known as Usāma's 'memoirs', is predominantly concerned with retailing the exploits of its author while hunting or at war, but it was immediately recognised as a rare and entertaining Muslim perspective on the Frankish Crusaders, and on daily life in general in Syria during the age of the Crusades. Today it has, for better or for worse, become the standard, go-to book for understanding how medieval Muslims understood their Frankish neighbours. It has been translated into virtually every major European language, and many non-European languages too.[6] On that score at least, it qualifies as a 'bestseller' today even if it languished in relative obscurity for much of its existence. But why? How do we account for the wide popularity of this work today, known only in one, unique and damaged Escorial manuscript? To answer that question requires a consideration of the book's 800-year afterlife.

The book after Usāma

To begin with, what was the standing of the *Book of Contemplation* among audiences in the Middle Ages? Usāma composed, and probably dictated, the work towards the end of his life in Damascus, around 1185 or so. His intent, to judge from the surviving portion, was to produce a collection of anecdotes that encouraged the reader to contemplate the power of God's will and the ineffable nature of Fate – using examples from his own adventure-filled life to illustrate this theme. The work is thus not, despite the common appellation, a narrative-driven 'memoir', but rather a thematic literary anthology that uses accounts from Usāma's own life or from the lives of those whom he knew – and sometimes a good story he just happened to have heard. It includes his famous accounts of the Frankish Crusaders and their manners and customs, but also of his family at his home castle of Shayzar, battles with Muslim rivals, poetry, court intrigues, hunting exploits and tales of miraculous healing, among other subjects. It is a perceptibly intimate work, and this may partially account for its modest circulation after Usāma's day.

Aside from this notable sense of intimacy, and heavy reliance on autobiographical tales, the work is entirely in keeping with other literary anthologies that Usāma composed, such as works devoted to walking sticks, refinement, old age and so on. But it was poetry, not these literary anthologies, that made Usāma's reputation as an *adīb* or man of letters among his peers.[7] Usāma possessed a reputation for being a walking encyclopaedia of Arabic poetry, both the classics and the more recent 'New Poetry' of the *badīʿ* movement, and he was himself the author of his own collection or *Dīwān*, which was said to be a favourite of Saladin. His companion, the young courtier ʿImād al-Dīn al-Iṣfahānī (d. 1201), said that 'Usāma was, in the power of his poetry and prose, like his name ("lion").' His former student, Ibn ʿAsākir of Damascus (d. 1175), shared a fellow pupil's review of his work:

> The amir Usāma was one of the poets of the age, holding the reins of poetry and prose … He cannot be described by one sole quality, nor can one explicate his poetry by the tongue alone. His lengthy odes are almost indistinguishable from those of [the great Arab poet] Ibn al-Walīd, nor would it be denied if they were attributed to [the

> great poet] Labīd. They come as if from the tip of his tongue thanks to the clarity of his expression; they are not overly long, nor does his elevated style become mixed up in useless digression. As for his shorter poems, they are sweeter than honey, and more delicious than sleep after a long period of wakefulness, in every one is rare meaning and a delightful resonance.[8]

Nevertheless, although Usāma's poetic prowess overshadowed most of his other works, the *Book of Contemplation* was not completely unknown in its day. At least one scholar appears to have owned a copy of it, namely the Syrian historian al-Dhahabī (d. 1348), who quoted from it in his own work and preserves for us some account of its now-lost introduction. It is also cited or paraphrased by a handful of other authors, such as Ibn al-ʿAdīm (d. 1262) in his history of Aleppo, Abū Shāma (d. 1268) in his anthology of poetry from the Zangid and Ayyubid periods, Ibn Wāṣil in his history of the Ayyubids, Abū al-Fidāʾ (d. 1331) in his chronicle of Islamic history, and al-Maqrīzī (d. 1442) in his chronicle of the Fatimids. In some cases, the citations preserve parts of the work that are now lost from the surviving Escorial manuscript. Finally, the Ottoman polymath Ḥajjī Khalīfa (d. 1657) included the title of the book in his bibliographical encyclopaedia, though whether he ever saw a copy or not is a moot point.[9]

As for the Escorial manuscript, it is itself a copy of a first, now-lost copy made on 4 July 1213 – this first copy being vetted (according to the colophon) by Murhaf, Usāma's own son. The Escorial copy appears on palaeographical grounds to date to the late thirteenth or early fourteenth centuries. Either copy could well have been the text used by any of the medieval authors mentioned above. But how did it get to Spain and to the Escorial? Unfortunately, there is no clear record of the manuscript's acquisition, and a fire that badly damaged the Escorial in 1681 (and probably caused the damage visible in our manuscript) makes this situation impossible to rectify.

However, it is almost certain that the manuscript arrived by the same means that brought most of the Arabic manuscripts to the Escorial, all at the same time in 1612. In that year, Mūlay Zaydān (d. 1627), the Sultan of Morocco, fleeing an uprising in Marrakesh, decamped to the city of Safi on the Atlantic coast. He entrusted much of his treasury, including around 4,000 manuscripts from his private library, to a French sea-captain to transport safely up the coast. Mūlay Zaydān cherished his library, most of which had apparently been acquired by purchase or by the work of copyists for his father, Aḥmad al-Manṣūr (d. 1603). However, and unfortunately for Mūlay Zaydān, the French sea-captain he had hired was not to be trusted, and he made off with the sultan's treasure ship and his library, headed for France. But merely a week later, a Spanish fleet intercepted him and his precious cargo. The Arabic manuscripts caught the attention of the Spanish authorities, and these were eventually deposited in the Escorial.[10] It seems likely, then, that our fourteenth-century copy of Usāma's twelfth-century *Book of Contemplation* found its way somehow to Marrakesh by the late sixteenth century, before winding up in the Escorial in the seventeenth, thanks to a jittery sultan and a slow-sailing pirate.

Derenbourg and *fin-de-siècle* medievalism

Taken in context, then, Usāma can be described as at best a well-known regional author in his day, appreciated for, if anything, his poetry and his mastery of the classical poetic heritage. If he was known for any one book (besides his *Dīwān*), it would be his book on rhetoric, the *Kitāb al-Badīʿ*, not the *Book of Contemplation*. In other words, the *Book of Contemplation* was very far from being a medieval 'bestseller'. To its contemporary medieval audience, it was neither an important nor a representative work. So why is it so well known and well loved today?

The answer brings us back to Hartwig Derenbourg, but this is not a simple story of a European Orientalist 'discovering' a medieval work and 'rescuing' it from oblivion. The answer to the question *does* hinge partly on Derenbourg, but for reasons that are more subtle than mere discovery. First of all, Derenbourg didn't just discover the manuscript of the *Iʿtibār*: he also edited it in 1886, wrote a massive study of Usāma's life and times based upon it in 1889, and finally and most importantly, translated it for the first time into any language in 1895. The sequence of those events is interesting, and says something about Derenbourg's methods: coming to terms first with the text, *then* its author and his context, and only *then* hazarding to translate it.[11] That said, pathfinders are always awarded the privilege of making the first mistakes, and his edition and translation are now largely superseded.

Derenbourg's nineteenth-century context is important, since it is that context that allowed his rather recondite work in Arabic philology to cross over into other fields, notably the history of the Crusades, which gave the work far greater 'legs' than would have been the case if it had remained merely a rediscovered text by a twelfth-century poet.[12] Thanks to Derenbourg's careful scholarship, Usāma's book became a regular feature in Francophone histories of the Crusades in the early twentieth century, and when it appeared extensively referenced in René Grousset's monumental 1934 *Histoire des Croisades et du royaume franc de Jérusalem*, Usāma had, as it were, arrived.[13] More subtly, Derenbourg's impact was felt even in non-French-speaking realms, as the early twentieth century saw some of the first translations, some of them intended for a non-academic audience, of the *Book of Contemplation* into other European languages. But these were *not* new translations based upon Derenbourg's edition of the Arabic text, but rather simple renderings of Derenbourg's French translation. These include the first German translation in 1909, the first Russian translation in 1922 and Potter's English translation in 1929. It is thus not so much Derenbourg's discovery of the manuscript that made the *Book of Contemplation* a widely cited text, but rather his presentation of the work and its use by an ever-increasing community of non-Arabists, including medieval historians, that situated this book firmly as the most commonly cited Arabic source on the Crusades.

It helped that Usāma – as presented by Derenbourg – also spoke to the values of the day. The late nineteenth and early twentieth centuries were the heyday on the Continent as well as in the trans-atlantic realm for a kind of reflowering of romantic medievalism in which a particular understanding of the Crusades and its lessons played a specific role. This was the popular fad for crusading and chivalric imagery that inspired the young T. E. Lawrence to go cycling across France to sketch cathedrals, for example, and later to carry Malory's *Morte d'Arthur* with him during the Arab Revolt;[14] and that prompted the Rockefellers and Carnegies and others to perfect the Collegiate Gothic style in the architecture of the college campuses they built across the United States;[15] and that compelled Kaiser Wilhelm to restore the tomb of Saladin in Damascus on the eve of the First World War.[16] In Derenbourg's day – in art, architecture, ornament, religion, public space and, most especially, national identity – 'the Middle Ages belong[ed] to France', and the Crusades were thrown in into the bargain.[17] That this vision of a medieval past was rooted in the modern nation-state and growing anxieties about Christian identity seems clear with the advantage of hindsight. But for Derenbourg, a prominent Jewish scholar of Semitic languages at a French university, hailing from a family with German roots, this atmosphere must have posed some challenges. Derenbourg's academic interests and even his personal identity itself seemed to thwart such a simple understanding of nation and history. Nevertheless, this atmosphere may also have presented some opportunities: before that sweltering Madrid summer of 1880, Derenbourg was just a philologist; in the intervening decade, he became a minor aficionado of the Crusades.[18]

In Derenbourg's estimation, Usāma represented an example to serve as a counterpart to the English, French, German and Belgian Crusader heroes who were so lionised as emblems of civilisation.[19] Usāma was a medieval version of the cultured men of action that the modern era seemed to want so badly, consonant with a revived Western cult surrounding Saladin that began with Sir Walter Scott and continues until now.[20] Indeed, in the massive biography he wrote for Usāma, Derenbourg tried to sculpt this specific image of his pet hero. He dwelt on his troubled yet formative upbringing and distinguished him from his pious father, for example:

> As for the soul of the young Usāma, it leapt into action from the sting of reproof. These circumstances created a hero, full of deference and admiration for [his father], but determined to imitate him more as the warrior than the ascetic, the adversary of the Franks more than the calligrapher, the man of resolute action more than the mystic absorbed in reciting and copying the Qur'ān.[21]

This was the Usāma the West first encountered in the decades on either side of the new century, through Derenbourg's own monumental works and in those other works that relied upon them. Derenbourg's Usāma was a figure who appealed to the tastes of the day, not just because he was cast as a chivalrous warrior, but also because he was largely shorn of his Muslim context, at least in Derenbourg's presentation. It is undoubtedly significant that Derenbourg contrasts

Usāma with his more spiritually inclined father. Derenbourg's Usāma, then, was retrieved from relative medieval obscurity, dusted off, and presented as a medieval Muslim who was destined to appeal to modern, secular sensibilities about the medieval past in Europe and, crucially, America.

Dana Munro, Philip Hitti and academic capitalism

Among the first American scholars to make use of Derenbourg's translation was Dana Carleton Munro (d. 1933), formerly of the University of Pennsylvania (1893–1902) and later of Princeton (1916–33), and the first academic historian of the Crusades in the United States. Munro, an Episcopalian who came from a family of historians, churchmen and academics that had settled in Rhode Island in its early colonial years, undoubtedly inhabited the medievalism of the age rather differently from Derenbourg. His interests in philology and the institutions of medieval Latin Christendom were perfectly aligned with academic trends in Europe. Indeed, Munro spent part of his post-baccalaureate time studying at Strasburg and Freiburg and is usually celebrated for bringing the training in diplomatics and philology that he gained there to the US and impressing it upon his students. In this way, Munro became an almost unwitting agent in bringing Usāma to American audiences. In a 1901 essay, Munro, who was not himself an Arabist but was very sympathetic to the sorts of perspectives that Arabic sources could offer on the Crusades, cited the *Book of Contemplation* at length for what it revealed of Muslim attitudes towards the Franks.[22] The work contains no notes or bibliography, but his distinctive rendering of Usāma's name as 'Ousâma' throughout the text shows that he learned of him through a French text – undoubtedly Derenbourg. Munro may well have been first drawn to the Crusades as a subject of inquiry during his student days in Germany as was later claimed, though his surviving notebooks from that time barely make reference to them except in the context of other subjects – church history or the Hohenstaufen dynasty, for example.[23] A list of sources that he compiled at that time certainly does not mention Derenbourg's work.[24] However, later teaching bibliographies he produced to accompany his widely used textbook, *A History of the Middle Ages*, do cite the work of the British Orientalist Stanley Lane-Poole (d. 1931), who made good use of Derenbourg's translation of Usāma's work in his classic *Saladin and the Fall of the Kingdom of Jerusalem* (1898), and this seems to be the most likely vector by which Munro became such a fan of Usāma.[25] Thanks to Munro, the parts of Usāma's work on Frankish customs that he drew upon for his 1901 essay have been considered the highlight of the text ever since, reprinted time and again in readers and textbooks to the point that the real glories of the book – its poetry, nostalgia and hunting anecdotes, all of great interest to Derenbourg – are almost entirely forgotten. And *this*, when it comes down to it, accounts for much of the work's popularity today.

Munro was very much a pioneer in the study of the Crusades. But although he wrote a number of influential essays and textbooks on medieval history broadly, it is through his many students, trained at Pennsylvania, Wisconsin and Princeton, that the field of Crusades studies truly flourished in the US. He is above all credited with being the intellectual grandfather of the project that became known as the 'Pennsylvania History' (later the 'Wisconsin History') of the Crusades, a sprawling, multi-volume collaborative history that would first be realised only under Munro's successor at the University of Pennsylvania, Kenneth Setton.[26] Although he was most at home as a student of the Latin texts produced by the Franks and as a historian of Western medieval institutions, his synthetic work, intended for a broader public, displays a marked sensitivity and sympathy for the Middle Eastern context of the Crusades and the societies that the Franks encountered. During his career at Princeton, he expressed a desire to write a large synthetic narrative history of the Crusades, which he hoped would be 'based on an exhaustive and critical use of contemporary sources and vivified by a careful study on the ground of the regions traversed and occupied by the Crusaders'.[27] To that end, in 1924 Munro left for a tour of Turkey, Syria and Lebanon, and it was during this trip that the seeds of Usāma's even greater popularity were sown.

It is not known precisely when and how Munro met the young Lebanese Orientalist Philip Hitti (d. 1978). But Hitti is quite clear that it took place sometime during this 1924 visit to Lebanon, when Hitti was serving as Professor of Oriental History at the American University in Beirut. It was then that Munro invited Hitti 'to accompany him on a visit to the Crusading castles of the area and hopefully to collaborate with him on writing their "biographies"'.[28] One must assume that Munro, already familiar with and impressed by Derenbourg's work on Usāma, made visiting Shayzar one of the goals of this journey. And indeed, the Hitti papers at the University of Minnesota preserve an envelope bearing Munro's Princeton home address and containing a series of photographs of Crusader castles and monuments from the Near East, among them Shayzar – undoubtedly taken during this 1924 visit.[29]

Within a year after Munro's return to Princeton from this voyage, the university had acquired the library of former lawyer and lifelong Egyptology enthusiast David Paton (Princeton Class of 1874) and a bequest from his parents that became the William and Annie S. Paton Foundation to support Oriental Studies at Princeton. And in the meantime, Hitti, still teaching in Beirut, had coincidentally brokered a deal with Princeton alumnus and benefactor Robert Garrett (Class of 1897) to purchase a collection of Arabic manuscripts from one Murād Bey al-Bārūdī (d. 1918), an AUB acquaintance, which was added to the already rich Garrett Collection of manuscripts housed in Princeton's library since 1900.[30] When it was evident that there was no member of the faculty at Princeton capable of working with the Garrett Collection, Munro appears to have recalled his wanderings with Hitti and recommended him for the job. Certainly, Hitti would later link these three occurrences – the Paton Foundation, the Garrett Collection and travelling with Munro – as driving his move to Princeton, where he started as Assistant Professor of Semitic Literature in February 1926: 'Such were the fortuitous happenings – two hobbies of two graduates and an incidental visit of a professor of Princeton – that prompted the university to invite the professor of Oriental history at Beirut to join its faculty as assistant professor of Semitic literature.'[31] As Hitti later put it in a 1971 interview:

> Again chance took a hand in my life. A professor of history from Princeton, Dana Munro, took a trip to Lebanon and came to the university asking for someone to go with him to visit Crusader castles. You see, that was in my field, Arab history, so I accompanied him and his wife to Sidon, Byblos, Tripoli and other castles in the area ... [Once the Garrett Collection of manuscripts was established at Princeton, the university] felt that it might be well to have somebody give courses that would make use of these manuscripts, so a new

> chair – in Semitic literature – was established, funded by the William and Annie S. Paton Foundation. Munro suggested the name of 'that fellow in Beirut who took me around' and that's how I happened to come to Princeton.[32]

It is worth pointing out that, prior to his involvement with Munro, and despite his reference to 'my field', Hitti had shown no professional interest whatsoever in the Crusades, Usāma or other Arabic texts addressing the crusading phenomenon. After graduating from AUB, and before he returned to Beirut to teach there, Hitti came to the United States and pursued graduate study at Columbia University, where he received his PhD in 1915. At Columbia, Hitti worked primarily with the Semiticist Richard Gottheil (d. 1936), and dedicated his first work to him, the published version of his dissertation, which was an annotated translation of part of a medieval Arabic chronicle about the early Islamic conquests.[33] His other works written before his arrival at Princeton concern the history of the Druze and of modern Syrian immigration to America, in addition to sundry philological projects.[34] Until he met Munro, then, the Crusades – and Usāma – were of little if any interest to Philip Hitti.

But in the late 1920s, Munro was contacted by his Columbia counterpart, the medievalist Austin P. Evans, who also happened to be the editor of the 'Columbia Records of Civilization' series for Columbia University Press, a collection of primary sources in translation that were deemed to be especially rich or representative of various world cultures. By this time Hitti and Munro were both ensconced in Princeton, and Munro had long since earned himself a reputation as a bibliographer of medieval sources and their translations.[35] It was thus natural that Evans would seek Munro out for suggestions about medieval sources to include in his series. It was also equally natural that Munro, the 'lifelong friend of Usamah', as Hitti would later call him, would be eager to include an English translation of Usāma's 'memoirs' in this series, and once again he proposed his erstwhile travel-companion and now Princeton colleague Hitti as the man for the job. In the preface to the translation that he produced, Hitti acknowledged this debt: 'The initiative for the production of this work was taken by Professor Dana C. Munro, a lifelong friend of Usamah, at whose suggestion the Editor of the "Records of Civilization" asked the writer to undertake a fresh study of the life and memoirs of Usamah.'[36] The result was the first

English translation, Hitti's classic *An Arab-Syrian Gentleman and Warrior in the Period of the Crusades. The Memoirs of Usamah ibn Munqidh*, published in 1929, followed by his own edition of the Arabic text in 1930.

Hitti was clear to the point of unsparing in describing why he thought the text merited another 'fresh study', this time in English: Derenbourg's readings, while pioneering, were 'suspect'.[37] In his introduction to the translation, Hitti gives some pertinent details.[38] Derenbourg frequently misread the Arabic text because of missing diacritical dots, supplying the wrong vowels, confusing proper names with common nouns, putting quotations in the mouths of the wrong speakers, reading foreign loan-words as if they were Arabic, and being ignorant of the Levantine colloquialisms that punctuate the work. Such bungling, Hitti points out, 'made Derenbourg in one instance cause the wrong man to fly off his saddle, in another to fall unconscious, and in a third to cut off the leg of a patient'.[39] However, Hitti was nothing but kindness personified to his predecessor, offering as a final, pointed, word: 'On the whole, however, it must be said that Derenbourg did a very creditable and honest piece of work, considering the handicaps under which he labored.'[40]

Just as Hitti set out to produce an English translation that would improve upon Derenbourg's pioneering French translation, so too did he see it necessary to produce, in 1930, a thoroughly new edition of the Arabic text. If his English translation would make Usāma's memoirs a well-known text among students and even the general public, Hitti's new Arabic edition would become the *editio princeps* and put the original Arabic text on a solid academic footing for specialists. It is worth noting that Hitti conceived of a new Arabic edition *after* he produced his English edition and became aware of the many problems with Derenbourg's early readings of the text. As with his translation, Hitti found many problems with Derenbourg's Arabic edition, and enumerated them in detail in the introduction to his new edition. This time, however, his parting words regarding the old edition were, from one philologist to another, altogether kinder: 'Here I must admit that Professor Derenbourg has preceded me by producing pioneering scholarly work in solving the manuscript's many riddles and puzzles. I am indebted to him in many instances regarding the readings of the original text and understanding its intending meaning.'[41]

To produce his edition, Hitti had to overcome certain obstacles. For one, the manuscript of Usāma's work was still housed in the Escorial Library where Derenbourg had found it, and Hitti, for reasons unknown, was unable to travel to Spain to analyse it. Instead, he had a photostatic reproduction of the entire manuscript produced and shipped to him, 'through the kind offices of the United States embassy at Madrid'.[42] Hitti's edition and translation were thus *not* based on an examination of the original manuscript, but rather on this single photostatic reproduction.

It happens that the photostat that Hitti had made survives to this day. In the Rare Book and Manuscript Library of Columbia University, a bound tome mislabelled as 'Kilab al-I'tibar' by 'Isamah ibn Murchid' can be found. Its original card-catalogue entry, dated 7 July 1930, describes it as a 'Photostat from copy in the Library of the Escorial' and notes that it was donated to the collection by Philip Hitti in 1930, the year he completed his edition. The photostat was thus deposited by Hitti, one presumes, as the gift of a grateful alumnus.[43] It was one of many manuscript photostats produced on demand at the Escorial by an Augustinian friar named Macario Sánchez López.[44]

With a copy of the Escorial manuscript obtained, Hitti faced a second obstacle: how to print an Arabic text. It so happened that Hitti was just the one to tackle this problem as well. In his Editor's Note to the edition, Hitti notes with pride that his edition of Usāma's Arabic text was 'the first Arabic book to be printed in a university press in America', though this is true only on a technicality.[45] Arabic printing in the US, of course, extends back well before 1930 if we consider the printing of Qur'āns, Arabic Bibles and community newspapers for the various Arabophone immigrant populations of the United States, most of whom arrived in the 1870s. Hitti himself had already edited and published another medieval Arabic text in the States, though it was through a small *private* press, not an academic one, the Syrian-American Press of New York, run by Hitti's acquaintance (and fellow Maronite), Salloum Mokarzel.[46] It happened that Mokarzel was also the publisher of the major Arabic newspaper *al-Hoda*, which served New York's large Syrian and Lebanese immigrant community from 1898 until 1972.[47] There, in 1910, Mokarzel had partnered with the Mergenthaler Printing Company to adapt a new printing technology – linotype printing – for Arabic, making for a much more efficiently produced and readable Arabic text. On the basis of this experience, then, Hitti followed suit and contacted the Mergenthaler Company about producing his new edition of Usāma's Arabic text using their linotype machine, in collaboration with Princeton University Press – thus Hitti's qualified statement that his Usāma edition was the first Arabic text produced by an *American university press*.[48] Hitti appears to have negotiated with the Mergenthaler Company to donate one of their machines to Princeton, a convenience that would have great repercussions.[49] For Hitti's edition of Usāma's work was just the first linotype Arabic text produced at Princeton, volume one of its long-lived 'Princeton Oriental Texts' series.[50]

Hitti did his best to market his new translation. He published excerpts from it in Salloum Mokarzel's monthly magazine, *The Syrian World*, in an attempt to drum up interest from potential readers.[51] A marketing flyer and order form that Columbia University Press produced to promote the book came complete with reassuring testimonials from eminent Orientalists and medievalists. But at a price of $4.50 in hardback (around $65.00 in 2019 values, adjusted for inflation), it was not likely to be a bestseller. His edition of the Arabic for Princeton, priced at $3.50 (roughly equivalent to $51.00), was hardly much more affordable, and certainly less likely to find a readership.[52] The translation sold a little over 100 copies each year for the first few years, with annual sales dwindling to a few dozen. In November 1951 Columbia University Press wrote to Hitti that its stock of the book was finally exhausted.[53]

Although Columbia renewed its copyright in 1957, for the rest of Hitti's life finding an outlet for a second printing of *An Arab-Syrian Gentleman*, the work that one editor indicated was Hitti's 'favorite book', would be a minor preoccupation.[54] In 1958, after a meeting in Damascus and subsequent negotiation by letter, Hitti persuaded the Arabic Language Association under Khalīl Mardam Bey (d. 1959) to produce a second edition of the Arabic text.[55] However, the translation was in limbo. Columbia demurred from reprinting it, so Hitti contacted his Beirut acquaintance, Paul Khayat, who was known for precisely such reprint work, supplying the student market at the American University in Beirut and beyond from his bookshop on Bliss Street. Khayat Publishing formally requested permission in 1960. Hitti wrote to Columbia University Press, reminding them, snippily, 'You [*sic*] records will show that a few years ago I suggested that you reprint this volume but you did not see fit to do so.'[56] Columbia responded by suggesting that it relinquish the copyright to Hitti, which it did in 1961.[57] Perhaps reluctant to entrust a book with such potential to a Beirut publisher with only limited reach such as Khayat, Hitti wrote to the Macmillan Company, the publisher of his wildly successful survey, *History of the Arabs*, a book that truly dominated his career, but it too refused him. He wrote one last time to his editor there, trying to be as persuasive as possible, while still keeping his dignity:

> Your interest ... [in the Usāma translation] is deeply appreciated. I honor you for your insight and long view. Admittedly, this is not going to be a 'best-seller,' but assuredly it will survive many of what is today your best sellers. It is a source book, unique, full of human and historic interest and is destined to live as long as there are students of the Crusades, medieval times and East-West interrelationship ... Your colleagues are right if they expect an immediate return of investment plus profit and overhead. But if a leading American publishing house is not willing to invest in such a scholarly long-range book, well...[58]

But Macmillan was unmoved and Khayat began reprinting a second edition in 1964.[59] The translation seems to have survived the migration quite well: eventually, and fittingly, Princeton obtained the copyright in 1987, and – crucially – it was the first press to publish the text in paperback. When the rights reverted to Columbia again in 2000, it continued the practice. By then, of course, the book had become an affordable and therefore common presence on reading lists and syllabuses at universities and schools across the Anglophone world. Whether the same will come to be said of the latest English translation, from Penguin Classics (2008), remains to be seen.[60]

Conclusion: Usāma's performance

In tracing the history of Usāma ibn Munqidh's *Kitāb al-I'tibār* or *Book of Contemplation*, from its dictation in Damascus in the twelfth century to its setting on a Linotype press in Brooklyn in the twentieth and beyond, one is struck by the role that contingency – what Usāma would no doubt call the vicissitudes of Fate – has played in that history. Usāma probably never intended this unusually personal and meditative work to be read beyond those who might secure a place for him in Saladin's firmament of courtiers. But books have a way of ruining their authors' plans.

Usāma could not have predicted that one of the few copies of his work in circulation after his death would itself be copied and find its way into the library of the Saʿdī Sultans of Morocco, nor that it would be stolen by pirates, rescued by Spaniards and ensconced in the Escorial where, weathering fire and flood, it would be recognised centuries later by a French Jew who was just too overheated to do anything else. That this Frenchman's work would then catch the eye of a Philadelphia medievalist, who would then encourage a Lebanese colleague he had met by chance in Beirut to publish it, would, of course, be equally incomprehensible. And that this Lebanese scholar would have the perfect combination of philological skills, chutzpah and personal connections in the worlds of Arabic printing, American publishing and self-promotion would, to Usāma, only seem the smallest of minor miracles surrounding his book. 'If any book is the man,' Hitti once wrote, '*Kitab al-I'tibar* is certainly Usamah.'[61] Like its author, this book is a survivor.

Now, one could make a materialist argument that it was Hitti and not Derenbourg who made Usāma a true 'modern medieval bestseller', since his edition was seen by specialists as an improvement upon Derenbourg (and indeed replaced Derenbourg altogether even in French academic studies by the 1940s) *and* it was published as part of the Records of Western Civilization, one of only three works of Islamic literature included in the series, intended as supplements for use in Columbia's Core Curriculum or what would be called today 'the textbook market'. Certainly, the historical records show that no other translator of Usāma besides Hitti so resolutely pursued its reprinting, marketing and copyright. And certainly, as a result, Hitti's translation, now in its third printing, in paperback no less, is the most common gateway that Anglophones have had to access the *Book of Contemplation.* Hitti's translation and edition became a staple in full or in excerpts in textbooks and readers, and was the subject of literary and historical scrutiny throughout the world and across the twentieth century.

But in making such a materialist argument about scholarly genealogies and textbook series and paperback sales, we miss a point that is of equal explanatory value: namely that the *Book of Contemplation* became a modern bestseller not just because of its translators, but because of its author-subject. For Usāma was, like

Marco Polo or Beowulf, subject to constant reinterpretation and hence constantly appealed to modern audiences.

When Derenbourg first presented Usāma to Western audiences as a charismatic man of action, he and his subject were in complete agreement, for this was certainly the side of his personality that Usāma, no stranger to vanity, tried to stress in his *Book of Contemplation*. Hitti's Usāma was a rather different sort of man, but here too it is unlikely that Usāma himself would dispute the picture:

> If Usāma lived today, then he would undoubtedly be an active member of the Arab Academy, and his home in Damascus would be a *salon* for belles-lettres. He would contribute to *al-Hilāl* and *al-Muqaṭṭam*, and spend much of his life in the open air, studying the nature of animals and observing the growth of plants. The excellence of his Arabic would win him the top prizes in Beirut, and he would have, without hesitation, enlisted during the Great War among a contingent of volunteers, even taking charge of them himself.[62]

No doubt Usāma emerges as an equally different sort of person in the hands of all his different translators.

But, to be accurate, Usāma never played more than a supporting role in the dramas of his day, and if his peers valued his literary work at all, it was not as a result of the *Book of Contemplation*. Usāma did his best to portray himself as an attractive personality, and so it is easy to see how, for Derenbourg and others, he might fit into a heroic mould that could be adapted to many ends. And so it is Usāma who must be at the centre of any inquiry about the changing popularity of this work. Derenbourg, Munro, Hitti and even the Sultan of Morocco all played their part, but the *Book of Contemplation* would be nothing without Usāma, and not merely because he wrote the thing. The book survives and thrives among latter-day audiences because Usāma crafted an image of himself that lent itself to redefinition. Usāma is at once a romantic man of action, a bourgeois Syrian gentleman, a warrior wary of *jihād*, a joke-teller and spinner of yarns, a falconry nerd hectoring us with unsolicited advice, and a melancholic, shaky-handed old poet reviewing his long life of adventures, one eye on the ruins of Shayzar, the other on the grave. Usāma wrote himself this way for Saladin and for all his readers, and, with a little help from some unexpected strangers over the centuries he thereby created his most memorable character.

Notes

1 Derenbourg gave an account of his summer of discovery in the foreword he wrote to Georg Schumann's German translation of his work. Hartwig Derenbourg, 'Comment j'ai découvert en 1880 à l'Escurial le manuscrit arabe contenant l'Autobiographie d'Ousâma Ibn Mounkidh (1095–1188)', in Usāma ibn Munqidh, *Kitāb al-iʿtibār*, trans. G. Schumann as *Memoiren eines syrischen Emirs aus der Zeit der Kreuzzüge* (Innsbruck: Wagner, 1905), pp. v–ix. The quotation occurs on p. v: 'Trois mois de séjour extrêmement laborieux sous un ciel torride, par une temperature brûlante d'Orient ... avait épuisé mes forces et soumis à une rude épreuve celles de ma femme, ma compagne inseparable.'

2 Derenbourg, 'Comment j'ai découvert', p. v: 'les mathématiques, terre inconnue, sur laquelle je n'ai pas osé m'aventurer'.

3 Derenbourg, 'Comment j'ai découvert', p. vi: 'Les derniers jours de notre captivité studieuse au couvent de San Lorenzo étaient arrives et nous comptions bien ne pas y mourir tristement at mélancoliquement, comme Phillippe II en 1598.'

4 See the collation and codicological comments in Usāma ibn Munqidh, *Kitāb al-iʿtibār*, ed. Qāsim al-Sāmarrāʾī (Riyad: Dār al-Aṣāla, 1987), pp. xxv–xxvii [in Arabic].

5 Escorial Library Arabic MS 1947.

6 On translating Usāma, see my comments in my own translation, Usāma ibn Munqidh, *The Book of Contemplation: Islam and the Crusades*, trans. Paul M. Cobb (London: Penguin, 2008), pp. xxxviii–xli.

7 On Usāma's reputation among his contemporaries, and his literary output in context, see the short biography, Paul M. Cobb, *Usama ibn Munqidh: Warrior-Poet of the Age of Crusades* (Oxford: Oneworld, 2005), pp. 51–65.

8 These assessments can be found in Ibn ʿAsākir, *Taʾrīkh madīnat dimashq*, ed. 'U. al-'Amrāwī (Beirut: Dār al-Fikr, 1998), vol. VIII, pp. 90–1: '[al-amīr usāma] shāʿir ahl al-dahr mālik ʿinān al-naẓm wa'l-nathr ... laysa yustaqṣā waṣfahu bi-maʿānin wa-lā yuʿabbaru ʿan sharḥihā bi-lisānin. fa-qaṣāʾiduhu al-ṭiwāl lā yufarraq baynahā wa-bayna shiʿr ibn al-walīd wa-lā yunkir ʿalā munshidihā nisbatahā ilā labīd wa-hiya ʿalā ṭarf lisānihi bi-ḥusn bayānihi ghayr muḥtafal bi-ṭawlihā wa-lā yataʿaththar lafẓuhu al-ʿālī fī shayʾin min fuḍūlihā; wa-ammā al-muqṭaʿāt fa-aḥlā min al-shahd wa-aladhdh min al-nawm baʿda ṭūl al-sihr. fī kulli maʿānin gharīb wa-sharḥ ʿajīb.'

9 All of these citations have been collected and discussed rather heroically by al-Sāmarrāʾī in the introduction to his edition of the Arabic text, cited above, pp. 7–16. Those that appear to be from lost sections of the

work appear for the first time in English translation in Usāma, *Book of Contemplation*, trans. Cobb, pp. 241–5.

10 Mohammed ibn Azuz, 'La biblioteca de Muley Zaidan en El Escorial', *Cuadernos de la Biblioteca Española de Tetuán* 17/18 (1978): 117–53; Daniel Hershenzon, 'Traveling Libraries: The Arabic Manuscripts of Muley Zidan and the Escorial Library', *Journal of Early Modern History* XVIII (2014): 535–58; Oumelbanine Zhiri, 'A Captive Library between Morocco and Spain', in M. Keller and Javier Irigoyen-Gárcia (eds), *The Dialectics of Orientalism in Early Modern Europe* (Basingstoke: Palgrave Macmillan, 2018), pp. 17–32.

11 Arabic edition: Usāma ibn Munqidh, *Kitāb al-iʿtibār*, ed. Hartwig Derenbourg as *Ousâma ibn Mounkidh: Un Êmir syrien au premier siècle des Croisade. (1095–1188). Texte arabe* (Paris: E. Leroux, 1886); study: Hartwig Derenbourg, *Ousâma ibn Mounkidh: Un Êmir syrien au premier siècle des Croisade (1095–1188). Vie d'Ousâma* (Paris: E. Leroux, 1889); translation: *Souvenirs historiques et récits de chasse par un emir syrien de douzième siècle* (Paris: E. Leroux, 1895).

12 Derenbourg's similarly monumental work on the Yemeni poet ʿUmāra (d. 1174), which is almost entirely forgotten today, is an instructive counter-example of this point.

13 René Grousset, *Histoire des Croisades et du royaume franc de Jérusalem*, 3 vols (Paris: Plon, 1934–36).

14 M. D. Allen, *The Medievalism of Lawrence of Arabia* (University Park, PA: Pennsylvania State University Press, 1991).

15 Michael J. Lewis, *The Gothic Revival* (London: Thames and Hudson, 2003).

16 See, in general, the papers collected in Thorsten Beigel and Sabine Mangold-Will (eds), *Wilhelm II: Archäologie und Politik um 1900* (Stuttgart: Franz Steiner, 2017), and especially the chapter by Mangold-Will, 'Die Orientreise Wilhelms II.: Archäologie und die Legitimierung einer hohenzollernschen Universalmonarchie zwischen Orient und Okzident', pp. 74–104, which points out, among other things, that Wilhelm's Saladin was the Saladin of Romantic era literature, not of history.

17 Elizabeth Emery and Laura Morowitz, *Consuming the Past: The Medieval Revival in fin-de-siècle France* (Aldershot: Ashgate, 2003), quoting the title of their chapter 1.

18 That Derenbourg's field of philology also flourished in tandem with romantic medievalism and European nationalism is probably no accident. See Richard Utz, 'Academic Medievalism and Nationalism', in Louise D'Arcens (ed.), *The Cambridge Companion to Medievalism* (Cambridge: Cambridge University Press, 2016), pp. 119–34. And it goes without

saying that Orientalist discourses prevailing in French academic circles were also a major part of Derenbourg's intellectual context.

19 On this phenomenon, see, for example, Elizabeth Siberry, *The New Crusaders: Images of the Crusades in the Nineteenth and Early Twentieth Centuries* (Aldershot: Ashgate, 2000), and the specific cases in Michael Horswell, *The Rise and Fall of British Crusader Medievalism, c. 1825–1945* (Abingdon: Routledge, 2019).

20 For a vigorous survey of Saladin's modern afterlife, see Jonathan Philips, *The Life and Legend of the Sultan Saladin* (London: Bodley Head, 2019), pp. 309–86.

21 Derenbourg, *Vie*, p. 41: 'Quant à l'âme du jeune Ousâma, elle bondit sous l'aiguillon des épreuves. Les circonstances en firent un héros, plein de deference et d'admiration pour un père tel que Mourschid, mais décidé à imiter chez lui le guerrier plutôt que l'ascète, l'adversaire des Francs plutôt que le calligraphe, l'homme d'action résolu plutôt que le mystique absorbé dans la récitation et dans la copie du Coran.'

22 Dana C. Munro, 'Christian and Infidel in the Holy Land', *International Quarterly* IV (1901): 690–704, 726–41. The essay is better known in its reprinted form in Dana C. Munro (ed.), *Essays on the Crusades* (New York: Fox, Duffield, 1903), pp. 1–41, by which time Munro had already moved to the University of Wisconsin.

23 Dana Carleton Munro papers, 1888–1949, Ms. Coll. 1168, Kislak Center for Special Collections, Rare Books and Manuscripts, University of Pennsylvania. Folders 1 and 2 contain Munro's notes from his post-baccalaureate year in Strasburg and Freiburg, in mixed German and English.

24 See ibid., Folder 4.

25 Dana C. Munro, *The Teaching of Medieval History* (New York: D. Appleton, 1903), p. 30, citing Lane-Poole. Stanley Lane-Poole, *Saladin and the Fall of the Kingdom of Jerusalem* (London: G. P. Putnam, 1898), explicitly cites Derenbourg on p. xv.

26 On Munro, the 'Pennsylvania History' and Crusades studies in the US more broadly, see Kenneth M. Setton (ed.), *A History of the Crusades*, 6 vols (Philadelphia: University of Pennsylvania Press, 1958), vol. I, pp. xiii–xvii; and Hans Eberhard Meyer, 'America and the Crusades', *Proceedings of the American Philosophical Society* 125 (1981): 38–45.

27 s.v. 'D.C. Munro', in Dumas Malone (ed.), *Dictionary of American Biography*, 2nd edn (New York: Scribner's, 1962).

28 Philip Khuri Hitti papers, IHRC894, Immigration History Research Center Archives, University of Minnesota [henceforth PKH papers], Box 21, Folder 1 Manuscript: 'From Lebanon to Princeton (In Lebanon)', 1972, p. 63.

29 PKH papers, Box 23, Folder 5. Photographs: Crusader Castles and Cities. The typed envelope is addressed to Munro at 119 Fitz-Randolph Road, but is labelled in a later hand in pencil, 'Pictures of Palestine & Syria'. The photos of Shayzar are, unsurprisingly, identical to the ones used by Hitti to illustrate his translation of Usāma's *Kitāb al-iʿtibār*.

30 Al-Bārūdī had studied pharmacology at AUB and was a minor philologist, collector and bibliophile. A few of his writings were published in the Lebanese science and literary magazine *al-Muqaṭaf*. His own work as an antiquarian and collector is worthy of a separate study. I thank my Penn colleague Huda Fakhreddine and Bilal Orfali of AUB, and Ms Samar Mikati of the AUB Archives for these tips.

31 PKH papers (see note 28 above). On Hitti's involvement with Garrett's 1925 manuscript purchases, see P. K. Hitti, N. A. Faris and B. 'Abd al-Malik (eds), *Descriptive Catalog of the Garrett Collection of Arabic Manuscripts in the Princeton University Library* (Princeton, NJ: Princeton University Press, 1938), p. iii.

32 John R. Starkey, 'A Talk with Philip Hitti', *Saudi ARAMCO World* 22.4 (1971): 23–31.

33 Aḥmad ibn Jābir al-Balādhurī, *Kitāb futūḥ al-buldān*, trans. Philip Hitti as *The Origins of the Islamic State* (New York: Columbia University Press, 1916).

34 For example, Philip K. Hitti, *The Syrians in America* (New York: George H. Doran, 1923); *The Origins of the Druze People and Religion* (New York: Columbia University Press, 1928).

35 From 1894 until 1904 Munro was the editor of the series 'Translations and Reprints from the Original Sources of History', published by the University of Pennsylvania Press, a kind of predecessor to Columbia's series.

36 Usāma ibn Munqidh, Kitāb al-iʿtibār, trans. Philip K. Hitti as *An Arab-Syrian Gentleman and Warrior in the Period of the Crusades. The Memoirs of Usamah ibn Munqidh* (New York: Columbia University Press, 1929), p. v.

37 Ibid., p. v.

38 Ibid., pp. 18–20.

39 Ibid., p. 19.

40 Ibid., p. 20. It should be pointed out that many other reviews of Derenbourg's work were equally critical.

41 Usāma ibn Munqidh, *Kitāb al-iʿtibār*, ed. P. K. Hitti (Princeton, NJ: Princeton University Press, 1930), p. xl [in Arabic]: 'wa-lā budda liyya hunā min al-iʿtirāf anna al-ustādh dirinbūrgh jāhada qablī jihād al-ʿulamāʾ al-abṭāl fī ḥall alghāz al-makhṭūṭa al-ʿarabiyya wa-kashf muʿamiyātihā

wa-innanī madīn lahu bi'l-shay' al-kathīr min haythi qirā'at al-aṣl wa-fahm al-murād.'

42 Ibid., 'Editor's Note' (unpaginated). See also Usāma, *Kitāb al-i'tibār*, trans. Hitti, p. v., where he says much the same thing.

43 Columbia University Libraries, Rare Book and Manuscript Collection, shelf-mark X893.7 Us1 S4. I am grateful to Jane Siegel of Columbia University Libraries' Rare Book and Manuscript Collection for helping me track down Hitti's photostat after I stumbled upon it in an informal hand-list of manuscript holdings at Columbia prepared by Peter Magierski, Middle East and Islamic Studies Librarian.

44 An identifying tag reading 'Fr. Macario Sanchez. Fot. Escorial' appears on the last page of the photostat, a modern colophon to the medieval colophon, as it were. Brother Macario was imprisoned and executed with some fifty others of his order by Republican troops in 1936. http://agustinosmadrid.com/conocernos/provincia-agustiniana-matritense/retratos-de-familia/sanchez-lopez-macario/ (accessed 22 December 2019).

45 Usāma, *Kitāb al-i'tibār*, ed. Hitti, 'Editor's Introduction' (unpaginated).

46 Al-Suyūṭī, *Naẓm al-iqyān fī a'yān al-a'yān*, ed. P. Hitti as *As-Suyuti's Who's Who in the Fifteenth Century* (New York: Syrian-American Press, 1927).

47 On the history of this newspaper and its press, see the commemorative volume, *Al-Hoda, 1898–1968* (New York: Al-Hoda Press, 1968). Salloum inherited control of the company from its founder, his brother Naoum, but only after Naoum's widow's attempt to sell it to, of all people, Ibrahim Hitti – Philip's brother – failed. The press was originally located in Philadelphia, using text typeset by hand. Naoum relocated it to New York, where its readership was greater, in 1902.

48 Hitti, in his introduction to the edition, thanks the Mergenthaler Company warmly, and this aspect of the publication features in most of the contemporary press releases about the edition.

49 The *Princeton Herald* at the time announced that 'Installation of a type-setting machine completely equipped with Arabic characters at the University Press has furthered the project of the publication of the Princeton oriental texts which have been planned for several years', adding that 'The machine was presented to the Press by the Mergenthaler Linotype Company.' 'Press Completes Work on First Oriental Book', *Princeton Herald*, 17 October 1930. But a departmental profile in the *Princeton Alumni Weekly*, written by Hitti's department chair, Herman Bender, specifically states that the department 'procured for the University Press a gift' of the machine. Herman H. Bender 'Oriental Studies', *Princeton Alumni Weekly* XXXI.34 (5 June 1931): 862.

50 An industry newsletter, *Linotype News*, produced by the Mergenthaler Company, makes the not unrelated point that the machines in question 'are equipped to compose Greek, Russian, Arabic, Turkish, Hebrew, Syriac, Coptic, Sanskrit, Persian, Urdu, Hindustani, Burmese, Armenian, and other Oriental languages'. 'Another Scholarly Work in Arabic Composed Entirely on the Linotype', *Linotype News*, December 1930, p. 2.

51 For example, Philip K. Hitti, 'An Arab-Syrian Gentleman and Warrior of the Crusades', *The Syrian World* 3 (1928): 3–10, 13–20; 'A Chapter from Usama', *The Syrian World* 3 (1928): 21–5.

52 PKH papers, Box 24, Folder 22. Order forms for 'Usamah's Memoirs' and 'An Arab-Syrian Gentleman and Warrior in the Period of the Crusades'.

53 PKH papers, Box 6, Folder 12. Sales reports from Columbia University Press.

54 PKH papers, Box 14, Folder 7. Correspondence from A. L. Hart of Macmillan, dated 28 June 1962: 'I have run into considerable opposition with regard to our reprinting your favorite book.'

55 PKH papers, Box 14, Folder 6. Correspondence with Khalīl Mardam Bey, dated 2 March 1958–8 March 1958 [in Arabic].

56 PKH papers, Box 14, Folder 7. Correspondence with Columbia University Press, dated 11 August 1960.

57 PKH papers, Box 14, Folder 7. Correspondence from Robert A. Gravallese, Foreign Rights Editor, Columbia University Press, dated 10 October 1961; Certified Copyright Registration document, dated 13 October 1961, sealed 6 November 1961.

58 PKH papers, Box 14, Folder 7. Correspondence with A. L. Hart of the Macmillan Company, dated 1 September 1962.

59 With a slight title change: *Memoirs of an Arab-Syrian Gentleman, Or, An Arab Knight in the Crusades* (Beirut: Khayat, 1964).

60 Usāma, *The Book of Contemplation*, trans. Cobb. This translation also includes autobiographical excerpts culled from Usāma's other works, many unknown to Derenbourg or Hitti. Mention should also be made of George R. Potter's *The Autobiography of Ousama* (London: Routledge, 1929), which was published as Hitti was preparing his new Arabic edition. Potter was a medievalist at the University of Sheffield and something of a pop biographer. He did not know Arabic, so his 'translation' is simply an English translation of Derenbourg's French.

61 Usāma, *I'tibār*, trans. Hitti, p. 15.

62 Usāma, *I'tibār*, ed. Hitti, p. iii [Arabic introduction]: 'wa-law anna usāma 'āsha al-yawma la-kāna bi-lā rayba 'uḍwan 'āmilan fī al-majma' al-'ilmī al-'arabī, wa-la-kāna baytuhu ṣālawnan li'l-adab bi-dimashq, wa-la-rāsala al-hilāl wa'l-muqaṭṭam wa-la-akthara min al-'aysh fī al-hawā' al-ṭalīq

yadrusu ṭabāʾiʿ al-ḥayawān wa-yarqubu numūw al-nabāt wa-la-nālat jiyāduhu al-ʿarabiyya jawāʾiz al-sabq fī bayrūt wa-la-kāna bi-lā taraddud fī ithnāʾ al-ḥarb al-ʿuẓmā daywana firqatin min al-mutaṭawwiʿa tawallā qiyādatahā bi-nafsihi.' Here, and tellingly, Hitti sees Usāma as a member of that generation of Syrian notables who fought during the First World War (he demurs from saying on which side) who then became members of the bourgeois *literati*, writing for literary journals and participating in the Arab cultural renaissance known as the *Nahḍa*. *Muqaṭṭam* and *Hilāl* were a prominent Egyptian newspaper and magazine respectively, both founded, it should be noted, by Lebanese immigrants. Elsewhere in his introduction, Hitti the professor imagines Usāma living today as a professor at a school of journalism, 'where students would receive lessons on how best to treat a narrative or recount events' (p. xxi): 'talaqqana ṭalabatuhā durūsan fī kayfiyyat muʿālajat al-mājariyyāt wa-sard al-ḥawādith.'

Works cited

Primary sources

Dana Carleton Munro Papers, 1888–1949, Ms. Coll. 1168, Kislak Center for Special Collections Rare Books and Manuscripts, University of Pennsylvania.

Philip Khuri Hitti papers, IHRC894, Immigration History Research Center Archives, University of Minnesota.

Usāma ibn Munqidh, *Kitāb al-ʿitibār* [*Book of Contemplation*], Escorial Library Arabic MS 1947.

— photostatic reproduction, Columbia University Libraries, Rare Book and Manuscript Collection, shelf-mark X893.7 Us1 S4.

— ed. Hartwig Derenbourg as *Ousâma ibn Mounkidh: Un Êmir syrien au premier siècle des Croisade (1095–1188). Texte arabe* (Paris: E. Leroux, 1886).

— ed. Philip K. Hitti (Princeton, NJ: Princeton University Press, 1930).

— ed. Qāsim al-Sāmarrāʾī (Riyad: Dār al-Aṣāla, 1987).

— trans. Hartwig Derenbourg as *Souvenirs historiques et récits de chasse par un emir syrien de douzième siècle* (Paris: E. Leroux, 1895); trans. Georg Schumann as *Memoiren eines syrischen Emirs aus der Zeit der Kreuzzüge* (Innsbruck: Wagner, 1905); trans. George R. Potter as *The Autobiography of Ousama* (London: Routledge, 1929).

— trans. Philip K. Hitti as *An Arab-Syrian Gentleman and Warrior in the Period of the Crusades. The Memoirs of Usamah ibn Munqidh* (New York: Columbia University Press, 1929); also reprinted as *Memoirs of an Arab-Syrian Gentleman, Or, An Arab Knight in the Crusades* (Beirut: Khayat, 1964).

— trans. Paul M. Cobb as *The Book of Contemplation: Islam and the Crusades* (London: Penguin, 2008).

Secondary sources

Allen, Malcolm D., *The Medievalism of Lawrence of Arabia* (University Park, PA: Pennsylvania State University Press, 1991).
Al-Balādhurī, Aḥmad ibn Jābir, *Kitāb futūḥ al-buldān*, trans. Philip Hitti as *The Origins of the Islamic State* (New York: Columbia University Press, 1916).
Beigel, Thorsten, and Sabine Mangold-Will (eds), *Wilhelm II: Archäologie und Politik um 1900* (Stuttgart: Franz Steiner, 2017).
Cobb, Paul M., *Usama ibn Munqidh: Warrior-Poet of the Age of Crusades* (Oxford: Oneworld, 2005).
Derenbourg, Hartwig, 'Comment j'ai découvert en 1880 à l'Escurial le manuscrit arabe contenant l'Autobiographie d'Ousâma Ibn Mounkidh (1095–1188)', in Usāma, *Kitāb al-iʿtibār*, trans. Georg Schumann, *Memoiren eines syrischen Emirs aus der Zeit der Kreuzzüge* (Innsbruck: Wagner, 1905), pp. v–ix.
— *Ousâma ibn Mounkidh: Un Êmir syrien au premier siècle des Croisade (1095–1188). Vie d'Ousâma* (Paris: E. Leroux, 1889).
Emery, Elizabeth, and Laura Morowitz, *Consuming the Past: The Medieval Revival in fin-de-siècle France* (Aldershot: Ashgate, 2003).
Grousset, René, *Histoire des Croisades et du royaume franc de Jérusalem*, 3 vols (Paris: Plon, 1934–36).
Hershenzon, Daniel, 'Traveling Libraries: The Arabic Manuscripts of Muley Zidan and the Escorial Library', *Journal of Early Modern History* XVIII (2014): 535–58.
Hitti, Philip K., *The Syrians in America* (New York: George H. Doran, 1923).
— *The Origins of the Druze People and Religion* (New York: Columbia University Press, 1928).
— 'An Arab-Syrian Gentleman and Warrior of the Crusades', *The Syrian World* 3 (1928): 3–10, 13–20.
— 'A Chapter from Usama', *The Syrian World* 3 (1928): 21–5.
Hitti, Philip K., N. A. Faris and B. 'Abd al-Malik (eds), *Descriptive Catalog of the Garrett Collection of Arabic Manuscripts in the Princeton University Library* (Princeton, NJ: Princeton University Press, 1938).
Al-Hoda Press, *Al-Hoda, 1898–1968* (New York: Al-Hoda Press, 1968).
Horswell, Matthew, *The Rise and Fall of British Crusader Medievalism, c. 1825–1945* (Abingdon: Routledge, 2019).
Ibn ʿAsākir, *Taʾrīkh madīnat Dimashq* [A History of the City of Damascus], 40 vols, ed. 'Umar al-'Amrāwī (Beirut: Dār al-Fikr, 1998).
Ibn Azuz, Mohammed, 'La biblioteca de Muley Zaidan en El Escorial', *Cuadernos de la Biblioteca Española de Tetuán* 17/18 (1978): 117–53.
Lane-Poole, Stanley, *Saladin and the Fall of the Kingdom of Jerusalem* (London: G. P. Putnam, 1898).

Lewis, Michael J., *The Gothic Revival* (London: Thames and Hudson, 2003).
Mangold-Will, Sabine, 'Die Orientreise Wilhelms II.: Archäologie und die Legitimierung einer hohenzollernschen Universalmonarchie zwischen Orient und Okzident', in Thorsten Beigel and Sabine Mangold-Will (eds), *Wilhelm II: Archäologie und Politik um 1900* (Stuttgart: Franz Steiner, 2017), pp. 74–104.
Meyer, Hans Eberhard, 'America and the Crusades', *Proceedings of the American Philosophical Society* 125 (1981): 38–45.
Munro, Dana C., 'Christian and Infidel in the Holy Land', *International Quarterly* IV (1901): 690–704, 726–41.
— *The Teaching of Medieval History* (New York: D. Appleton, 1903).
Munro, Dana C. (ed.), *Essays on the Crusades* (New York: Fox, Duffield, 1903).
Philips, Jonathan, *The Life and Legend of the Sultan Saladin* (London: Bodley Head, 2019).
Setton, Kenneth M. (ed.), *A History of the Crusades*, 6 vols (Philadelphia: University of Pennsylvania Press, 1958).
Siberry, Elizabeth, *The New Crusaders: Images of the Crusades in the Nineteenth and Early Twentieth Centuries* (Aldershot: Ashgate, 2000).
Starkey, John R., 'A Talk with Philip Hitti', *Saudi ARAMCO World* 22.4 (1971): 23–31.
Al-Suyūṭī, *Naẓm al-iqyān fī aʿyān al-aʿyān*, ed. Philip Hitti as *As-Suyuti's Who's Who in the Fifteenth Century* (New York: Syrian-American Press, 1927).
Utz, Richard, 'Academic Medievalism and Nationalism', in Louise D'Arcens (ed.), *The Cambridge Companion to Medievalism* (Cambridge: Cambridge University Press, 2016), pp. 119–34.
Zhiri, Oumelbanine, 'A Captive Library between Morocco and Spain', in M. Keller and Javier Irigoyen-Gárcia (eds), *The Dialectics of Orientalism in Early Modern Europe* (Basingstoke: Palgrave Macmillan, 2018), pp. 17–32.

2

Dons and dragons: *Beowulf* and 'popular reading'

Daniel C. Remein and Erica Weaver

A bit of sober reflection from the early eighth century, the most popular Old English poem forms a powerful meditation on life and death, good and evil – on what it means to live (and die) wisely and well. Garnering praise for its 'dry, deeply understated' style and 'intense emotion', it foregrounds unavoidable journeys, departures and judgements.[1] Throughout, the oral poet masterfully suspends the audience in 'a poised temporality' within which 'we feel the expansive vocabulary working perfectly against a sense of the compression of time'.[2] We are talking, of course, about *Bede's Death Song*:

For þam nedfere   næni wyrþeþ
þances snotera   þonne him þearf sy
to gehicgenne   ær his heonengange
hwæt his gaste   godes oþþe yfeles
æfter deaþe heonon   demed weorþe.[3]

[Before the inescapable trip, no one grows
wiser of thought than one compelled
to mull over, before his passage from here,
what to his soul of good or evil
will be accorded after death bears it away.]

Widely attested from the eighth century to the sixteenth, these five lines of vernacular poetry were supposedly composed by the venerable historian on his deathbed and survive today in at least thirty-four manuscripts.[4] Transmitted through the *Epistola de obitu Bedae* [Letter on the Death of Bede] of Cuthbert, Bede's own student and later abbot of Wearmouth and Jarrow, *Bede's Death Song* was regarded as the only surviving vernacular poem by the early medieval schoolroom author and today remains the best-attested Old English poem by far, even if it is now rarely taught or studied.[5]

In contrast, *Beowulf* survives in one half-burned copy, yet it is today both the star poem that begins countless surveys of British literature and one of the few medieval texts with sufficient name recognition to receive a major Hollywood movie adaptation under the same title as its scholarly edition.[6] When we think about Old English poetry, it is probably the first text that now comes to mind (an honour that, we are willing to wager, is never accorded to the *Death Song*). So, how might this unusual dyad help us rethink what constitutes a canonical Old English poem?

To be fair, at only five lines long, the *Death Song* is an easy addition to a compilation, while *Beowulf* requires far more parchment and planning. Moreover, as Peter Orton calculates, only 679 lines of Old English poetry – or 2.2 per cent of the extant corpus – survive in more than one copy, making the *Death Song*'s high manuscript count all the more remarkable and Beowulfian exceptionalism par for the course.[7] Yet Anglo-Latin poems tended to circulate more widely, so our sense of 'the corpus' of early medieval English literature is skewed by the undeniable fact that most 'early English literature' was not produced in English, at least as it has come down to us in manuscript. Aldhelm of Malmesbury's *Carmen de virginitate* [Verses on Virginity] – roughly the length of *Beowulf* and only one half of a full *opus geminatum* or 'twinned work' – survives in five copies, all written or owned in England before 1100,[8] while the longest surviving pre-Conquest English poem, Wulfstan Cantor's *Narratio metrica de S. Swithuno* [Metrical Life of St Swithun], totals nearly 3,400 lines extant in full in two copies, with a part in a third.[9] As Daniel Donoghue reminds us, however, 'the pervasive presence of oral poetry among the general population' may be fruitfully thought of as equivalent to the 'dark matter and dark energy, which together constitute 95 percent of all the mass-energy of the universe' and 'included women and men from all walks of life, from peasants like Cædmon to scholars like Aldhelm'.[10] For early medieval England, the manuscript count alone cannot account for true popularity or rarity, then, as the oral-literate spectrum stymies any tallying efforts.

By other metrics, *Beowulf* certainly participates in notions of what might have constituted 'popular' literature in the early medieval North Atlantic. It is impossible to say whether the poem would have been, in today's terms, canon or fan fiction, a definitive work in the legendarium of early medieval Germanic languages or a spin-off, but brief echoes and shared characters suggest that *Beowulf* was itself one part of a larger network of poems, sagas and didactic works, even if we now only have traces of the full legendary universe. Rather than surviving as a pure one-off, then, *Beowulf* shares poetic formulas with the Old English *Andreas*, a poetic account of the apostle Andrew's captivity in Mermedonia.[11] Many of *Beowulf*'s central characters even recur in texts on the Swedish–Geatish wars, which form a backdrop to the poem, as well as in schoolroom compendia. So, the Scyldings – the Danish dynasty of which the besieged Hrothgar forms a part – feature in dozens of Scandinavian and Icelandic texts from the later Middle Ages, while Hygelac – Beowulf's uncle and king – makes a brief cameo in the *Liber monstrorum*.[12] What constitutes a 'representative' or 'popular' text is thus a far more complex question than we might at first assume, both for the present and the past. And it becomes increasingly complicated when we remember that the past is itself a rapidly multiplying category, especially in poems such as *Beowulf* and *Bede's Death Song*, which experiment with dilating and contracting time-scales and with how individual lives can fit into geological, eschatological and even just human historical time.

Beowulf survives to us against seemingly incredible odds, but this may have more to do with evolving notions of taste and decorum (and whose taste? and when?), as well as the inevitably quirky survival record of literature in a language that had become largely unreadable by the time of the dissolution of the English monasteries (1536–41), and that remained incomprehensible to all but a very small group of readers well into the nineteenth century. As Brian O'Camb has demonstrated, George Hickes's 1705 *Thesaurus* had 'founded an Old English literary canon with gnomic poetry at the helm nearly a century before Beowulf was published for a reading public'.[13]

After centuries without any surviving record of attention to the poem, Humphrey Wanley's somewhat misleading mention of it in his catalogue of 1705 (as 'wars waged against princes of Sweden by a certain Dane named Beowulf…') was followed by another century of silence until Sharon Turner's 1805 *The History of the Manners, Landed Property, Government, Laws, Poetry, Literature, Religion, and Language, of the Anglo-Saxons*. As Haruko Momma reports, Turner's inclusion of translated passages from *Beowulf* 'introduced a hoard of inaccuracies including those resulting from the transposition of a single leaf in the manuscript' (an error that Momma notes was soon caught by John Josias Conybeare's posthumous *Illustrations of Anglo-Saxon Poetry*).[14] As Momma argues, both Conybeare and John Mitchell Kemble, who was engaged in the first modern edition of the poem, 'believed that *Beowulf* had not received enough attention' and 'argued for an intrinsic value of the language';[15] however, their differing philological approaches set the scholars at odds – an opposition that may have delayed coordinated attention to *Beowulf*'s literary merits.

In Chris Jones's account, the nineteenth century's popular idea of an Old English poem was drawn not from any medieval source but from Walter Scott's 1819 novel *Ivanhoe*.[16] So, how did *Beowulf* emerge from almost complete obscurity to gain a place in the canon? And if, as Momma writes, '"What has *Beowulf* to do with English?" is a genuine question, the answer to which may be either "nothing" or "a lot," depending on whom we ask', what makes *Beowulf* a 'bestseller' in a global, multilingual world?[17]

The traditional account of the poem's rise to prominence hinges on a single essay, but as we will show in the pages to come, its canonisation actually involved many more readers and critics. Teachers of Old English tell themselves and their students a story about how *Beowulf* came to be studied only relatively recently as a serious literary endeavour, pinpointing philologist and fantasy writer J. R. R. Tolkien's 1936 Israel Gollancz Memorial British Academy lecture, subsequently published as '*Beowulf:* The Monsters and the Critics', as a site of pure origin that opened up the possibility for modern English-language readers to encounter the poem as a unified text and a sophisticated literary accomplishment for the first time.[18] This assumption – and several others that, as we will see, come with it – takes Tolkien at his word that, when he spoke of '*Beowulf* as a poem, with an inherent poetic significance', he acted to cut a path, for the first time, through the work of the 'jabberwocks of historical and antiquarian research' who 'burble in the tulgey wood of conjecture, flitting from one tum-tum tree to another' and who supposedly all but guaranteed that, up to that point, 'the main interest which the poem has for us is thus not a purely literary interest', as Tolkien quotes from Archibald Strong.[19]

Already, we might ask precisely who comprises this first-person plural pronoun, this supposed *us* to whom Tolkien's infantilised and primitivised antiquarians have denied the *poesis* of *Beowulf*. And as Dorothy Kim reminds us,[20] we should pause, too, over the adjacency of this rhetoric to Tolkien's distinctly ethnicising and race-making investments in 'the ancient English temper' which he claims to identify in the poem's '*instinctive* historical sense' (emphasis ours);[21] his insistence that 'we have to deal with a poem by an *Englishman* using afresh ancient and largely traditional material' (emphasis ours) in order to understand its poetry;[22] and the inclusion of a specifically 'Gallic voice' complaining of 'beer-bemused Anglo-Saxons' in his list of parodied detractors.[23]

Moreover, even as Tolkien insists that *Beowulf*'s interest has not been 'purely literary', his own allusion to 'jabberwocks' (and his recognition that the poem already anchored British literature syllabuses) belies this claim. By mocking antiquarians in the terms of Lewis Carroll's 'Jabberwocky', Tolkien undermines his own narrative about the contemporary lack of interest in Old English verse qua verse, because he is quoting a poem that is itself presented by an 'Anglo-Saxon messenger' in Carroll's 1871 novel *Through the Looking Glass*, and is thus an intentional and recognisable send-up of an Old English poem about the killing of an adversary with 'jaws that bite' and 'claws that catch', whose dismembered head is ultimately carried back as a trophy. Carroll thus transmutes *Beowulf*, however subtly, into nonsense verse, attesting at least satirically to recognition of its literary appeal sixty-five years before 'The Monsters and the Critics'.

And yet, whatever awareness we may have of its problems, in critical and pedagogical practice scholars of Old English continue to venerate the lecture as marking the true dawn of the poem's modern readership, even in what from outside the field might appear as an attempted apotheosis: *Beowulf and the Critics*, which transforms what was originally a 36-page lecture printed with another 17 or so pages of appendices into a 479-page critical edition.[24] Including two unpublished versions of Tolkien's lecture (designated *A* and *B*), this later edition, however accidentally, amusingly recalls the two earliest known acts of 'modern' readership of *Beowulf*: the copies of the poem's unique manuscript made by the amanuensis hired by eighteenth-century Danish antiquarian Grímur Jónsson Thorkelín, and Thorkelín's own copy, known to students of *Beowulf* today as Thorkelín *A* and *B*, respectively.

More recently, however, the monumental status of Tolkien's lecture has been shaken. Kathy Lavezzo recounts Tolkien's role in shutting out a young, Jamaican-born, Black British Marxist theorist Stuart Hall from medieval studies and graduate work on *Piers Plowman*, playing the role, in Hall's recollection, of an 'ascetic South African professor' whose attachments to aristocratic, idealised rural white supremacy have long been apparent to scholars of modern fantasy narrative.[25] As a result, amplifying Lavezzo's work alongside an essay about the poem by Toni Morrison, Kim has issued a call to put Tolkien's lecture 'to bed and read *Beowulf* anew'.[26]

Many literary luminaries have done this already, from Bryher's queer, feminist novel *Beowulf* (1948) to John Gardner's *Grendel* (1971) to Michael Crichton's *Eaters of the Dead: The Manuscript of Ibn Fadlan Relating His Experiences with the Northmen in AD 922* (1976) to Maria Dahvana Headley's *The Mere Wife* (2018) to recent work by writers of colour such as Teju Cole, Natasha Trethewey and, of course, Morrison, which we will discuss at greater length below. As we will see, Tolkien – together with the British Academy – was not really singularly responsible for delivering *Beowulf* to the literature classroom, the publishing industry and Hollywood. Lending force to this argument, this chapter gives historical frames of reference for readers of *Beowulf* as a poem before Tolkien, as well as for subsequent readings that we hope might supersede his.

Indeed, if *Beowulf*'s canonical status in 'British literary history' was sealed by mid-century investments in 'Literature' as a privileged domain for relatively dehistoricised, formalist reading, all underwritten by an oddly Arnoldian, decidedly middle-brow philologist,[27] how was it that the poem held its place throughout the significant revisions of the canon during the poststructuralist and Marxist debates of the 1980s and 1990s – and how might it continue to earn its keep in ongoing efforts to decolonise the canon? Surely, there must have been other processes, other now obscured vectors for the poem's canonical apotheosis. We thus ask what other stories we can tell about the poem, both in terms of its enduring appeal and its course through different institutional spaces and historical moments. Our answers are exploratory, rather than exhaustive – a partial inventory of often overlooked elements of the processes that yielded *Beowulf*'s canonisation and the contemporary popular belief in its representative status (many of which have received or would benefit from fuller analyses in their own right from other scholars with more specific expertise) rather than a case for what *Beowulf* decidedly is, does, or should be now.

Here, Tolkien's focus on 'the Critics' – and, more precisely, on the most 'potent' criticism – proves instructive.[28] Although it now reads as an indictment of a broad field of scholars, it was, for Tolkien and his auditors, a much narrower category comprised largely of Oxford dons seeking to legitimate English as a serious scholarly discipline. Tellingly, two years after Tolkien's lecture, Virginia Woolf lamented that 'the noble courts and quadrangles of Oxford and Cambridge often appear to educated men's daughters like petticoats with holes in them, cold legs of mutton, and the boat train starting for abroad while the guard slams the door in their faces'.[29] Jana Schulman notes that Tolkien himself voted to make certain that Dorothy Whitelock, one of the greatest medievalist scholars of her moment, would not inherit the Rawlinson and Bosworth Professorship after him in the interests of a less well-published man.[30]

As it happens, however, precisely during the period when Tolkien found his professorial predecessors failing to grant *Beowulf* sufficient importance in British arts and letters, the teaching of Old English in the United States – and, in particular, in elite women's colleges and historically Black colleges and universities – was yielding literary attention to *Beowulf* and contributing to ensconcing the poem in late nineteenth- and early twentieth-century American literary history, as Mary Dockray-Miller and Matthew X. Vernon have uncovered.[31] Some of these curricula can be documented as having included passages of *Beowulf*, and resulted in a number of dissertations on *Beowulf* by women around the turn of the century.[32] As Dockray-Miller explains, this phenomenon in women's colleges drew on and contributed to the women's suffrage movement while at the same time intersecting with various strands of white supremacist Anglo-Saxonism, wherein 'these women used training in Anglo-Saxon to expand their social and professional mobility, even as it reinforced the racialized and racist hierarchies of the era'.[33]

Against this history of white supremacy, however, Old English – and the teaching of *Beowulf* specifically – also emerged in the early twentieth century as an important subject in HBCUs in the United States. As Vernon has demonstrated, for instance, the renowned African American philologist Lorenzo Dow Turner regularly taught Old English at Howard University from 1917 to 1928; during those years, he also offered courses on Old English poetry and on *Beowulf* specifically at the University of Chicago, where he received his PhD after completing an MA at Harvard.[34] While at Harvard, Turner had also studied Old French, so careful work on medieval languages provided the first indication of his linguistic interests and, we would argue, laid the groundwork for his later research on Gullah. Today, his 1949 magnum opus, *Africanisms in the Gullah Dialect*, remains a foundational text for African American studies. Indeed, after leaving Howard, this teacher of *Beowulf* established the first African studies department at Fisk University.[35]

Elsewhere, Nathaniel Tillman taught Old English at Atlanta University from 1927 to 1957, likewise bridging medieval studies and careful study of African American vernaculars after completing a dissertation on Lydgate,[36] while the all-women Spelman College offered its first Old English class in 1932.[37] As one of Tillman's former students, A. Russell Brooks, recalled, 'His approach to the study of language was organic and dynamic rather than prescriptive', truly bringing texts to life rather than drowning them in pedantry.[38] Perhaps unsurprisingly, then, Tillman's formative mentor, the African American scholar and Morehouse College professor Benjamin Griffith Brawley, was likewise a sensitive reader of Old English literature long before Tolkien's 'Monsters and the Critics', devoting several pages of his landmark 1925 *A New Survey of English Literature* to *Beowulf* specifically, about which he observed, 'Above all other virtues are courage and love of kin. Beowulf boasts as well as acts, but he is ever a man of deeds rather than words.'[39] By shaping countless other students – particularly in the case of Brawley's textbook, which went on to a second edition – these inspired professors of Old English thus helped to construct *Beowulf* as a literary object in the modern world, and particularly in HBCUs in the American South.

American women also published their own poetic translations from *Beowulf* in the late nineteenth and early twentieth centuries, likewise attesting to the poem's recognisable literary merits. Anna

Robertson Brown, a poet with a PhD in later medieval English literature, published 'The Passing of Scyld' and 'The Battle with the Water-Sprite' in the 1890 issue of *Poet Lore*, an important (and still-running) journal that would also publish the likes of Rabindranath Tagore, Rainer Maria Rilke, Anton Chekhov and Paul Verlaine in its early years.[40] Also of note are the translations from *Beowulf* and the 206-line poem 'The Ballad of Hart Hall' (adapted from the first third of *Beowulf*) by Mary Gwinn,[41] whose work Dockray-Miller recovered from obscurity among Gwinn's husband's papers.[42] Dockray-Miller argues that Gwinn's 'Ballad' uses couplets and numerous mythographical elements to create a fictional 'source' for *Beowulf*,[43] and so the poem registers the obvious importance of *Beowulf* to Gwinn *as a poet* as well as a scholar.

Gwinn was entirely self-taught and held no degrees other than her 1888 PhD on *Beowulf* from Bryn Mawr, which likewise registers a pre-Tolkien critic committed to accounting for its poesy.[44] As Dockray-Miller observes, 'her topic is not philological at all', as she 'argues for "a purely literary enjoyment and appreciation" of the poem and focuses on the poem's use of imagery'.[45] Gwinn's proposed methodology is a kind of late nineteenth-century anticipation of reader-response criticism: 'we shall do best to confine ourselves strictly to the poem itself, and be very honest with ourselves about the impressions we receive from it, and scrupulous in our way of noting them'.[46] And in contrast to Tolkien's motionless, balanced elegy, for Gwinn, the 'poetry' of *Beowulf* has 'an air of abundance', of 'interminable flow'.[47]

Many people, although not Oxford dons (however otherwise privileged), were thus reading *Beowulf* as a poem before Tolkien, including four of the best-known nineteenth-century poets and aesthetes – Henry Wadsworth Longfellow, Sidney Lanier, Alfred Lord Tennyson and William Morris – who all reworked the Old English in contemporary poetry and testify to a growing readership on both sides of the Atlantic. While Tennyson's imperialist and racialising Anglo-Saxonism is probably most readily identified in his 'Brunanburh', Chris Jones locates a thread that runs continuously from the Poet Laureate's undergraduate work with Old English (including a glossary full of Old English words and a fragmentary translation from *Beowulf*) to his later 'Brunanburh', lodging *Beowulf* and Tennyson's friend from Cambridge and *Beowulf*'s first editor,

John Mitchell Kemble, in the canonical heart of Tennyson's corpus.[48] As Jones argues, Tennyson's 'Sonnet to J. M. K[emble]' is ostensibly about Kemble's commitment to the Anglican Church, but 'seems to hint at Kemble's philological interests' precisely when Kemble resolved to leave off his pursuit of a clerical life and focus on philological activities.[49] This sonnet not only sutures the subject of Tennyson's corpus into the production of that famous complete edition of *Beowulf* (the second volume of which – the translation – Kemble inscribed as a gift to Tennyson),[50] but also, we would suggest, points to the more surprising implications of a letter Jones describes from Arthur Henry Hallam in 1832. In 'mock grievance', Hallam, who had been staying with Kemble just before his first 1833 volume of *Beowulf* was published and would soon help him out as a proofreader, describes Kemble as so absorbed in his manuscripts that he can only respond to a greeting with notes on the text.[51] Hallam would soon suggest to Kemble that he 'select some very ancient passage in an Edda' as 'puff collateral' to help sell Tennyson's new book, and, when Kemble wrote to Tennyson to announce that *Beowulf* was published, Tennyson responded with, 'I am heartily glad you have got *Beowulf* out.'[52] Hallam's role as the mediator of sorts between Tennyson's 'mainstream' poetry and the production of *Beowulf* installs, if indirectly, Tennyson's seeming adjacency to the construction of a canonical *Beowulf* into the heart of perhaps his most famous poetic project, the lengthy *In Memoriam A. H. H.*, first published in 1850, but mourning Hallam's sudden death from a cerebral haemorrhage in 1833, just after these exchanges around the publication of Kemble's *Beowulf* – making *Beowulf* an unlikely ghost haunting the margins of *In Memoriam*.

Meanwhile, the poem was supposedly absent from American literary circles. In 1878 Lanier lamented that, although 'One will go into few moderately appointed houses in this country without finding a Homer in some form or other … it is probably far within the truth to say that there are not fifty copies of *Beowulf* in the United States.'[53] A former Confederate soldier, Lanier appropriated the dialects of both Black Americans and poor whites from the American South in his poetry,[54] and takes his own place within the historically specific inheritance of racist uses of Old English in the American South.[55] As John D. Kerkering argues, in the interests of a post-bellum project of national reconciliation for white Americans,

Lanier posits a theory of poetry and music that casts 'Anglo-Saxon' and *Beowulf* in particular in terms of a 'race-specific sound' that he contrasts with what he sees as the less developed sounds of Black American speech (even producing editions of Old English poetry 'to introduce children to Anglo-Saxon rhythms', replacing '[Thomas] Jefferson's reliance on Anglo-Saxon legal codes for instilling national character with a pattern of sound perpetuating Anglo-Saxon racial identity').[56] Kerkering points out that Lanier claimed that *Beowulf* might at first sound 'strange and rugged' but that careful attention yields 'a very familiar face' – presumably a white one – 'speaking to you in the voice of an old friend' thanks to a rhythm that is 'well-nigh universal in our race'.[57] Lanier thus laments that *Beowulf*:

> is not found in the tatters of use, on the floors of our children's playrooms; there are no illuminated boy's editions of it; it is not on the booksellers' counters at Christmas; it is not studied in our common schools; it is not printed by our publishers; it does not lie even in the dusty corners of our bookcases; nay, the pious English scholar must actually send to Germany for Grein's Bibliothek in order to get a compact reproduction of the body of Old English poetry.[58]

Yet two decades later, *Beowulf* was more easily available to the American reading public, with Lanier conceding in a footnote, 'Since this was written (in the winter of 1878–9), two editions of the work have been published here', attesting to growing interest.[59]

At the same moment, as Jones notes, 'as early as 1886 [William] Morris was publically proclaiming *Beowulf* a poem "worthy of a great people"'.[60] A collaboration with A. J. Wyatt, Morris's *Beowulf* was first published in 1895 in a deluxe Kelmscott Press edition. Part of a larger trend by which the New Philology seems to have resulted in a 'heightened etymological awareness' for a number of nineteenth-century English poets,[61] Morris's translation takes the archaising impulse that still haunts much translation from Old English poetry to an extreme.[62] The translation, with lines such as 'Brake the bale-heedy, he with wrath bollen',[63] 'often needs the same glossing that the original does', and indeed includes a glossary.[64] Even if later critics have been unenthused, its immediate reception deemed it a success.[65]

In 1899 Lanier's hope for Beowulfian nursery fare would even be answered by Clara Thomas's *The Adventures of Beowulf*, which offered a paraphrase for use in elementary education and was quickly followed by several adaptations that explicitly sought to put the poem on the playroom floor.[66] Henrietta Elizabeth Marshall's 1908 *Stories of Beowulf*, for instance, begins:

> '*Beowulf* is known to every one.' Some months ago I read these words, and doubted if they were true. Then the thought came to me that I would help to make them true, for *Beowulf* is a fine story finely told, and it is a pity that there should be any who do not know it. So here it is 'told to the children.'[67]

As Lise Jaillant has observed, however, this was hardly a purely literary project; rather, these early children's *Beowulf*s encoded nationalist and frequently racist Victorian medievalism in their typography, illustrations and cover art in order to market the poem as a foundational text for white English identity.[68] Over the course of the twentieth century, children's *Beowulf*s would continue to hit the market, with Manuel Vallvé publishing a moralising Spanish *Beowulf* in 1934 and Robert L. Schichler even suggesting that Grendel might underpin Theodor Geisel's (Dr Seuss's) Grinch – a supposition that receives more weight when we remember that the young Geisel had studied Old English at Oxford.[69]

Publications such as these serve to remind us of at least two things. First, that the history of modern literary studies itself and its installation within university education is relatively recent. And, second, concomitantly, that the picture outside the halls of Oxford might look very different (after all, in its early nineteenth-century form, the Rawlinson chair itself 'had no resemblance to a modern professorship' and was occupied by a number of persons who had never published on Old English at all).[70] It may have been that few of Tolkien's 'critics' read the poem 'as poetry', but plenty of other readers certainly did, including the queer American poet and labour rights activist Edna St Vincent Millay, who – just as Morris's *Beowulf* was being put to music – was hard at work on *The King's Henchman*, a libretto set in tenth-century England that would take her two years of intensive study to complete and would be hailed as 'the Great American opera' on its premiere at New York City's Metropolitan Opera in 1927.

Although Millay was commissioned by the Met, the story was left entirely up to her, and she found her ultimate topic in the 'era that had fascinated her during her Vassar years and studies of the language using Henry Sweet's *Anglo-Saxon Reader*, which included Beowulf's fight with Grendel's Mother as its poetic apogee, with Sweet's introduction noting that the lines comprised 'one of the most vivid and picturesque passages in the whole poem'.[71] Indeed, Millay had first studied Old English with Vassar Professor Christabel Fiske and maintained her interests in early medieval England.[72] While she found her central plotline in the *Anglo-Saxon Chronicle*, a 'well-thumbed' copy of Sweet can still be found in her library at Steepletop along with Holthausen's German edition of *Beowulf*, which was a gift from her mother Cora and contained a scholarly introduction, glossary and critical apparatus as well as 'much handwritten notation' from Millay herself.[73] Although her mother gave her this edition after *Henchman* had already premiered, the gift attests to Millay's sustained work on early medieval England while likewise suggesting that *Beowulf* was of sufficient interest to her that a rigorous scholarly edition – in German at that – would constitute a welcome gift.[74] Millay's *Beowulf* 'has extensive written annotations throughout, mostly appearing to be translations of words and phrases', and in Mark O'Berski's summation, 'Needless to say, the book is well-read.'[75]

Moreover, while *Henchman*'s overarching plot derives from the *Chronicle*, the story is set in *Beowulf*'s world of banquets and scops. Millay provides several pages of stage directions to set the opening scene, which features King Edgar and his court listening to a scop at the end of a banquet: an arrangement that vividly recalls Hrothgar's court at Heorot. Moreover, the scop's opening song initiates the play in an imitative alliterative metre complete with a caesura running down the page that further testifies to Millay's work with Old English poetry in the original and with *Beowulf* in particular: 'Wild as the white waves / Rushing and roaring, Heaving the wrack / High up the headland; Hoarse as the howling / Winds of winter'.[76] Ladies in attendance, including a 'Hildeburh', weep for the murdered king, while the lords lament that none of his retainers came to his aid, another detail reminiscent of *Beowulf*. Like Bryher's *Beowulf*, Millay's *Henchman* thus offers what Peter Buchanan has termed a 'queer historical palimpsest' of the poem.[77]

As Bryher's and Millay's reworkings of Old English reveal, the story we tell about *Beowulf* and Oxford falls subject to the same problems that the poem itself faced in the early to mid-twentieth century (and beyond): the obsession with singular dates and names and with excavating a history in and for the poem rather than reading it. From this perspective, the obsession with Tolkien and with 1936 is another symptom of the desire to date the poem and to thereby legitimise it within a certain kind of elitist framework. But there is a distortion effect caused by focusing myopically on Oxford – and, relatedly, on Harvard in the history of *Beowulf*'s afterlives, with Tolkien's lecture serving as a midpoint between the poem's early translation by Fireside Poet and Harvard professor Henry Wadsworth Longfellow and its later uptake by Harvard oral-formulaic theorists.

But just as Harvard also offered medieval linguistic training to Lorenzo Dow Turner and therefore to the formation of African American studies even as Stuart Hall was being turned away from medieval studies at Oxford, so too might Oxford's contribution to *Beowulf*'s literary status be reimagined, at least in fiction if not in real life, through the work of Nigerian American novelist and cultural critic Teju Cole, whose novel *Open City* imagines newer, more generative lines of transmission for *Beowulf* and other medieval English poems. Whereas Tolkien pushed Hall away from graduate work on *Piers Plowman*, Cole gives us a fictional Oxbridge that welcomes a Japanese American DPhil student whose crowning achievement is an annotated translation of *Piers*. The fictional young scholar ultimately becomes an early medieval literature professor in New York City, where he teaches and mentors the novel's protagonist and narrator, Julius, a Nigerian immigrant and a research fellow in psychiatry; but in between, he and his family are interned during the Second World War. As Julius explains, 'The war had broken out just as he was finishing his D. Phil, and he was forced to leave England and return to his family in the Pacific Northwest. With them, shortly afterward, he was taken to internment in the Minidoka Camp in Idaho', where he takes consolation in memorising poetry, so that, years later, the lines '*In summer season when soft was the sun, I wore a shroud as I a shepherd were*' come back to him with the unanswered question for his former student: 'Do you recognize it?'[78] Again, medieval English poetry offers Cole a means of retracing lines of transmission, so that the medieval becomes a consoling touchstone for memory and identity in times of profound racism and crisis.

In the novel's opening pages, Julius visits Professor Saito, whose 'English Literature Before Shakespeare' seminar he had taken as a junior, and who, he relates, 'had taken me under his wing' and 'invited me to meet with him several times in his office', where 'we drank coffee, and talked: about interpretations of *Beowulf* ... and of his studies just before the Second World War'.[79] While the war and the poem are thus entangled, the poem offers a means of undoing the racist violence of internment as well as the larger war, and Julius notes that 'those meetings became cherished highlights of my last two years at Maxwell. I came to view him as a grandfatherly figure.' When he returns to New York after medical school, Julius resumes the visits, which transport the elderly professor back to his graduate school days: 'It was the late thirties again, and he was back in Cambridge', reminiscing about how his tutor, Chadwick, had 'been taught by Skeat himself' and 'taught me the value of memory, and how to think of it as mental music, a setting to iambs and trochees'.[80] Here, we have 1930s Oxbridge, *Beowulf* and even the editor and first Elrington and Bosworth Professor of Anglo-Saxon W. W. Skeat, together fostering kinship and providing 'mental music' for Julius and Professor Saito.

Extending his *Beowulf*ian interests, Cole's 2016 collection of essays literally begins with the first three lines of the poem and the revelation that

> When I am trying out a new pen in a shop, I write out the first words of *Beowulf* as translated by Seamus Heaney. Years ago, I memorized the opening page. After a while, those were the words that came most readily to hand when I was testing the flow of ink.[81]

As his go-to pen trial, the poem thus serves an important function for Cole's writing, getting the ink flowing and becoming the arbiter for his writing implements. Indeed, we might even hear an echo of it in Cole's debut novel, *Open City*, which opens similarly *in medias res*: 'And so'.[82] So, while the non-fiction collection that his 'Heaney-wulf' anecdote opens with takes its title from another Heaney poem, suggesting that Cole's primary interest might be in Heaney rather than *Beowulf* itself, his medieval interests are in fact sustained throughout his work.

As a native of Kalamazoo, Michigan, the home of the International Congress on Medieval Studies, this medieval enthusiasm comes naturally, so that *Beowulf*'s opening lines flow seamlessly together with his quip when anyone asks him about Yoruba, the language of Nigeria, where he spent his childhood and teenage years: 'Opolopo opolo ni ko mo pe opolopo eniyan l'opolo l'opolopo' ('Many frogs do not know that many people are very intelligent').[83] As he riffs, 'I reiterate *Beowulf*. I recite my Yoruba tongue-twister, I tell Lucian Freud's joke: we are creatures of private convention. But we are also the ways in which we enlarge our coasts.'[84] *Beowulf* and Yoruba and the joke Cole uses to test the microphone before talks and readings are thus both 'private convention[s]' and radical means of both mapping and reorienting the self. Indeed, the self enlarging its own coasts through reading and remembering texts takes its guiding image from *Beowulf*'s subsequent lines, which trace Scyld Scefing, or 'Shield Sheafson' in Heaney, as he circumnavigates the North Sea to become the influential leader to whom 'each clan on the outlying coasts / beyond the whale-road had to yield', and who, when dead, is taken 'out to the sea's flood', where 'A ring-whorled prow rode in the harbour, / ice-clad, outbound.'[85] In Cole's reading, however, coast enlarging is mapped into migration rather than conquest.

For Poet Laureate and Pulitzer Prize winner Natasha Trethewey, *Beowulf* is also intimately woven into her experience of reading, writing and memory writ large. When asked about her 'first encounter with poetry', Trethewey replied, 'my father used to recite parts of *Beowulf* to me as a bedtime story'.[86] *Beowulf* in Old English, that is, with her father's particular speciality being Grendel's terrifying entrance through the doors of Heorot. As she reminisced, laughing,

> I think I was charmed by my father's performance of it; he had a big, booming voice and he could do part of it in Old English, so that was pure sound. Then, the translation was the story, which was gripping. After all that, he'd turn off the lights and I'd have to go to sleep.[87]

Relating the same anecdote in another interview, she explains that 'the stories he told me undergird our relationship and our shared relationship to my mother', thus weaving *Beowulf*, however faintly, through her poems on family, race and her native Mississippi.[88] Indeed, in her first book, *Domestic Work*, she recounts how 'Late, / when my dreams turned / to nightmare, you were there- / Beowulf to slay Grendel / at my door'.[89]

An episode of the television series *Star Trek: Voyager* also registers a history – and a speculative future – for *Beowulf*'s popularity that resists and revises the role that white supremacy has played in constructing and sustaining *Beowulf*'s particular hypercanonicity.[90] Written by Naren Shankar and aired in the United States on 24 April 1995, the episode, 'Heroes and Demons', features Ensign Harry Kim (played by Garrett Wang) playing the role of the eponymous hero in a holographic simulation of *Beowulf*. After Kim's mysterious disappearance, the role of Beowulf is then taken up first by the Vulcan Tuvok (played by African American actor Tim Russ) and then by Chakotay, a Native American character (played by the Latindio actor Robert Beltran), before the ship's holographic doctor and a 'shield maiden' simulation character free the missing crew members together with the simulation's 'Grendel', a sentient star-energy life-form that had become trapped in the ship's computer system. For at least one member of the cast, the racial inclusiveness of this speculative *Beowulf*-future was specifically important, as Wang reported that being an Asian American actor had limited his opportunities to appear in period drama.[91]

Delivered as a lecture over the course of many years and retrospectively published as 'Grendel and his Mother' in 2019, Nobel Laureate Toni Morrison's contribution to the future popularity of *Beowulf* proceeds by amplifying the perspective on the poem espoused by her teacher John Gardner and his novel *Grendel*. As she and the other thinkers cited above reveal, we can thus make *Beowulf* continue to be canonical by appealing to the potentially radical possibilities opened up by the poem itself. Thinking with *Beowulf*, Morrison is able to conclude, 'I like to think that John Gardner's view will hold: that language – informed, shaped, reasoned – will become the hand that stays crisis and gives creative, constructive conflict air to breathe, startling our lives and rippling our intellect.'[92]

The language of *Beowulf* can thus itself open new horizons. Even though it only comes down to us in a single manuscript, the poem can continually find new readerships, because it remains just as rethinkable as it was in the early Middle Ages. In fact, in Roger Reeves's poem 'Grendel', which was published in *The New Yorker* during the revision phase of this chapter, 'the beast Grendel' signifies James Baldwin's rendition of 'Precious Lord' as a fragile 'absolute prophecy … Bringing humans the best vision of themselves, / Which, of course, must be slaughtered'.[93] *Beowulf* is a poem that modulates and re-paces its own timescales as it dramatises the uncontrollable circulation and destruction of heroes, objects and, above all, stories. Good poems, like language in Morrison's and Gardner's view, escape their traditional contexts and give air to new discussions, so that – rather than requiring Tolkien's 'potent' criticism – *Beowulf* can still offer Morrison 'fertile ground'.[94] Indeed, this sense of the ground that offers up new stories is intimately bound up in *Beowulf* itself.

At the very end of the poem, the poet briefly alludes to a thousand-year gap between the burial of the treasure that would furnish the dragon's hoard and the slaying of the dragon that now lies dead beside it: 'Him big stodan bunan ond orcas, / discas lagon ond dyre swyrd, / omige, þurhetone, swa hie wið eorðan fæðm / þusend wintra þær eardodon' (ll. 3047–50) ['By him there stood cups and flagons, plates lay stacked and expensive swords eaten through with rust – just as they had spent a thousand winters, there in the lap of the earth']. We learn that, at the moment of burial, these dishes were wrapped in a curse, presumably unknown to Beowulf and his men. Now, after another thousand-year gap, from the copying of the sole surviving manuscript to our own, provisional account of its course through several later literary histories, these lines still offer us treasures whose stories we may not fully understand.

Notes

1 Howell D. Chickering, 'Some Contexts for Bede's *Death-Song*', *PMLA* 91.1 (1976): 93, 94.

2 Ibid., 98, 99.

3 We quote here the West Saxon Version, which survives in seventeen manuscripts from the British Isles, as edited by Elliott Van Kirk Dobbie, *The Anglo-Saxon Minor Poems*, ASPR 6 (New York: Columbia University Press, 1942), p. 108.

4 The count is Michael W. Twomey's from 'On Reading *Bede's Death Song*: Translation, Typology, and Penance in Symeon of Durham's Text of the *Epistola Cuthberti de obitu Bedae*', *Neuphilologische Mitteilungen* 84.2 (1983): 171, supplemented with the copy in The Hague, Royal Library, MS 70.H.7, which he does not count.

5 Cuthbert, *Epistola de obitu Bedae*, ed. and trans. Bertram Colgrave and R. A. B. Mynors, in *Bede's Ecclesiastical History of the English People* (Oxford: Oxford University Press, 1969), pp. 579–87.

6 *Beowulf*, dir. Robert Zemeckis (Paramount, 2007).

7 Peter Orton, *The Transmission of Old English Poetry* (Turnhout: Brepols, 2000).

8 Helmut Gneuss and Michael Lapidge, *Anglo-Saxon Manuscripts: A Bibliographical Handlist of Manuscripts and Manuscript Fragments Written or Owned in England up to 1100* (Toronto: Toronto University Press, 2014), nos. 12, 82, 542, 584 and 661.

9 For more information, see Michael Lapidge, *The Cult of St Swithun* (Oxford: Oxford University Press, 2003).

10 Daniel Donoghue, *How the Anglo-Saxons Read their Poems* (Philadelphia, PA: University of Pennsylvania Press, 2018), p. 6.

11 For a recent exploration of these correspondences, see Irina Dumitrescu, '*Beowulf* and *Andreas*: Intimate Relations', in Daniel C. Remein and Erica Weaver (eds), *Dating Beowulf: Studies in Intimacy* (Manchester: Manchester University Press, 2020), pp. 257–78.

12 For an overview of the Scylding backdrop to the poem, see Roberta Frank, '*Beowulf* and the Intimacy of Large Parties', in Remein and Weaver (eds), *Dating Beowulf: Studies in Intimacy*, pp. 54–72.

13 Brian O'Camb, 'George Hickes and the Invention of the Old English *Maxims* Poem', *English Literary History* 85.1 (2018): 2. On the earliest editions of *Beowulf*, see J. R. Hall, 'The First Two Editions of *Beowulf*: Thorkelin's (1815) and Kemble's (1833)', in D. G. Scragg and Paul Szarmach (eds), *The Editing of Old English* (Cambridge: D. S. Brewer, 1994), pp. 239–50.

14 Haruko Momma, *From Philology to English Studies: Language and Culture in the Nineteenth Century* (Cambridge: Cambridge University Press, 2013), pp. 87–8, citing Sharon Turner, *The History of the Manners, Landed Property, Government, Laws, Poetry, Literature, Religion and Language, of the Anglo-Saxons* (London: Printed for Longman, Hurst, Rees, and Orme, 1805), and John Josias Conybeare, *Illustrations of Anglo-Saxon Poetry by John Josias Conybeare, M.A. &c., Late Prebendary of York and Vicar of Bath Easton, Formerly Student of Christchurch and Successively Professor of Anglo-Saxon and of Poetry in the University of Oxford, ed. with addition notes, introductory notices, &c., by his brother William Daniel Conybeare, MA, &c., Rector of Sully* (London: Printed for Harding and Lepard, 1826), p. 31.

15 Momma, *From Philology to English Studies*, p. 87.

16 For more details, see chapter 1 of Chris Jones, *Fossil Poetry: Anglo-Saxon and Linguistic Nativism in Nineteenth-Century Poetry* (Oxford: Oxford University Press, 2018).

17 Haruko Momma, 'What Has *Beowulf* to Do with English? (Let's Ask Lady Philology!)', in Mary Hayes and Allison Burkette (eds), *Approaches*

to Teaching the History of the English Language: Pedagogy in Practice (Oxford: Oxford University Press, 2017), p. 219.

18 This sense is routinely reaffirmed in the 'handbook' genre of critical literature; for example, Thomas A. Shippey refers to the essay as 'the most influential essay ever written on the poem' in 'Structure and Unity', in Robert E. Bjork and John D. Niles (eds), *A Beowulf Handbook* (Lincoln, NE: University of Nebraska Press, 1997), p. 162; while Seth Lerer, even while critiquing the critical rhetoric that Tolkien's essay underwrites, still identifies it as the 'originary piece of modern *Beowulf* criticism' in '*Beowulf* and Contemporary Critical Theory', in Bjork and Niles (eds), *A Beowulf Handbook*, p. 328.

19 J. R. R. Tolkien, '*Beowulf*: The Monsters and the Critics', *Proceedings of the British Academy*, vol. 22 (London: Oxford University Press, 1936), p. 8; and Archibald Strong, *A Short History of English Literature* (Oxford, 1921), pp. 2–3, quoted in Tolkien, 'Monsters and the Critics', p. 5.

20 Dorothy Kim, 'The Question of Race in *Beowulf*', *JSTOR Daily*, 25 September 2019, https://daily.jstor.org/the-question-of-race-in-beowulf/ (accessed 7 January 2022).

21 Tolkien, 'Monsters and the Critics', pp. 5–6.

22 Ibid., p. 6.

23 Ibid., p. 7.

24 Michael D. C. Drout (ed.), *J.R.R. Tolkien: Beowulf and the Critics*, 2nd rev. edn (Tempe, AZ: ACMRS, 2002).

25 Kathy Lavezzo, '"New Ethnicities" and "Medieval Race"', *Addressing the Crises: The Stuart Hall Project* 1.6, p. 2. See also the speculative fiction writer and Marxist China Miéville, who famously called Tolkien 'the wen on the arse of fantasy': Miéville, 'Debate', n.d., *China Miéville Official Website* [now defunct], http://web.archive.org/web/20050115043853/http://www.panmacmillan.com/features/china/debate.htm.

26 Kim, 'The Question of Race in *Beowulf*'.

27 We thank Nicholas Watson for this characterisation of Tolkien and his tastes.

28 Tolkien, 'Monsters and the Critics', p. 1.

29 Virginia Woolf, *Three Guineas* (London: Hogarth, 1938), p. 5.

30 Jana Schulman, 'An Anglo-Saxonist at Oxford and Cambridge: Dorothy Whitelock (1902–1982)', in Jane Chance (ed.), *Women Medievalists and the Academy* (Madison, WI: University of Wisconsin Press, 2005), p. 555.

31 Mary Dockray-Miller, *Public Medievalists, Racism, and Suffrage in the American Women's Colleges* (New York: Palgrave, 2017); and Matthew X. Vernon, *The Black Middle Ages: Race and the Construction of the Middle Ages* (New York: Palgrave, 2018), especially 'Medieval

Self-fashioning: the Middle Ages in African-American Scholarship and Curricula'. Dockray-Miller catalogues 32 women's institutions, including Spelman College, that offered coursework in Old English in the late nineteenth and early twentieth centuries (p. 8), while Vernon identifies Old English courses at Howard University and Atlanta University.

32 See Dockray-Miller's Appendix 1, in *Public Medievalists, Racism, and Suffrage*, pp. 75–84, and Appendix 2, especially pp. 91–6.

33 Ibid., 2. Salient examples from Dockray-Miller's bibliography on the longer history of racist Anglo-Saxonism in the United States dating at least to Thomas Jefferson are worth rehearsing: Stanley R. Hauer, 'Thomas Jefferson and the Anglo-Saxon Language', *PMLA* 98.5 (1981): 879–98; Reginald Horseman, *Race and Manifest Destiny: The Origins of American Racial Anglo-Saxonism* (Cambridge, MA: Harvard University Press, 1981); Gregory A. VanHoosier-Carey, 'Byrthnoth in Dixie: The Emergence of Anglo-Saxon Studies in the Postbellum South', in Allen J. Frantzen and John D. Niles (eds), *Anglo-Saxonism and the Construction of Social Identity* (Gainesville, FL: University Press of Florida, 1997); Eric Kaufmann, 'American Exceptionalism Reconsidered: Anglo-Saxon Ethnogenesis in the "Universal" Nation, 1776–1850', *Journal of American Studies* 33.3 (1999): 437–57; and Richie Devon Watson, *Normans and Saxons: Southern Race Mythology and the Intellectual History of the American Civil War* (Baton Rouge, LA: Louisiana State University Press, 2008). See also more recent contributions on race and Old English studies by scholars of colour, for example Adam Miyashiro, 'Decolonizing Anglo-Saxon Studies: A Response to ISAS in Honolulu', blog post, *In the Medieval Middle*, http://www.inthemedievalmiddle.com/2017/07/decolonizing-anglo-saxon-studies.html (accessed 7 January 2022); Mary Rambaran-Olm, 'Anglo-Saxon Studies, Academia, and White Supremacy', *Medium* post, 27 June 2018, https://mrambaranolm.medium.com/anglo-saxon-studies-academia-and-white-supremacy-17c87b360bf3 (accessed 7 January 2022); and Kim, 'The Question of Race'.

34 Vernon, *The Black Middle Ages*, pp. 79–80. Dockray-Miller has also identified an earlier Old English poetry course taught by Professor Gordon David Houston at Howard, prompting Mary Rambaran-Olm to uncover more about Houston's career as a medieval philologist in '"Houston, we have a problem": Erasing Black Scholars in Old English Literature', *Medium* post, *The Sundial*, 3 March 2020, https://medium.com/the-sundial-acmrs/houston-we-have-a-problem-erasing-black-scholars-in-old-english-821121495dc (accessed 7 January 2022).

35 Smithsonian Anacostia Community Museum, *Word, Shout, Song: Lorenzo Dow Turner Connecting Communities through Language*, exhibition brochure, 9 August 2010.

36 Vernon, *Black Middle Ages*, p. 81, n. 91; Nathaniel Patrick Tillman, 'Lydgate's *Rimes* as Evidence of his Pronunciation', PhD dissertation, University of Wisconsin-Madison, 1941.
37 Dockray-Miller, *Public Medievalists, Racism, and Suffrage*, p. 43.
38 A. Russell Brooks, 'Nathaniel Patrick Tillman (1898–1965): A Tribute to a Distinguished Teacher', *CLA Journal* 9.2 (1965): 207–8.
39 Benjamin Griffith Brawley, *A New Survey of English Literature: A Text Book for Colleges* (New York: Alfred A. Knopf, 1925), p. 7. In the opening section on Old English literature, Brawley also gives an overview of the four major codices that today preserve the bulk of Old English verse (p. 3) and delves into several texts, recounting Bede's story of Cædmon (p. 9), noting the runic signatures that link the poems of Cynewulf (p. 10) and summarising 'the famous *Anglo-Saxon Chronicle*' (p. 12), among other highlights that give a learned overview of Old English literature.
40 The poems may be found in *Poet-Lore* 2 (1890): 133–4 and 185–7, and, as Marijane Osborn notes, they comprise verse translations of *Beowulf* lines 26–53 and 1493–1571, in her 'Annotated List of Beowulf Translations', forthcoming in *Medieval Perspectives* 35 (2021).
41 Dockray-Miller, *Public Medievalists, Racism, and Suffrage*, Appendix 1, p. 115.
42 Ibid., Appendices 3–4, pp. 96–126.
43 Ibid., p. 116.
44 Ibid., p. 92.
45 Ibid., p. 93.
46 Mary Gwinn, 'The First Part of Beowulf', PhD dissertation, Bryn Mawr College, 1888, p. 8.
47 Ibid., p. 13. Cf. Tolkien, 'Monsters and the Critics', p. 30.
48 On this point, Jones differentiates his account of Tennyson's knowledge and attention – including even which books he owned or accessed – from that of Damian Love, 'Hengist's Brood: Tennyson and the Anglo-Saxons', *The Review of English Studies*, 60 (2009): 460–74; and Edward B. Irving, Jr, 'The Charge of the Light Brigade: Tennyson's Battle of Brunanburh', in Donald Scragg and Carole Weinberg (eds), *Literary Appropriations of the Anglo-Saxons from the Thirteenth to the Twentieth Century* (Cambridge: Cambridge University Press, 2000), pp. 174–93.
49 Jones, *Fossil Poetry*, p. 238, citing, on the timing of the poem, Clare Simmons, 'Iron-Worded Proof: Victorian Identity and the Old English Language', *Studies in Medievalism* 4 (1992): 202–18.
50 Jones, *Fossil Poetry*, p. 239.

51 Ibid.
52 Here we merely rehearse in a new context Jones's already superb account of the primary sources: see *Fossil Poetry*, pp. 239–40, citing Jack Kolb (ed.), *The Letters of Henry Hallam* (Columbus, OH: Ohio State University Press, 1981), pp. 646, 738; and other quotations from Irving, 'The Charge of the Light Brigade', pp. 176–7.
53 Sidney Lanier, 'The Death of Byrhtnoth: A Study in Anglo-Saxon poetry', in his *Music and poetry: essays upon some aspects and inter-relations of the two arts* (1898), pp. 136–58, at 138.
54 For example, Sidney Lanier and Clifford Lanier, 'The Power of Prayer, or, the First Steamboat up the Alabama' and 'Uncle Jim's Baptist Revival', in *The Centennial Edition of the Works of Sidney Lanier*, 10 vols (Baltimore, MD: Johns Hopkins University Press, 1945), vol. I, pp. 215–17. And see John D. Kerkering, *The Poetics of National and Racial Identity in Nineteenth-Century American Literature* (Cambridge: Cambridge University Press, 2003), pp. 114–51.
55 On Southern Anglo-Saxonism, see also Donna Beth Ellard, *Anglo-Saxon(ist) Pasts, Postsaxon Futures* (Goleta, CA: Punctum Books, 2019), especially chs 1, 6–7.
56 Kerkering, *Poetics of National Identity*, pp. 120, 153–54.
57 Sidney Lanier, 'Lecture I', in *Shakespeare and His Forerunners* in *The Centennial Edition of the Works of Sidney Lanier*, vol. III, p. 23; Lanier, *The Science of English Verse in The Centennial Edition of the Works of Sidney Lanier*, vol. II, p. 113. Quoted in Kerkering, *Poetics of National Identity*, p. 121.
58 Lanier, 'Death of Byrhtnoth', pp. 136–7.
59 Ibid., p. 138, n. 1.
60 Jones, *Fossil Poetry*, p. 184, citing William Morris, 'Early England', in *The Unpublished Lectures of William Morris* (Detroit, MI: Wayne State University Press, 1969), pp. 158–78.
61 Ibid., p. 183.
62 Ibid. And see Denis Ferhatović's characterisation of this phenomenon as 'familiar defamiliarization' in his 'A Portrait of the Translator as Grendel's Mother: The Postcolonial Feminist Polyphony of Meghan Purvis's *Beowulf*', in Irina Dumitrescu and Eric Weiskott (eds), *The Shapes of Early English Poetry: Style, Form, History* (Kalamazoo, MI: Medieval Institute Publications, 2019), p. 73.
63 William Morris and A. J. Wyatt (trans.), *The Tale of Beowulf Done Out of the Old English Tongue*, in *The Collected Works of William Morris*, vol. X (London: Longmans, Green, 1898), p. 723.
64 Ibid., p. 186.
65 Ibid., p. 165.

66 Clara Thomas, *The Adventures of Beowulf* (London: H. Marshall & Son, 1899).
67 H. E. Marshall, *Stories of Beowulf* (London: T.C. & E.C. Jack, 1908), p. i.
68 Lise Jaillant, '*A fine old tale of adventure*: *Beowulf* Told to the Children of the English Race, 1898–1908', *Children's Literature Association Quarterly* 38.4 (2013): 399–419.
69 Manuel Vallvé, *Beowulf* (Barcelona: Araluce, 1934); Robert L. Schichler, 'Understanding the Outsider: Grendel, Geisel, and the Grinch', *Popular Culture Review* 11 (2000): 99–105. We thank Damian Fleming for bringing the possibility of a Grendel-inspired Grinch to our attention.
70 Momma, *From Philology to English Studies*, p. 80.
71 James A. Pegolotti, *Deems Taylor: A Biography* (Boston, MA: Northeastern University Press, 2003), p. 143; Henry Sweet, *An Anglo-Saxon Reader in Prose and Verse: With Grammatical Introduction* (Oxford: Clarendon Press, 1879), p. 119.
72 Elizabeth Hazelton Haight, 'Vincent at Vassar', *Vassar Quarterly* XXXVI.5, May 1951.
73 The condition of Sweet's *Reader* is according to Elaine Bremer Apczynski, as recorded in Pegolotti, *Deems Taylor*, p. 371, n. 18. We were unable to locate Elaine Bremer Apczynski, 'The Making of *The King's Henchman*: An American Opera', MA thesis, State University of New York at Buffalo, 1991, pp. 61–2, but Pegolotti also reports that she posits that Millay derived her topic from a reading of William of Malmesbury's *Chronicles of the Kings of England*. For more on Millay's *Beowulf*, see F. Holthausen and L. Morsbach, 'Beowulf. nebst den kleineren Denkmälern der Heldensage… 2. T., Einleitung, Glossar und Anmerkungen', Steepletop Library: the books of Edna St. Vincent Millay, https://steepletoplibrary.org/items/show/1274 (accessed 26 December 2019).
74 The catalogue of Millay's library is, at present, only half-finished, so it is difficult to ascertain whether Millay owned other editions of *Beowulf* as well, but we are grateful to Mark O'Berski of the Edna St Vincent Millay Society for his insights into Millay's collection.
75 Private communication from Mark O'Berski, 2 February 2020.
76 Edna St Vincent Millay, *The King's Henchman: A Play in Three Acts* (New York: Harper and Brothers, 1927), p. 7.
77 Peter Buchanan, '*Beowulf*, Bryher, and the Blitz', in Remein and Weaver (eds), *Dating Beowulf: Studies in Intimacy*, p. 299.
78 Teju Cole, *Open City* (New York: Random House, 2011), pp. 9, 14.
79 Ibid., p. 9.
80 Ibid., pp. 10, 14.

81 Teju Cole, *Known and Strange Things: Essays* (New York: Random House, 2016), p. xiii.
82 Cole, *Open City*, p. 3. Seamus Heaney famously – and somewhat controversially – begins his *Beowulf* with 'So', explaining his logic in his *Beowulf: A New Verse Translation* (New York: Farrar, Straus and Giroux, 2000), p. xxvii.
83 Cole, *Known and Strange Things*, p. xii.
84 Ibid., p. xiv.
85 Heaney, *Beowulf*, ll. 9–10, 30, 32–3.
86 Remica L. Bingham, 'Interview with Natasha Trethewey', *PMS poemmemoirstory* 8 (2008): 1–20; repr. in Joan Wylie Hall (ed.), *Conversations with Natasha Trethewey* (Jackson, MS: University Press of Mississippi, 2013), p. 62.
87 Ibid.
88 Ibid.
89 Natasha Trethewey, 'Mythmaker', in *Domestic Work: Poems* (Minneapolis, MN: Graywolf Press, 2000), p. 31.
90 This recalls André M. Carrington's breakthrough analysis of *Deep Space Nine* (another *Star Trek* spin-off from the 1990s) as 'not only an SF narrative, but a racial narrative, embedded in American cultural traditions alongside the Black–White buddy comedy and the captivity narrative', in his *Speculative Blackness: The Future of Race in Science Fiction* (Minneapolis, MN: University of Minnesota Press, 2016), ch. 5.
91 Edward Gross and Mark A. Altman, *Captain's Log: Supplemental: The Unauthorized Guide to the New Trek Voyages* (Boston, MA: Little, Brown, 1996), pp. 143–4.
92 Toni Morrison, 'Grendel and his Mother', in *The Source of Self-Regard: Selected Essays, Speeches, and Meditations* (New York: Alfred A. Knopf, 2019), p. 262.
93 Roger Reeves, 'Grendel', *The New Yorker*, 14 September 2020, p. 48.
94 Morrison, 'Grendel and his Mother', p. 255.

Works cited

Primary sources

Beowulf, dir. Robert Zemeckis (Paramount, 2007).
Cole, Teju, *Open City* (New York: Random House, 2011).
— *Known and Strange Things: Essays* (New York: Random House, 2016).
Cuthbert, *Epistola de obitu Bedae*, ed. and trans. Bertram Colgrave and R.A.B. Mynors, in *Bede's Ecclesiastical History of the English People* (Oxford: Oxford University Press, 1969), pp. 579–87.

Heaney, Seamus, *Beowulf: A New Verse Translation* (New York: Farrar, Straus and Giroux, 2000).
Marshall, H. E. *Stories of Beowulf* (London: T.C. & E.C. Jack, 1908).
Miéville, China, 'Debate', n.d., *China Miéville Official Website* [now defunct], http://web.archive.org/web/20050115043853/http://www.panmacmillan.com/features/china/debate.htm.
Millay, Edna St Vincent, *The King's Henchman: A Play in Three Acts* (New York: Harper and Brothers, 1927).
Morris, William, 'Early England', in *The Unpublished Lectures of William Morris* (Detroit, MI: Wayne State University Press, 1969), pp. 158–78.
Morris, William, and A. J. Wyatt (trans.), *The Tale of Beowulf Done Out of the Old English Tongue*, in *The Collected Works of William Morris*, vol. X (London: Longmans, Green, 1898).
Morrison, Toni, 'Grendel and his Mother', in *The Source of Self-Regard: Selected Essays, Speeches, and Meditations* (New York: Alfred A. Knopf, 2019), pp. 255–62.
Reeves, Roger, 'Grendel', *The New Yorker*, 14 September 2020, p. 48.
Robertson Brown, Anna, 'The Passing of Scyld' and 'The Battle with the Water-Sprite', *Poet-Lore* 2 (1890): 133–4, 185–7.
Thomas, Clara, *The Adventures of Beowulf* (London: H. Marshall & Son, 1899).
Trethewey, Natasha, 'Mythmaker', in *Domestic Work: Poems* (Minneapolis, MN: Graywolf Press, 2000), p. 31.
Vallvé, Manuel, *Beowulf* (Barcelona: Araluce, 1934).
Woolf, Virginia, *Three Guineas* (London: Hogarth, 1938).

Secondary sources

Apczynski, Elaine Bremer, 'The Making of *The King's Henchman*: An American Opera', MA thesis, State University of New York at Buffalo, 1991.
Bingham, Remica L., 'Interview with Natasha Trethewey', *PMS poemmemoirstory* 8 (2008): 1–20; repr. in Joan Wylie Hall (ed.), *Conversations with Natasha Trethewey* (Jackson, MS: University Press of Mississippi, 2013), pp. 61–76.
Brawley, Benjamin Griffith, *A New Survey of English Literature: A Text Book for Colleges* (New York: Alfred A. Knopf, 1925).
Brooks, A. Russell, 'Nathaniel Patrick Tillman (1898–1965): A Tribute to a Distinguished Teacher', *CLA Journal* 9.2 (1965): 207–8.
Buchanan, Peter, '*Beowulf*, Bryher, and the Blitz', in Daniel C. Remein and Erica Weaver (eds), *Dating Beowulf: Studies in Intimacy* (Manchester: Manchester University Press, 2020), pp. 279–303.
Carrington, André M., *Speculative Blackness: The Future of Race in Science Fiction* (Minneapolis, MN: University of Minnesota Press, 2016).
Chickering, Howell D., 'Some Contexts for Bede's *Death-Song*', *PMLA* 91.1 (1976): 91–100.

Conybeare, John Josias, *Illustrations of Anglo-Saxon Poetry by John Josias Conybeare, M.A. &c., Late Prebendary of York and Vicar of Bath Easton, Formerly Student of Christchurch and Successively Professor of Anglo-Saxon and of Poetry in the University of Oxford, ed. with addition notes, introductory notices, &c., by his brother William Daniel Conybeare, MA, &c., Rector of Sully* (London: Printed for Harding and Lepard, 1826).

Dobbie, Elliott Van Kirk (ed.), *The Anglo-Saxon Minor Poems*, ASPR 6 (New York: Columbia University Press, 1942).

Dockray-Miller, Mary, *Public Medievalists, Racism, and Suffrage in the American Women's Colleges* (New York: Palgrave, 2017).

Donoghue, Daniel, *How the Anglo-Saxons Read their Poems* (Philadelphia, PA: University of Pennsylvania Press, 2018).

Drout, Michael D. C. (ed.), *J.R.R. Tolkien: Beowulf and the Critics*, 2nd rev. edn (Tempe, AZ: ACMRS, 2002).

Dumitrescu, Irina, '*Beowulf* and *Andreas*: Intimate Relations', in Daniel C. Remein and Erica Weaver (eds), *Dating Beowulf: Studies in Intimacy* (Manchester: Manchester University Press, 2020), pp. 257–78.

Ellard, Donna Beth, *Anglo-Saxon(ist) Pasts, Postsaxon Futures* (Goleta, CA: Punctum Books, 2019).

Ferhatović, Denis, 'A Portrait of the Translator as Grendel's Mother: The Postcolonial Feminist Polyphony of Meghan Purvis's *Beowulf*', in Irina Dumitrescu and Eric Weiskott (eds), *The Shapes of Early English Poetry: Style, Form, History* (Kalamazoo, MI: Medieval Institute Publications, 2019), pp. 59–81.

Frank, Roberta, '*Beowulf* and the Intimacy of Large Parties', in Daniel C. Remein and Erica Weaver (eds), *Dating Beowulf: Studies in Intimacy* (Manchester: Manchester University Press, 2020), pp. 54–72.

Gneuss, Hemut, and Michael Lapidge, *Anglo-Saxon Manuscripts: A Bibliographical Handlist of Manuscripts and Manuscript Fragments Written or Owned in England up to 1100* (Toronto: Toronto University Press, 2014).

Gross, Edward, and Mark A. Altman, *Captain's Log: Supplemental: The Unauthorized Guide to the New Trek Voyages* (Boston, MA: Little, Brown, 1996).

Gwinn, Mary, 'The First Part of Beowulf', PhD dissertation, Bryn Mawr College, 1888.

Haight, Elizabeth Hazelton, 'Vincent at Vassar', *Vassar Quarterly*, XXXVI.5 (May 1951): 14–20.

Hall, J. R., 'The First Two Editions of *Beowulf*: Thorkelin's (1815) and Kemble's (1833)', in D. G. Scragg and Paul Szarmach (eds), *The Editing of Old English* (Cambridge: D. S. Brewer, 1994), pp. 239–50.

Hauer, Stanley R., 'Thomas Jefferson and the Anglo-Saxon Language', *PMLA* 98.5 (1981): 879–98.

Holthausen, F., and L. Morsbach, 'Beowulf. nebst den kleineren Denkmälern der Heldensage… 2. T., Einleitung, Glossar und Anmerkungen', Steepletop Library: the books of Edna St. Vincent Millay, https://steepletoplibrary.org/items/show/1274 (accessed 26 December 2019).

Horseman, Reginald, *Race and Manifest Destiny: The Origins of American Racial Anglo-Saxonism* (Cambridge, MA: Harvard University Press, 1981).

Irving, Jr, Edward B., 'The Charge of the Light Brigade: Tennyson's Battle of Brunanburh', in Donald Scragg and Carole Weinberg (eds), *Literary Appropriations of the Anglo-Saxons from the Thirteenth to the Twentieth Century* (Cambridge: Cambridge University Press, 2000), pp. 174–93.

Jaillant, Lise, '*A fine old tale of adventure*: *Beowulf* Told to the Children of the English Race, 1898–1908', *Children's Literature Association Quarterly* 38.4 (2013): 399–419.

Jones, Chris, *Fossil Poetry: Anglo-Saxon and Linguistic Nativism in Nineteenth-Century Poetry* (Oxford: Oxford University Press, 2018).

Kaufmann, Eric, 'American Exceptionalism Reconsidered: Anglo-Saxon Ethnogenesis in the "Universal" Nation, 1776–1850', *Journal of American Studies* 33.3 (1999): 437–57.

Kerkering, John D., *The Poetics of National and Racial Identity in Nineteenth-Century American Literature* (Cambridge: Cambridge University Press, 2003).

Kim, Dorothy, 'The Question of Race in *Beowulf*', *JSTOR Daily*, 25 September, 2019, https://daily.jstor.org/the-question-of-race-in-beowulf/ (accessed 7 January 2022).

Kolb, Jack (ed.), *The Letters of Henry Hallam* (Columbus, OH: Ohio State University Press, 1981).

Lanier, Sidney, 'The Death of Byrhtnoth: A Study in Anglo-Saxon Poetry', in *Music and poetry: essays upon some aspects and inter-relations of the two arts* (1898), pp. 136–58.

— *The Science of English Verse and Essays on Music.* Vol. II of *The Centennial Edition of the Works of Sidney Lanier* (Baltimore, MD: Johns Hopkins University Press, 1963).

— *Shakespeare and His Forerunners.* Vol. III of *The Centennial Edition of the Works of Sidney Lanier* (Baltimore, MD: Johns Hopkins University Press, 1963).

Lanier, Sidney, and Clifford Lanier, 'The Power of Prayer, or, the First Steamboat up the Alabama', and 'Uncle Jim's Baptist Revival', in *The Centennial Edition of the Works of Sidney Lanier* (Baltimore, MD: Johns Hopkins University Press, 1945), vol. I, pp. 215–17.

Lapidge, Michael, *The Cult of St Swithun* (Oxford: Oxford University Press, 2003).

Lavezzo, Kathy, '"New Ethnicities" and "Medieval Race"', *Addressing the Crisis: The Stuart Hall Project* 1 (2019), https://doi.org/10.17077/2643-8291.1003 (accessed 8 February 2022).

Lerer, Seth, '*Beowulf* and Contemporary Critical Theory', in Robert E. Bjork and John D. Niles (eds), *A Beowulf Handbook* (Lincoln, NE: University of Nebraska Press, 1997), pp. 325–39.

Love, Damian, 'Hengist's Brood: Tennyson and the Anglo-Saxons', *The Review of English Studies* 60 (2009): 460–74.

Miyashiro, Adam, 'Decolonizing Anglo-Saxon Studies: A Response to ISAS in Honolulu', blog post, *In the Medieval Middle*, http://www.inthemedievalmiddle.com/2017/07/decolonizing-anglo-saxon-studies.html (accessed 7 January 2022).

Momma, Haruko, *From Philology to English Studies: Language and Culture in the Nineteenth Century* (Cambridge: Cambridge University Press, 2013).

— 'What Has *Beowulf* to Do with English? (Let's Ask Lady Philology!)', in Mary Hayes and Allison Burkette (eds), *Approaches to Teaching the History of the English Language: Pedagogy in Practice* (Oxford: Oxford University Press, 2017), pp. 211–22.

O'Berski, Mark, private communication, 2 February 2020.

O'Camb, Brian, 'George Hickes and the Invention of the Old English *Maxims* Poem', *English Literary History* 85.1 (2018): 1–31.

Orton, Peter, *The Transmission of Old English Poetry* (Turnhout: Brepols, 2000).

Pegolotti, James A., *Deems Taylor: A Biography* (Boston, MA: Northeastern University Press, 2003).

Rambaran-Olm, Mary, 'Anglo-Saxon Studies, Academia, and White Supremacy', *Medium* post, 27 June 2018, https://mrambaranolm.medium.com/anglo-saxon-studies-academia-and-white-supremacy-17c87b360bf3 (accessed 7 January 2022).

— '"Houston, we have a problem:" Erasing Black Scholars in Old English Literature'. *Medium* post for *The Sundial*, 3 March 2020, https://medium.com/the-sundial-acmrs/houston-we-have-a-problem-erasing-black-scholars-in-old-english-821121495dc (accessed 7 January 2022).

Schichler, Robert L., 'Understanding the Outsider: Grendel, Geisel, and the Grinch', *Popular Culture Review* 11 (2000): 99–105.

Schulman, Jana, 'An Anglo-Saxonist at Oxford and Cambridge: Dorothy Whitelock (1902–1982)', in Jane Chance (ed.), *Women Medievalists and the Academy* (Madison, WI: University of Wisconsin Press, 2005), pp. 553–64.

Shippey, Thomas A., 'Structure and Unity', in Robert E. Bjork and John D. Niles (eds), *A Beowulf Handbook* (Lincoln, NE: University of Nebraska Press, 1997), pp. 149–74.

Simmons, Clare, 'Iron-Worded Proof: Victorian Identity and the Old English Language', *Studies in Medievalism* 4 (1992): 202–18.

Smithsonian Anacostia Community Museum, *Word, Shout, Song: Lorenzo Dow Turner Connecting Communities through Language*, exhibition brochure, 9 August 2010.

Strong, Archibald, *A Short History of English Literature* (Oxford: Oxford University Press, 1921).

Sweet, Henry, *An Anglo-Saxon Reader in Prose and Verse: With Grammatical Introduction* (Oxford: Clarendon Press, 1879).

Tillman, Nathaniel Patrick, 'Lydgate's *Rimes* as Evidence of his Pronunciation', PhD dissertation, University of Wisconsin-Madison, 1941.

Tolkien, J. R. R., '*Beowulf:* The Monsters and the Critics', *Proceedings of the British Academy*, vol. 22 (London: Oxford University Press, 1936).
Turner, Sharon, *The History of the Manners, Landed Property, Government, Laws, Poetry, Literature, Religion and Language, of the Anglo-Saxons* (London: Printed for Longman, Hurst, Rees, and Orme, 1805).
Twomey, Michael W., 'On Reading *Bede's Death Song*: Translation, Typology, and Penance in Symeon of Durham's Text of the *Epistola Cuthberti de obitu Bedae*', *Neuphilologische Mitteilungen* 84.2 (1983): 171–81.
VanHoosier-Carey, Gregory A., 'Byrthnoth in Dixie: The Emergence of Anglo-Saxon Studies in the Postbellum South', in Allen J. Frantzen and John D. Niles (eds), *Anglo-Saxonism and the Construction of Social Identity* (Gainesville, FL: University Press of Florida, 1997), pp. 157–72.
Vernon, Matthew X., *The Black Middle Ages: Race and the Construction of the Middle Ages* (New York: Palgrave, 2018).
Watson, Richie Devon, *Normans and Saxons: Southern Race Mythology and the Intellectual History of the American Civil War* (Baton Rouge, LA: Louisiana State University Press, 2008).

3

Ibn Ḥazm's *Ṭawq al-ḥamāma* (*The Neck-Ring of the Dove*)

Boris Liebrenz

Today, the *Ṭawq al-ḥamāma* [*The Neck-Ring of the Dove*] is the most widely known work by the Andalusian scholar and statesman ʿAlī b. Aḥmad b. Saʿīd Ibn Ḥazm (384/994–456/1064).[1] As far as Arabic literary classics go, this one has become a nearly ubiquitous text: in the Arabic-speaking world, it is found on school curricula and in popular editions; on a global scale it has been translated into numerous languages; and it has not only sparked much scholarship, but also inspired modern literary adaptations. It is considered a quintessential guide to the theme of love in medieval Arabic literature. Although its Andalusian author was a prolific writer in the fields of law, theology and philosophy, today Ibn Ḥazm's only surviving literary work remains his strongest claim to lasting fame and a broad readership.[2] Yet, remarkably, this, his most famous work, survives in but a single copy. As is shown in the first part of this chapter, however, careful examination of that physical manuscript reveals a fascinating history, for its movements among owners and readers, from Mamluk Palestine through Ottoman Constantinople and finally to a library in Leiden, were recorded in notes inscribed on the first and final pages of the codex.

Even once it was transferred to Leiden by the Dutch Resident in Constantinople, Levinus Warner, it lay almost entirely ignored by scholars for some 250 years.[3] Its impact in Western literature was thus belated when compared to *Kalīla wa-Dimna* [Kalīla and Dimna] with its medieval translations and long history of printing that started in the incunabula era,[4] or Ibn Ṭufayl's *Ḥayy Ibn Yaqẓān* [Alive son of Awake], which found vivid interest already in the Enlightenment era;[5] and it cannot match the global phenomenon of *The Thousand and One Nights*, a steady success ever since its first translation by Antoine Galland in 1704–08.[6] Yet in the twentieth century, *The Neck-Ring of the Dove* has emerged as one of the most universally acclaimed pieces of pre-modern Arabic literature. The concluding section of this chapter recounts the manuscript's 'discovery' and its first publication by D. K. Pétrof in 1914,[7] since when it has seen no less than five editions with philological-critical apparatus (alongside a great number of popular printings),[8] as well as translations, sometimes multiple ones, into many languages.[9]

In the East

The nucleus for Pétrof's editorial work and all the ensuing popularity was and is the only surviving manuscript of the text, MS Leiden Or. 927. This manuscript was acquired in Constantinople, sometime in the 1650s or 1660s, by the then Resident of the Dutch Republic, Levinus Warner (1618/1619–65).[10] It has since remained in the *Legatum Warnerianum* in Leiden University Library, today under the shelfmark Or. 927.

With such a history, one question could not but puzzle anyone who reflected on the impact of the *Ṭawq*: how could it be that a text so ubiquitous today was transmitted to us on the feeble thread of a single manuscript? Does this reality betray a level of interest squarely at odds with the work's more recent global success? Did no one care to transmit the text prior to some twentieth-century Orientalist scholars? Was the route to Leiden a necessary detour for this text to gain a relevance it was clearly not having among its erstwhile audience?

In grappling with these questions, it is essential to unearth the history of this unique witness. Yet when describing what the fact of its present uniqueness might mean, it should be borne in mind that this was not always the case. While another copy of the text is not recorded anywhere today, the Leiden manuscript cannot always have been the only one. There certainly was a manuscript that made it from Andalusia to the East, namely the exemplar from which the *unicum* in Leiden was copied, either directly or through any number of intermediary copies. (One day, these intermediary copies might well resurface, probably masked by an incorrect title page or the lack of a beginning and end, in some hitherto ill-catalogued collections.) And there was, in 738/1337, a patron who was willing to have a fine copy executed from one of them, or a scribe who found it worth his while to produce one for his own enjoyment, namely the copy presently in Leiden.[11]

But to return to our present state, we can show that this manuscript was not resting idly and obscure on a bookshelf. Rather, it bears multiple traces of sustained interest over the centuries. This interest is manifest in the form of manuscript notes left on the first and last pages of the codex by a variety of readers and owners. Scholarship has long acknowledged the potential of, but only recently actively engaged with, manuscript notes in any systematic fashion.[12] There are many reasons to account for this, not least the difficulty with which many of these notes can be deciphered.[13] Furthermore, the name of a reader or owner is often without immediate insights if it is not supplemented by information systematically gathered either from literary sources or from snippets of information in other, often widely dispersed manuscript notes. Such systematic gathering has only recently been undertaken in several publicly available databases,[14] and the nascent project *Bibliotheca Arabica* proposes to accumulate, consolidate and considerably expand this material.[15] Literary sources can give us the necessary background information to situate a person in their geographical, chronological, societal and cultural context. The Middle East during the lifetime of this manuscript was home to an astoundingly rich tradition of biographical and chronistic writing that allows us to identify a surprising number of people from many backgrounds. Yet not everyone who wrote, read or owned a book was deemed worthy to be remembered by the compilers of those literary texts.

Those problems and limitations are visible in the manuscript of the *Ṭawq* as well. The following discussion will propose a biographical background based on literary sources for only two of the many who left a trace in the manuscript. Nonetheless, much can be learned even in the absence of such supplementary sources. In this section, I shall present the notes that have survived in this manuscript and what they can tell us about the routes it took and the people who held it in their hands before Warner finally bought it in Constantinople.

The creation of the manuscript

The first phase in the life of any manuscript is its creation, and information on that is often found in the colophon at the very end of a text. In our case, we find no mention of the scribe's name, nor that of a patron, and no place of creation. Of the data we can usually expect in such a text we are left merely with the date of the copy's completion, namely the beginning (*mustahill*) of the month of Rajab in the year 738, which corresponds to January 1338. However, and equally important, it has been noted before that the copyist informs us about his method. We learn that he did not faithfully transcribe the original text of Ibn Ḥazm as it was in front of him.[16] Although the crucial word is unreadable, the context is sufficiently clear for us to learn that the copyist abbreviated his source text where he found it wordy, especially where the poetry of the author was concerned.

Yet in this case, the colophon is not the only place where we learn about the creation of the manuscript. Some hitherto unnoticed codicological observations can shed additional light on the manufacturing process. First, we can gauge the materiality of the source text through traces of its original appearance that are now lost. The whole volume must have been originally bound in an older – most likely Mamluk and possibly original – binding with stamped leather doublures. This we can conclude because faint traces of the pattern of these stamps can still be seen on the original flyleaf (now fol. iii*r*), which today follows after two modern flyleaves. Such a refined leather binding speaks for the care with which the book was produced and would have given the whole codex a much more splendid aspect than we see today.

Additionally, and more importantly, the manuscript displays at least two distinct stages of production that differ in subtle but discernible ways. There is a clear shift in layout and rubrication, if not hand. Style I is maintained until folio 20 and then starts again from folio 79. It distinguishes itself by three red points to mark verse divisions (also applied on fol. 78*v*), as well as the rubrication of headings and other highlighted divisions such as the word *khabar*. Style II is employed in the intermediary folios. Does this mean that two copyists were working simultaneously on the *Ṭawq*? Or that a fragment, the intermediary folios of Style II, was completed by another writer, in itself not an uncommon process? If so, would this collaboration be the reason why we do not find a name in the colophon? The script is close enough to make this an unlikely scenario, though why the copyist would have chosen to change his style during the work process and then reverse that decision is impossible to tell. And we will see shortly that there is another possible clue to the identity of the copyist.

Between the creation and Warner

It did not take long for the blank spaces of the title page to attract those who saw the manuscript to leave their marks. In the upper left corner of the title page, we find an acephalous note by one Muḥammad b. ʿUthmān al-Nahāwandī al-Ṣūlī, dated to the very year the copy was achieved, 738 AH [1338 CE]:

[...]
العبد الضعيف [الى
ربه اللطيف محمد [بن[17]
ابن عثمان النهاوندي
الصولي[18] عفا الله تعالى [عنه
في سنة ٨٣٧ هجرية

[...] al-ʿabd al-ḍaʿīf [ilā] / rabbihī al-laṭīf Muḥammad [b.] / Ibn ʿUthmān al-Nahāwandī / al-Ṣūlī ʿafā Allāh taʿālā [ʿanhū] / fī sanat 735 hijriyya

[...] the weak slave [in the face of] his kind master Muḥammad [b.] Ibn ʿUthmān al-Nahāwandī al-Ṣūlī may God, exalted is He, forgive [him] in the year 738 of the Flight]

This man is Sharaf al-Dīn Muḥammad b. ʿUthmān b. Abī Bakr al-Nahāwandī (d. 740/1340).[19] His biographers describe him mainly in professional terms as a judge who held the position in Ṣafad, then ʿAjlūn, Ṭarābulus and Nābulus, constantly in and out of favour with superior judges and rulers. He spent the last years of his life unemployed (*baṭālan*) in his home in Ṣafad for roughly four years, then joined his patron, the governor of Ṣafad, in Cairo, where he eventually died. It was in either of these last two locations that he would have acquired, read or probably even produced the manuscript of the *Ṭawq* roughly two years prior to his death. The manuscript, if it was indeed still his at this point, could thus have stayed in Cairo.

The year 738 AH also appears in the colophon, and early on Nykl would 'safely conclude' that al-Nahāwandī was the copyist,[20] a conclusion also postulated by van Koningsveld,[21] while Witkam later speculated, though more carefully, that this could well be the case given the proximity of the handwriting.[22] The survival of one of the highlights of Arabic literature could thus be the outcome of a period of involuntary leisure on the part of an unemployed middle-rank jurist. Another possibility is that although al-Nahāwandī appears to have come from a well-to-do family (his father, d. 698/1298, had already served as judge of Ṣafad),[23] he might have fallen on hard times after his dismissal. Ṣafadī even states clearly that al-Nahāwandī's end was marked by poverty and constraints.[24] Could he have made a living in his forced retirement by copying books? Could the interventions into the text, mentioned above, be due to his wish to appeal to certain readers and make his product more marketable?

Nahāwandī is not described by his biographers as the owner of a splendid library or as an avid reader. But Ṣafadī's remark that he was a pleasant and refined conversationalist hints at his familiarity with just the kind of literature that the *Ṭawq* represents. In that sense, al-Nahāwandī stands for a common trend that saw an increasing number of trained legal scholars as authors of entertaining literature and put more impetus into the mastery of poetry as an important social skill for the advancement of a judicial career. In recent scholarship this trend is termed the *adabisation* of the jurists, that is, the showcasing of *adab* or a highly refined yet entertaining and edifying mixture of poetry and often rhymed prose by actors who previously would rely on their expertise in law alone.[25]

The whereabouts of the volume are then shrouded in silence for some decades, and the next palpable date is nearly seventy years later, when the *Ṭawq* was bought in 804/1401–02:

من كتب
محمد بن احمد بن (الصاحب)
سنة
٨٠٠٤

min kutub / Muḥammad b. Aḥmad b. (al-Ṣāḥib) / sanat / 8004

[From the books of Muḥammad b. Aḥmad b. (al-Ṣāḥib) [in the] year 8004 [= 804]]

Unfortunately, I could neither read the name of this owner with certainty nor find a person who matched my proposed reading. If we are still in Ṣafad at this point, it would be quite understandable that the sources are silent on this person. What we do know, however, is that this man also owned the manuscript Paris, BnF Arabe 3939, a multi-text manuscript with Muḥibb al-Dīn al-ʿAkbarī's (d. 616/1219) commentary to the *Maqāmāt* of al-Ḥarīrī (*Sharḥ mā ghamaḍa min al-alfāẓ al-lughawiyya min al-Maqāmāt al-ḥarīriyya* / Explanation of what was obscure in the *Maqāmāt* of al-Ḥarīrī), picaresque tales of extreme linguistic sophistication, as well as other treatises on the Arabic language. This fine copy in a rare *safīna* format (an oblong form with the text running parallel to the spine) was bought in Cairo in the seventeenth century, so this owner could have had an Egyptian background.

For reasons elaborated in the following lines, I will argue that the chronologically following note was now placed after the colophon and consists of a couplet. Poetry constitutes a form of notes through which readers would occasionally engage with a manuscript.[26] The Leiden manuscript of *Ṭawq al-ḥamāma* exhibits several more examples on the title page and the back flyleaf, although not all have a discernible name attached to them or were originally signed. In encountering verses signed by their creator, be it as copyist or author, we can assume that such a writer was at least an attentive reader of the book he used. In this case the phrasing *li-kātibihī* makes it clear that these verses were indeed the product (*li-*) of their signing writer (*kātib*).

لكاتبه علي بن الرصاص الحنفي
واجمل ما افني المحب فواده على حب من لا فيك للعـ[.] مرضـ[
فاما الذي يهوي <و(يضي)> فواده على حَب ذواق فذا[ك] مضـ[

li-kātibihī ʿAlī b. al-Riṣāṣ al-Ḥanafī
wa-ajmalu mā afnā l-muḥibba fawāddahū ʿalā ḥubbi man lā fīka li-l-ʿ[.] murḍ[
fa-ammā l-ladhī yuhwī wa-yuḍīʾu fuʾāduhū ʿalā ḥubbi dhawāqin fa-dhā[ka] maḍ[

> [By its writer, ʿAlī b. al-Riṣāṣ al-Ḥanafī:
> The most beautiful thing that consumes a lover and makes him love // [...]
> And concerning that which his heart pounces upon and which it enlightens // [...]][27]

It is tempting to identify this ʿAlī b. al-Riṣāṣ al-Ḥanafī with a man mentioned only in passing by the chroniclers and biographers, one ʿAlāʾ al-Dīn ʿAlī b. al-Riṣāṣ, who died in 803/1400–01.[28] Just like al-Nahāwandī several decades before him, this man, on 4 Dhū l-Qaʿda, 771/30 May 1370, was appointed to the Ḥanafī judgeship of Ṣafad. This remarkable spatial and occupational congruence would suggest that the manuscript was produced in Ṣafad and stayed there throughout the eighth/fourteenth century, or otherwise that it might have returned to Ṣafad with its governor to whose entourage al-Nahāwandī had belonged. And since ʿAlī Ibn al-Riṣāṣ, the judge of Ṣafad, died in 803/1400–01, could it be more than an interesting coincidence that one of the few dated ownership statements on the title page stems from the year 804/1401–02? Wasn't it likely that the book entered the market again after al-Riṣāṣ's death?

Yet however probable that identification seemed at first, our ʿAlī b. al-Riṣāṣ al-Ḥanafī was in fact another man of that same name, ʿAlāʾ al-Dīn ʿAlī b. Taqī al-Dīn Abū Bakr b. ʿIsā al-Anṣārī al-Maqdisī al-Ḥanafī, known as Ibn al-Riṣāṣ (822/1419–882/1477), a scholar who headed several madrasas in Jerusalem and Hebron.[29] Sakhāwī explicitly mentions his skilled and beautiful handwriting, such as is on display in these verses, and that he used it to copy books on law (*fiqh*), exegesis (*tafsīr*) and other matters. Indeed, ʿAlī Ibn al-Riṣāṣ was probably the copyist of two undated manuscripts in Rabat[30] and Damascus.[31] What tipped the balance in his favour was the finding of another note that he left, this time in a legal manuscript that is today preserved in the Khalidi Library in Jerusalem. Although this was a much more prosaic text, namely a marginal commentary on the question of when the spilling of blood would disturb ritual purity and thus invalidate a prayer, the calligraphic boldness is the same (MS Jerusalem, Khalidi Library 328, fol. 6v). What is important for our purpose, however, is that the Khalidi Library manuscript was only copied in 869/1464–65, making the later ʿAlī Ibn al-Riṣāṣ the only possible identification. This, in turn, allows us to locate the *Ṭawq* in late Mamluk Palestine, and possibly in or around Jerusalem, more than a century after its creation. And another valuable insight is that, again, we find in the person of ʿAlī Ibn al-Riṣāṣ, as well as his habits of annotation, the proximity of *adab* and law that we observed already in the figure of the *Ṭawq*'s copyist.

Other notes are harder to place, such as the following undated reading note. But since it is couched next to the preceding note of 804/1401–02, following its spatial configuration to the point that its *ḥamdallah* [Praise be to God] is placed to the left where Muḥammad's name would not allow it to be centred above its own note, and since a later note of 1049/1639–40 partly overwrites it, this note must have been written sometime in between these dates. But besides its coarse writing and disregard for the grammatical rule that would have made Abū into Abī, nothing definitive can be said about this reader, Muḥammad b. Aḥmad b. Abū Bakr:

الحمد لله
طالعه
محمد بن احمد
ابن ابو بكر
عفا الله عنه
ولمن دعا له
بالمغفرة
ولجميع المسلمين

al-ḥamdu li-llāh / ṭālaʿahū / Muḥammad b. Aḥmad / Ibn Abū Bakr / ʿafā Allāh ʿanhū / wa-li-man daʿā la-hū / bi-l-maghfara / wa-li-jamīʿ al-muslimīn

[Praise be to God! Muḥammad b. Aḥmad b. Abū Bakr read it, may God forgive him and those who pray for him for forgiveness and all Muslims!]

Right beneath al-Nahāwandī's initial note, in fact even slightly touching its last line, we find another mark of ownership:

حسبي الله
في نوبة
ابرهيم بن محمد بن الحسام

ḥasbī Allāh / fī nawbat / Ibrāhīm b. Muḥammad b. al-Ḥusām

[God is sufficient for me! In the possession of Ibrāhīm b. Muḥammad b. al-Ḥusām]

Structurally and stylistically, this note, although also undated, is characteristic of the ninth/fifteenth and tenth/sixteenth centuries: squeezed to the left edge of the page, the *ḥasbala* in the top line, followed by a simple but bold *fī nawba* the length of the name following in the last line.

Some eighty years before the last ownership note was penned on the title page, one more reader was inspired to express his impressions poetically, and he used the verso side of the back flyleaf to do so. We do not know who owned the book at this point, but this note shows us a very different audience:

نظر في هذ الكتاب الفقير الحاج علي ابن الحاج ابو بكر ابن السمان
غفر الله له ولولد ولجميع المسلمون امين كتبه بتاريخ عشرين شهر
صفر الخير سنة ستة وخمسين وتسعماية

naẓara fī hāḏ al-kitāb al-faqīr al-ḥājj ʿAlī Ibn al-ḥājj Abū Bakr Ibn al-Sammān / ghafara Allāh la-hū wa-li-walad wa-li-jamīʿ al-muslimūn amīn katabahū bi-tārīkh ʿashrīn shahr / Ṣafar al-khayr sanat sitta wa-khamsīn wa-tisʿmīya

[The poor Ḥājj ʿAlī b. Ḥājj Abū Bakr Ibn al-Sammān looked into this book. May God forgive him and his parents and all Muslims. Amen. He wrote it on the 20th of Ṣafar in the year 956 [1549–50]]

Not only did this reader look into the *Ṭawq*, but Ibn al-Sammān also left the following verses of his own:

وقال هد البيت خد كلامي مجرباً وامتحنه وبميزان عقل نفسك زنه
كل شي يضق صدرك منه ينبغي ان تصد نفسك عنه

wa-qāla hād al-bayt:
khud kalāmī mujarraban wa-mtaḥinhū wa-bi-mīzāni ʿaqli nafsika zanhū
kull shay yaḍiqu ṣadruka minhū yanbaghī an taṣudda nafsaka ʿanhū

[And he said this verse:
Take my words as a tested [recipe], examine it and weigh it on the scale of your own intellect.
Everything that your heart is oppressed by, you should turn your soul away from it!]

He then copied verses by other authors:

تجهز للدي لا بد منه فان الموت ميقات العبا[دي
اترضا ان تكون رفيق قوم لهم زاد وانت بغير [زا..

بلاد مصر هي الدنيا وسكنها هم النام فقلناها [فتقلـ.
يا من يوبماهي ببغداد ودجلتها مصر مقدامت والـ[شق...
للبدى

tajahhaz li-l-ladī lā budda minhū fa-inna l-mawt mīqātu l-ʿibā[dī
ʾa tarḍā an takūna rafīqu qawmin lahum zādun wa-anta bi-ghayr [
bilādu Miṣrin hiya l-dunyā wa-sukkānuhā hum al-anām fa-qulnāhā [
yā man yubāhī bi-Baghdād wa-Dijlatihā Miṣrun muqaddima wa-[

[Prepare for what cannot be avoided! Death is the deadline for all men.
Can you accept to be companion to a people who have provisions while you are without [...]?
Egypt is the world and those who live in it are mankind. We said [to?] her [...].
You who vie with Baghdad and its Tigris, Cairo is the preface and the [...].]

The last double-verse belongs, albeit in a markedly different form, to a contemporary of this copy, the Mamluk poet Zayn al-Dīn ʿUmar b. al-Wardī (d. 749/1349),[32] and it is frequently quoted by Mamluk authors such as Ibn Taghrī Birdī (d. 874/1469) in his *al-Nujūm al-zāhira* [The Radiant Stars],[33] as an exemplary poem of praise for Egypt, and Khalīl Ibn Aybak al-Ṣafadī (d. 764/1363) in the biography of his friend Ibn al-Wardī, included in *Aʿyān al-ʿaṣr* [Notables of the Age].[34]

This verse in praise of Egypt and Cairo in particular might possibly reveal that the writer was a resident in that country, even though this is far from certain. But his note does inadvertently reveal something else about Ibn al-Sammān, namely where we can situate him on a scale of linguistic competence. Both in his own writing and when he copies a text, Ibn al-Sammān commits a great number of significant grammatical and orthographic mistakes (e.g. ده instead of هذا; لولد instead of لوالديه; جميع المسلمون instead of جميع المسلمين, while يباهي inexplicably ends up becoming يوبماهي), which are quite incomprehensible in someone with literary ambitions. And yet he was a lover of poetry and a poet himself. With these characteristics, Ibn al-Sammān is emblematic of a group of people who probably existed earlier, but who become more visible in the written sources of the Ottoman period. However we want to classify them as a group, there are a number of shared traits that characterise them in the manuscript notes: their un-recoverability in other sources;

grammatical and orthographic weaknesses, though not an embrace of colloquialisms; and coarse handwriting.[35] How these characteristics map on to any social or economic classification of society is not entirely clear (for example, one could be rich and illiterate, one could have earnestly studied and still taken up a craft), yet we certainly have here a group that the narrative and biographical sources do not identify with bookishness, and certainly not with the sort of high literature that the *Ṭawq* represents. The scope and timing of the advent of these people – classified in the literature for lack of better signifiers as 'commoners', 'the middle class' or 'craftsmen' – into the world of reading and writing is a topic of much interest in recent scholarship.[36] As yet another puzzle-piece in this ongoing examination, it would seem that the *Ṭawq al-ḥamāma* fitted their taste in the sixteenth century.

In Ibn al-Sammān's case, we possess an additional small hint of what else he liked. Namely, we learn that he also owned MS Leiden Or. 42,[37] which he probably bought in 967/1559–60.[38] In his ownership note, he calls himself Zayn al-Dīn b. Abū Bakr al-shahīr bi-Ibn al-Sammān. The volume in question contains al-Nawājī's (d. 859/1455) *Ḥalbat al-Kumayt* [The Racecourse of the Bay], the mostly anthologised collection of verse and prosimetric anecdotes on wine.[39] With this, stories about wine and intoxication become the fitting companion to Ibn Ḥazm's reflections on love.

Dated some ninety years after the reading of Ibn al-Sammān, one last note on the title page is again an ownership statement:

الله الكريم
استصحبه العبد الفقير اليه سبحانه
احمد بن احمد الشهير بطفلي
عفا الله تعالى
عنهما
سنة تسع واربعين والف

Allāh al-karīm / istaṣhabahū al-ʿabd al-faqīr ilayhi subḥānahū / Aḥmad b. Aḥmad al-shahīr bi-Ṭiflī / ʿafā Allāh taʿālā / ʿanhumā / sanat tisʿ wa-arbaʿīn wa-alf

[God is benevolent! The poor slave in the face of Him, praised be He, Aḥmad b. Aḥmad known as Ṭiflī, claimed ownership of it. May God forgive them both. In the year 1049.]

This last documented owner of the *Ṭawq al-ḥamāma*, Aḥmad b. Aḥmad known as Ṭiflī,[40] could only recently be identified after some struggle. Yet again, even initially, it was possible to infer something about his background from the note itself. In aesthetic terms, he distinguishes himself through elegant handwriting. It also seems that with this note we have left the Arab world. The writer employed a formula in Arabic which was most in favour with the Ottoman learned elite.[41] All this points to a man who was most likely from the higher echelons of society, well educated, and originating from the Ottoman heartland. Furthermore, I was lucky enough to find seven more books that this man possessed. It was again Levinus Warner who acquired all but one of these additional volumes from Ṭiflī's library: Leiden Or. 465 is *Ṣafwat al-Ṣafā ʾ* [Quintessence of Felicity], the hagiography, authored in Persian by Tawakkulī Ibn Bazzāz around 759/1358, of the Sufi and eponymous forefather of the Safavid dynasty, Shaykh Ṣafī al-Dīn (d. 735/1334); Leiden Or. 310 contains two Persian texts by Farīd al-Dīn ʿAṭṭār (d. 586/1190);[42] Leiden Or. 574 contains another Persian work, Muḥammad b. Hindushāh al-Nakhjiwānī's secretarial handbook *Dustūr al-kātib fī taʿyīn al-marātib* [Regulation of the Scribe in Discerning Ranks], authored around the year 760/1359; Leiden Or. 580 is the Arabic *ḥadīth* collection *Fawāʾid al-ḥadīth* [Benefits of the Prophetic Transmission] by Tammām Ibn al-Junayd al-Rāzī (d. 414/1023) in a sixth-/twelfth-century copy from Damascus; Leiden Or. 586 contains Bahāʾ al-Dīn Muḥammad b. al-Muʾayyad al-Baghdādī's (fl. 6th c. AH) Persian *al-Tavassul ilā al-tarassul* [Entreatment to the Art of Correspondence]; additionally, we find in Or. 696 a commentary, by Jalāl al-Dīn al-Khujandī (d. 802/1399), on al-Būṣīrī's (d. 694/1294) famous devotional poem *Qaṣīdat al-Burda* [The Mantle Ode]; and, finally, a single manuscript outside of Warner's purchases (MS Paris, BnF Arabe 3414) contains an anthology of Arabic poetry.

One note of Ṭiflī's in particular reveals some more details. Although the ownership notes in all cases are again in Arabic, Ṭiflī also signs a Turkish note in Leiden Or. 310, giving further credence to the speculation about his origin. In this last note, Ṭiflī claims that corrections found in the text are in the hand of one Ṣabūḥī efendī, shaikh of the Mevlevī-khāne in the vicinity of the Yeni Kapu.[43] Two things can be learned from this note about Ṭiflī. One is that he was in contact with a Mevlevī dervish in Istanbul, even though he does not identify as a Mevlevī himself. The other, since Ṣabūḥī efendī is a known Sufi and poet who died in 1057/1647[44] and in the note he is identified as being dead (*qaddasa sirruhū*), is that Ṭiflī owned these

Persian works even after the *Ṭawq*, and that he acquired his books when Warner was already in Istanbul. With Ṭiflī, we find the *Ṭawq* incorporated into the trilingual environment of the Ottoman learned elite, exemplified by the contemporary ideal of 'the three tongues' (*al-alsina al-thalātha / alsine-i selāse*), in which Persian mystical poetry, hagiography and secretarial arts were read together with Arabic love and devotional poetry and *ḥadīth* (prophetic traditions) by speakers of Turkish. And all this seems to have happened in a particularly Sufic environment.

We can now attempt to combine this information and make an identification of Aḥmad Ṭiflī with a poet of that name who lived in Istanbul in those years (d. 1070/1659–60).[45] A fine calligrapher whose collection of poetry (*divan*) is extant, this man was also a companion (*nedim*) of the sultan Murad IV. And indeed, it was in Istanbul that the book was acquired by the Dutch Resident Levinus Warner sometime between 1645 and 1665, that is, only a few years after our Aḥmad Ṭiflī bought the volume. So it is tempting to see in this last owner the man who brought the *Ṭawq al-ḥamāma* to the Ottoman capital and maybe the direct source for Warner's purchase, whether as a vendor or in an auction from his estate, which would have happened during the last years of Warner's stay.

An attempt should at least be made here to interpret the price extant on the title page, even though such an interpretation cannot be conclusive without a date and place to put it into a satisfying context. Such a context could be had under the hypothetical assumption that the price belongs to the ownership note of Aḥmad Ṭiflī, which I believe to be the case. In this case, the actual ownership note would be hemmed in on the upper and lower end by the price and the date, respectively. Both are slightly detached from the main body of the note.

مشتراه شاهيات
١٧

mushtarāhu shāhiyyāt 17

[Its price is 17 *shāhīs*.]

The word *mushtarā* indicates a price.[46] The signs beneath the word *shāhiyyāt* are *Rūmī* numerals (a form of numbers developed from

Greek Coptic antecedents) and mean seventeen.[47] The *shāhī*[48] was a large silver piece, usually exchanging with the *akce* at a rate of 1:4. It was minted mainly in the eastern and Arabic provinces of the Ottoman Empire and it remained stable throughout the sixteenth century, though it shared the devaluation of the *'uthmānī / akce* after 1585. While they used to weigh around 4 grammes, *shāhī*s gradually deteriorated to between 2.2 and 3.1 grammes.[49] Most importantly, despite this deterioration the coins were widely accepted and the market constantly overvalued their exchange rate in relation to their silver content. This, despite the fact that the Ottoman authorities wanted to get rid of the *shāhī* in the seventeenth century, would lead to silver being exported from the centre to the eastern provinces and *shāhī*s in turn flooding to the centre. In the manuscripts, it appears only at this very late stage. In my extensive corpus of manuscript notes, I only found three prices indicated with *shāhiyyāt*, two of them dated 1054/1644–45 and 1064/1653–54 (most likely in the Persian Gulf region) respectively.[50] The date of Ṭiflī's note would therefore fit this pattern very well.

But what does this tell us about the value of the *Ṭawq*? Without knowing the precise exchange rate of the *shāhī* and without much of a systematic corpus of book prices from mid-seventeenth-century Istanbul for comparison, it is hard to tell. Abū l-Wafā' al-'Urḍī, the Aleppan scholar who, sometime after 1068/1658, bought six books for Warner from the estate of Kātib Celebī for a total of 53 *ghurūsh* and 300 *'uthmānī*, provides some scarce context.[51] The individual prices of his purchases, which he reported to Warner in a letter, range from one *ghursh* for a part of Ibn 'Abd Rabbih's *al-'Iqd al-farīd* [The Unique Necklace] to 16 *ghurūsh* for Ibn Ḥamdūn's *Tadhkira* [The Memoir], two literary-historical anthologies. Incidentally, the two cheapest manuscripts on the list were both by Andalusian authors like Ibn Ḥazm, namely Ibn 'Abd Rabbih (with his own 'necklace', the *'Iqd*) and a commentary to Ibn 'Abdūn's (d. 529/1134) poem, *Sharḥ al-'Abdūniyya* [Explanation of the *'Abdūniyya*], for two *ghursh*. 'Urḍī does not indicate what coin he meant by the *ghursh*, but it must have been either the Spanish eight-real piece (*riyāl*) or the Dutch Leeuwendaaler (*asadī*), which exchanged with the *shāhī* at different rates between around 1:10 and 1:20. Thus, 17 *shāhī*s appears to indicate that our manuscript of the *Ṭawq* sold for a medium to low price.

The variety of notes and the (presumed) backgrounds of their writers, while certainly not unheard of, is still telling in a work of such high stylistic claims. They document a sustained and varied interest, an appeal that was moreover not confined to a narrow set of scholars and that is often labelled 'popular'. We can spot very professional hands and notes in a refined language side by side with rather crude ones. The two readership notes as well as the poems also attest to the book not lying dormant on someone's bookshelf. Consecutive owners left their notes for three centuries, as did a diverse group of readers, and the *Ṭawq* inspired some of them to add their own poetical takes on the theme of love in productive interaction. In other words, there was a welcoming audience.

All this suggests that this book was no ugly duckling in a dark corner of a library waiting for modern scholarship to show the world what a beautiful swan it really was! This, of course, leads right back to the initial conundrum of why this interest, now an established fact, did not lead to more production. Why this scarcity of textual witnesses? In what follows, we can merely offer a number of possible reasons without elevating any above the realm of speculation.

Possible reasons for a lack of copies

One has to stress again that Constantinople was not this work's place of origin. Since it originated in Islamic Spain, the *Ṭawq al-ḥamāma* had to travel a long distance to end up in the capital of the Ottoman Empire. Acknowledging this origin makes the text's virtual disappearance much more understandable since much of the rich manuscript heritage of al-Andalus had been destroyed. For the considerable literature that nonetheless did survive, it still was a long way to the Ottoman realm. The *Ṭawq* was evidently one of those works that were received in the Mamluk realm already by the eighth/fourteenth century.

The author Ibn Ḥazm was certainly not unknown to the East. He is included in several of the most important biographical collections by Egyptian and Syrian authors[52] and those biographies feature extensive work lists.[53] Yet while many knew of the prolific author Ibn Ḥazm, a comparison between biographical mentions and manuscripts gives the picture of an Andalusian scholar whose name travelled farther than his books. It was not only the *Ṭawq* that was hard to lay one's hands on: manuscripts of Ibn Ḥazm's works are rare, full stop. The vast collections of Leiden appear to hold only two of his other works, one from Warner (Or. 480) and the other a much later addition (Or. 3006). The principal collections in Germany, the Staatsbibliothek zu Berlin (Petermann II 594) and the Staatsbibliothek München (Cod. arab. 1332), as well as the Bibliothèque nationale in Paris (Arabe 5829), seem to have only one each. None of his works appears to have come to Princeton or Leipzig. It seems significant that at the same time that the *Ṭawq* found its place in Istanbul, the city also hosted the only known copy of Ibn Ḥazm's massive work on law, *al-Muḥallā* [The Bejewelled], which came through the palace library of Bayezid II.[54] Quite apart from the struggle to explain the *Ṭawq*'s lack of transmission, the broader success of Ibn Ḥazm's overall corpus might have been hindered by the fact that most of his theological and juridical works expound the Ẓāhirī doctrine, which found few followers in either East or West.[55]

Specific to the *Ṭawq*, another possible explanation could rest on stylistic grounds. It has been mentioned above that the copyist of the Leiden manuscript was not simply rendering the text as he found it in his exemplar. The colophon informs us that the copy was completed after 'abridging most of its poems and leaving their best ones, to beautify it, reveal its good qualities, and to reduce its size'.[56] Put differently, although he took up the task of producing this book, the copyist nonetheless saw problems with the work with regard to his possible audience or his own taste. In particular, its size (*ḥajmihā*) needed some attention. In other words, the *Ṭawq* was, in its copyist's estimation, not particularly reader-friendly, its gems hidden behind too many unnecessary words that obscured rather than highlighted its value.

The *Ṭawq* is renowned mostly for its anecdotes about contemporary lovers and the poetry that accompanied them. But since this was a work intended not merely to entertain but also to moralise, and as the borders between genres were often not clear-cut, the reading was enlivened by the incorporation of texts from other fields, such as Qur'ān and *ḥadīth* studies, that reflected Ibn Ḥazm's stance as a jurist and theologian as well, and that would please even readers specialised in these fields such as the two judges we encountered earlier.[57] Yet Ibn Ḥazm, by conscious choice, and although he would also refer to many texts from different genres, was not an anthologist, while virtually all the other authors who wrote on the theory of love were.[58] Instead, he wrote in the *Ṭawq* that he was relying on his own experiences, his own poetry, and did not wish to deck himself with borrowed plumes (or, rather, borrowed jewellery, in his own words).[59] Did the age of anthology not value what Ibn Ḥazm was so proudly offering? Was it too boring to listen to only one voice?

Tastes, however, can and do change, and this is not without precedent. Other works from the Islamic West also had to be rediscovered or discovered in the first place. Had the *Ṭawq* stayed in Istanbul, who is to say that it might not have seen a renewed surge of interest concomitant to the vogue for Andalusian texts started in Egypt and Syria by the later émigré al-Maqqarī,[60] whose voluminous *Nafḥ al-ṭīb* [Spreading the Scent] preserved and introduced to the East another belletristic work of Ibn Ḥazm that was otherwise lost, the *Risāla fī faḍl al-Andalus* [Treatise on the Precedence of Andalusia].[61] A burgeoning interest in love poetry can be observed in the sixteenth and seventeenth centuries. James White has recently analysed a group of seventeenth-century readers whose interests in poetical collections intersected with another work connected with one of the *Ṭawq*'s readers, Ibn al-Sammān, namely al-Nawājī and his *Ḥalbat al-kumayt*.[62] In quite the same fashion, a renaissance for *Ṭawq al-ḥamāma* could be imagined. But the purchase of the only surviving manuscript by Warner precluded this possibility, if it ever existed.

In the West

Compared with what we find regarding the manuscript before it reached its current resting place, the history of the *Ṭawq al-ḥamāma* in Leiden up until its initial published edition in 1914 is connected with decidedly fewer names. Foremost among them is, of course, the man who brought the copy to Leiden, Levinus Warner. How did he get his hands on the book? The frustrating answer is that we do not know. In the Ottoman capital, Warner is known to have availed himself of the services of several Muslim scholars and book dealers. One of them was the Aleppan scholar Abū l-Wafāʾ Muḥammad b. ʿUmar al-ʿUrḍī (993/1585–1071/1660).[63] This allowed the Dutchman very favourable access to the book market and estate auctions. Through one of the latter, al-ʿUrḍi managed to buy several volumes from the famed library of the secretary and bibliographer Muṣṭafā b. ʿAbdallāh, known as Kātib Celebī or Ḥājjī Khalīfa, sometime after his death in 1657.[64] Yet the *Ṭawq* would not have been one of those volumes, since Ḥājjī Khalīfa, the persnickety bibliographer, does not mention the work in his *Kashf al-ẓunūn*.[65] It is, in fact, astonishing to contemplate that what is today considered one of the major works of Arabic literature could have escaped the world's most devoted bibliographer of this language while sitting right under his nose. Whichever way Warner came to it, he was responsible for having the volume shipped as part of a bequest to his erstwhile alma mater in Leiden in 1665. The shipments started to arrive in 1668 and this substantial collection formed the backbone of one of Europe's finest collections of Oriental manuscripts which, as a whole, became known as the *Legatum Warnerianum*.

What happened to the *Ṭawq* after it reached Leiden has been told numerous times. It is a story of sudden and unforeseen success. After more than two centuries in the Leiden University Library, the edition of Pétrof set into motion a sustained series of publications, and it was succeeded by several Arabic editions, both critical and popular.[66] More importantly for a broad dissemination and lasting global success, translations into nearly all the major languages made the text available not only to specialists.

What this account leaves out, though, are the years of obscurity. This success was two and a half centuries in the making. During that time, Leiden was not only the host to one of the largest collections of Oriental manuscripts in Europe, its university was also home to many of the most accomplished Orientalist philologists, and its library attracted visitors from all over Europe. As impressive as is the line of those who would, in the twentieth century, devote their scholarship to Ibn Ḥazm's work, it is just as enlightening to picture the number of illustrious Orientalist scholars who actually took no interest in the *Ṭawq*. To pick just one of Leiden's most famous and industrious visitors: Johann Jacob Reiske (1716–74), a devoted and tireless philologist with a deep interest in Arabic poetry (not least from al-Andalus),[67] travelled from Leipzig to Leiden on foot to study its riches, left with a wealth of copies that he had made, and also catalogued the collection.[68] Yet not even he seems to have noticed the importance of Ibn Ḥazm's treatise.

This task of discovery, amazingly, was left to a writer, Dmitrii Konstantinovich Pétrof (1872–1925), who was not even an Arabist to begin with and who travelled the even greater distance from Russia. An important Hispanist in Tsarist Russia who translated the poems of Calderon and Lope, his venture into Arabic literature was an unlikely and, to my knowledge, singular one. The available bibliographical tools list him as the author of works on Spanish poets and Russian socialists, with the *Ṭawq* as a remarkable intruder. We learn from Ignace Kratchkowsky's autobiographical essays that Pétrof started to learn Arabic with Victor Rosen in St Petersburg in 1906; that the inspiration for the edition of the *Ṭawq* came from Christian Friedrich Seybold (1859–1921) in Tübingen, where Pétrof studied in 1908; and that Kratchkowsky himself took part in the editing process in some not clearly detailed collaboration.[69]

Thus, while Pétrof's edition was not responding to the urgent calls of scholars who felt deprived of a text they longed to read, it was nonetheless greeted warmly and with growing enthusiasm in the academy and beyond. The appeal of the *Ṭawq* to Western readers might be that it covers an important intersection: while other works of similar analytical acumen exist, the *Ṭawq* distinguishes itself due to its anecdotal and lively style, while at the same time it does not dwell on the pornographic, as do other works of similar anecdotal riches.

Conclusion

This chapter grew out of the urge to explain an apparent dichotomy between the importance of a text and its feeble transmission, a dichotomy that has mystified many, including myself. The discrepancies between the interests of today's scholarship and contemporary manuscript production are indeed important signifiers for re-evaluating the emphasis put on certain texts by each. But as this investigation has shown, the conventional wisdom that a lack of copies reflects a concomitant degree of popular neglect and thus marks a literary failure needs to be complicated.

Instead, the lively and numerous interactions of Ibn Ḥazm's readers in the Leiden *unicum* betray a sustained attraction. The pages of few manuscripts, even of works that were eagerly reproduced, are as crowded as those of the *Ṭawq*. We can only speculate whether any number of readers might have wished to own a copy of the *Ṭawq*, but did not have the means to buy it or to pay for a copyist, or lacked the prolonged access needed to make a copy. And it should be kept in mind that Levinus Warner, the buyer of the *Ṭawq al-ḥamāma*, brought home among his roughly 1,000 manuscripts many other texts that have not been found anywhere else or are known from only one other copy.[70] So far, it is not even clear to what extent being a *unicum* was so unique.

Notes

1 The state of the art in scholarship on Ibn Ḥazm is collected in Camilla Adang, Maribel Fierro and Sabine Schmidtke (eds), *Ibn Ḥazm of Cordoba: The Life and Works of a Controversial Thinker* (Leiden: Brill, 2012).

2 The famous assertion of Ibn Ḥazm's son Abū Rāfiʿ al-Faḍl that he was in possession of 400 volumes of his father's works, containing some 80,000 folios, is cited in Ibn Khallikān, *Wafayāt al-aʿyān wa-anbāʾ abnāʾ al-zamān*, ed. Iḥsān ʿAbbās (Beirut: Dār Ṣādir, 2005), vol. III, p. 326.

3 Some faint earlier interest in the nineteenth century (early cataloguing and Dozy's early translation of a passage in his *Histoire des musulmans d'Espagne*; a plan, in the 1890s, by Francisco Pons Boigues to edit the text) is recorded in Ibn Ḥazm, *Ṭauḳ al-ḥamâma, publié d'après l'unique manuscrit de la Bibliothèque de l'Université de Leide*, ed. D. K. Pétrof (Leiden: Imprimérie Orientale ci-devant E.J. Brill, 1914), pp. vii–viii, and Jan Just Witkam, 'Establishing the Stemma: Fact or Fiction?', *Manuscripts of the Middle East* 3 (1988): 90.

4 The Spanish version, titled *Exemplario contra los engannos y peligros del mundo*, was published in 1493 in Zaragoza. Thanks to Professor Kristina Richardson for this reference.

5 The far-flung claims to inspirations for *Robinson Crusoe* and similar works as presented in Samar Attar, *The Vital Roots of European Enlightenment: Ibn Tufayl's Influence on Modern Western Thought* (Lanham, MD: Lexington Books, 2007), are critiqued by Remke Kruk in her review of the work in *Middle Eastern Literatures* 14 (2011): 91–5.

6 Michael Lailach, Carola Pohlmann and Christoph Rauch (eds), *Reisende Erzählungen. Tausendundein Nacht zwischen Orient und Europa* (Berlin: Insel, 2019).

7 Ibn Ḥazm, *Ṭauḳ al-Ḥamâma*, ed. Pétrof.

8 On the textual history, see Qasim al-Samarrai, 'New Remarks on the Text of Ibn Ḥazm's *Ṭawq al-ḥamāma*', *Arabica* XXX (1983): 57–72; Witkam, 'Establishing the Stemma', 90–2, list of editions on p. 100.

9 A list of chief translations is in Witkam, 'Establishing the Stemma', 100.

10 Warner arrived in Constantinople in 1645, where he was appointed chargé d'affaires in 1655 and Resident (a rank below that of ambassador) in 1657. On his life, see Arnoud Vrolijk and Richard van Leeuwen, *Arabic Studies in the Netherlands: A Short History in Portraits, 1580–1950* (Leiden: Brill, 2013), pp. 48–59.

11 The first half of the eighth/fourteenth century seems to have marked a high point for the transmission of Ibn Ḥazm's corpus in the East in general. Of the few Eastern copies that I could find, MS Berlin Petermann II 594 lacks a date but Ahlwahrdt puts it 'around 700' (Wilhelm Ahlwardt, *Verzeichnis der arabischen Handschriften der Königlichen Bibliothek zu Berlin*, vol. IX [Berlin: A. Asher, 1897], p. 111); MS Dublin, Chester Beatty Library (= CBL) Ar 4824 was copied 714 in Damascus; the texts in CBL Ar 4856 are dated 740; the three connected volumes of *al-Fiṣal fī l-milal* (CBL Ar 3845; MS Istanbul, Rāghib Pāshā 815 and 816) were completed between 742 and 744. Apart from the testimony of the manuscripts, this is also the time when Ibn Ḥazm's oeuvre influenced the ideas of Ibn Qayyim al-Jawzīya (d. 751/1350) in Damascus, one of the very rare authors who cite specifically from the *Ṭawq al-ḥamāma*; see Livnat Holtzman, 'Elements of Acceptance and Rejection in Ibn Qayyim al-Jawziyya's Systematic Reading of Ibn Ḥazm', in Adang, Fierro and Schmidtke (eds), *Ibn Ḥazm of Cordoba: The Life and Works of a Controversial Thinker*, pp. 608–11; P. S. van Koningsveld, 'De oorspronkelijke versie van Ibn Ḥazms Ṭawq al-ḥamâma', *Sharqiyyât* 5 (1993): 23–38, treats Ibn Qayyim's citations of the *Ṭawq* only very cursorily, probably because they largely agree with the Leiden manuscript and do not seem to support his theory that Ibn Ḥazm would have authored a different version of his work.

12 In Adam Gacek, 'Ownership Statements and Seals in Arabic Manuscripts', *Manuscripts of the Middle East* 2 (1987): 88–95; Ayman Fuʾād Sayyid, 'Les marques de possession sur les manuscrits et la reconstitution des anciens fonds des manuscrits arabes', *Manuscripta Orientalia* 9 (2003): 14–23; Boris Liebrenz, 'Lese- und Besitzvermerke in der Leipziger Rifāʿīya-Bibliothek', in Andreas Görke and Konrad Hirschler (eds),

Manuscript Notes as Documentary Sources (Beirut: Orient-Institut, 2012), pp. 141–62. It is telling that one of the early successful attempts to use Arabic manuscript notes (in this case the readership notes left by al-Ḥasan al-Wazzān during his captivity in Rome) as documentary sources to further a broader narrative comes from outside the field, namely Natalie Zemon Davis, *Trickster Travels: A Sixteenth-Century Muslim Between Worlds* (New York: Hill and Wang, 2006); the Arabic notes are depicted after p. 181. The potential of this line of study is demonstrated in the contributions to Boris Liebrenz (ed.), *The History of Books and Collections through Manuscript Notes* (Leiden: Brill, 2018) [= *Journal of Islamic Manuscripts* 9.2–3 (2018)].

13 A case in point would be the only other published attempt I know of to make sense of the manuscript notes on the title page of the *Ṭawq* manuscript, namely the fabulous misreadings in Abdallah Benaïssa, 'Vers une nouvelle interprétation paléographique du manuscript *Tawq al-Hamama* du théologien andalou Ibn Hazm (994–1063)', *Études Maghrébines* 5–6 (1997): 21. A. R. Nykl, one of the work's translators, had previously read the notes with much more accuracy, as Josef Ženka (Prague) informs me based on papers from Nykl's estate. But the footnote he devotes to them skips names and identifications and basically uses them to establish dates, and indeed that is all he could have done at this point; see Ibn Ḥazm, *A Book Containing the Risāla Known as the Dove's Neck-Ring about Love and Lovers*, trans. A. R. Nykl (Paris: Geuthner, 1931), p. 236, n. 145. Nykl also seems to locate the first owner, al-Nahāwandī, in the Persianate East, based on his name which refers to the city of Nahāwand in today's Iran. I owe knowledge of Nykl's work to Josef Ženka.

14 Specific databases for manuscript notes containing material collected by the author do exist, so far for the collections in Leipzig (https://www.refaiya.uni-leipzig.de), Berlin (http://orient-digital.staatsbibliothek-berlin.de) and Gotha (http://www.manuscripts-gotha.uni-jena.de); the project *Ex Libris Ex Oriente*, headed by Professor Frédéric Bauden (Liège), proposes to collect notes from Islamic manuscripts on a global scale; the project *Stories of Survival – Recovering the Connected Histories of Eastern Christianity in the Early Modern World* plans to integrate manuscript notes in its database of Christian Arabic manuscripts.

15 The project *Bibliotheca Arabica* (located at the Saxon Academy of the Sciences and Humanities in Leipzig and supported by the Union of Academies in Germany), headed by Professor Verena Klemm, sets out to combine a broad bibliography of Arabic literary production until the nineteenth century with the evidence of its physical transmission through manuscript notes.

16 Lois A. Giffen, '*Ibn Ḥazm and the* Ṭawq al-ḥamāmā', in Salma Khadra Jayyusi (ed.), *The Legacy of Muslim Spain* (Leiden: Brill, 1992), p. 421. I do not subscribe to van Koningsveld's ('De oorspronkelijke versie', 23) theory that the editorial changes were carried out by a person different from the copyist (he also speculates whether it could have been a version redacted by Ibn Ḥazm himself), based on his assumption that the end of the manuscript constitutes two distinct colophons. There is nothing in this colophon that would suggest this to me, as it was usual to employ special phrases (in this case *wa-farigha min naskhihā*) to begin the dating part of a colophon.

17 After inspecting the manuscript *in situ*, I interpret this superfluous 'بن' not as an indication that another ism is missing between Muḥammad and ʿUthmān. There is simply not enough space in the margin to have another name follow. This would, therefore, be a simple scribal lapse.

18 This could well be interpreted as *al-ṣūfī*, although the *fā*ʾ would then be the only letter in the note that did not receive its point. Neither possible reading, however, appears in the biographies.

19 The best biography is Khalīl Ibn Aybak al-Ṣafadī, *Aʿyān al-ʿaṣr wa-aʿwān al-naṣr*, ed. Nabīl Abū ʿAmsha, Muḥammad Mawʿad and Maḥmūd Sālim Muḥammad (Beirut: Dār al-Fikr al-Muʿāṣir and Damascus: Dār al-Fikr, 1998), vol. IV, pp. 569–70; also Khalīl Ibn Aybak al-Ṣafadī, *al-Wāfī bi-l-Wafayāt*, ed. Sven Dedering (Stuttgart: Steiner, 1974), vol. IV, pp. 90–91. Much shorter Ibn Ḥajar al-ʿAsqalānī, *al-Durar al-kāmina* (Beirut: Dār Iḥyāʾ al-Turāth al-ʿArabī, n.d.), vol. IV, p. 39.

20 See Ibn Ḥazm, *A Book Containing the Risala*, trans. Nykl, p. 236, n. 145.

21 van Koningsveld, 'De oorspronkelijke versie', 24.

22 Jan Just Witkam, *Inventory of the Oriental Manuscripts of the Library of the University of Leiden*, vol. I: *Manuscripts Or. 1–Or. 1000* (Leiden: Ter Lugt Press, 2007), p. 387.

23 His biography is found in Ṣafadī, *Aʿyān al-ʿaṣr*, vol. III, p. 218.

24 Ṣafadī, *Aʿyān al-ʿaṣr*, vol. IV, p. 569: 'wa-qāsā fī ākhir ʿumrihī qillatan wa-faqran kabīran.'

25 Konrad Hirschler, *Medieval Damascus. Plurality and Diversity in an Arabic Library: The Ashrafīya Library Catalogue* (Edinburgh: Edinburgh University Press, 2016), p. 118; Elias Muhanna, 'Encyclopaedism in the Mamluk Period: The Composition of Shihāb al-Dīn Nuwayrī's (d. 1333) *Nihāyat al-Arab fī Funūn al-Adab*', PhD dissertation, Harvard University, 2012, pp. 185–91.

26 These texts have received only sparse systematic attention so far. See James White, 'Mamlūk Poetry, Ottoman Readers, and an Enlightenment Collector: An Appendix to the *Nuzha* of Ibn Sūdūn', *Journal of*

Islamic Manuscripts 9.2–3 (2018): 272–307; poetry is also part of the collection of interesting material found on the flyleaves of manuscripts and compiled by Muḥammad Khayr Ramaḍān Yūsuf, *al-Ghurar ʿalā l-ṭurar. Ghurar al-fawāʾid ʿalā ṭurar al-makhṭūṭāt wa-l-nawādir*, 2 vols (Beirut: Dār al-Bashāʾir al-Islāmīya, 2004).

27 Since the last part of each line is unintelligible, the full meaning of each is also obscured, and the verse, which on top of that certainly rests on double entendres, is rendered even more untranslatable.

28 Taqī al-Dīn Aḥmad al-Maqrīzī, *al-Sulūk li-maʿrifat duwal al-mulūk*, vol. IV, ed. Muḥammad ʿAbd al-Qādir ʿAṭā (Beirut: Dār al-Kutub al-ʿIlmiyya, 1997), p. 335; al-Sakhāwī, *al-Ḍawʾ al-lāmiʿ*, vol. XI, p. 238. The death date is mentioned by al-Sakhāwī as the only information on him besides the appointment in Ṣafad.

29 Muḥammad b. ʿAbd al-Raḥmān al-Sakhāwī, *al-Ḍawʾ al-lāmiʿ li-ahl al-qarn al-tāsiʿ* (Beirut: Dār al-Jīl, n.d.), vol. V, p. 206. Here we also find the vocalisation as Riṣāṣ instead of Raṣṣāṣ.

30 ʿAlī b. al-Raṣṣāṣ al-Ḥanafī al-Anṣārī, MS Rabat, al-Khizāna al-ʿāmma 250q, a historical fragment unidentified in the catalogue; see https://digitallibrary.al-furqan.com/our_is_item/manid/1020318/groupid/0 (accessed 8 February 2022).

31 ʿAlī Ibn al-Raṣṣāṣ MS Damascus, Ẓāhirīya 5258, a copy of *Tarjīḥ madhhab Abī Ḥanīfa ʿalā sāʾir al-madhāhib* by Akmal al-Dīn Muḥammad b. Muḥammad al-Bābartī al-Rūmī (d. 786/1384); see Muḥammad Muṭīʿ al-Ḥāfiẓ, *Fihris makhṭūṭāt Dār al-Kutub al-Ẓāhiriyya: al-Fiqh al-ḥanafī* (Damascus: Majmaʿ al-Lugha al-ʿArabiyya bi-Dimashq, 1980), vol. I, p. 205

32 The verse is found in Zayn al-Dīn ʿUmar Ibn al-Wardī, *Dīwān Ibn al-Wardī*, ed. ʿAbd al-Ḥamīd Hindāwī (Cairo: Dār al-Āfāq al-ʿArabiyya, 2006), p. 175. The edited version reads as follows:

ديار مصر هي الدنيا وساكنها // هم الانام فقابلهم بتقبيل
يا من يباهي ببغداد ودجلتها // مصر مقدمة والشرح للنيل

diyāru Miṣrin hiya l-dunyā wa-sākinuhā // hum al-anāmu faqābilhum bi-taqbīlī
yā man yubāhī bi-Baghdādin wa-Dijlatihā // Miṣrun muqaddimatun wa-l-sharḥu li-l-Nīlī
[Egypt is the world and those who live in it are mankind, encounter her with a kiss!
You who boasts about Baghdad and its Tigris: Cairo takes the lead (*muqaddama*) / is the preface (*muqaddima*) and the Nile is the proof / commentary.]

Thanks to Adam Talib (Durham) who helped identify and translate the *tawriya* of the last line.

33 Yūsuf Ibn Taghrī Birdī, *al-Nujūm al-zāhira fī mulūk Miṣr wa-l-Qāhira*, vol. I, ed. Muḥammad Ḥusayn Shams al-Dīn (Beirut: Dār al-Kutub al-ʿIlmiyya, 1992), p. 67.

34 Ṣafadī, *Aʿyān al-ʿaṣr*, vol. III, p. 694.

35 I talk about this chimeric and vaguely defined group in Boris Liebrenz, 'The Library of Aḥmad al-Rabbāṭ. Books and their Audience in 12th to 13th/18th to 19th Century Syria', in Ralf Elger and Ute Pietruschka (eds), *Marginal Perspectives on Early Modern Ottoman Culture: Missionaries, Travellers, Booksellers* (Halle/Saale: Zentrum für Interdisziplinäre Regionalstudien, 2013) [= *Orientwissenschaftliche Hefte* 32], pp. 17–59, esp. pp. 33–6.

36 Nelly Hanna, *In Praise of Books. A Cultural History of Cairo's Middle Class, Sixteenth to the Eighteenth Century* (Syracuse, NY: Syracuse University Press, 2003); Dana Sajdi, *The Barber of Damascus. Nouveau Literacy in the Eighteenth-Century Ottoman Levant* (Stanford, CA: Stanford University Press, 2013); see, for a new discussion and a different chronology, Boris Liebrenz and Kristina Richardson (eds), *The Notebook of Kamāl al-Dīn the Weaver: Aleppine Notes from the End of the 16th Century* (Beirut: Orient-Institut Beirut, 2021), pp. 41–55.

37 Although it ended up in the same Dutch collection, this volume was brought to Leiden not by Warner but, a few decades earlier, by Jacob Golius.

38 The date is given in *rūmī* numerals (a form of numbers developed from Greek Coptic antecedents), and although the 67 is clear, I could not make out the preceding number. It is only logical to assume, given the date in the *Ṭawq*, that it would be a 9.

39 Geert Jan van Gelder, 'A Muslim Encomium on Wine: *The Racecourse of the Bay (Ḥalbat al-Kumayt)* by al-Nawājī (d. 859/1455) as a Post-Classical Arabic Work', *Arabica* XLII (1995): 222–34. Interestingly, Gelder juxtaposes the impression of 'timelessness' in al-Nawājī's work and other anthologies with the 'refreshingly personal approach' of Ibn Ḥazm in his *Ṭawq*; see ibid., p. 233.

40 I arrived at this transliteration only after some iterations, and therefore the process should be traced here. The reading of this name poses particular difficulty due to an unusual connection of the letters which I initially read as *fāʾ-qāf*, and the name therefore as Fiqlī. Paul Babinski and Evren Sünnetçioğlu, when shown this name, have strongly and with good arguments suggested reading the name as Ṭiflī (طفلي) and identified him with a known poet of that name whose dates (d. 1070/1659–60) and life in Istanbul match with the date provided in the note (Mehmed Süreyya, *Sicill-i osmanî*, vol. V [Istanbul, 1996], p. 1634). However, despite the allure of this identification, I maintained my own reading of

Fiqlī, which, I admit, only occurred to me when by chance I happened upon that very same graphic form of *fāʾ-qāf* in the word *al-faqīr* in a historical note in Leiden Or. 315, this one by the well-known poet Veysī (Leiden Or. 315, fol. 1r; the note is undated but written after 1006AH). Once attuned to it, I found numerous other instances of this writing of *al-faqīr* in notes in Leiden Or. 377 (undated but probably earlier than the others), Or. 409b (undated), Or. 450b and Or. 450c (dated after 1000AH). It stands to reason that this ligature could well also stand for the reversal of these two letters, which would have resulted in the name Qiflī, although this name, too, was unattested.

A strong counter-argument which was put forward against my initial reading is that the form of *fāʾ* as seen in the name does not correspond at all with the same letter as written otherwise in Fiqlī's notes (compare in particular the word *al-faqīr* just beneath the presumed Fiqlī in Leiden Or. 310). Yet the same is true, for example, for the very long note of Veysī, where this particular ligature of *fāʾ-qāf* only appears in the word *al-faqīr*, for which there is no alternative reading. While everything, thus, pointed to a particular *fāʾ-qāf* ligature, the last-minute finding of a note clearly reading Ṭiflī in Leiden Or. 586 finally cleared the matter in favour of Babinski/Sünnetçioğlu's reading.

41 In the absence of a comprehensive study of the terminology employed, the following numbers are meant to give some statistical credence to this remark on the as yet very poorly understood nuances of formula in manuscript notes: in the Rifāʿiyya (a Damascene library of a rather local character; see Boris Liebrenz, *Die Rifāʿīya aus Damaskus. Eine Privatbibliothek im osmanischen Syrien und ihr kulturelles Umfeld* [Leiden: Brill, 2016]), the term *istaṣḥabahū* appears in no more than eight ownership statements as opposed to 95 instances of *malakahū*, 91 of *fī mulk* and 67 with *nawba* (to name only those that can easily be caught with a simple search); the Arabic manuscripts in Gotha, mostly assembled in the Arabic provinces of the Ottoman Empire, again have eight instances of *istaṣḥabahū*, against 81 of *malakahū*, 74 of *fī mulk* and 171 composed with *nawba*; yet Gotha's much smaller number of Persian and Turkish manuscripts have fifteen instances of *istaṣḥabahū*. Of those owners employing the *istaṣḥabahū* formula, most bear names composed with *zāde*. In the manuscripts preserved in Istanbul's Fazilahmadpasha Köprülü library, despite them numbering only a quarter of those I saw in Gotha and the Rifāʿiyya, I counted no less than 35 occurences of *istaṣḥabahū*.

42 Witkam, *Inventory*, vol. I, p. 155.

43 Jan Schmidt, *Catalogue of Turkish Manuscripts in the Library of Leiden University and other Collections in the Netherlands*, vol. 1:

Comprising the Acquisitions of Turkish Manuscripts in the Seventeenth and Eighteenth Centuries (Leiden: Legatum Warnerianum, 2000), p. 67, called this an ownership note of Ṣabūḥ efendī.

44 Mehmet Sari, 'Sabûhî (صبوحي)', in *TDV İslâm Ansiklopedisi*, vol. 35 (Istanbul: Türkiye Diyanet Vakfı İslâm Araştirmaları Merkezi, 2008), pp. 357–8.

45 Bekir Çinar, 'Tiflî Ahmed Çelebi (ö. 1070/1660)', in *TDV İslâm Ansiklopedisi*, vol. 41 (Istanbul: Türkiye Diyanet Vakfı İslâm Araştirmaları Merkezi, 2012), pp. 89–90.

46 See Boris Liebrenz, 'Note on the Term *al-mushtarī* and the Dating of Leiden Or. 1020a', *Journal of Islamic Manuscripts* 5 (2014): 63–70.

47 See, on those numerals, François Déroche et al., *Islamic Codicology: An Introduction to the Study of Manuscripts in Arabic Script* (London: Al-Furqan Islamic Heritage Foundation, 2006), p. 97.

48 Şevket Pamuk, *A Monetary History of the Ottoman Empire* (Cambridge: Cambridge University Press, 2000), pp. 101–5; Şule Pfeiffer-Taş and Nikolaus Schindel, 'Ein Münzkonvolut aus der Regierungszeit des osmanischen Sultans Ahmed I. (1603–1617) im Museum von Tire', *Wiener Zeitschrift für die Kunde des Morgenlandes* 99 (2009): 257–9.

49 Pamuk, *A Monetary History*, p. 104.

50 MS Princeton, Firestone Library, Garrett no. 569Yq, fol. 1r (2½ *ghurūsh* and 3 *shāhiyyāt dallāliyya* in Rajab 1054/1644); MS Copenhagen, Royal Library, Cod. Arab. A.C. 24, fol. 1r (most likely from Iraq, 50 *shāhiyya fiḍiyya* of Baṣran mint in 1064/1654, though this is probably not an actual price but an indication of the worth of the manuscript, since it is described as 'if one wanted to sell it / *idh urīda l-bay*ʿ'); MS Leiden Or. 313 7½ *ghurūsh* and 2 *shāhī*s (between 7.984/1576 and the early 1600s).

51 M.Th. Houtsma, *Uit de Oostersche Correspondentie van Th. Erpenius, Jac. Golius en Lev. Warner* (Amsterdam: Johannes Müller, 1887), p. 108.

52 One of the important biographies is found in Ibn Khallikān, *Wafayāt*, vol. III, pp. 325–30.

53 The sources are listed in Samir Kaddouri, 'Ibn Ḥazm al-Qurṭubī (d. 456/1064)', in Oussama Arabi, David S. Powers and Susan A. Spectorsky (eds), *Islamic Legal Thought: A Compendium of Muslim Jurists* (Leiden: Brill, 2013), p. 212.

54 Himmet Taşkömür, 'Books on Islamic Jurisprudence, Schools of Law, and Biographies of Imams from the Hanafi School', in Gülrü Necipoğlu, Cemal Kafadar and Cornell Fleischer (eds), *Treasures of Knowledge: An Inventory of the Ottoman Palace Library (1502/3–1503/4)*, vol. I: *Essays* (Leiden: Brill, 2019), pp. 396, 401.

55 However, Camilla Adang cautions that it is far from certain that Ibn Ḥazm was already converted to Ẓāhirism when he wrote the *Ṭawq*; see Camilla Adang, 'Ibn Ḥazm on Homosexuality: A Case-Study of Ẓāhirī Legal Methodology', *Al-Qanṭara* XXIV (2003): 12.

56 '[ikhtiṣār] akthar ashʿārihā wa-ibqāʾ al-ʿuyūn minhā taḥsīnan la-hā wa-iẓhāran li-maḥāsinihā wa-taṣghīran li-ḥajmihā'. Interestingly, another work by Ibn Ḥazm has seen a similar treatment by a copyist cum redactor, namely MS Gotha orient. A 640, which was based on *Ibṭāl al-qiyās wa-l-raʾy wa-l-istiḥsān wa-l-taqlīd wa-l-taʿdīl*, but on which the copyist remarked: *wa-qad katabtu mā nafaʿa lī bi-hī l-kifāya wa-ḥadhaftu al-asānīd* ('and I wrote out what was useful to me and cut the lines of transmission'); see Wilhelm Pertsch, *Die Orientalischen Handschriften der Herzoglichen Bibliothek zu Gotha*. Vierter Theil: *Die Arabischen Handschriften*, vol. II (Gotha: Perthes, 1880), p. 2. The same concern with size and the unwieldy length of the material seems to have prevailed here.

57 Joel Blecher discusses how Ibn Ḥazm's citation of and commentary to a *ḥadīth* advanced a complex legal agenda that one would rather have expected to find in a specialised work: *Said the Prophet of God: Hadith Commentary across a Millennium* (Oakland, CA: University of California Press, 2018), p. 42.

58 Lois A. Giffen situates the *Ṭawq* in the tradition of texts on love theory in '*Ibn Ḥazm and the* Ṭawq al-ḥamāma', pp. 422–7.

59 Ibn Ḥazm, *Ṭawq*, ed. Pétrof, p. 4.

60 Ralf Elger, 'Adab and Historical Memory: The Andalusian Poet/Politician Ibn al-Khaṭīb as Presented in Aḥmad al-Maqqarī (956/1577–1041/1632), *Nafḥ aṭ-ṭīb*', *Die Welt des Islams* 42 (2002): 289–306; Liebrenz, *Die Rifāʿīya*, p. 312.

61 According to Giffen, 'Ibn Ḥazm and the *Ṭawq al-ḥamāma*', p. 421.

62 White, 'Mamlūk Poetry, Ottoman Readers', 282.

63 Muḥammad Amīn al-Muḥibbī, *Khulāṣat al-athar fī aʿyān al-qarn al-ḥādī ʿashar*, vol. I, ed. Muḥammad Ḥasan Muḥammad Ḥasan Ismāʿīl (Beirut, 2006), pp. 167–80, no. 111; Khayr al-Dīn al-Ziriklī, *al-Aʿlām. Qāmūs tarājim li-ashhar al-rijāl wa-l-nisāʾ min al-ʿarab wa-l-mustaʿribīn wa-l-mustashriqīn*, vol. VI (Beirut: Dār al-ʿIlm li-l-Malāyīn, 2002), p. 317; Muḥammad Rāghib al-Ṭabbākh, *Iʿlām al-nubalāʾ bi-tārīkh Ḥalab al-shahbāʾ*, vol. VI (Aleppo: Dār al-Qalam al-ʿArabī, 1988), p. 308. Several of al-ʿUrḍī's own manuscripts also ended up with Warner, e.g. Leiden Or. 275 (which al-ʿUrḍī purchased in 1048) and Or. 300.

64 See the letters in Houtsma, *Uit de oostersche correspondentie*, p. 108, letter XXIII. G. W. J. Dreewes, 'The Legatum Warnerianum of the Leiden University Library', in *Levinus Warner and his Legacy. Three Centuries*

Legatum Warnerianum in the Leiden University Library (Leiden: Brill, 1970), p. 18. Warner did not, as John-Paul Ghobrial recently claimed ('The Archive of Orientalism and its Keepers: Re-Imagining the Histories of Arabic Manuscripts in Early Modern Europe', *Past and Present* 230 [2016]: 97), buy the library of Ḥajjī Khalīfa, but rather several volumes from it at the auction of his estate through an intermediary.

65 Neither Ḥājjī Khalīfa in his *Kashf al-ẓunūn* nor the later additions such as Ismāʿīl Bāshā al-Bābānī al-Baghdādī in his *Hadiyyat al-ʿārifīn* or the *Īḍāḥ al-maknūn* knew about it. Both men cite other works with the title *Ṭawq al-ḥamāma*, but that does not alert them to the lacuna of Ibn Ḥazm's text.

66 Chief editions and translations are cited in al-Samarrai, 'New Remarks', 58–9; Witkam, 'Establishing the Stemma', 100. The list has grown since then. Witkam also points out (p. 92) that none of the subsequent editions are based on revisiting the manuscript but rather make emendations based on philological grounds.

67 Johann Jacob Reiske (ed. and trans.), *Abi'l Walidi Ibn Zeidvni Risalet seu Epistolivm* (Leipzig: Gleditsch, 1755).

68 For that cataloguing work, see Boris Liebrenz, *Arabische, Persische und Türkische Handschriften in Leipzig. Geschichte ihrer Sammlung und Erschließung von den Anfängen bis zu Karl Vollers* (Leipzig: Leipziger Universitätsverlag, 2008), p. 59.

69 I. J. Kratschkowski, *Über arabische Handschriften gebeugt*, trans. Oskar P. Trautmann (Leipzig: Koehler und Amelang, 1949), pp. 163–5; and in the English translation, I. J. Kratchkowsky, *Among Arabic Manuscripts: Memories of Libraries and Men*, trans. Tatiana Minorsky, 2nd edn (Leiden: Brill, 2017), pp. 123–4. Pétrof himself posthumously thanks Rosen in the acknowledgements of his edition for having taken up the task of teaching the Arabic alphabet to a man of 33 years, Ibn Ḥazm, *Ṭauḳ al-ḥamâma*, ed. Pétrof, p. v. He does not, however, allude to any substantial involvement by Kratchkowsky and does not mention Seybold at all.

70 Cases of *unicum* manuscripts are Muḥammad b. Lājīn al-Ṭarābulusī's book on cavalry tactics (Or. 490), the account of the battles of the Ottoman governor Yemenli Ḥasan Pasha in Yemen, *al-Rawḍ al-ḥasan fī akhbār siyar mawlānā ṣāḥib al-saʿāda al-bāshā Ḥasan fī ayyām wilāyatihi bi-iqlīm al-Yaman* (Or. 477), a Kipchak Turkish grammar and vocabulary for Arabic speakers by Khalīl b. Muḥammad al-Qūnawī (Or. 517), the *Tārīkh Makka* by Muḥammad b. Isḥāq al-Fākihī (Or. 463), *Kitāb al-Muʿjib fī talkhīṣ Akhbār al-Maghrib* by ʿAbd al-Wāḥid b. ʿAlī al-Tamīmī al-Marrākushī (Or. 546), the *Dhikr Akhbār Iṣbahān* by Abū Nuʿaym al-Iṣbahānī (Or. 568) and the *Dīwān* of Muslim b. al-Walīd al-Ghawānī (Or. 888).

Works cited

Primary sources

al-Bāghdādī, Ismāʿīl Bāshā, *Hadiyyat al-ʿārifīn. Asmāʾ al-muʾallifīn wa-āthār al-muṣannifīn*, vol. I (Beirut: Dār Iḥyāʾ al-Turāth al-ʿArabī; repr. Istanbul, 1951).

Ibn Ḥajar al-ʿAsqalānī, *al-Durar al-kāmina*, vol. IV (Beirut: Dār Iḥyāʾ al-Turāth al-ʿArabī, n.d.).

Ibn Ḥazm, *Ṭauḳ al-ḥamâma, publié d'après l'unique manuscrit de la Bibliothèque de l'Université de Leide*, ed. D. K. Pétrof (St Petersburg/Leiden: Imprimérie Orientale ci-devant E.J. Brill, 1914).

— *A Book Containing the Risāla Known as the Dove's Neck-Ring about Love and Lovers*, trans. A. R. Nykl (Paris: Geuthner, 1931).

Ibn Khallikān, *Wafayāt al-aʿyān wa-anbāʾ abnāʾ al-zamān*, ed. Iḥsān ʿAbbās, 8 vols (Beirut: Dār Ṣādir, 2005).

Ibn Taghrī Birdī, Yūsuf, *al-Nujūm al-zāhira fī mulūk Miṣr wa-l-Qāhira*, vol. I, ed. Muḥammad Ḥusayn Shams al-Dīn (Beirut: Dār al-Kutub al-ʿIlmiyya, 1992).

Ibn al-Wardī, Zayn al-Dīn ʿUmar, *Dīwān Ibn al-Wardī*, ed. ʿAbd al-Ḥamīd Hindāwī (Cairo: Dār al-Āfāq al-ʿArabiyya, 2006).

al-Maqrīzī, Taqī al-Dīn Aḥmad, *al-Sulūk li-maʿrifat duwal al-mulūk*, vol. IV, ed. Muḥammad ʿAbd al-Qādir ʿAṭā (Beirut: Dār al-Kutub al-ʿIlmiyya, 1997).

al-Muḥibbī, Muḥammad Amīn, *Khulāṣat al-athar fī aʿyān al-qarn al-ḥādī ʿashar*, vol. I, ed. Muḥammad Ḥasan Muḥammad Ḥasan Ismāʿīl (Beirut: Dār al-Kutub al-ʿIlmiyya, 2006).

al-Ṣafadī, Khalīl Ibn Aybak, *al-Wāfī bi-l-Wafayāt*, vol. IV, ed. Sven Dedering (Stuttgart: Steiner, 1974).

— *Aʿyān al-ʿaṣr wa-aʿwān al-naṣr*, ed. Nabīl Abū ʿAmsha, Muḥammad Mawʿid and Maḥmūd Sālim Muḥammad, vols III–IV (Beirut: Dār al-Fikr al-Muʿāṣir and Damascus: Dār al-Fikr, 1998).

al-Sakhāwī, Muḥammad b. ʿAbd al-Raḥmān, *al-Ḍawʾ al-lāmiʿ li-ahl al-qarn al-tāsiʿ*, 12 vols (Beirut: Dār al-Jīl, n.d.).

Secondary sources

Adang, Camilla, 'Ibn Ḥazm on Homosexuality: A Case-Study of Ẓāhirī Legal Methodology', *Al-Qanṭara* 24 (2003): 5–31.

Adang, Camilla, Maribel Fierro and Sabine Schmidtke (eds), *Ibn Ḥazm of Cordoba: The Life and Works of a Controversial Thinker* (Leiden: Brill, 2012).

Ahlwardt, Wilhelm, *Verzeichnis der arabischen Handschriften der Königlichen Bibliothek zu Berlin*, vol. IX (Berlin: A. Asher, 1897).

Attar, Samar, *The Vital Roots of European Enlightenment: Ibn Tufayl's Influence on Modern Western Thought* (Lanham, MD: Lexington Books, 2007).

Benaïssa, Abdallah, 'Vers une nouvelle interpretation paléographique du manuscript *Tawq al-Hamama* du théologien andalou Ibn Hazm (994–1063)', *Études Maghrébines* 5–6 (1997): 7–21.

Blecher, Joel, *Said the Prophet of God: Hadith Commentary across a Millennium* (Oakland, CA: University of California Press, 2018).

Çinar, Bekir, 'Tiflî Ahmed Çelebi (ö. 1070/1660)', in *TDV İslâm Ansiklopedisi*, vol. 41 (Istanbul: Türkiye Diyanet Vakfı İslâm Araştirmaları Merkezi, 2012), pp. 89–90.

Déroche, François, et al., *Islamic Codicology: An Introduction to the Study of Manuscripts in Arabic Script* (London: Al-Furqan Islamic Heritage Foundation, 2006).

Dreewes, G. W. J., 'The Legatum Warnerianum of the Leiden University Library', in *Levinus Warner and his Legacy. Three Centuries Legatum Warnerianum in the Leiden University Library* (Leiden: Brill, 1970), pp. 1–31.

Elger, Ralf, 'Adab and Historical Memory: The Andalusian Poet/Politician Ibn al-Khaṭīb as Presented in Aḥmad al-Maqqarī (956/1577–1041/1632)', *Nafḥ aṭ-ṭīb', Die Welt des Islams* 42 (2002): 289–306.

Fuʾād Sayyid, Ayman, 'Les marques de possession sur les manuscrits et la reconstitution des anciens fonds des manuscrits arabes', *Manuscripta Orientalia* 9 (2003): 14–23.

Gacek, Adam, 'Ownership Statements and Seals in Arabic Manuscripts', *Manuscripts of the Middle East* 2 (1987): 88–95.

Ghobrial, John-Paul, 'The Archive of Orientalism and its Keepers: Re-Imagining the Histories of Arabic Manuscripts in Early Modern Europe', *Past and Present* 230 (2016): 90–111.

Giffen, Lois A., '*Ibn Ḥazm and the* Ṭawq al-ḥamāmā', in Salma Khadra Jayyusi (ed.), *The Legacy of Muslim Spain* (Leiden: Brill, 1992), pp. 420–42.

Hanna, Nelly, *In Praise of Books. A Cultural History of Cairo's Middle Class, Sixteenth to the Eighteenth Century* (Syracuse, NY: Syracuse University Press, 2003).

Hirschler, Konrad, *Medieval Damascus. Plurality and Diversity in an Arabic Library: The Ashrafīya Library Catalogue* (Edinburgh: Edinburgh University Press, 2016).

Holtzman, Livnat, 'Elements of Acceptance and Rejection in Ibn Qayyim al-Jawziyya's Systematic Reading of Ibn Ḥazm', in Camilla Adang, Maribel Fierro and Sabine Schmidtke (eds), *Ibn Ḥazm of Cordoba: The Life and Works of a Controversial Thinker* (Leiden: Brill, 2012), pp. 601–44.

Houtsma, M.Th., *Uit de Oostersche Correspondentie van Th. Erpenius, Jac. Golius en Lev. Warner* (Amsterdam: Johannes Müller, 1887).

Kaddouri, Samir, 'Ibn Ḥazm al-Qurṭubī (d. 456/1064)', in Oussama Arabi, David S. Powers and Susan A. Spectorsky (eds), *Islamic Legal Thought: A Compendium of Muslim Jurists* (Leiden: Brill, 2013), pp. 211–38.

Kratschkowski, I. J., *Über arabische Handschriften gebeugt*, trans. Oskar P. Trautmann (Leipzig: Koehler und Amelang, 1949).

— *Among Arabic Manuscripts: Memories of Libraries and Men*, trans. Tatiana Minorsky, 2nd edn (Leiden: Brill, 2017).

Kruk, Remke, 'Review of Samar Attar, *The Vital Roots of European Enlightenment*', *Middle Eastern Literatures* 14 (2011): 91–5.

Lailach, Michael, Carola Pohlmann and Christoph Rauch (eds), *Reisende Erzählungen. Tausendundein Nacht zwischen Orient und Europa* (Berlin: Insel, 2019).

Liebrenz, Boris, *Arabische, Persische und Türkische Handschriften in Leipzig. Geschichte ihrer Sammlung und Erschließung von den Anfängen bis zu Karl Vollers* (Leipzig: Leipziger Universitätsverlag, 2008).

— 'Lese- und Besitzvermerke in der Leipziger Rifāʿīya-Bibliothek', in Andreas Görke and Konrad Hirschler (eds), *Manuscript Notes as Documentary Sources* (Beirut: Orient-Institut, 2012), pp. 141–62.

— 'The Library of Aḥmad al-Rabbāṭ. Books and their Audience in 12th to 13th/18th to 19th Century Syria', in Ralf Elger and Ute Pietruschka (eds), *Marginal Perspectives on Early Modern Ottoman Culture: Missionaries, Travellers, Booksellers* (Halle/Saale: Zentrum für Interdisziplinäre Regionalstudien, 2013) [= *Orientwissenschaftliche Hefte* 32], pp. 17–59.

— 'Note on the Term *al-mushtarī* and the Dating of Leiden Or. 1020a', *Journal of Islamic Manuscripts* 5 (2014): 63–70.

— *Die Rifāʿīya aus Damaskus. Eine Privatbibliothek im osmanischen Syrien und ihr kulturelles Umfeld* (Leiden: Brill, 2016).

— (ed), *The History of Books and Collections through Manuscript Notes* (Leiden: Brill, 2018) [= *Journal of Islamic Manuscripts* 9.2–3 (2018)]

Liebrenz, Boris, and Kristina Richardson (eds), *The Notebook of Kamāl al-Dīn the Weaver: Aleppine Notes from the End of the 16th Century* (Beirut: Orient-Institut Beirut, 2021).

Muhanna, Elias, 'Encyclopaedism in the Mamluk Period: The Composition of Shihāb al-Dīn Nuwayrī's (d. 1333) *Nihāyat al-Arab fī Funūn al-Adab*', PhD dissertation, Harvard University, 2012.

Muṭīʿ al-Ḥāfiẓ, Muḥammad, *Fihris makhṭūṭāt Dār al-Kutub al-Ẓāhiriyya: al-Fiqh al-ḥanafī*, vol. I (Damascus: Majmaʿ al-Lugha al-ʿArabiyya bi-Dimashq, 1980).

Pamuk, Şevket, *A Monetary History of the Ottoman Empire* (Cambridge: Cambridge University Press, 2000).

Pertsch, Wilhelm, *Die Orientalischen Handschriften der Herzoglichen Bibliothek zu Gotha*. Vierter Theil: *Die Arabischen Handschriften*, vol. II (Gotha: Perthes, 1880).

Pfeiffer-Taş, Şule, and Nikolaus Schindel, 'Ein Münzkonvolut aus der Regierungszeit des osmanischen Sultans Ahmed I. (1603–1617) im Museum von Tire', *Wiener Zeitschrift für die Kunde des Morgenlandes* 99 (2009): 249–80.

Reiske, Johann Jacob (ed. and trans.), *Abi'l Walidi Ibn Zeidvni Risalet seu Epistolivm* (Leipzig: Gleditsch, 1755).

Sajdi, Dana, *The Barber of Damascus. Nouveau Literacy in the Eighteenth-Century Ottoman Levant* (Stanford, CA: Stanford University Press, 2013).

al-Samarrai, Qasim, 'New Remarks on the Text of Ibn Ḥazm's *Ṭawq al-ḥamāma*', *Arabica* XXX (1983): 57–72.
Sari, Mehmet, 'Sabûhî (صبوحي)', in *TDV İslâm Ansiklopedisi*, vol. 35 (Istanbul: Türkiye Diyanet Vakfı İslâm Araştirmaları Merkezi, 2008), pp. 357–58.
Schmidt, Jan, *Catalogue of Turkish Manuscripts in the Library of Leiden University and other Collections in the Netherlands*, vol. I: *Comprising the Acquisitions of Turkish Manuscripts in the Seventeenth and Eighteenth Centuries* (Leiden: Legatum Warnerianum, 2000).
Süreyya, Mehmed, *Sicill-i osmanî* (Istanbul: Tarih Vakfı Yurt Yayınları, 1996).
al-Ṭabbākh, Muḥammad Rāghib, *Iʿlām al-nubalāʾ bi-tārīkh Ḥalab al-shahbāʾ*, vol. VI (Aleppo: Dār al-Qalam al-ʿArabī, 1988).
Taşkömür, Himmet, 'Books on Islamic Jurisprudence, Schools of Law, and Biographies of Imams from the Hanafi School', in Gülrü Necipoğlu, Cemal Kafadar and Cornell Fleischer (eds), *Treasures of Knowledge: An Inventory of the Ottoman Palace Library (1502/3–1503/4)*, vol. I: *Essays* (Leiden: Brill, 2019), pp. 390–422.
van Gelder, Geert Jan, 'A Muslim Encomium on Wine: *The Racecourse of the Bay (Ḥalbat al-Kumayt)* by al-Nawājī (d. 859/1455) as a Post-Classical Arabic Work', *Arabica* XLII (1995): 222–34.
van Koningsveld, P. S., 'De oorspronkelijke versie van Ibn Ḥazms Ṭawq al-ḥamâma', *Sharqiyyât* 5 (1993): 23–38.
Vrolijk, Arnoud, and Richard van Leeuwen, *Arabic Studies in the Netherlands: A Short History in Portraits, 1580–1950* (Leiden: Brill, 2013).
White, James, 'Mamlūk Poetry, Ottoman Readers, and an Enlightenment Collector: An Appendix to the *Nuzha* of Ibn Sūdūn', *Journal of Islamic Manuscripts* 9.2–3 (2018): 272–307.
Witkam, Jan Just, 'Establishing the Stemma: Fact or Fiction?', *Manuscripts of the Middle East* 3 (1988): 88–101.
— *Inventory of the Oriental Manuscripts of the Library of the University of Leiden*, vol. I: *Manuscripts Or. 1–Or. 1000* (Leiden: Ter Lugt Press, 2007).
Yūsuf, Muḥammad Khayr Ramaḍān, *al-Ghurar ʿalā l-ṭurar. Ghurar al-fawāʾid ʿalā ṭurar al-makhṭūṭāt wa-l-nawādir*, 2 vols (Beirut: Dār al-Bashāʾir al-Islāmīya, 2004).
Zemon Davis, Natalie, *Trickster Travels: A Sixteenth-Century Muslim Between Worlds* (New York: Hill and Wang, 2006).
al-Ziriklī, Khayr al-Dīn, *al-Aʿlām. Qāmūs tarājim li-ashhar al-rijāl wa-l-nisāʾ min al-ʿarab wa-l-mustaʿribīn wa-l-mustashriqīn*, vol. VI (Beirut: Dār al-ʿIlm li-l-Malāyīn, 2002).

4

'Thirty pieces of silver': interpreting anti-Jewish imagery in the *Poema de mio Cid* manuscript

Ryan D. Giles

In 2014 Steven Hess published a biography of the best-known twentieth-century scholar of medieval Spanish literature, Ramón Menéndez Pidal, who completed the first modern critical edition of the *Poema de mio Cid* (*PMC*) [*The Poem of the Cid*]. Over the course of his long career, this gifted philologist continued to emphasise what he saw as the historical nature of the canonical poem's celebration of the deeds of the eleventh-century figure Rodrigo Díaz de Vivar (c. 1040s–1099). Influenced by the aims of nineteenth-century philology, he elevated the *PMC* to the status of national epic, a 'retrato del pueblo donde se escribió' ['portrait of the people from where it was written'].[1] He viewed the poem as being based on oral composition, expressing the spirit of the folk through the character of the Cid, who embodied trans-historical values, including equality, moderation, fidelity and justice.[2] Menéndez Pidal's work on the poem coincided with a national crisis, following Spain's disastrous war with the United States and resulting loss of Caribbean and Pacific colonies in 1898. He belonged to a generation of intellectuals seeking to renew their country's identity in the wake of this humiliating loss of empire. In the words of Michael Gerli, Menéndez Pidal offered his study of the Cid as 'a remedy for Spain's national malaise of skepticism and factionalism'.[3] His scholarship contested earlier assessments of the *PMC* as a 'French imitation', and Spain itself as trapped in a state of arrested development, unable to produce its own, homegrown epic tradition.[4] As María Eugenia Lacarra points out, Menéndez Pidal believed that contemporary society could benefit from the rediscovery of Spain's primordial virtues, epitomised by its epic hero. In doing so, he reacted against earlier characterisations of the Cid as a cruel 'mercenary' or a greedy 'rogue' and 'perjurer'.[5] In the biography, Hess noted that Menéndez Pidal 'could never divest himself of a patriotic interpretation that emphasised the positive aspects of Spain's historical mission and shunted aside the distasteful aspects', including 'racism' and 'intolerance'.[6] For this reason, in his work on the *PMC*, the Spanish philologist tried to justify an episode in which the hero mendaciously deceives two Jews in order to secure a loan that is never paid back.[7] Hess finds that Menéndez Pidal, through 'scholarly subterfuge', tried to avert an 'embarrassing blemish on the integrity of El Cid' by claiming that the hero only resorted to deception out of necessity, and attributing the lack of repayment in the poem to an authorial memory lapse.

Because the *PMC* only survives in one extant medieval codex (Biblioteca nacional de España, Vitr./7/17), Menéndez Pidal was unable to support this claim by consulting another manuscript. His only recourse was to cite later medieval chronicles and an early modern ballad in which the Cid is said to have returned the promised funds and even apologised for tricking the Jews.[8] This bears little resemblance to the story as recorded in the *unicum* codex, where the Cid expresses no such remorse and the Jews are, as we will show, portrayed in an emphatically negative light. The sole manuscript is a fourteenth-century copy of a lost version dated 1207, according to a colophon penned by a scribe called 'Per Abbat' (Pedro Abad). This otherwise anonymous text, known as the Vivar codex, retains evidence of orality, along with many clerical, legal and other learned elements.[9] The episode in question appears on folios 3–4, where the Jewish lenders are identified as 'Rachel' (usually understood as an alternative spelling or erroneous scribal rendering of the male Sephardic name, Rogel) and 'Vidas' (according to the consensus view, a Castilian version of the name Hayim, meaning 'life' in Hebrew).[10]

The *PMC* begins with the Cid being exiled and impoverished by the King of Castile and León, Alfonso VI. The poem implicitly seems to compare his unjust punishment with the betrayal of Christ by repeatedly evoking the crowing of roosters.[11] The image appears three times, in keeping with the Gospel account of Peter's prophesied denial of Christ (Matt. 26:34, Mark 14:30, John 13:38). In the *PMC*, this temporal marker is associated first with the loan from the Jews (v. 169), and thereafter with the Cid's arrival at a monastery named after St Peter, San Pedro de Cardeña. The hero has duped the Jewish characters by having two richly adorned chests filled with sand, and ordering his vassal Martín Antolínez to pass them off as security on a hefty loan of 'seysçientos marcos' (600 marks) (vv. 84, 147).[12] In his edition, Menéndez Pidal notes that the ruse could have been influenced by a tale found in an early twelfth-century collection, the *Disciplina clericalis* [Scholar's Guide].[13] This story, apparently derived from an earlier Arabic source, recounts a similar deception involving chests filled with gravel during a pilgrimage to Mecca. Unlike the *PMC*, this work survives in dozens of manuscripts (at least seventy-six, with five found in Spain), many of which predate the Vivar codex.[14] It was composed by a Jew who took the name Petrus Alfonsi (Pedro Alfonso) after coming of age in Muslim Al-Andaluz, and then immigrating to Aragon where he converted to Christianity and began his writing career.[15] His other 'bestseller' was, in fact, an anti-Jewish polemic known as the *Dialogi contra Judeos* [Dialogue against the Jews]. Not surprisingly, the works of Petrus Alfonsi have received much less attention from Hispano-medievalists than the *PMC*. Apart from being written in Latin instead of Castilian – which much later became the national language of Spain – these works complicate the pre-modern history of the nation by underscoring the cultural significance of religious 'others' and the problem of anti-Judaism in pre-modern Iberia. The often neglected *Disciplina clericalis* is a fictional, didactic book of prose that was widely popular outside the Iberian Peninsula during the Middle Ages.[16] On the other hand, the *PMC* – rediscovered in one badly damaged codex near the end of the sixteenth century and not published until 1779 – was used during the nineteenth and twentieth centuries to construct a national philology, as it celebrates the deeds of a historical Christian hero in the vernacular poetry of the Spanish homeland.[17]

In recent years José Ramírez del Río has analysed Arabic and Hebrew versions of the tale of the worthless chests in comparison to what is found in the *PMC*. In a Hebrew story recorded by Nissim ben Jacob in the eleventh century, nearly a hundred years before the *Disciplina clericalis*, it is a Jew who benefits from chests full of sand, as God intervenes on his behalf at the expense of the gentiles. Ramírez del Río points out that, for an audience familiar with the story as told from a Jewish perspective, the Cid's deception could be understood as a 'subversión', insofar as its Christian hero instead takes advantage of Sephardic moneylenders.[18] Whether or not the epic subverts this variation on the popular tale, I will show how it employs undeniably anti-Jewish images and how these relate to Iberian history and echo often ignored Latin legends – legends that, unlike the *PMC*, are attested by multiple surviving manuscripts. More specifically, my purpose in this chapter is to demonstrate how the episode of the sand-filled chests evokes transactions between Christians and Jews in medieval Iberia, as well as beliefs concerning the biblical figure of Judas Iscariot that fuelled accusations of Jewish avarice and usury during this period.

In the Vivar codex the story is told in painstaking detail. Making his way into the Jewish quarter of Burgos, Antolínez finds the two moneylenders counting their profits (v. 101). After asking them to keep the loan a secret, and to swear not to open the chests for one year, he agrees that the Cid will pay whatever interest they deem necessary.[19] Rachel and Vidas seem to believe that the Cid has amassed a fortune from an unauthorised raid on Muslim territories to the south, and over the course of the poem we will see how powerful enemies in the court have turned against him. Antolínez accepts a payment of thirty marks ('treínta marcos') from the lenders for helping arrange the transaction (v. 196). Receipt of the chests and the expectation of further profit greatly please Rachel and Vidas: 'al cargar las arcas veriedes gozo tanto … grádanse Rachel y Vidas con averes monedados' ['as they pick up the chests you could see such joy … Rachel and Vidas are pleased with their income in coins'] (vv. 170, 172). Later in the poem, after the exiled hero has conquered Valencia and enriched his family and allies, the lenders complain about the unpaid loan. The Cid's commander, Minaya Álvar Fañez, claims that he will take up the issue with his lord to make things right (v. 1437).[20] Following this encounter, the narrative relates how the Cid reconciled himself with the king and successfully sought justice for wrongs suffered by his daughters at the hands of villainous, cowardly nobles. The lenders never again appear in the narrative, nor is any further information given concerning the unsettled debt, as I mentioned earlier.

The Rachel and Vidas episode is among the most thoroughly studied of the *PMC*. Critical debates have primarily centred on whether the Cid's treatment of these characters is anti-Jewish. Such discussions often hinge on whether the hero should be understood as having ultimately repaid his loan, as Menéndez Pidal insisted.[21] In an important early study, Leo Spitzer found this stance to be anachronistic: 'he [Menéndez Pidal] tries hard to deny any trace of medieval anti-Semitism in his hero ... let us avoid confusions: medieval morality is not our own'.[22] In keeping with Spitzer, a majority of later critics have understood the episode to be anti-Jewish.[23] Many also view the courteous language used to address the moneylenders – whose greed presumably blinds them to the obvious ruse – as ironic, their hollow complaints as ridiculous, and the later promise to repay the loan as disingenuous. For example, Colin Smith argued that a twelfth-century audience would have lauded their hero's ability to trick moneylending Jews. In response to Menéndez Pidal, he also observed that previously referenced royal chronicles probably added the Cid's repayment to the story in order to encourage 'a reluctant populace to pay its debts to Jews', as this minority group loaned money and carried out other financial activities under the protection of the king – not to mention their participation in compiling such texts under royal direction.[24] Donald McGrady similarly described the lenders' portrayal in the poem as an 'anti-Semitic satire', as it shows the Jews 'avariciously counting their money (v. 101) ... and drooling at the prospect of becoming the owners of gold worth far more than the loan, should the Cid not redeem his pledge within the appointed time' (vv. 170–3).[25] In another study, Edna Aizenberg connected the passage to a formulaic prayer in which Jimena, the Cid's wife, refers to Jews collectively as deicides (vv. 347–8).[26] While critics of the episode have often employed the modern term anti-semitism, and some even refer to race, my approach follows that of scholars who specify that anti-Jewish imagery in the poem targets the moneylenders' religious identity and social function, rather than supposedly inborn traits.[27]

One aspect of the negative depiction of Rachel and Vidas that merits further exploration is a possible allusion first noticed by Seymour Resnick. This critic wondered whether the poet chose to have the lenders pay 'the figure of thirty [marks] because of its unpleasant association with the betrayal of Christ'.[28] He then observes in a footnote that 'under Sancho IV' (1258–95) Jews 'were required to pay a tax of thirty *dineros* to remind them of the thirty pieces of silver alleged to have been paid by their ancestors to bring about the death of Jesus'.[29] This connection would have worked in tandem with the previously cited scriptural reference to cocks crowing three times. Some critics have dismissed Resnick's interpretation, such as Nicasio Salvador Miguel, who asserts that a loyal vassal's receipt of 'treínta marcos' for arranging the Cid's loan could not evoke the treachery of taking thirty pieces of silver from the Sanhedrin.[30] On the other hand, Luis López González has argued that evoking the biblical sum could also allude to the anti-Jewish story of Titus selling thirty Jews in exchange for one denarius to avenge the betrayal of Christ by Judas. He also notes that, in 1240, Fernando III imposed upon the Burgos jewry an annual tithe of thirty 'dineros', to be paid to the city's cathedral.[31] While I agree that the marks should not be viewed as solely a scriptural reference, we will see how the historical context that Resnick briefly refers to in his note, and that López González has followed up, does further elucidate the episode.

Without mentioning the *PMC*, two historians have in recent years examined the phenomenon of Iberian Jews paying a symbolic fee of thirty coins, partly as a means of commemorating their perceived guilt in the crucifixion. Lucy Pick demonstrates that eleventh-century bishops of León began receiving royal taxes collected from the city's Jewish quarter when Fernando I donated three hundred *solidi*. From these funds, Bishop Pelayo set aside thirty silver *solidi* annually to keep candles lit before the altars of the Saviour, Mary and St Cyprian. His donation began in 1074, during the reign of Alfonso VI and the lifetime of the historical Cid. The exact sum, as Pick makes clear, 'was not chosen arbitrarily; it evokes the price of thirty coins paid to Judas to betray Jesus', a practice that continued into the early twelfth century, when 'Bishop Diego expanded the gift again by an additional 30*s*, still taken out of the bishop's portion of the royal tax on the Jews'.[32]

In his earlier study, Javier Castaño traced the tradition of requiring Iberian Jews to pay 'triginta denarios annuatim', or thirty units of coinage per year, from Navarra to the newly conquered territories of Castile, from the High Middle Ages to the expulsion of the Iberian Jews in 1492:

> not only does it explicitly symbolize … the Passion … they were to pay for having a sanctioned status within medieval society … a 'sacred

> fisc' ... the 'thirty monies' form part of larger discourse that revolved around the Passion. By punishing the Jews, the Christian community avenged the crucifixion and assured its salvation.[33]

Pick builds on Castaño's work, finding that the way in which the taxes were put to use by early bishops made these 'spiritually laundered' donations represent the treacherous profit received by Judas, transforming and recirculating it to fund Christian devotion.[34] What was viewed as Jewish blood money was in this way converted into a pious sum. Bishop Pelayo, in fact, is recorded as having prayed that the yearly candles purchased with thirty silver coins would provide 'temporal light' before the altars of the Redeemer and his Mother, and illuminate the 'darkness of the heart', so that his soul could glory with the saints in the 'inextinguishable light' of the afterlife.[35]

I would argue that what Pick aptly calls 'laundering' as means of Christianising monies is implicated in the *PMC*, as the coins taken from Rachel and Vidas are partially transformed into a kind of spiritual debt owed to God and his ministers. Not long after Antolínez takes the symbolic 'treínta marcos' from Rachel and Vidas and the Cid receives his loan, which the Jews count out in two sums of three hundred marks, the hero prays for the protection of God and the Virgin. In exchange, he promises to furnish an altar with 'buenas donas e rricas' ['fine and rich offerings'] and to return the 'debdo' ['debt'] owed to his heavenly protectors by paying for 'mill missas' ['one thousand Masses'] (vv. 224–5).[36] He then donates part of the funds acquired from the moneylenders to the monastery of San Pedro de Cardeña, pledging to provide more in the future, and asking its abbot to take care of his wife and daughters (vv. 250–3). Again the Cid describes himself as being indebted, 'só vuestro pagado', to the monastery (v. 248). The remainder of the borrowed money makes it possible for the hero and his followers to amass further wealth by raiding and conquering Muslim territories to the east. Just before Minaya encounters Rachel and Vidas, who have come to protest about the outstanding loan, he makes another monetary donation to the monastery on behalf of the Cid (v. 1423).

The Cid's debt to the Jewish moneylenders is thus converted into a spiritualised monetary obligation that the hero pays out in the text of the epic – unlike his original loan. As Pick puts it in her study of how money collected from Jews was piously repurposed by the crown and the Church, 'material donation *pro anima* was intended to set in motion a process that required both the gift itself and its donor to be spiritually transformed or converted to sacred use'.[37] The meaning of this 'sacred fisc', as Castaño puts it, with its commemoration of the thirty coins paid to Judas, suggests that scholars should avoid imposing 'a false dichotomy between fiscal concerns and theological ones' and instead consider how these might work 'in harmony', recognising how Christian relations with Jews on the Peninsula at times 'seamlessly blended theological, political, and economic concerns, and indeed could not conceive of these as separate'.[38] Monies collected in Jewish quarters and cleansed by the Church contributed, on the one hand, to the ability of kings, their ministers – and, by extension, bishops – to control and protect the value provided by this minority group (including its role in moneylending), in effect monetising their separateness and its theological underpinnings.

On the other hand, the harmonious relationship between Christian belief and the power of money could also fuel outbursts of religious violence. One such example, cited by Pick, occurred during the reign of Alfonso XI of León, not long before the only extant manuscript of the *PMC* was dated in 1207. This king was excommunicated by the pope in 1196 after he attacked neighbouring Castile with the help of Muslim forces from the south. That same year the Jewish quarter of León was sacked by an Aragonese and Castilian alliance – the very community whose taxes during the reign of Alfonso VI had supplied thirty silver coins annually to illuminate altars in the city's cathedral. As Pick points out, surviving Jews were said to have been 'taken captive', since 'the motivations for this destruction were certainly grounded in both politics and economics … the Jews were prosperous, and … closely associated with the army's target, the king of León. But when armies or mobs attack Jews, theological righteousness coincides with economic self-interest.'[39]

Castaño traced the pre-modern monetisation of Jewish captives and the sacred fisc – believed to be a testimony to and consequence of the death of Jesus – back to a widely circulated Latin legend known as the *Vindicta Salvatoris* [Vengeance of the Saviour], first written during the eighth century. This anonymous narrative provides a fictionalised account of the 70 CE destruction of Jerusalem during

Passover, claiming that the Roman conquerors under the future Emperor Titus, recast here as a convert to Christianity, sold groups of thirty captive Jews for one silver coin in order to exact revenge for the treachery of Judas. The popularity of this story can be attested by its inclusion in a variety of influential Latin and vernacular works that survive in numerous manuscripts, from Petrus Comestor's *Historia Scholastica* [History of the Church] to the Old French epic poem, *La Venjeance Nostre Seigneur* [The Vengeance of our Lord], both written during the twelfth century, to thirteenth-century works such as the *Legenda aurea* [*Golden Legend*] of Jacobus de Voragine, the Iberian anti-Muslim polemic called *Sobre la secta mahometana* [On the Mohammedan Sect], and, as López González points out, the *Estoria de España* [History of Spain] attributed to the Castilian King Alfonso X.[40] A commentary on the *Historia Hierosolymitana* [History of Jerusalem] (c. 1107) even alleged that Tancred repeated the imagined revenge of Titus during the First Crusade, selling Jewish captives for the same amount after the Holy City was sacked.[41] This legend of monetised vengeance illustrates how the payment to Judas resonated in ways that could not only convert it into pious donations, as we have seen, but also military plunder. In each of these retellings, the biblical transaction of thirty for one was converted into funds gained by and for Christian conquest, comparable to the Cid's utilisation of the money he and Antolínez receive from Rachel and Vidas.

Apart from the *Vindicta Salvatoris*, a related tradition further illustrates how the profit of Judas was understood during the time the *PMC* was composed. It drew on typological connections between the books of Genesis and Zechariah and the Gospel of Matthew. Biblical commentators consistently associated the twenty pieces of silver paid to the brothers of the prophet Joseph (Gen. 37:28) with the 'thirty pieces of silver' of the gospel as a way of prefiguring the price for which Christ was sold (Matt. 26:15). Medieval exegetes also understood the thirty coins that Zechariah threw into the 'house of the Lord' (Zech. 11:12–13) as prophesying the money a repentant Judas brought back to the chief priests of the temple and flung to the ground (Matt. 27:3–6). Both interpretations can be found, for instance, in the early thirteenth-century *Fazienda de ultramar* [Deeds from across the Seas], which features an early Castilian translation of biblical passages.[42]

In other works, the conventional reading of Joseph as a type of Christ seems to have influenced the legend of the thirty coins themselves – that is, how the physical objects were said to reappear at different times in sacred history. This can be seen most notably in the widely diffused *Pantheon* or *Liber universalis* of Godfrey of Viterbo, completed during the 1180s and later quoted by Alfonso X's chroniclers. Preserved in numerous manuscripts, like the *Vindicta Salvatoris* (and previously discussed works by Petrus Alfonsi), it describes how the coins received by Joseph's brothers made their way into Solomon's temple, and eventually came into the hands of the Magi.[43] Whereas the *Fazienda de ultramar* claims that the price of twenty coins paid for the prophet in Genesis were worth the same amount as the thirty *denarii* in the gospel, this text gives no explanation of the discrepancy between the sums. Given as a gift to the infant Jesus, it claims that the Holy Family hid the thirty coins in Egypt, where they were later found by an astrologer who brought them to the Second Temple prior to the Passion.[44] According to this popular account, the same coins earned from Joseph's betrayal had already been repurposed as a blessed donation prior to the treachery of Judas. Such beliefs no doubt provided an additional analogue for how monies received from Jews such as Rachel and Vidas could be recast as a sacred fisc in medieval Spain.

In addition to beliefs surrounding the thirty coins, a concurrent legend elaborated on the association of Judas with avarice by providing details not present in Matthew. In the *Legenda aurea* (c. 1260), preserved in hundreds of extant medieval manuscripts across Europe, Jacobus Voragine recounts what he calls an earlier 'apocryphal history', apparently derived from a *Hystoria de Juda* that circulated in pre-existing sermonic collections and has been shown to date back to the twelfth century.[45] The first part of the narrative relates the Oedipal story of Judas, characterised as a cursed foundling who grows up to marry his mother and kill his father before becoming an apostle. The second part follows the Gospel of John by portraying him as the keeper of alms received by the followers of Christ who took advantage of his role by regularly stealing from this treasury (John 12:6). Motivated by avarice, he protested when the Magdalene anointed Christ's feet with perfume that could have been sold for three hundred *denarii*. Once again drawing on an earlier Latin *Hystoria*, Voragine then explains how Judas made a practice of stealing one-tenth of all of the money donated to Christ, in what seems to be a kind of travesty of the Old Testament tithe. Judas therefore sold his Lord for one-tenth of the lost price of the perfume: since it would have yielded three hundred, he took the thirty pieces of silver, 'trecentos denarios valebat ... dominum XXX denariis vendidit'.[46] This legend of Judas demonstrates how sums of three hundred *and* thirty coins were both closely connected to the infamous apostle's greed. Such a connection might have informed the use of these particular amounts in the episode of the two moneylenders in the *PMC*: 'tendieron un almofalla ... a tod el primer colpe *trezientos* marcos de plata echaron ... los otros *trezientos* en oro ge los pagavan ... dámosvos en don a vós *treínta* marcos' ['they spread a rug ... all at once they poured out *three hundred marks* of silver ... the other *three hundred* they paid them in gold ... we give you as a gift *thirty marks*] (vv. 182–6, 196, emphasis mine).

In pre-modern iconography, Judas often appears receiving a bag of coins from the Sanhedrin. In her study of *Bibles moralisées*, or picture Bibles produced in France during the thirteenth century, Sara Lipton examines an example of the greedy apostle, dressed in medieval clothing, taking his moneybag from one of the chief priests.[47] Such bags, according to Lipton, were 'the traditional emblem associated with moneylending', and were often 'suspended outside the houses of professional moneylenders to indicate their occupation'.[48] Rachel and Vidas probably would have handed Antolínez his thirty pieces of silver in one of these objects, typically made of animal skins and tied with a long drawstring.[49] An illuminated manuscript of Alfonso X's thirteenth-century *Cantigas de Nuestra Señora* [Songs of Our Lady] includes an image of a Jewish moneylender, identified by his pointed hat, counting coins and handing his Christian customer a moneybag.[50] Repeatedly in the *Bibles moralisées* Jews appear wearing the same kind of medieval garb as Judas, holding bags of coins to visualise usury. The *PMC* makes it abundantly clear that Rachel and Vidas fit the medieval definition of usurers, as the two are first shown counting profits from earlier loans, and then discussing, negotiating and celebrating the interest they expect to earn from the Cid: 'nós huebos avemos en todo de ganar algo ... ¿qué ganacia nos dará por todo aqueste año? ... grádanse Rachel e Vidas con averes monedados, / ca mientra que visquiessen refechos eran amos' ['what we need above all is to profit from this ... what interest will you give us for all of this year? … Rachel and Vidas are pleased with their income in coins / for as long as they lived the two would be recompensed'] (vv. 123, 130, 172–3). Their expectation is to make money from money – in keeping with Jacques Le Goff's definition of usury in the context of the Middle Ages, as taking interest 'where there is no production or physical transformation of tangible goods'.[51] As we will see, this usurious reproduction of monies was understood in the medieval imaginary as a kind of unnatural form of procreation.

Le Goff observes how usury became closely associated with Jews as a consequence of the Church's continuing condemnation of the practice. In spite of this ban, both religious groups participated in what was recognised as a necessary activity, sanctioned through a number of legal stipulations and exceptions, in the growing money economies of the High Middle Ages.[52] Preachers and theologians described usury as a sin 'against nature', partly because it involved earning one's livelihood without physical work. For instance, in his late twelfth-century treatise on penitence, Thomas of Chobham wrote that 'the usurer wants to make a profit without doing any work … which goes against the precepts of the Lord, who said to Adam, "by the sweat of your face shall you get bread to eat" (Gen. 3:19)'.[53] Such a distinction is made in the *PMC* between the Cid earning 'bread' for his men in battle (v. 1682) and the moneylending of Rachel and Vidas.[54] In addition to the biblical prescription of work, usurers were accused of violating another precept laid out in Genesis: the divinely ordained nature of reproduction.[55] The penitential writings of Chobham again provide a clear example: 'money that lies fallow does not naturally produce any fruit, but the vine bears fruit naturally'.[56] Already by the mid-twelfth century, notions of money's infertility and the perverse nature of making it 'breed' can be found in Gratian's *Decretum*. This work, which quickly became the scholastic textbook for teaching canon law, described how 'repeatedly, by the most vile cunning of usury, gold is born [*nascitur*] from gold'.[57] Later, Bonaventure would warn that 'in itself and by itself money does not bear fruit', and Thomas Aquinas similarly cautioned that, according to nature, 'money does not reproduce itself'.[58]

This context could shed light on the way in which the *PMC* combines the scene of Rachel and Vidas counting their money with an image that seems to echo a verse from Genesis – the same verse that established the conditions for human procreation through the coupling of Adam and Eve: 'they shall be two in one flesh' (Gen. 2:24): 'Rachel y Vidas *en uno estavan amos* / en cuenta de sus averes de los que avién ganados' ['Rachel and Vidas *were together as one* / counting their wealth gained through profit'] (vv. 100–1, emphasis mine). The lenders' 'breeding' of money as a barren thing to create more money would have been viewed as – among other things – a perversion of the natural law guiding reproduction. As Sander Gilman puts it in his study of anti-Jewish discourse, 'money, not being alive, could not reproduce. Jews, in taking money, treated money as if it were alive.'[59] In addition to the decree in Genesis, ecclesiastical authorities also insisted that usury was explicitly prohibited in the Gospel of Luke, when Christ advises his followers to forgo receiving full repayment for loans, and then urges them to 'give: and it will be given to you' (Luke 6:34–5, 38). When Antolínez suggests that he might secure the loan without collateral, the *PMC* includes a description of Rachel and Vidas's business that fittingly inverts the meaning of this same biblical verse: 'Non se faze assí el mercado, / sinon *primero prendiendo e después dando*' ['deals are not made like that, but instead by *first getting and then giving*'] (vv. 139–40, emphasis mine).

The Cid claims to be taking the usurious loan reluctantly, 'fer lo he amidos, de grado non avrié nada' ['I will do this grudgingly, otherwise I would have nothing'] (v. 84). While this justification is subject to irony – since the avaricious lenders are characterised as deserving to be swindled – it comes as no surprise, considering that Alfonso VI had forbidden the exile from receiving any assistance in his realm, putting him in a desperate situation. Another reason the poet might have chosen to emphasise his reluctance can be gleaned once more from Chobham's extensive, late twelfth-century discussion of usury. He finds that Christians, including nobles and royal families, 'who transfer to their own use the money they have received from Jews, since the Jews have no other possessions than those earned by usury … become the accomplices of usurious practices and usurers themselves'.[60] This idea of guilt by association constitutes another potential risk that the Cid runs by doing business with usurers, to the extent that Antolínez twice urges Rachel and Vidas to keep the deceptive transaction a secret from 'Moors' and 'Cristianos' (vv. 107, 145). Such a risk would provide additional motivation for the previously discussed spiritual cleansing of the Cid's tainted money. His donations to the monastery and promise to fund 'a thousand masses' brings to mind examples of Christians from the period, who had in some way profited from usury, hoping to redeem themselves by 'giving gifts' and trying to 'buy the Church's prayers'.[61]

Probably the most striking example of the lengths to which medieval Christians would go to purify themselves from the stigma of usury can be seen in a series of frescoes painted by Giotto di Bondone in Padua's Scrovegni chapel, completed around 1305. Usurers such as members of the Scrovegni family were often criticised by fellow Catholics as 'indistinguishable' from Jews.[62] In fact, Bernard of Clairvaux, writing in the first half of the twelfth century, had already 'used the term *judaizere* to mean any form of moneylending'.[63] Later in the twelfth century, the preacher and cardinal bishop Jacques de Vitry called Christian moneylenders 'our Jews, although they are worse than the Jews. For the Jews do not lend at usury to their brothers.'[64] In the *Inferno*, Dante famously spoke to a sinner who epitomised usury and who was identified as the poet's contemporary, Reginaldo Scrovegni, by the family crest on a moneybag hanging around his neck. As Anne Derbes and Mark Sandona note in their analysis of Giotto's fresco programme, Reginaldo's son Enrico 'had the chapel built and decorated to expiate the sin of usury', having 'renounced the enterprise' of his father.[65] As a result, one central feature in the frescoes is the '*coincidentia oppositorum*' or 'confrontation of meaningful opposites' represented by Judas, pictured as a usurer, together with images of redemptive 'fecundity, which was understood throughout the Middle Ages as usury's antithesis'.[66] In other words, the chapel provides a telling visualisation of the same sort of confrontation that I have been exploring.

In Giotto's *Visitation of Mary and Elizabeth*, for example, the visible pregnancies of the women parallel and contrast with the bulging moneybag of the avaricious apostle as he stands before one of the Sanhedrin.[67] Another painting counterposes the treacherous kiss of Judas with the embrace of Joachim and Anne – parents of Mary as the new Eve, and grandparents of Christ as the new Adam – embracing 'as if their bodies and faces had become "one flesh"'.[68] While this image of the Virgin's aged parents innovates traditional iconography, the decision to include images from Genesis in a depiction of the sins of avarice and usury was not unprecedented. In one of the previously mentioned thirteenth-century *Bibles moralisées* (Vienna ÖNB cod. 1179, fol. 4c) studied by Lipton, Adam and Eve appear as one flesh in the Garden of Eden, their bodies coupled in the same posture before God, having just eaten from the Tree of Knowledge. Directly beneath this scene is another roundel showing a Jew with moneybags.[69] It is this long-standing opposition between natural fertility and the sin of usurious reproduction that, as we have found, also feeds into the portrayal of Rachel and Vidas.

Lipton observes that, because the figure of Judas 'was often taken to epitomize all of the Jews', images of him selling Christ raise questions such as: 'Are medieval Jews considered the accomplices of Judas? … Does he become "like" the medieval Jews through his actions?'[70] This chapter has shown that images of Jewish moneylending in the *PMC* can be understood as evoking the usury of Judas in scripture and lore. However, money tainted by this greed is transformed over the course of the narrative: the loan made by Rachel and Vidas – comparable to taxes paid by medieval Sephardic communities and redirected to the Church in symbolic sums of coins – becomes an 'accomplice' in acts of Christian charity. The epic hero also repurposes usurious money to fund his military campaign, reminiscent of legends recounting how the payment to Judas was converted into plunder through the righteous vengeance of Christian warriors. In medieval culture, the economic and religious value of the coins was interlinked. Believers envisioned the cursed money recirculating in sacred history as a blessed gift, and invented a story in which Judas took thirty coins as a percentage of three hundred lost *denarii*, the same amounts counted and doled out by Rachel and Vidas.

It is not surprising that the probable impact of such Latin legends on the episode has been overlooked, despite the fact that they survive in multiple manuscripts and enjoyed extremely wide circulation throughout Europe – and date back to the period when the story told in the *unicum PMC* manuscript is believed have been composed (late twelfth to very early thirteenth century). We have seen how the tendency to disregard this kind of anti-Judaism in the poem was initiated by Menéndez Pidal, who repeatedly attempted to justify the Cid's relationship with Jews. His exoneration of the hero reflected the aims of an emerging national philological project during the late nineteenth and first half of the twentieth century, that sought to promote the hero of a Castilian epic as an internal model of Spain's essential values and transhistorical identity. Decades after the publication of his edition, Menéndez Pidal maintained that 'El Cid poético *no puede* obrar movido por un vulgar anti-semitismo' ['the conduct of the Cid in the poem *cannot* be motivated by some vulgar antisemitism'].[71] This chapter has shown how the characterisation of Rachel and Vidas draws on an age-old anti-Jewish tradition of understanding and picturing usury as a perverse form of reproduction that stands in opposition to the gospel tenet to give first, and without expectation of being recompensed, before receiving. Christian practitioners and accomplices in usurious transactions could only hope to cleanse themselves and their corrupt money by completely rechannelling it for what they believed to be sacred purposes and the defence of the faith.

Notes

1 Quoted in Steven Hess, *Ramón Menéndez Pidal: The Practice and Politics of Philology in Twentieth-Century Spain* (Newark, DE: Juan de la Cuesta, 2014), p. 143.

2 These values are discussed in the classic article by María Eugenia Lacarra, 'La utilización del Cid de Menéndez Pidal en la ideología rnilitar franquista', *Ideologies and Literature* 3 (1980): 100–1.

3 Michael Gerli, 'Inventing the Spanish Middle Ages: Ramón Menéndez Pidal, Spanish Cultural History, and Ideology in Philology', *La corónica* 30.1 (2001): 111–26.

4 Nadia R. Altschul, *Geographies of Philological Knowledge: Postcoloniality and the Transatlantic National Epic* (Chicago: University of Chicago Press, 2012), p. 118. This was the position of European scholars Gaston Paris and Ferdinand Wolf, and later the South American intellectual Andrés Bello, who edited the *PMC* before Menéndez Pidal (see also Altschul, *Geographies*, pp. 104, 118, 162).

5 Altschul, *Geographies*, p. 108; Lacarra, 'La utilización del Cid', 100. This was the assessment of Reinhart Dozy. See also Richard A. Fletcher, *The Quest for El Cid* (Oxford: Oxford University Press, 1989), pp. 200–1.

6 Hess, *Ramón Menéndez Pidal*, p. 196.

7 Menéndez Pidal had serious reservations, however, about how the Franco regime co-opted the figure of the Cid (see Lacarra, 'La utilización del Cid', 100–1).

8 Ramón Menéndez Pidal, 'Poesía e historia en el *Mio Cid*', *Nueva revista de filología hispánica* 3.2 (1949): 120. He had also made this argument in his edition (*Poema de mio Cid*, ed. Ramón Menéndez Pidal [Madrid: La Lectura, 1923], pp. 35–6).

9 For a detailed description of the manuscript, see the recent study of Alberto Montaner, 'The *Poema de mio Cid* as Text: Manuscript Transmission and Editorial Politics', in Irene Zaderenko and Alberto Montaner (eds), *A Companion to the Poema de mio Cid* (Leiden: Brill, 2018), pp. 43–88. On the learned, clerical background of the *PMC*, see Irene Zaderenko, 'The Question of Authorship', in Zaderenko and Montaner (eds), *A Companion to the Poema de mio Cid*, pp. 89–118. Matthew Bailey has convincingly identified oral qualities: Matthew Bailey, 'Oral Expression in the Poema de mio Cid', in Zaderenko and Montaner (eds), *A Companion to the Poema de mio Cid*, pp. 247–70. Most scholars agree that the Vivar codex contains, as Leonardo Funes puts it, 'the confluence of both oral and written discursive practices': Leonardo Funes, 'Episodic Logic and the Structure of the *Poema de mio Cid*', in Zaderenko and Montaner (eds), *A Companion to the Poema de mio Cid*, p. 290.

10 *Cantar de mio Cid*, ed. and trans. Matthew Bailey, https://miocid.wlu.edu (accessed 9 January 2022). Subsequent citations are from the critical edition of Ian Michael, *Poema de mio Cid* (Madrid: Castalia, 1973). For a more thorough treatment of the names, see Nicasio Salvador Miguel, 'Reflexiones sobre el episodio de Rachel y Vidas en el *Cantar de mio Cid*', *Revista de Filología Española* 59.1 (1977): 187–93; and Gisela Roitman, 'El episodio de Rachel y Vidas, polifónico y al mismo tiempo velado', *Revista de literatura medieval* 23 (2011): 239–45. On Vidas as a possible 'scribal misreading' of Judas, see Luis F. López González, 'Stereotypes and the Unpaid Debt in the Episode of Rachel and Vidas in *Cantar de Mio Cid*', *Revista canadiense de estudios hispánicos* 43.2 (2019): 342.

11 I am grateful to Michael Gerli, who offered a number of helpful comments on an earlier version of this chapter, for emphasising the importance of this allusion. In his study of how the Cid is mythically linked to Christ, Cesáreo Bandera argued that the hero's trickery of the moneylenders reflects the theological concept of the Messiah's true, spiritual nature being hidden from unbelieving Jews – as a kind of holy deception (Cesáreo Bandera, *El 'Poema de mío Cid': Poesía, historia, mito* [Madrid: Gredos, 1969], pp. 115–36).

12 I have consulted the English version of Matthew Bailey, but translations unless otherwise indicated are my own. Rodríguez Díaz de Vivar was in fact exiled twice by Alfonso VI. For more information on his life,

see Joseph F. O'Callaghan, *A History of Medieval Spain* (Ithaca, NY: Cornell University Press, 1975), pp. 200–16.

13 *Poema de Mio Cid*, ed. Menéndez, p. 32.

14 John Tolan, *Petrus Alfonsi and His Medieval Readers* (Gainesville, FL: University Press of Florida, 1993), pp. 199–204.

15 On Petrus Alfonsi and his reception during the Middle Ages, see Tolan, *Petrus Alfonsi.*

16 The same story made its way in the popular late thirteenth-century *Gesta Romanorum* (*'Gesta Romanorum' or Entertaining Moral Stories*, ed. and trans. Charles Swan and Wynnard Hooper [New York: Dover, 1959], no. 118).

17 In his 'Introducción', Ian Michael discusses damage to the manuscript in some detail (*Poema de Mio Cid*, ed. Michael, pp. 52–8).

18 José Ramírez del Río, 'El *Poema de Mio Cid* y las colecciones de cuentos árabes y hebreos. Las arcas de los judíos Rachel y Vidas', *Sefarad* 79.2 (2019): 406.

19 These neighbourhoods were typically situated in the district of a city's castle, in keeping with the Jews' relationship with the monarchy (v. 99). See Salvador Miguel, 'Reflexiones', 193–6.

20 Invoking 'el Criador' (the Creator), the two claim they will come looking for the Cid in Valencia (vv. 136–7).

21 Menéndez Pidal, decades after the publication of his edition, maintained that 'El Cid poético *no puede* obrar movido por un vulgar anti-semitismo' ['the conduct of the Cid in the poem cannot be motivated by some vulgar antisemitism'] (Ménendez Pidal, 'Poesía e historia', p. 121). Menéndez Pidal was in part reacting against the commentary of Andrés Bello who described the episode as anti-Jewish in his nineteenth-century edition (Ménendez Pidal, 'Poesía e historia', pp. 201–11). One recent critic to argue that the Cid repaid the loan is Alfonso Boax Jovaní, 'El Cid pagó a los judíos', *La corónica: A Journal of Medieval Hispanic Languages, Literatures, and Cultures* 35.1 (2006): 67–81.

22 Leo Spitzer, 'Sobre el carácter histórico del *Cantar de Mio Cid*', *Nueva Revista de Filología Hispánica* 2.2 (1948): 108–9: 'Se esfuerza en negar toda huella de antisemitismo medieval en su héroe … no hagamos confusiones: la moralidad medieval no es la nuestra.' Spitzer then explains: 'para un aristócrata del siglo XI contaba la obligación moral de pagar mil misas prometidas al abad de San Pedro; no tanto la de pagar 600 marcos a judíos' ['for an aristocrat in the eleventh century, the obligation to the abbot of St Peter to pay for a thousand masses counted; not so much the promise to repay 500 marks to Jews']. Colin Smith also found that Menéndez Pidal was influenced by 'modern ideas

... about anti-Semitism' (Colin Smith, 'Did the Cid Repay the Jews?', *Romania* 36.344 [1965]: 528).

23 Almost all critics also agree that the moneylenders are both Jewish men. Francisco Cantera tried to argue that they are a married couple, as did Josep M. Solà-Solé (Francisco Cantera, 'Raquel e Vidas', *Sefarad* 18 [1958]: 99–108; Josep M. Solà-Solé, *Sobre árabes, judíos y marranos y su impacto en la lengua y literatura españolas* [Barcelona: Puvill, 1983]). This view has since been ruled out, mostly due to the poet's consistent use of *don* (sir) as opposed to *doña* (lady) in front of 'Rachel' (*don* can only mean 'sir' in front of a name beginning with a consonant) (see Salvador Miguel, 'Reflexiones', 192; Roitman, 'El episodio de Rachel y Vidas', 240). To my knowledge, the only critic who has tried (unconvincingly) to argue that Rachel and Vidas were not Jews is Miguel Garci-Gómez, 'El burgos de mio Cid', in *Temas socio-económicos y escolásticos, con revisión del antisemitismo* (Burgos: Disputación provincial, 1982). Roitman – as part of an intriguing study of how the exiled Cid and the Jews can be understood as 'outsiders' – argues against 'antijudaísmo directo', as the poet does not specify that the two charge excessive interest (Roitman, 'El episodio de Rachel y Vidas', 248, 258). It is true that usury would become more acceptable on the basis of moderated interest rates. However, the first clear evidence of this only seems to emerge later, following the Fourth Lateran Council in 1215 (see Jacques Le Goff, *Your Money or Your Life. Economy and Religion in the Middle Ages*, trans. Patricia Ranum [New York: Zone Books, 1988], pp. 70–2). In medieval Iberia, it appears during the second half of the thirteenth century in the *Siete Partidas* (Seven Parts) of Alfonso X (Alfonso X, *Las siete partidas. Family, Commerce, and the Sea: The Worlds of Women and Merchants*, ed. Robert I. Burns, trans. Samuel Parsons Scott, vol. IV [Philadelphia, PA: University of Pennsylvania Press, 2001], p. xl).

24 Smith, 'Did the Cid Repay the Jews', 528, 535.

25 Donald McGrady, 'Did the Cid Repay the Jews? A Reconsideration', *Romania* 106.424 (1985): 523.

26 'Los iudíos te dexeste prender ... pusieronte en cruz por nombre en golgotá' ['You allowed the Jews to seize you ... they put you on the cross'] (vv. 347–8). This is part of a narrative prayer that appears in a number of other thirteenth-century Castilian texts (see, for example, Gerli). Aizenberg also compares the episode to later fictional instances of anti-Jewish violence in Gonzalo de Berceo's *Milagros de Nuestra Señora* (Miracles of Our Lady, c. 1260) when the Jews of Toledo are attacked after being accused of crucifying a wax figure of Jesus (Edna Aizenberg, 'Myth, Stereotype, Humor', *Hispania* 63.3 [1980]: 480;

Gonzalo de Berceo, *Milagros de Nuestra Señora*, ed. E. Michael Gerli, 8th edn [Madrid: Cátedra, 1996], pp. 142–4). In the final miracle of Berceo's text, Theophilus, guided by a Jewish sorcerer, sells his soul, and this is repeatedly compared to the betrayal of Judas (Gonzalo de Berceo, *Milagros*, pp. 195–219). On the anti-Jewish nature of the prayer, see also López González, 'Stereotypes', 343–4.

27 For a different view, see the recent work of Geraldine Heng, who finds that the consequences and legacy of pre-modern forms of discrimination against minority groups can be fruitfully compared to elements of modern racism (Geraldine Heng, *The Invention of Race in the Middle Ages* [Cambridge: Cambridge University Press, 2018]). On the question of Jews and race in late medieval Spain, see David Nirenberg, 'Was there Race before Modernity? The Example of "Jewish" Blood in Late Medieval Spain', in Miriam Eliav-Feldon, Benjamin Isaac and Joseph Ziegler (eds), *The Origins of Racism in the West* (Cambridge: Cambridge University Press, 2009), pp. 232–64.

28 Seymour Resnick, '"Raquel e Vidas" and the Cid', *Hispania* 39.3 (1956): 303.

29 Resnick, '"Raquel e Vidas"', 304. In his edition, Ian Michael also mentions that the number could refer to Judas's coins (*Poema de Mio Cid*, p. 91, n. 197).

30 Salvador Miguel, 'Reflexiones', 202, 223.

31 López González, 'Stereotypes', 340–1.

32 Lucy Pick, 'Toledo and Beyond: Bishops and Jews in Medieval Iberia', in Ryan D. Giles and E. Michael Gerli (eds), *The Routledge Companion to Medieval Iberia: Unity and Diversity* (New York: Routledge, 2021), p. 259.

33 Javier Castaño, 'Una fiscalidad sagrada: los "treinta dineros" y los judíos de Castilla', *Studi Medievali* 42 (2001): 167–8. 'No sólo simboliza explícitamente … la Pasión … debían pagar para ver sancionado su estatus dentro de la sociedad medieval … una "fiscalidad sagrada" … las "trienta dineros" son parte de un discurso más amplio que giraba en torno a la Pasión. Al castigar a los judíos, la comunidad cristiana venga la crucifixión y asegura su salvación.' Castaño also cites late medieval texts that provide further evidence by considering whether Sephardic communities could be exempted from the tax – if they had been established prior to the time of Christ's betrayal (Castaño, 'Una fiscalidad sagrada', 193, 195).

34 Pick, 'Toledo and Beyond', 259.

35 Manuel Risco, *España sacrada*, vol. 35 (Madrid: Pedro Marín, 1786), p. 117.

36 Antolínez verifies that the count is correct, but does not weigh them. The first three hundred are silver, while the second three hundred are

made of gold (vv. 184–6). On the weight and minting of the coins, see the note in Ian Michael's edition (*Poema de Mio Cid*, ed. Michael, pp. 88–9, no. 161).

37 Pick, 'Toledo and Beyond', 259

38 Ibid., 269, 259, 262.

39 Ibid., 260.

40 Petrus Comestor, *Historia Scholastica*, ed. J. P. Migne, Patrologia Latina 198, cols. 1053–1722, http://patristica.net/latina/, col. 125c; Gaël Milin, *Le Cordonnier de Jérusalem: la véritable histoire du Juif Errant* (Rennes: Presses Universitaires de Rennes, 1997), pp. 27–8; Jacobus Voragine, *Legenda aurea*, ed. T. Graesse, 2nd edn (Leipzig: Impensis Librariae Arnoldianae, 1850), p. 302; *Golden Legend*, ed. William Granger Ryan and Eamon Duffy (Princeton, NJ: Princeton University Press, 2012), p. 276; Fernando González Muñoz, *Sobre la se[c]ta mahometana* (Valencia: Universitat de València, Publications de la Universitat de València, 2011), p. 201; López González, 'Stereotypes', p. 340; Alfonso X, *Primera crónica general: Estoria de España*, ed. Ramón Menéndez Pidal (Madrid: Bailly-Bailliere, 1906), p. 136. For more sources testifying to this legend, see David Hook, 'Some Problems in Andrés Bernáldez's Account of the Spanish Jews', *Michael* 11 (1989): 234–5.

41 Castaño, 'Una fiscalidad sagrada', 170.

42 *Fazienda de ultramar*, ed. Moshé Lazar (Salamanca: Universidad de Salamanca, 1965), pp. 51, 195: 'Vendieronle por xx arientos ... valia ... xxx dineros ... aquí es la sacrificanza de los xxx dineros de que vendió Judas el traydor a Nuestro Sennor Jhesu Cristo ... pris los xxx e eché los ... en la casa del Criador' ['they sold him for twenty coins of silver ... that were worth ... thirty *denarii* ... this is the sacrifice of the thirty *denarii* for which Judas the traitor sold our Lord Jesus Christ ... I took the thirty and threw them ... into the house of the Creator'].

43 Stephen Wright discusses the *Vindicta Salvatoris*'s 'enormous popularity throughout medieval Europe' (Stephen K. Wright, *The Vengeance of Our Lord: Medieval Dramatizations of the Destruction of Jerusalem* [Toronto: Pontifical Institute of Mediaeval Studies, 1989], p. 29). Maria Dorninger cites seventy-six surviving manuscripts of Godfrey's work, with a 'broad distribution, which is pan-European, extending from Poland to Spain and from England to Italy' (Maria E. Dorninger, 'Modern Readers of Godfrey', in Thomas Foerster [ed.], *Godfrey of Viterbo and his Readers: Imperial Tradition and Universal History* [New York: Routledge, 2015], p. 20).

44 Erica Reiner, 'Thirty Pieces of Silver', *Journal of the American Oriental Society* 88.1 (1968): 189. Paulo Cherchi argues that the early fourteenth-century Castilian author Juan Manual (grand-nephew of Alfonso X)

alluded to the text, further attesting to its influence in medieval Iberia (Paolo Cherchi, 'Juan Manuel's *Libro de los estados* (2:6–32) and Godfrey of Viterbo's *Panteon* (books 13–14)', *Romance Philology* 38 [1985]: 300–3). For a full account of the story of the coins in late medieval Spain, see David Hook, 'The Legend of Thirty Pieces of Silver', in Ian Macpherson and Ralph Penny (eds), *The Medieval Mind: Hispanic Studies in Honour of Alan Deyermond* (Woodbridge: Tamesis: 1997), pp. 205–22.

45 Voragine, *Legenda aurea*, ch. 45; *Golden Legend*, p. 167. On earlier sources that inform Voragine's legend, see the work of Edward Kennard Rand, 'Mediaeval Lives of Judas Iscariot', in William Allan Neilson, Fred Norris Robinson and Edward Stevens Sheldon (eds), *Anniversary Papers by Colleagues and Pupils of George Lyman Kittredge* (Boston: Ginn, 1913), pp. 305–16, and Paull Franklin Baum, *The Mediaeval Legend of Judas* (New York: Modern Language Association, 1916), pp. 484–97. According to Pieter W. Van der Horst it survives in 'almost a thousand Latin manuscripts' (*Studies in Ancient Judaism and Early Christianity* [Leiden: Brill, 2014], p. 248). The Biblioteca nacional de España, where the *PMC* is housed, contains a number of *Legenda aurea* manuscripts dating from the fourteenth and fifteenth centuries.

46 Voragine, *Legenda aurea*, p. 185.

47 Sara Lipton, *Images of Intolerance: The Representation of Jews and Judaism in the 'Bible moralisée'* (Berkeley, CA: University California Press, 1999), p. 25. These Bibles are especially telling; as Lipton points out, in their depiction 'of contemporary figures and situations ... they constitute an unprecedented visual polemic against the Jews' (*Images of Intolerance*, p. 1).

48 Lipton, *Images of Intolerance*, p. 32.

49 Moneybags could also be implicated in the episode's opening scene when the two are seen counting what they have earned through lending, 'en cuenta de sus averes, de los que avién ganados', and later when they pour hundreds of 'marcos' on to a carpet (vv. 101, 182–6).

50 Alfonso X, *Cantigas de Nuestra Señora*, ed. Walter Mettman, 3 vols (Madrid: Castalia, 1986–1988), no. 25, 1:117. In this story, a Christian receives a loan from a Jew after invoking Christ and Mary as guarantors. He later fills a chest full of money gained through his business dealings in another land, and prayerfully sets it afloat in the sea as a way of repaying his loan. When later the moneylender will not admit that he miraculously received the chest, a statue of Mary comes to life and testifies that the money was indeed returned, leading to the Jew's conversion. A version of this tale also appears in Berceo's *Milagros de Nuestra Señora* (no. 23). The use of pointed hats to identify Jews

during the period has been studied by Lipton, *Images of Intolerance*, pp. 15–19.

51 Le Goff, *Your Money or Your Life*, p. 18.

52 Thomas Aquinas wrote: 'human law ... allows the taking of interest, not because it deems this to be just but because to do otherwise would hinder the "utilities" of a great many people' (qtd. in Le Goff, *Your Money or Your Life*, p. 49). Le Goff discusses a number of legal stipulations and exceptions that emerged during the thirteenth century (*Your Money or Your Life*, pp. 70–5).

53 Le Goff, *Your Money or Your Life*, p. 42.

54 Louise Mirrer concluded that the poet strips Rachel and Vidas of masculine qualities by portraying them as 'passively collecting interest on their loans', in contrast to the military prowess of the Cid and his warriors (Louise Mirrer, *Women, Jews, and Muslims in the Texts of Reconquest Castile* [Ann Arbor, MI: University of Michigan Press, 1996], pp. 70–1).

55 For this reason, usury was sometimes linked with sodomy; see, for example, James A. Arieti, 'Magical Thinking in Medieval Anti-Semitism: Usury and the Blood Libel', *Mediterranean Studies* 24.2 (2016): 193–218.

56 Quoted in Le Goff, *Your Money or Your Life*, p. 30. As Odd Langhold explains, this notion ultimately traces back to the meaning Aristotle assigned to money, *nomisma*, as a means of exchange that is not meant to be used as an end by making it reproduce itself: '*tokos* in Greek means offspring, as well as usury, thus suggesting a most powerful simile: usury is that form of acquisition which consists in making money breed money and it is against nature because only natural organisms can breed an offspring' (Odd Langhold, *Economics in the Medieval Schools: Wealth, Exchange, Value, Money and Usury According to the Paris Theological Tradition, 1200–1350* [Leiden: Brill, 1992], p. 265). Describing Rachel and Vidas as scapegoats, Raymond Barbera seems to have been the first to suggest that their usury would have been considered a crime against nature (Raymond Barbera, 'The "Pharmakos" in the *Poema de Mio Cid*', *Hispania* 50.2 [1967]: 239).

57 Quoted in Anne Derbes and Mark Sandona, 'Barren Metal and the Fruitful Womb: The Program of Giotto's Arena Chapel in Padua', *The Art Bulletin* 80.2 (1998): 277.

58 Quoted in Le Goff, *Your Money or Your Life*, p. 29.

59 Sander Gilman, *The Jew's Body* (New York: Routledge, 1991), p. 124.

60 Quoted in Le Goff, *Your Money or Your Life*, p. 49.

61 Ibid., p. 52.

62 Ibid., p. 37.

63 Lipton, *Images of Intolerance*, p. 34.

64 Le Goff, *Your Money or Your Life*, pp. 37–8. Vitry refers to a prohibition in the Hebrew Bible (Deut. 23:20). Christian usurers, hoping to save themselves from punishment in the afterlife, were expected to make full restitution for the profits they had made through moneylending (see Le Goff, *Your Money or Your Life*, p. 80).
65 Derbes and Sandona, 'Barren Metal and Fruitful Wombs', 274–5.
66 Ibid., 275.
67 Giotto's *Last Judgment* portrays the death of Judas, combining the account in Matthew of his suicide by hanging (Matt. 27:5) with the description in Acts of his disembowelment (Acts 1:18), in what Derbes and Sandona call 'a grim version of childbirth' ('Barren Metal and Fruitful Wombs', 208). As they also note, Voragine refers to the 'bowels' of Judas that 'conceived the betrayal' being made to 'burst and spill out' (*Golden Legend*, p. 168; *Legenda aurea*, p. 186).
68 Derbes and Sandona, 'Barren Metal and Fruitful Wombs', 282.
69 Lipton, *Images of Intolerance*, p. 39.
70 Ibid., pp. 39, 25.
71 Ménendez Pidal, 'Poesía e historia', 121.

Works cited

Primary sources

Alfonsi, Petrus, *The Scholar's Guide: A Translation of the Twelfth-Century 'Disciplina Clericalis' of Pedro Alfonso* (Toronto: Pontifical Institute of Mediaeval Studies, 1969).

Alfonso X, *Primera crónica general: Estoria de España*, ed. Ramón Menéndez Pidal (Madrid: Bailly-Bailliere, 1906).

— *Cantigas de Nuestra Señora*, ed. Walter Mettman, 3 vols (Madrid: Castalia, 1986–88).

— *Las siete partidas. Family, Commerce, and the Sea: The Worlds of Women and Merchants*, ed. Robert I. Burns, trans. Samuel Parsons Scott, vol. IV (Philadelphia: University of Pennsylvania Press, 2001).

Alighieri, Dante, *Divine Comedy*, ed. and trans. Charles S. Singleton, vol. I (Princeton, NJ: Princeton University Press, 1980).

Berceo, Gonzalo de, *Milagros de Nuestra Señora*, ed. E. Michael Gerli, 8th edn (Madrid: Cátedra, 1996).

Bible, Parallel Latin Vulgate, Douay-Rheims and King James, http://www.latinvulgate.com (accessed 3 March 2016).

Comestor, Petrus, *Historia Scholastica*, Patrologia Latina 198, ed. J. P. Migne, cols. 1053–1722, http://patristica.net/latina/ (accessed 9 January 2022).

Fazienda de ultramar, ed. Moshé Lazar (Salamanca: Universidad de Salamanca, 1965).

'*Gesta Romanorum*' *or Entertaining Moral Stories*, ed. and trans. Charles Swan and Wynnard Hooper (New York: Dover, 1959).

Poema de mio Cid, ed. Ramón Menéndez Pidal (Madrid: La Lectura, 1923).
Poema de mio Cid, ed. Ian Michael (Madrid: Castalia, 1973).
Cantar de mio Cid, ed. and trans. Matthew Bailey, William and Lee University, https://miocid.wlu.edu (accessed 9 January 2022).
Poema del Cid. Obras completes, ed. Andrés Bello, vol. II (Santiago, Chile: Pedro G. Ramírez, 1881).
Voragine, Jacobus, *Legenda aurea*, ed. T. Graesse, 2nd edn (Leipzig: Impensis Librariae Arnoldianae, 1850).
— *Golden Legend*, ed. William Granger Ryan and Eamon Duffy (Princeton, NJ: Princeton University Press, 2012).

Secondary sources

Aizenberg, Edna, 'Myth, Stereotype, Humor', *Hispania* 63.3 (1980): 478–86.
Altschul, Nadia R., *Geographies of Philological Knowledge: Postcoloniality and the Transatlantic National Epic* (Chicago: University of Chicago Press, 2012).
Arieti, James A., 'Magical Thinking in Medieval Anti-Semitism: Usury and the Blood Libel', *Mediterranean Studies* 24.2 (2016): 193–218.
Bailey, Matthew, 'Oral Expression in the Poema de mio Cid', in Irene Zaderenko and Alberto Montaner (eds), *A Companion to the Poema de mio Cid* (Leiden: Brill, 2018), pp. 247–70.
Bandera, Cesáreo, *El 'Poema de mío Cid': Poesía, historia, mito* (Madrid: Gredos, 1969).
Barbera, Raymond, 'The "Pharmakos" in the *Poema de Mio Cid*', *Hispania* 50.2 (1967): 236–41.
Baum, Paull Franklin, *The Mediaeval Legend of Judas* (New York: Modern Language Association, 1916).
Boix Jovaní, Alfonso, 'El Cid pagó a los judíos', *La corónica* 35.1 (2006): 67–81.
Cantera, Francisco, 'Raquel e Vidas', *Sefarad* 18 (1958): 99–108.
Castaño, Javier, 'Una fiscalidad sagrada: los "treinta dineros" y los judíos de Castilla', *Studi Medievali* 42 (2001): 164–204.
Cherchi, Paolo, 'Juan Manuel's *Libro de los estados* (2:6–32) and Godfrey of Viterbo's *Panteon* (books 13–14)', *Romance Philology* 38 (1985): 300–3.
Fletcher, Richard A., *The Quest for El Cid* (Oxford: Oxford University Press, 1989).
Garci-Gómez, Miguel, 'El burgos de mio Cid', in *Temas socio-económicos y escolásticos, con revisión del antisemitismo* (Burgos: Disputación provincial, 1982).
Derbes, Anne, and Mark Sandona, 'Barren Metal and the Fruitful Womb: The Program of Giotto's Arena Chapel in Padua', *The Art Bulletin* 80.2 (1998): 274–91.
Dorninger, Maria E., 'Modern Readers of Godfrey', in Thomas Foerster (ed.), *Godfrey of Viterbo and his Readers: Imperial Tradition and Universal History* (New York: Routledge, 2015), pp. 13–36.

Fletcher, Richard A., *The Quest for El Cid* (Oxford: Oxford University Press, 1989).
Funes, Leonardo, 'Episodic Logic and the Structure of the *Poema de mio Cid*', in Irene Zaderenko and Alberto Montaner (eds), *A Companion to the Poema de mio Cid* (Leiden: Brill, 2018), pp. 271–96.
Gerli, Michael E., 'The *Ordo Commendationis Animae* and the Cid Poet', *Modern Language Notes* 95.2 (1980): 436–41.
— 'Inventing the Spanish Middle Ages: Ramón Menéndez Pidal, Spanish Cultural History, and Ideology in Philology', *La corónica* 30.1 (2001): 111–26.
Gilman, Sander, *The Jew's Body* (New York: Routledge, 1991).
González Muñoz, Fernando, *Sobre la se[c]ta mahometana* (Valencia: Universitat de València, Publications de la Universitat de València, 2011).
Heng, Geraldine, *The Invention of Race in the European Middle Ages* (Cambridge: Cambridge University Press, 2018).
Hess, Steven, *Ramón Menéndez Pidal: The Practice and Politics of Philology in Twentieth-Century Spain* (Newark, DE: Juan de la Cuesta, 2014).
Hook, David, 'Some Problems in Andrés Bernáldez's Account of the Spanish Jews', *Michael* 11 (1989): 231–55.
— 'The Legend of Thirty Pieces of Silver', in Ian Macpherson and Ralph Penny (eds), *The Medieval Mind: Hispanic Studies in Honour of Alan Deyermond* (Woodbridge: Tamesis, 1997), pp. 205–22.
Lacarra, María Eugenia, 'La utilización del Cid de Menéndez Pidal en la ideología rnilitar franquista', *Ideologies and Literature* 3 (1980): 95–127.
Langhold, Odd, *Economics in the Medieval Schools: Wealth, Exchange, Value, Money and Usury According to the Paris Theological Tradition, 1200–1350* (Leiden: Brill, 1992).
Le Goff, Jacques, *Your Money or Your Life. Economy and Religion in the Middle Ages*, trans. Patricia Ranum (New York: Zone Books, 1988).
Lipton, Sara, *Images of Intolerance: The Representation of Jews and Judaism in the 'Bible moralisée'* (Berkeley, CA: University of California Press, 1999).
López González, Luis F., 'Stereotypes and the Unpaid Debt in the Episode of Rachel and Vidas in *Cantar de Mio Cid*', *Revista canadiense de estudios hispánicos* 43.2 (2019): 329–45.
McGrady, Donald, 'Did the Cid Repay the Jews? A Reconsideration', *Romania* 106.424 (1985): 518–27.
Menéndez Pidal, Ramón, 'Poesía e historia en el *Mio Cid*', *Nueva revista de filología hispánica* 3.2 (1949): 113–29.
Michael, Ian, 'Introducción', in *Poema de mio Cid* (Madrid: Castalia, 1973), pp. 11–59.
Milin, Gaël, *Le Cordonnier de Jérusalem: la véritable histoire du Juif Errant* (Rennes: Presses Universitaires de Rennes, 1997).
Mirrer, Louise, 'Jewish Men in the *Cantar de mio Cid*', in *Women, Jews, and Muslims in the Texts of Reconquest Castile* (Ann Arbor, MI: University of Michigan Press, 1996).

Montaner, Alberto, 'The *Poema de mio Cid* as Text: Manuscript Transmission and Editorial Politics', in Irene Zaderenko and Alberto Montaner (eds), *A Companion to the Poema de mio Cid* (Leiden: Brill, 2018), pp. 43–88.

Nirenberg, David, 'Was there Race before Modernity? The Example of "Jewish" Blood in Late Medieval Spain', in Miriam Eliav-Feldon, Benjamin Isaac and Joseph Ziegler (eds), *The Origins of Racism in the West* (Cambridge: Cambridge University Press, 2009), pp. 232–64.

O'Callaghan, Joseph F., *A History of Medieval Spain* (Ithaca, NY: Cornell University Press, 1975).

Pick, Lucy, 'Toledo and Beyond: Bishops and Jews in Medieval Iberia', in Ryan D. Giles and E. Michael Gerli (eds), *The Routledge Companion to Medieval Iberia: Unity and Diversity* (New York: Routledge, 2021), pp. 256–67.

Ramírez del Río, José, 'El *Poema de Mio Cid* y las colecciones de cuentos árabes y hebreos. Las arcas de los judíos Rachel y Vidas', *Sefarad* 79.2 (2019): 289–410.

Rand, Edward Kennard, 'Mediaeval Lives of Judas Iscariot', in William Allan Neilson, Fred Norris Robinson and Edward Stevens Sheldon (eds), *Anniversary Papers by Colleagues and Pupils of George Lyman Kittredge* (Boston: Ginn, 1913), pp. 305–16.

Reiner, Erica, 'Thirty Pieces of Silver', *Journal of the American Oriental Society* 88.1 (1968): 186–90.

Resnick, Seymour, '"Raquel e Vidas" and the Cid', *Hispania* 39.3 (1956): 300–4.

Risco, Manuel, *España sacrada*, vol. 35 (Madrid: Pedro Marín, 1786).

Roitman, Gisela, 'El episodio de Rachel y Vidas, polifónico y al mismo tiempo velado', *Revista de literatura medieval* 23 (2011): 237–59.

Salvador Miguel, Nicasio, 'Reflexiones sobre el episodio de Rachel y Vidas en el *Cantar de mio Cid*', *Revista de Filología Española* 59.1 (1977): 182–224.

Smith, Colin, 'Did the Cid Repay the Jews?', *Romania* 36.344 (1965): 520–38.

Solà-Solé, Josep M., *Sobre árabes, judíos y marranos y su impacto en la lengua y literatura españolas* (Barcelona: Puvill, 1983).

Spitzer, Leo, 'Sobre el carácter histórico del *Cantar de Mio Cid*', *Nueva Revista de Filología Hispánica* 2.2 (1948): 105–17.

Tolan, John, *Petrus Alfonsi and His Medieval Readers* (Gainesville, FL: University Press of Florida, 1993).

Van der Horst, Pieter W., *Studies in Ancient Judaism and Early Christianity* (Leiden: Brill, 2014).

Wright, Stephen K., *The Vengeance of Our Lord: Medieval Dramatizations of the Destruction of Jerusalem* (Toronto: Pontifical Institute of Mediaeval Studies, 1989).

Zaderenko, Irene, 'The Question of Authorship', in Irene Zaderenko and Alberto Montaner (eds), *A Companion to the Poema de mio Cid* (Leiden: Brill, 2018), pp. 89–118.

5

'Let no bad song be sung of us': fame, memory and transmission in/and the *Chanson de Roland*

Sharon Kinoshita

La Chanson de Roland was both a solitary masterpiece and a medieval bestseller: a solitary masterpiece in the sense that the text we today know as the *Song of Roland* survives in a single manuscript; but a 'bestseller' in the sense that the story it tells – of Roland's death fighting the Saracens in Spain – was well known throughout the Middle Ages, as attested not only in the variant versions collectively known as *Roncevaux* but in a range of literary allusions, translations, visual representations and even onomastic evidence. No work from the French Middle Ages is better known, or has been more argued about: it is one of the texts most likely to figure in school curricula and, since the nineteenth century, has been used to exemplify the precociousness of both medieval French literature and French national identity. More recently, it has been taken as a prime example of Orientalism or cited for its representation of racial others. This chapter explores some of the discrepancies between the *Roland*'s political and literary significance in the modern era and the precariousness of its textual tradition. This includes a consideration of its history as a *lieu de mémoire* – beginning from the text itself, which encodes at least two distinct modalities of memory, both oral and written.

'To be a medievalist,' wrote the French philologist Bernard Cerquiglini in 1981, 'is to take a stand on the *Chanson de Roland*.'[1] Yet despite its iconic status, the poem in the version we know today survives, as noted above, in a single copy. The manuscript, MS Digby 23, housed in Oxford's Bodleian Library, dates from the second quarter of the twelfth century.[2] This is remarkably old for a vernacular text; by way of comparison, most of the manuscripts containing the romances of Chrétien de Troyes, composed in the last third of the twelfth century, date from the mid-thirteenth century or later.[3] The Digby manuscript preserves a version of the poem that, based on linguistic evidence, is thought to have been composed around 1100. It is modest: small, measuring approximately 17.5 x 12.5 cm (about 7 x 5 in.), and consisting of 'mediocre, sometimes poor, quality' parchment that is 'thick and somewhat coarse, often discoloured, sometimes torn, holed, and repaired'. Its seventy-two folios, in twelfth-century Anglo-Norman script, present the text in a single column, in pages mostly containing twenty-eight lines.[4] The manuscript also contains a Latin translation of Plato's *Timaeus*.

The *Chanson de Roland* is a highly mythified version of the Spanish campaigns of the Emperor Charlemagne, building on the smallest historical kernel of an incident that took place in 778 (more than two decades before Charles was crowned emperor in 800). It consists of just over 4,000 decasyllabic lines – each divided into units of 4 + 6 syllables – bundled into *laisses* (stanzas) bound together by a common assonance. When the poem opens, the emperor and his Franks have been in Spain for seven long years; after successfully conquering numerous towns and fortresses, they are bogged down besieging Saragossa, the last remaining Saracen stronghold. Its king, Marsile, makes the Franks an offer: if they agree to lift their siege and return to 'sweet France', he will pay the emperor a vast tribute and follow him back to his capital, there to convert to Christianity and become Charlemagne's 'man'. A debate breaks out between those war-weary Franks who favour accepting the peace and going home, and Roland, the emperor's nephew, who vehemently exhorts Charlemagne not to trust the Saracen king. When the consensus goes against him, Roland nominates his stepfather, Ganelon, a vociferous proponent of the peace, to carry the Franks' acceptance to the Saracens. At this, Ganelon abjures all feudal connection with his stepson – 'Tu n'ies mes hom ne jo ne sui tis sire … Jo ne vus aim nïent' ['You are not my man nor am I your lord … I do not love you at all'] (ll. 297, 306) – and, during his embassy to Saragossa, he plots with Marsile to destroy Roland, whom he casts as the instigator of Charlemagne's apparently endless pursuit of war. Back among the Franks, Ganelon nominates Roland to head the rearguard: a dangerous assignment with the crucial burden of guarding the main body of Charlemagne's army during their hazardous retreat through the high mountain passes of the Pyrenees.

The remainder of the story moves from one dramatic scene to the next. As the Franks retreat, the Saracens break the peace and attack the rearguard. Just before battle is joined, Roland and his boon companion Oliver argue over whether to sound the horn – the oliphant – that will alert Charlemagne to the danger and call the main army back to aid them. Oliver says yes, to save the rearguard from destruction; but Roland says no: as vassals, they are sworn to endure any hardship, including death, in order to protect their lord. The battle, recounted in some 1600 lines, claims the lives of Roland, Oliver and all the 'twelve peers' of France. Near its conclusion, Roland – against Oliver's protests – sounds the oliphant to recall Charlemagne and the main army of the Franks. The effort causes his temples to burst and blood to spurt from his mouth; it is this, not the wounds sustained in battle, that finally kills him.

With Roland dead just past the halfway point of the poem that bears his name, attention turns to Charlemagne's revenge: first, of course, against the Saracens, in a great apocalyptic battle pitting him against the forces of Marsile's overlord, the emir Baligant from over-the-seas (an episode that, on stylistic grounds, has been judged a later interpolation); and against Ganelon, in a trial held after the Franks' return to Aix (actually two trials, since the first one fails to render the verdict Charles desires). In the poem's concluding *laisses*, Ganelon is executed, and the queen of Saragossa – the lone Saracen not killed or forcibly converted earlier – willingly embraces Christianity. Together, the death of the declared 'traitor' and the spiritual rebirth of the Saracen queen seem to offer an ideologically satisfying resolution both to Charlemagne's tragic loss of Roland and the rearguard, and his triumph in subduing Spain and securing it for Christianity.

In its time, this version of the *Roland* was a solitary masterpiece; as we have seen, it survives in a single, and singularly unimposing, manuscript. Yet other evidence shows that versions of the legend circulated widely in the decades both preceding and contemporary with the composition of the Oxford *Roland*. Charter evidence shows witnesses named after two of our epic characters, with a tantalising change occurring around the turn of the twelfth century: before this, documents are witnessed by pairs of brothers named Oliver and Roland; after that date, the pairs are named Roland and Oliver. This suggests that somewhere around 1075 (allowing twenty-five years or so for the infants so named to grow to adulthood), the version of the tale in popular circulation shifted, promoting Roland to the position of prominence (thus inspiring the name of the elder of two brothers) previously occupied by Oliver.[5] Around the same time, art history provides plentiful examples of the legend's popularity. Scenes from the legend are sculpted on the historiated capitals of the abbey of Sainte Foy de Conques (c. 1097–1107) and on the lintel above the right portal of the west façade of the cathedral of Angoulême (c. 1120s).[6] Later in the twelfth century, scenes associated with variant versions of the Roland legend are depicted in bas-relief at the cathedral of Modena and in pavement mosaics at the cathedrals of Otranto (c. 1165–66) and Brindisi (late twelfth century).[7]

When it comes to textual transmission, expanded versions of the story in Old French survive in seven 'substantial' manuscripts and three fragments.[8] The seven manuscripts fall into two groups: those in assonance, like the Oxford *Roland* and other relatively early *chansons de geste*; and rhymed versions, typical of poems from the later Middle Ages. Collectively known as the *Roman de Roncevaux*, these poems, on the one hand, follow the plot of the Oxford *Roland* very closely and, on the other, feature huge interpolations – for example, expanding the episode of Roland's fiancée Aude, told in some thirty lines in the Oxford version, to over 800 lines in some manuscripts, radically altering the proportions and the tenor of the earlier text.[9] This, of course, is not unusual: as Joseph Duggan reminds us in the General Introduction to the three-volume edition of the seven manuscripts and three fragments (published in 2005): 'In the Middle Ages, literary texts of renown typically underwent modifications at the hands of successive revisors … Recasting a literary work, which the modern eye tends to view as an act of desecration, was in the Middle Ages a gesture of homage and renewal.'[10]

The *Chanson de Roland* in literary-historical context

The *Chanson de Roland* is a *chanson de geste*. This Old French term is usually translated into English as 'epic', which links it not only with near-contemporary works such as the *Poema de mio Cid* or the *Nibelungenlied*, but with the *Iliad*, the *Odyssey* and the *Aeneid*, helping to secure its privileged place both in literary history and in genealogies of 'Western Civilisation'. This is not, however, how contemporaries viewed the genre. Just before the turn of the thirteenth century, when we begin to see epics composed by known authors, the Arrageois poet Jehan Bodel (1167–1210) famously divided the vernacular literature of his day into three *matières*: the matter of Rome (stories of antiquity, translated from Latin), the matter of France ('historical' matter, including the legends of Charlemagne) and the matter of Brittany (stories inspired by the Celtic tradition, including the story of Arthur).[11] At about the same time, the Champenois Bertrand de Bar-sur-Aube (in his poem *Girart de Vienne*) further divided the 'matter of France' into three 'cycles': *la geste du roi* (poems about Charlemagne and his lineage); *la geste de Garin de Monglane* (poems about Guillaume d'Orange and his lineage); and *la geste de Doon de Mayence* (poems about the so-called 'rebel barons', ill-served by their overlords, who revolt against feudal authority).[12]

For all its canonical status, the *Roland* is only one of about a hundred surviving *chansons de geste*; the fact that most of these others remain unknown outside a small circle of specialists has produced a highly distorted vision of medieval 'epic'. The final chapter of historian Robert Southern's classic study *The Making of the Middle Ages* is entitled 'From Epic to Romance', suggesting a kind of civilisational evolution from the stark masculine world of the former (as in the *Roland*) to the more feminine and courtly sphere of the latter.[13] This, as Sarah Kay has shown, is a double misconception: first, *chansons de geste* remained popular throughout the late Middle Ages and beyond: not only were old poems recopied (as our manuscript histories show) but new ones were composed – often (as in modern popular culture) as sequels or prequels to core texts such as the *Roland* or the *Chanson de Guillaume*.[14] 'Far from being "primitive" or "originary",' as Robert Stein writes, 'the medieval epic is a new representation of the same contemporary situation that simultaneously brings romance and historical chronicle into being, and the epic is intended to make an intervention in that situation.'[15] Second, women play significant, even central roles in many of these poems. The vision of early masculinist epic giving way to a later, feminising romance is the misleading result of a selective cultural memory that designates the *Roland* and a handful of other texts, though in fact atypical, to stand in for the genre as a whole.

Canonising the *Chanson de Roland*

The story of the canonisation of the Oxford *Roland* and the marginalisation of the multiple versions of *Roncevaux* brings us back to Cerquiglini's assertion that 'To be a medievalist … is to take a stand on the *Chanson de Roland*'. Although the various manuscripts collectively called *Roncevaux* were already known, Bodleian Digby 23 was 'discovered' by the young Frenchman Francisque Michel only in 1833, and published, at his own expense, four years later.[16] *Le Monde* immediately declared it 'peut-être notre plus ancienne, notre véritable épopée nationale'.[17] In the ensuing decades, scholars with duelling stemmata tussled over the relationship between the Oxford *Roland* and the *Roncevaux* texts. That German philologists took the lead in these debates proved a matter of some consternation to the French. Then, in the wake of the siege of Paris during the Franco-Prussian War, the Catholic nationalist Léon Gautier enshrined the *Roland* as a French nationalist text, publishing over two dozen editions and translations (between 1872 and 1895) – and in 1880 getting it inserted into the school curriculum of the fledgling Third Republic. In the meantime, debates also arose on the question of the poem's composition. Early proponents of a romantic folk nationalism saw the poem's origins in short songs – *cantilènes* – dating back to the kernel 'event' itself. Then, in 1912, Joseph Bédier, 'the most influential French medievalist of the twentieth century', published an essay that, combined with his subsequent work and his editorial practice, was to establish the 'pre-eminence' of the Oxford text: for though he was not alone in believing 'that the Oxford text had as much authority as all the others combined, he refused to correct it except in what he considered the most obvious cases of error'.[18] Then, in the third volume of his *Légendes épiques*, Bédier, who saw its consummate artistry as incompatible with oral 'folk' composition, declared the Oxford text to be the work of a gifted and learnèd author – probably a monk in one of the monasteries on the Santiago pilgrimage trail (which crosses the battlefield of Roncevalles at the strategic point where it emerges from the Pyrenees) – a theory memorably conveyed in his eminently quotable line, 'Au commencement était la route' ['In the beginning was the road']. In the 1970s the debate was revived, with a twist, by Joseph J. Duggan, who – based on the density of its formulaic language (identified through an early application of computer-aided analysis) – borrowed from the Parry-Lord thesis on the oral-formulaic composition of the Homeric epics to argue for the oral composition of the *Roland* and other early *chansons de geste*.

Cutting through the either/or binarism of this debate, Robert Stein sees medieval epic as embedded in a moment of 'transitional literacy', encoding 'a degree of textual self-consciousness' no less significant than that found in romance.[19] In the *Roland*, this self-consciousness is manifested in the way orality and literacy are imagined as two distinct modes of memory and transmission. Just past the quarter way point of the poem, the rearguard consisting of Roland and the twelve peers are preparing for battle against the pursuing army of the Saracen king of Saragossa. Seeing their shining armour glinting brilliantly in the sun and hearing the overwhelming din of their bugles, Oliver laconically states: 'in my view / We shall have the opportunity to fight some Saracens' (ll. 1006–7)

> Respont Rollant: « E Deus la nus otreit !
> Ben devuns ci ester pur nostre rei:
> pur sun seignor deit hom susfrir destreiz
> e endurer e granz chalz e granz freiz,
> si'n deit hom perdre e del quir e del peil.
> Or guart chascuns que granz colps i empleit
> male cançun de nus chantét ne seit[20]
> Paien unt tort e chrestïens unt dreit.
> Malvaise essample n'en serat ja de mei. » (L. 79, ll. 1008–16; compare 1517)

> [Roland replies: 'May God grant it to us!
> It is our clear duty to be here for our king:
> For his lord a man should suffer great hardship
> And endure both extreme heat and extreme cold,
> And be willing to lose his skin and hair.
> Now let every man make sure he inflicts great blows,
> Let no bad song be sung about us.

Pagans are wrong and Christians are right.
No bad example will ever be made of me.']

This *laisse* is one of the most important in the poem, both for Roland's graphic account of the duties of the faithful vassal and for his uncompromising assertion pitting 'pagans' against 'Christians' – articulating an intransigent 'clash of civilisations' worldview with which the poem has become associated. Significantly, however, both these central points are cast in a proleptic mode of the way his and his companions' acts will be remembered and, crucially, remembered in song. As battle is joined, Roland shouts encouragement to his boon companion, Oliver:

Jo i ferrai de Durendal m'espee,
E vos, compainz, ferrez de Halteclere.
En tantes teres les avum nos portees,
Tantes batailles en avum afinee !
Male chançun n'en deit estre cantee. (L. 112, ll. 1462–6)

[I will strike there [in battle] with my sword Durendal,
And you, companion, will strike with Halteclere.
We have carried them in so many lands;
We've finished so many battles with them!
No bad song should be sung about them.]

For Roland, there is no higher motivation than imagining the songs that future generations will sing about him, his companions, and even their swords. The same sentiment is echoed immediately by Archbishop Turpin:

Pur Deu vos pri que ne seiez fuiant
que nuls prozdom malvaisement n'en chant. (L. 113, ll. 1473–4)

[For God's sake, I beg you not to flee;
let no brave man sing ill of us.]

In addition to this incitement to future memory, the archbishop – whose participation in battle flies in the face of the ideology of the 'three orders of feudal society', which divides the clergy (*oratores*, those who pray) from knights and warriors (*bellatores*, those who fight) – has something else to offer:

Mais d'une chose vos soi jo ben guarant:
Seint pareis vos est abundunant;
As Innocenz vos en serez sëant. (L. 113, ll. 1478–80)

[But there is one thing I can promise you:
Holy paradise is yours.
You will sit with the Holy Innocents.]

A master motivator, Turpin couples the glory of memory with a Crusade indulgence: those who die in battle are guaranteed their place in heaven.

Yet as a cleric, Turpin is associated not with the world of heroic song but with Latinate texts and archives. Earlier, witnessing the Franks slaughtering the pagans in battle, the archbishop had observed:

Nostre hume sunt mult proz;
Suz ciel n'ad rei plus en ait de meillors.
Il est escrit en la Geste Francor[21]
Que bons vassals out nostre empereür. (L. 111, ll. 1443–4)

[Our men are very brave:
No king on earth has better ones.
It is written in the Geste Francor
that our emperor had good vassals.]

And later, perhaps not incidentally in the same *laisse* in which Roland praises the archbishop as a 'very good knight' (*mult bon chevalier*) (l. 1673), the narrator grounds his evocation of the great number of men they have killed by citing his (written) sources:

Il est escrit es cartres e es brefs,
Ço dit la Geste, plus de quatre milliers. (L. 127, ll. 1684–5)

[It is written in records and documents;
The Geste says: more than four thousand.]

A thousand lines later, when things are going very badly for the Franks, Turpin acquits himself valiantly to the end:

Puis le dist Carles qu'il n'en espargnat nul:
tels quatre cenz i troevet entur lui,
alquanz nafrez, alquanz parmi ferut,
s'i out d'icels ki les chefs unt perdut.
Ço dist la Geste e cil ki el camp fut,
li ber seinz Gilie, por qui Deus fait vertuz
e fist la charter el muster de Loüm;
ki tant ne set ne l'ad prod entendut. (L. 155, ll. 2091–8)

[Charles said afterwards that he had spared no one,
So the four hundred bodies he found around him:

Some wounded, some pierced through.
There were also those who had lost their heads.
Thus state the Geste and the one who was on the battlefield,
The noble Giles, for whom God performs miracles,
And who made the charter at the monastery of Laon.
He who does not know this has not properly understood.]

This cryptic passage refers to the legend of 'Charlemagne's sin'. One day, as the emperor's confessor was about to give him absolution, an angel descended with a document that named a sin that Charles had failed to confess: an incestuous relation with his sister.[22] The future saint, who was there the recipient of a written text revealing Charlemagne's lapse, here becomes the presumed author – or informant? – of another *written* text recording the emperor's subsequent *oral* report ('dist Carles') of the bodily evidence of the archbishop's valour.

In the poem, Roland himself, as I have argued elsewhere, is the principle of memory. As he is dying, he eulogises his sword, Durendal, recalling all the lands they have conquered together:

Jo l'en cunquis e Anjou e Bretaigne,
Si l'en cunquis e Peitou e le Maine;
Jo l'en cunquis Normendie la franche,
Si l'en cunquis Provence e Equitaigne
E Lumbardie e trestute Romaine,
Jo l'en cunquis Baiver e tute Flandres
E Buguerie e trestute Puillanie,
Costentinnoble, dunt il out la fiance,
E en Saisonie fait il ço qu'il demandet;
Jo l'en cunquis e Escose e Irlande,
E Engletere, que il teneit sa cambre. (L. 172, ll. 2322–32)

[With it I conquered for him Anjou and Brittany,
and with it I conquered for him Poitou and Maine,
and with it I conquered for him Normandy the free.
With it I conquered Provence and Aquitaine,
and Lombardy and the whole region of Romagna.
With it I conquered for him Bavaria and all of Flanders,
And Burgundy and the whole of Apulia,
Constantinople, whose homage he received,
And Saxony, he does what he pleases.
With it I conquered for him Scotland and Ireland,
And England, while he kept to his chamber.]

In contrast to the opening Frankish council scene in which Roland reminds Charlemagne of the many places in Spain he has conquered for him during their ongoing seven-year campaign (*laisse* 14), Roland here, with his dying breath, recalls a previous moment; highlighted by the anaphora 'with it I conquered…', his speech reveals that the very nations now composing Charlemagne's army are themselves recent conquests – a layered history at odds with the stark binary opposition of his earlier pronouncement that 'Paien unt tort e chrestïens unt dreit' ['Pagans are wrong and Christians are right'] (l. 1015). In this light, the catalogue of troops appearing earlier in the poem does not so much describe Frankish unity as perform it, assimilating former enemy tribes such as the Bavarians or the Saxons into the imagined community of *douce France*. From this perspective, Roland *must* die so that his recollection of the historical layering underlying the nascent Frankish state – the memory of the violence that has gone into the formation of Charlemagne's empire – may die with him.[23]

A modern bestseller

In contrast to the tenuousness of its medieval survival, the *Chanson de Roland* is a modern 'bestseller' – as may be gauged by the plethora of translations available to the English-language reader: Penguin has two (by Dorothy Sayers in 1957 and Glyn Burgess in 1990), followed by the Modern Library (1957), W. W. Norton (1978), Signet Classic and Hackett (both in 2012), and Oxford World's Classics (2017). As a direct consequence of its nineteenth-century canonisation, the *Chanson de Roland* has become an iconic text, anthologised and figuring in undergraduate survey courses (Great Books, Medieval History, Western Civilisation) and PhD lists for professional medievalists-in-training.[24]

This wide dissemination has several consequences. If in the late nineteenth century the *Chanson de Roland* became a *lieu de mémoire* for a precocious French nationalism, since the late 1990s it has become another kind of *lieu de mémoire* for a medieval studies inflected by postcolonial theory and Critical Race studies.[25] In some essays by prominent medievalists, the *Roland* has become the go-to text for scholars wishing to underscore the medieval roots of modern racism or the intransigence of the poem's binary construction of Christianity versus its Saracen Other.[26] This phenomenon frequently involves a process of selective quotation. In his 1998 article, 'The Color of Salvation', for example, Bruce Holsinger characterised the *Roland* as 'one of the most violent and widely diffused pieces of anti-Muslim literature in the years surrounding the First Crusade'. He expands:

> Here the religious alterity of the Saracen Abisme, who 'fears not God, the Son of Saint Mary,' is writ large on his countenance: 'Black is that man as molten pitch that seethes.' Roland himself gazes upon other such 'misbegotten men,' who appear 'more black than ink is on the pen, / With no part white but their teeth.' Samir Marzouki has gone so far as to argue that for the *Roland* author skin color was 'un indice moral ainsi qu'un indice social,' in which the Saracen, 'hâlé par le soleil, était considéré comme laid et par conséquent immoral.'[27]

Strikingly, Holsinger conflates 'religious alterity' with a racialised otherness, marked by skin pigment – an association derived from selective quotation (buttressed by a citation from Samir Marzouki, a Tunisian poet, professor of French and Francophone literature who is a specialist in Apollinaire and Mallarmé).[28] Abisme appears in *laisse* 125, near the culmination of the battle of Roncevaux; in the series of one-on-one combats that characterise this section of the poem, he will be slain by Turpin – the feat that triggers Roland's pronouncement that the archbishop is 'a very good knight' (*mult bon chevalier*) (l. 1673). Before and during the battle, the poet introduces a series of pagans: King Marsile's nephew Aëlroth (ll. 860, 1188), the Barbary king Corsablix (ll. 885, 1235), Turgis de Turteluse (l. 916, 1282), Escremiz de Valterne (ll. 931, 1291), Estorgans (ll. 940, 1297), Estramariz (ll. 941, 1304) and a host of others, none of whom is marked for colour. These include King Marsile's brother Falsaron, with a monstrously wide half-foot gap between his eyes (ll. 879, 1213, 1219–20), the emir (*amurafles*) of Balaguer, with a 'noble body and proud, bright face' (*cors … mult gent e le vis fier e cler*) (ll. 893–5), and Margariz of Seville, who attracts many lady-friends (*amies*) on account of his good looks (*Pur sa beltét*) (ll. 955, 957). In other words, Abisme's blackness, which for Holsinger stands in for the poem's depiction of all Saracens, in fact contributes to the wide spectrum of diversity to be found among Marsile's Saracen vassals.

And yet Abisme's blackness is once again highlighted (this time together with the blackness of the troops of another Saracen ruler, Marganice) by Jeffrey Jerome Cohen in his article 'On Saracen Enjoyment':

> Like monsters, racist representations inevitably conjoin desire and disgust. The Saracens were no exception. The extended visualizations of 'lusty, black-skinned people' in the *Chanson de Roland*, for example, brought 'the darkness of Africa' queerly close to Christianity, a temptation within a threat. The poem describes both Margariz, whose beautiful body attracts the lingering eyes of Saracen ladies and Christian men, and Abisme, a Saracen 'neirs cume peiz ki est demise' [black as molten pitch] whose skin color and character are inseparable (he enjoys perfidy, murder, and heresy). Another Saracen leader, Marganice, rules over Africa (Ethiopia, Carthage, Alfrere, Garmalie), where he holds 'the black race' [la neire gent] under his command; / their noses are big and their ears broad' (1917–18; cf. 1933–34: '[they] are blacker than ink / and have nothing white but their teeth').[29]

In this example, Cohen focuses on two particular Saracens, in descriptions totalling five lines strongly marked for 'race'. Again, however, this reading is buttressed by an internal citation:

> For the Europe of the *Chanson de Roland*, Iberia was the land of the Saracens, a lusty, black-skinned people that brought the darkness of Africa dangerously close; so too the temptations of the soul's darker side ... Roland's Saracens are implicitly defined by a sexuality that exceeds the bounds of a Christian normativity, one that subverts the teleology of sex and emblematizes the shadow side of European culture. Indeed, in Christian accounts of Muslim Iberia, sexual excess seems inevitably to cross with cultural (or racial) otherness, and at times becomes its unique mode of expression.[30]

This quotation, we find, comes from Gregory Hutcheson and Josiah Blackmore's Introduction to their 1999 edited volume, *Queer Iberia*. As I have noted elsewhere, this is the book's *lone* mention of the *Chanson de Roland*, which does not even figure in the volume's index; yet here, on the very first page, it is called upon to exemplify everything that is most intransigent and reprehensible in medieval 'European' culture. Moreover, by a logic of association, the volume's focus on sexuality and queerness is taken to permeate the *Roland* as well. Thus Saracens are necessarily 'lusty' and 'implicitly defined by a sexuality that exceeds the bounds of a Christian normativity'.

In fact, none of the three articles cited above is 'about' the *Roland* per se, and none of the four authors is a specialist of medieval French literature. Their descriptions and quotations taken from the poem – which all together amount to just a handful of lines out of 4,000 – are likely to ring just familiar enough to casual readers to secure acceptance of their more general, and questionable, characterisations. And in this, I suggest, it resembles nothing so much as the workings of Orientalist discourse. In the following, I take a passage from Said, replacing 'the Orient' with 'the *Roland*' and 'place' with 'text':

> In the system of knowledge about the *Roland*, the *Roland* is less a text than a *topos*, a set of references, a congeries of characteristics, that seems to have its origin in a quotation, or a fragment of a text, or a citation from someone's work on the *Roland*, or some bit of previous imagining, or an amalgam of all of these. Direct observation or circumstantial description of the *Roland* are the fictions presented by writing on the *Roland*, yet invariably these are totally secondary to systematic tasks of another sort.[31]

More recently, in *The Invention of Race in the European Middle Ages*, Geraldine Heng adduces the *Roland*'s representation of Saracens as illustrative of two distinct points: that '[a]t its most demonic', the racialisation of Saracens makes them 'appear monstrous by being fused with animals, so that ... they have spiny bristles like a boar, or skin hard as iron, or they bark like dogs'; and that 'admired' Saracens such as 'the gallant Margariz of Seville' are never depicted as black.[32] The first quotation alludes to three different Saracen peoples mentioned in the Baligant episode (as noted earlier, a later addition to the textual tradition): the Micens (ll. 3220–2) and those from Occïan (l. 3246) and Arguille (l. 3527). The second assertion, while accurate, fails to note the numerous other Saracens – both the individuals named in Roland's battle against Marsile and the collective groups or ethnicities named in Charlemagne's battle against Baligant – who likewise are never depicted as black. In fact, however, the range of examples Heng cites, together with those she glosses over, illustrate the importance of resisting the impulse either to read the *Roland* through the lens of simple binary oppositions or prematurely to subsume any and all differences under the category of 'race'.[33]

Roland in the museum

Earlier, we saw that when Roland imagined the songs that future generations would sing of him, his sword Durendal (along with Oliver's sword Halteclere) would have pride of place. In fact, in the modern world, the memory of Durendal has faded; rather, it is Roland's oliphant that has become something of a *lieu de mémoire* of the history and legend of Roland and Charlemagne.[34] An oliphant, of course, plays a key role in the *Chanson de Roland*.[35] At the crucial moment when the rearguard led by Roland is facing attack by Marsile's army, Roland and his close companion Oliver fall out about whether to sound an oliphant to alert Charlemagne to the danger. For Oliver, it is logical to recall the main body of the army to save the lives of some of the emperor's most valued vassals. But Roland refuses: in accepting leadership of the rearguard, he has sworn to uphold his duty *whatever the cost*; to recall the Frankish forces would shame his entire lineage and, as we have seen, cause bad songs to be sung of him. In the bloody battle that ensues, and when the badly outnumbered rearguard is on the verge of extinction, Roland announces his intention to sound the oliphant. Oliver erupts in rage: you did not summon Charlemagne when he could have saved us; why call him back now, when we are all doomed? Roland does not respond, but Archbishop Turpin, in his effort to make peace between the two companions, supplies two crucial justifications: so that the emperor will take vengeance for their deaths, and so that their bodies will receive a Christian burial, rather than being consumed by wild animals. Roland then sounds the horn with such force that blood spurts from his mouth and his brain bursts in his temples (ll. 1762–4; reprised ll. 1785–6). This is significant: he dies, not slain by Saracens, but from the force of his own exertion.[36] As he is in his death throes, a Saracen approaches and tries to take his sword, Durendal; enraged, Roland bashes his attacker with the oliphant, shattering his helmet and skull. But his horn does not escape damage: 'Fenduz en est mis olifans el gros, / caiüz en est li cristals e li ors' ['My big oliphant is split from [the bashing]; the crystal and gold have fallen out of it'] (L. 170, ll. 2295–6). After a long apostrophe to Durendal, Roland stages his own death scene, climbing to the top of a hill and arranging himself facing Spain, with his sword and oliphant under him.[37] This final act suggests perhaps the main reason why Roland insisted on recalling Charlemagne: so there will be witnesses to his valour, ensuring his future reputation. And so it happens: the emperor returns, destroys the Saracen army, then gathers up the corpses of his dead vassals and transports them home to Aix-la-Chapelle – stopping along the way to depose the body of his nephew and companions and the oliphant he left behind.

> Vint a Burdeles, la citét de renun,
> desur l'alter seint Sevrin le baron
> met l'oliphan plein d'or e de manguns
> li pelerin le veient ki la vunt. (L. 267, ll. 3684–6)

> [Charlemagne] came to Bordeaux, the famous city;
> on the altar of the noble Saint Severinus
> he places the oliphant, full of gold and coins.
> Pilgrims who go there see it.]

The *Chanson de Roland*, in other words, provides a medieval 'object biography' for a relic that pilgrims might see on a visit to Bordeaux. This biography is 'corroborated' in another contemporary source, the *Liber Sancti Jacobi*, a guide to the French pilgrimage routes to the shrine of Santiago de Compostela.[38] One detail, however, is at odds with the account found in the *Roland*: 'while sounding his horn [*tubam*], his breath split it down the middle … The ivory horn [*tuba eburnea*], in truth, thus split, is in the city of Bordeaux.'[39] This discrepancy, however slight, highlights the divergence between the ethos of the vernacular epic, composed for and about the feudal nobility, in which the oliphant is damaged when Roland smashes a pagan enemy with it, and the chronicle, composed in Latin for a more learned and clerical audience, where it is split by the same heroic blast that causes Roland's own death: two explanations for the broken object presumably displayed to pilgrims at the church of Saint Seurin de Bordeaux.[40]

Now oliphants, in the form of carved ivory elephant tusks ('olifant' doubles as the Old French word for 'elephant') dating from approximately the late eleventh century, survive in reasonable numbers in museum collections across Europe and elsewhere. One such artefact (London, British Museum OA+1302) is in the British Museum. Its online profile describes it as a 'drinking horn' featuring 'carved decoration with a frieze of water buffaloes and gazelles couchant against a spiral scroll ground, with two repoussé silver bands with scrolls or vine scrolls and a ring for slinging on each'.[41] In the museum itself, it features in the recently inaugurated (2018) Albukhary Foundation Gallery of the Islamic World, under the rubric 'Raw Materials: Ivory' in a display case devoted to 'Global Trade: Land and Sea'.[42] The accompanying description reads:

> Elephant ivory was imported into the Mediterranean world from Africa in the form of tusks … Hollowed out tusks known as 'oliphants' were made into horns in Egypt and Sicily. This example features water buffaloes and gazelles [carved] along the top. According to legend, the French hero Roland blew on an oliphant in an appeal for help at the battle of Roncesvalles against the Arab forces in 778.[43]

This same object also appears in the British Museum's 2018 volume, *The Islamic World: A History in Objects*, in the chapter on 'Interconnected Worlds, 750–1500'. The photo caption presents what seems like a variation of the information found on the gallery panel:

> According to the *Chanson de Roland*, an epic poem written in the age of Charlemagne (742–814), the hero Roland blew on an oliphant appealing for help before his death in the battle of Roncevaux against the Arab forces in 778. According to the epic poem, the oliphant entered the church treasury of St Seurin in Bordeaux and hung over the church altar. Combining Mediterranean with Islamic designs, ivory horns such as this one, made from a complete elephant's tusk, are generally associated with the Fatimid era or Norman Sicily. Many have been found in Europe, preserved in church treasuries and kept as relics, in memory of the martyrdom of Roland and embodying the myth of his tragic demise. Hooks on the metal bands would have held the carrying straps.[44]

The middle part of this account, like the first part of the museum plaque, speaks to art historical debates over where such oliphants originated – the stakes being the extent to which they can be categorised as 'Islamic' art.[45] In its mention of the 'legend' of 'the French hero Roland' in a battle against 'Arab forces in 778', the museum display collapses three hundred years of history: the ambush that the Franks suffered in the Pyrenees was a joint attack by supporters of the Muslim governor of Barcelona (Charles's erstwhile ally whom he had taken hostage) and local Basques; there is little or no evidence of a historical 'Roland' associated with Charles's court; and the *Chanson de Roland* was not 'written in the age of Charlemagne' but composed over the intervening centuries and set down in writing sometime in the twelfth century.[46] Together, the museum plaque and book caption for British Museum OA+1302 offer up an object biography that fails to distinguish between 'history' – itself the product of narrative (re)constructions – and what we might today call literary fiction.[47]

Conclusion

Since the Romantic period, writes Robert Stein, the *Chanson de Roland* has served as the 'one true epic' of the Middle Ages.[48] As such, it has borne enormous cultural weight, conscripted to the ideological obsessions of each age, from nineteenth-century nationalism to twenty-first-century Critical Race studies. At the same time, if it remains a 'bestseller', it is, I submit, not by serving as a conduit for simple meanings or messages, but because its way of managing the multiple cross-currents – political, social and cultural as well as discursive, generic and literary – of the historical moment in which it was produced proves good to think with for successive generations of readers.

Notes

1 '[L]a *Chanson de Roland* joue pour les études médiévales en tant que discipline, en tant qu'institution, un rôle fondateur … Être médiéviste c'est, au plus vrai, prendre position sur la C.R.' Bernard Cerquiglini, '*La chanson de Roland* et la traïson des clercs', *Littérature* 42 (1981): 40.

2 Ian Short, 'Introduction: The Oxford Version', in Joseph J. Duggan (ed.), *La Chanson de Roland/The Song of Roland: The French Corpus*, 3 vols (Turnhout: Belgium, 2005), vol. I, p. 19.

3 *Les Manuscrits de Chrétien de Troyes/The Manuscripts of Chrétien de Troyes*, ed. Keith Busby et al., 2 vols (Amsterdam: Rodopi, 1993), vol. II, pp. 15–16.

4 Short, 'Introduction', p. 15. See http://image.ox.ac.uk/show?collection=bodleian&manuscript=msdigby23b (accessed 29 December 2019).

5 Paul Aebischer, 'Trois personnages en quête d'auteurs: Roland, Oliver, Aude. Contribution à la génétique de la *Chanson de Roland*', in *Rolandiana et Oliveriana: Recueil d'études sur les chansons de geste* (Geneva: Droz, 1967), pp. 153–4.

6 Conques, in south-central France, was located along one of the four main pilgrimage routes to Santiago de Compostela; the priory of Roncesvalles was its dependent. For Conques, see Rita Lejeune and Jacques Stiennon, *La Légende de Roland dans l'art du moyen âge*, 2nd edn, 2 vols (Brussels: Arcade, 1967), vol. I, pp. 19–24, and vol. II, figs. 1, 6; for Angoulême, ibid., vol. I, pp. 29–42, and vol. II. figs. 14–19.

7 Lejeune and Stiennon, *La Légende de Roland*, vol. I, pp. 101, 103.

8 Joseph J. Duggan (ed.), *La Chanson de Roland/The Song of Roland: The French Corpus* (Turnhout: Brepols, 2005), vol. I, p. 5. For versions in other medieval languages, see Joseph J. Duggan, 'Beyond the Oxford Text: The *Songs of* Roland', in William W. Kibler and Leslie Zarker Morgan (eds), *Approaches to Teaching the* Song of Roland (New York: Modern Language Association, 2006), pp. 70–2.

9 A succinct summary of the manuscript tradition of versions in French and Franco-Italian, as well as translations into other medieval languages, may be found in Duggan, 'Beyond the Oxford Text'.

10 *La Chanson de Roland*, ed. Duggan, vol. I, p. 5.

11 Jehan Bodel, *La Chanson des Saisnes*, ed. Annette Brasseur, 2 vols (Geneva: Droz, 1989), l. 7. This quotation is from Ms A (Paris, Arsenal 3142). Bodel also wrote *Le Jeu de Saint Nicolas* (one of the earliest miracle plays in Old French), several fabliaux, pastourelles and his *Congés* – his farewell to public life after contracting leprosy.

12 In addition to Doon de Mayence, examples include the epics of Renaud de Montauban, Girart de Rousillon and Raoul de Cambrai.

13 R. W. Southern, *The Making of the Middle Ages* (New Haven, CT: Yale University Press, 1953). Compare M. M. Bakhtin's chapter on 'Epic and Novel', in *The Dialogic Imagination: Four Essays*, ed. Michael Holquist, trans. Caryl Emerson and Michael Holquist (Austin, TX: University of Texas Press, 1981), pp. 1–40.

14 Sarah Kay, *The Chansons de Geste in the Age of Romance: Political Fictions* (New York: Oxford University Press, 1995).

15 Robert M. Stein, *Reality Fictions: Romance, History and Governmental Authority, 1025–1180* (Notre Dame, IN: University of Notre Dame Press, 2006), p. 170.

16 On his remarkable and colourful career, see William Roach, 'Francisque Michel: A Pioneer of Medieval Studies', *Proceedings of the American Philological Society* 114.3 (1970): 168–78.

17 Joseph J. Duggan, 'General Introduction: Editing the *Song of Roland*', in *La Chanson de Roland*, ed. Duggan, vol. I, p. 8.

18 *La Chanson de Roland*, ed. Duggan, vol. I, pp. 23, 24. Duggan cites the studies of Alain Corbellari, 'Joseph Bédier, Philologist and Writer', in R. Howard Bloch and Stephen J. Nichols (eds), *Medievalism and the Modernist Temper* (Baltimore, MD: Johns Hopkins University Press, 1996), pp. 269–85, and *Joseph Bédier écrivain et philologue* (Geneva: Droz, 1997) (*La Chanson de Roland*, ed. Duggan, p. 23 n.13). On the way Bédier's scholarship was inflected by his origins on the French colony of Réunion, see Michelle R. Warren, *Creole Medievalism: Colonial France and Joseph Bédier's Middle Ages* (Minneapolis, MN: University of Minnesota Press, 2011).

19 Stein, *Reality Fictions*, p. 171.

20 Compare l. 1466, 'Male chançun n'en deit estre cantee' [about our swords].

21 Presumably, Geste Francor is meant to refer here to annals concerning Charlemagne and his Franks. Today, the name is given to the collection of seven *chansons de geste* compiled in the fourteenth-century Franco-Italian manuscript Venice, Biiblioteca Nazionale Marciano Francese Z. 13 (= 256), https://fit-ace-frenchofitaly-medieval.azurewebsites.net/?page_id=128 (accessed 1 May 2020).

22 On the complex history of this legend, including variants in which the emperor's sin is necrophilia (in the German tradition) or sodomy, see Susanne Hafner, 'Charlemagne's Unspeakable Sin', *Modern Language Studies* 32.2 (2002): 1–14.

23 This section is slightly adapted from Sharon Kinoshita, *Medieval Boundaries: Rethinking Difference in Old French Literature* (Philadelphia, PA: University of Pennsylvania Press, 2006), p. 30. On Roland's display of memory (versus the other Franks' willingness to forget) in the opening council scene, see Kinoshita, *Medieval Boundaries*, pp. 24–5.

24 Its popularity as a classroom text is confirmed by a volume devoted to it in the Modern Language Association's Approaches to Teaching World Literature series. See William W. Kibler and Leslie Zarker Morgan (eds), *Approaches to Teaching the* Song of Roland (New York: Modern Language Association, 2006).

25 On the *Chanson de Roland* as a site of French nationalism, see Joseph J. Duggan, 'Franco-German Conflict and the History of French Scholarship on the *Song of Roland*', in Patrick Gallacher and Helen Damico (eds), *Hermeneutics and Medieval Culture* (Albany, NY: State University of New York Press, 1989), pp. 97–106; Sharon Kinoshita, '"Pagans are wrong and Christians are right": Alterity, Gender and Nation in the *Chanson de Roland*', *Journal of Medieval and Early Modern Studies*

31.1 (2001): 80–1; and Simon Gaunt, 'The *Chanson de Roland* and the Invention of France', in Robert Shannan Peckham (ed.), *Rethinking Heritage: Cultures and Politics in Europe* (London: I. B. Tauris, 2003), pp. 90–101.

26 A word is in order here regarding the term 'Saracen'. I do not subscribe to Shofookeh Rajabzadeh's claim that it is necessarily a 'derogatory label' that shows 'Islamophobia at work in its most genius and powerful form' ('The Depoliticized Saracen and Muslim Erasure', *Literature Compass* 16 [2019]: 3, 4). In the *Chanson de Roland*, *Sarrazin* (Saracens), alongside *paien* (pagan), are used to refer to those under the lordship of Marsile and Baligant. 'Saracen' appears thirty times in the text and 'pagan' 109 times; the choice is determined by syllable count (three versus two), conditioned by the *Roland*'s strict decasyllabic meter, with each line further divided into groups of four + six syllables. The adjectival form *paienur* and variants (used to modify *gent* [people] or *enseigne* [battle standard]) appear five times. See Joseph J. Duggan, *A Concordance of the Chanson de Roland* (Columbus, OH: Ohio State University Press, 1969), pp. 282–83, 418.

27 Bruce Holsinger, 'The Color of Salvation: Desire, Death, and the Second Crusade in Bernard of Clairvaux's *Sermons on the Song of Songs*', in David Townsend and Andrew Taylor (eds), *The Tongue of the Father: Gender and Ideology in Twelfth-Century Latin* (Philadelphia, PA: University of Pennsylvania Press, 1998), p. 170.

28 www.kassataya.com/culture/15683-samir-marzouki-poete-nouvelliste-universitaire (accessed 4 May 2017).

29 Jeffrey Jerome Cohen, 'On Saracen Enjoyment: Some Fantasies of Race in Late Medieval France and England', *Journal of Medieval and Early Modern Studies* 31.1 (2001): 119–20.

30 Gregory S. Hutcheson and Josiah Blackmore, 'Introduction', in Gregory S. Hutcheson and Josiah Blackmore (eds), *Queer Iberia: Sexualities, Cultures, and Crossings from the Middle Ages to the Renaissance* (Durham, NC: Duke University Press, 1999), p. 1.

31 Edward Said, *Orientalism* (New York: Vintage, 1979), p. 177. The modifications are mine, inspired by Catherine Brown, 'In the Middle', *Journal of Medieval and Early Modern Studies* 30:3 (2000): 549. In comparison, Said's characterisation in *Orientalism* is judiciously restrained; in the *Chanson de Roland*, he notes, 'the worship of Saracens is portrayed as embracing Mahomet *and* Apollo' (p. 61); its author – like other pre- and early modern poets including Ariosto, Milton, Shakespeare and Cervantes – drew on the 'prodigious cultural repertoire' associated with the East (p. 63), representing 'the Orient and Islam … as outsiders having a special role to play *inside* Europe' (p. 71).

32 Geraldine Heng, *The Invention of Race in the European Middle Ages* (Cambridge: Cambridge University Press, 2018), pp. 118, 189.

33 See, for example, Kinoshita, 'Pagans are wrong and Christians are right', 81–3, and Sharon Kinoshita, 'Deprovincializing the Middle Ages', in Rob Wilson and Christopher Leigh Connery (eds), *The Worlding Project: Doing Cultural Studies in the Era of Globalization* (Santa Cruz, CA: New Pacific Press, 2007), pp. 67–70.

34 Shirin Khanmohamadi has recently refocused attention on Durendal as exemplary of Islamic 'object genealogies' in Old French *chansons de geste* ('Durendal, Translated: Islamic Object Genealogies in the *Chansons de geste*', *postmedieval* 8 [2017]: 321–33).

35 This section is adapted from Sharon Kinoshita, 'How to do Things with Things: Material Objects in the Multicultural Mediterranean', in Andrew James Johnston, Martin Bleisteiner and Jan-Peer Hartmann (eds), *'Strange Matter': How Things Disrupt Time* (forthcoming). For the way the oliphant troubles the transparency of communication in and easy readings of the poem, see Michelle Warren, 'The Noise of Roland', *Exemplaria* 16.2 (2004): 277–304.

36 Oliver's initial plea is laid out in the three 'similar' *laisses* (epic stanzas) 83–5 – the near-repetition among them (any differences largely dictated by changes in assonance) highlighting the drama of the moment. Oliver's condemnation of Roland's decision to sound the horn unfolds in *laisses* 129–31. Roland sounds the horn in *laisses* 133–4.

37 On his apostrophe to Durendal as a turning point in the 'meaning' of the poem, see Kinoshita, *Medieval Boundaries*, p. 30.

38 The *Liber Sancti Jacobi* is the fifth and final section of the so-called *Codex Calixtinus*, composed/compiled in the late 1130s or early 1140s (*The Pilgrim's Guide to Santiago de Compostela: A Critical Edition*, ed. Paula Gerson, Alison Stone and Jeanne Krochalis, 2 vols [London: Harvey Miller, 1998], vol. I, pp. 14–15). This makes it contemporary with the lone manuscript of the 'Oxford' *Roland* (Oxford, Bodleian Library, Digby 23), now dated, if not entirely securely, to the second quarter of the twelfth century (Short, 'Introduction', p. 19); the version of the poem it preserves is thought to date from the time of the First Crusade, so c. 1098 (Short, 'Introduction', p. 40). On the blend of fact and fiction in the poem, see William W. Kibler, 'Rencesvals: The Event', in William W. Kibler and Leslie Zarker Morgan (eds), *Approaches to Teaching the* Song of Roland (New York: Modern Language Association, 2006), pp. 53–6.

39 *The Pilgrim's Guide*, ed. Gerson et al., vol II, pp. 62–3.The *Liber*'s account of how the horn came to be split was taken from the Latin *Pseudo-Turpin Chronicle*, a purported eyewitness account of Charlemagne's adventures

also found in the *Codex Calixtinus* (*The Pilgrim's Guide*, ed. Gerson et al., vol. II, pp. 190–1, nn. 178–9). Elements of the *Pseudo-Turpin* are reflected in the so-called Charlemagne windows at Chartres and in the twelfth-century parodic epic *Le Pèlerinage de Charlemagne*.

40 In the *Chanson d'Aspremont*, a late twelfth-century 'prequel' to the *Chanson de Roland*, the 'biographies' of both Durendal and the oliphant are augmented by a Muslim provenance. A young Roland having captured them in battle from their original Saracen possessor, they do the 'translational work' of 'legitimating the transfer of rightful dominion and authority from one group to another' (Khanmohamadi, 'Durendal, Translated', 325).

41 See https://islamicworld.britishmuseum.org/collection/RRM128/ (accessed 4 August 2019).

42 On the Albukhary Galleries, see https://islamicworld.britishmuseum.org. For an overview of the display cases, click on 'Show gallery map'; for Case 13, scroll through 'Filter by display case'.

43 Here and in the following paragraph, observations about the gallery displays are based on a visit to the British Museum in April 2019.

44 Ladan Akbarnia, Venetia Porter and Fahmida Suleman, *The Islamic World: A History in Objects* (London: Thames and Hudson/The British Museum, 2018).

45 For the background to this debate, see Kinoshita, 'How to Do Things with Things'.

46 On the complexities of the evidence concerning 778, see Kibler, 'Rencesvals: The Event'. On the interpolation of a 'Roland' into the textual traditions of histories of Charlemagne, see Aebischer, 'Trois personnages en quête d'auteurs'.

47 Ironically, the plaques of three other oliphants displayed in the British Museum's Sir Paul and Lady Ruddock Gallery gallery of the European Middle Ages (Room 40) make no mention of the Roland–Charlemagne legend. Two oliphants displayed among other medieval objects in Vienna's Kunsthistorisches Museum are described as 'reliquary caskets', with the accompanying explanation that 'The term oliphant refers to an ivory horn such as the one used by the legendary hero Roland, one of Charlemagne's paladins, to sound the call for battle.'

48 Stein, *Reality Fictions*, p. 169.

Works cited

Primary sources

Bodel, Jehan, *La Chanson des Saisnes*, ed. Annette Brasseur, 2 vols (Geneva: Droz, 1989).

Les Manuscrits de Chrétien de Troyes/The Manuscripts of Chrétien de Troyes, ed. Keith Busby et al., 2 vols (Amsterdam: Rodopi, 1993).
The Pilgrim's Guide to Santiago de Compostela: A Critical Edition, ed. Paula Gerson, Alison Stone and Jeanne Krochalis, 2 vols (London: Harvey Miller, 1998).
La Chanson de Roland/The Song of Roland: The French Corpus, ed. Joseph J. Duggan, 3 vols (Turnhout: Brepols, 2005).
Song of Roland, trans. Dorothy L. Sayers (New York: Penguin, 1957).
Song of Roland, trans. W. S. Merwin (New York: Modern Library Books, 1957; repr. 2001 with Reading Guide).
Song of Roland, trans. Frederick Goldin (New York: W. W. Norton, 1978).
Song of Roland, trans. Glyn S. Burgess (London: Penguin, 1990).
Song of Roland, trans. Robert Harrison (New York: Signet Classic, 2012).
Song of Roland, trans. John DuVal (Indianapolis, IN: Hackett, 2012).
Song of Roland, trans. Simon Gaunt and Karen Pratt (Oxford: Oxford University Press, 2017).

Secondary sources

Aebischer, Paul, 'Trois personnages en quête d'auteurs: Roland, Oliver, Aude. Contribution à la génétique de la *Chanson de Roland*', in *Rolandiana et Oliveriana: Recueil d'études sur les chansons de geste* (Geneva: Droz, 1967), pp. 141–73.
Akbarnia, Ladan, Venetia Porter and Fahmida Suleman, *The Islamic World: A History in Objects* (London: Thames and Hudson/The British Museum, 2018).
Bakhtin, M. M., 'Epic and Novel', in *The Dialogic Imagination: Four Essays*, ed. Michael Holquist, trans. Caryl Emerson and Michael Holquist (Austin, TX: University of Texas Press, 1981), pp. 1–40.
Brown, Catherine, 'In the Middle', *Journal of Medieval and Early Modern Studies* 30.3 (2000): 547–74.
Cerquiglini, Bernard, '*La chanson de Roland* et la traïson des clercs', *Littérature* 42 (1981): 40–6.
Cohen, Jeffrey Jerome, 'On Saracen Enjoyment: Some Fantasies of Race in Late Medieval France and England', *Journal of Medieval and Early Modern Studies* 31.1 (2001): 113–46.
Duggan, Joseph J., *A Concordance of the Chanson de Roland* (Columbus, OH: Ohio State University Press, 1969).
— *The Song of Roland: Formulaic Style and Poetic Craft* (Berkeley, CA: University of California Press, 1973).
— 'Franco-German Conflict and the History of French Scholarship on the *Song of Roland*', in Patrick Gallacher and Helen Damico (eds), *Hermeneutics and Medieval Culture* (Albany, NY: State University of New York Press, 1989), pp. 97–106.
— 'General Introduction: Editing the *Song of Roland*', in Joseph J. Duggan (ed.), *La Chanson de Roland/The Song of Roland: The French Corpus*, 3 vols (Turnhout: Brepols, 2005), pp. 5–38.

— 'Beyond the Oxford Text: The *Songs of* Roland', in William W. Kibler and Leslie Zarker Morgan (eds), *Approaches to Teaching the* Song of Roland (New York: Modern Language Association, 2006), pp. 66–72.

Gaunt, Simon, 'The *Chanson de Roland* and the Invention of France', in Robert Shannan Peckham (ed.), *Rethinking Heritage: Cultures and Politics in Europe* (London: I. B. Tauris, 2003), pp. 90–101.

Hafner, Susanne, 'Charlemagne's Unspeakable Sin', *Modern Language Studies* 32.2 (2002): 1–14.

Heng, Geraldine, *The Invention of Race in the European Middle Ages* (Cambridge: Cambridge University Press, 2018).

Holsinger, Bruce, 'The Color of Salvation: Desire, Death, and the Second Crusade in Bernard of Clairvaux's *Sermons on the Song of Songs*', in David Townsend and Andrew Taylor (eds), *The Tongue of the Father: Gender and Ideology in Twelfth-Century Latin* (Philadelphia, PA: University of Pennsylvania Press, 1998), pp. 156–86

Hutcheson, Gregory S., and Josiah Blackmore, 'Introduction', in Gregory S. Hutcheson and Josiah Blackmore (eds), *Queer Iberia: Sexualities, Cultures, and Crossings from the Middle Ages to the Renaissance* (Durham, NC: Duke University Press, 1999), pp. 1–19.

Kay, Sarah, *The Chansons de geste in the Age of Romance: Political Fictions* (New York: Oxford University Press, 1995).

Khanmohamadi, Shirin A., 'Durendal, Translated: Islamic Object Genealogies in the *Chansons de geste*', *postmedieval* 8 (2017): 321–33.

Kibler, William W., 'Rencesvals: The Event', in William W. Kibler and Leslie Zarker Morgan (eds), *Approaches to Teaching the* Song of Roland (New York: Modern Language Association, 2006), pp. 53–6.

Kibler, William W., and Leslie Zarker Morgan (eds), *Approaches to Teaching the* Song of Roland (New York: Modern Language Association, 2006).

Kinoshita, Sharon, '"Pagans are wrong and Christians are right": Alterity, Gender, and Nation in the *Chanson de Roland*', *Journal of Medival and Early Modern Studies* 31.1 (2001): 79–111.

— *Medieval Boundaries: Rethinking Difference in Old French Literature* (Philadelphia, PA: University of Pennsylvania Press, 2006).

— 'Deprovincializing the Middle Ages', in Rob Wilson and Christopher Leigh Connery (eds), *The Worlding Project: Doing Cultural Studies in the Era of Globalization* (Santa Cruz, CA: New Pacific Press, 2007), pp. 61–75.

— 'Beyond Philology: Cross-Cultural Engagement in Literary History and Beyond', in Suzanne Conklin Akbari and Karla Mallette (eds), *A Sea of Languages: Rethinking the Arabic Role in Medieval Literary History* (Toronto: University of Toronto Press, 2013), pp. 25–42.

— 'How to Do Things with Things: Material Objects in the Multicultural Mediterranean', in Andrew James Johnston, Martin Bleisteiner and Jan-Peer Hartmann (eds), *'Strange Matter': How Things Disrupt Time* (forthcoming).

Lejeune, Rita, and Jacques Stiennon, *La Légende de Roland dans l'art du moyen âge*, 2nd edn, 2 vols (Brussels: Arcade, 1967).

— *The Legend of Roland in the Middle Ages* (New York: Phaidon, 1971).
Rajabzadeh, Shofookeh, 'The Depoliticized Saracen and Muslim Erasure', *Literature Compass* 16 (2019): 1–8.
Roach, William, 'Francisque Michel: A Pioneer of Medieval Studies', *Proceedings of the American Philological Society* 114.3 (1970): 168–78.
Said, Edward, *Orientalism* (New York: Vintage, 1979).
Short, Ian, 'Introduction: The Oxford Version', in Joseph J. Duggan (ed.), *La Chanson de Roland/The Song of Roland: The French Corpus*, 3 vols (Turnhout: Brepols, 2005), vol. I, pp. 13–107.
Southern, R. W., *The Making of the Middle Ages* (New Haven, CT: Yale University Press, 1953).
Stein, Robert M., *Reality Fictions: Romance, History, and Governmental Authority, 1025–1180* (Notre Dame, IN: University of Notre Dame Press, 2006).
Vance, Eugene, 'Roland and the Poetics of Memory', in Josué V. Harari (ed.), *Textual Strategies: Perspectives in Post-Structuralist Criticism* (Ithaca, NY: Cornell University Press, 1979), pp. 374–403.
Warren, Michelle R., 'The Noise of Roland', *Exemplaria* 16.2 (2004): 277–304.
— *Creole Medievalism: Colonial France and Joseph Bédier's Middle Ages* (Minneapolis, MN: University of Minnesota Press, 2011).

Part II

Medieval bestsellers: reading the 'medieval canon'?

6

World literature and its discontents: reading the Life of Aḥīqar

Daniel L. Selden

For Sharon Kinoshita

A scribe who knows no Sumerian,
what kind of scribe is he?

– Akkadian Proverb

What role does distributed authorship play – or, more accurately, what role should it play – in the emergent field of 'world literature'?[1] Roy Ascott, Britain's 'visionary pioneer' of the New Media who introduced cybernetics into the domain of art,[2] coined the term 'distributed authorship' in 1984 to describe non-hierarchised forms of telematic artwork based exclusively on interactive and remote types of connection.[3] 'Artists,' Marie Chatel explains, 'act here as mere participants, blurring the boundaries between the emitter and the receiver, with participants playing both roles as part of the systemic process.'[4] Ascott's best-known work, *La Plissure du Texte* (1983), engaged eleven different sites in Europe, the United States, Canada and Australia, each of which bore responsibility for elaborating a different actant (princess, sorcerer, hero, fairy godmother, beast, etc.) to create what Ascott described as a 'planetary fairy tale'.[5] Active online twenty-four hours a day for twelve days (11–23 December 1983), participants created and disbursed ASCII-based images and text asynchronously from multiple sites around the globe, spinning out a non-linear and multilayered tale with many forking paths.[6] Drawing eclectically on Vladimir Propp's *Morphology of the Folktale* (1928), André Breton's *Cadavre exquis* (1927)[7] and Roland Barthes' *The Pleasure of the Text* (1973), Ascott cites Barthes as his source of inspiration: 'the generative idea that the text is made, is worked out in a perpetual interweaving; lost in this tissue – this texture – the subject unmakes himself, like a spider dissolving in the constructive secretions of its web'.[8] For Ascott, then, telematic art – pleated and repleated by multiple authors and, at terminals placed publicly, random users – never closes itself off and never aims for or reaches a state of completion. As such, Ascott's telematics decentralise the artistic medium, which takes for its defining metaphor a web or net in which there is neither centre nor hierarchy, neither top nor bottom, thereby breaking not only the confines of the insular person but also the boundaries of institutions, territories and time zones.

In 2010 Axel Bruns, Professor of Digital Media at the Queensland University of Technology in Brisbane, Australia, reinflected Ascott's term to describe what he calls 'participatory poiesis', that is, projects in which a large number of participants contribute to a common pool of creative resources and artistic material, what in more politicising terms he describes as 'distributed citizen participation'.[9] Here, however, unlike Ascott's interdependent collaborations, participants act individually, taking their own steps in promoting the creative process such that they configure a modality of distributive production that no longer takes Breton's *Cadavre exquis* as its model.[10] Bruns's term for this creative process is produsage, a portmanteau that combines production with usage, designating user-led content creation that blurs the boundaries between passive consumption and active production. Participants shift easily from users to producers and vice versa,[11] occupying a medial role that Hayden White has called 'writing in the middle voice'.[12] Among the best-known and most extensively practised forms of produsage is fanfiction, that is, second-order literary compositions or videos in which a plurality of different authors (fandom) use copyrighted characters, settings and other intellectual properties from a prior work of film or fiction as the basis of their creative compositions.[13] Some fanfic seeks to close loopholes in the base text (canon) or to explore and deepen the character motivations that they find there. Some fanfic writers create texts to coexist with canon, whereas others rewrite canonical events that the produser dislikes because they are depressing, tedious or incomprehensible (fix-fix).[14] Some fanfic invents homosexual pairings between characters who otherwise appear normatively heterosexual in canon. Often, produsers translate the base text into a different genre – a television series becomes a noir detective film, or a play becomes a pornographic novel. The stress here falls on what Sean Cubitt calls the 'mutuality of making', a process in which the network artist no longer functions as a person.

A person, Cubitt argues, authors, assuming responsibility for his or her creation. Working within electronic networks, however, every artist humbles her or himself to the role of 'participant', a profoundly social act of self-abnegation with not only artistic but also political and cultural consequences: 'After the transnationals have demolished the last shards of nationhood, there will remain the transnations of those who have established, distinct from the cosmopolitan elite, those mutually constructed linkages that traverse the globe as diasporan musics do, always remade in every port they come to.'[15]

In drawing comparison between current, web-based produsage and earlier forms of collaborative fiction such as *Alf Layla wa-layla* [*The Thousand and One Nights*], a protean collection of Indic, Iranian, Jewish and Arabic tales which Daniel Heller-Roazen has described as 'a work in movement, caught in the passage from territory to territory, culture to language, language to language'[16] (any comparison between the mutability of *The Thousand and One Nights* and the ever-growing corpus of Harry Potter fanfic risks skating on the thin ice of anachronism), the disparities between scribal and digital forms of variance and participation remain irreducible.[17] This also requires a good deal of critical *léger de main*: in literary history it is not the similarities between texts or writers that ultimately count, but rather the differences – cultural, historical, linguistic and narratological.[18] Recently, however, Henry Colburn, a scholar fully aware of the need to historicise culture difference, has made a case for comparative studies that focus on the structure of pre-modern social systems rather than the particularities that they encode, in order to enable a dialectic between earlier and later forms of development without positing any necessary historical connection between them:

> Although globalization is generally thought of as a modern phenomenon, encompassing the entire world, its main systemic features existed in earlier periods as well, albeit on a reduced geographic scale. Moreover, the question of whether or not the Achaemenid Empire, or any other historical or archaeological phenomenon, was an instance of globalization is less important than how modern globalization can help us to better understand the past ... The main features of

> globalization are an increase in connectivity on an inter-regional scale and social, cultural, and economic change resulting from it. Connectivity arises from meaningful interactions between people, groups and institutions. These interactions can be meaningful either because of their frequent recurrence or because of their political, social, and economic significance.[19]

Among the means that the Achaemenid kings employed to promote complex, long-distance connectivity between the twenty far-flung provinces into which they divided their empire, Colburn singles out four main strategies: the network of roads and storehouses that linked Takṣaśilā in the east to Memphis and Sardis in the west; the mounted relay postal system that criss-crossed the Achaemenid domain; the promotion of Aramaic as the language of imperial administration; and the imposition of a uniform calendar for all provinces and peoples subject to what the Achaemenids called 'The State'. This enhanced connectivity, Colburn argues, resulted in three systemic features that also typify globalisation in the era of late capitalism: space-time compression, standardisation and the deterritorialisation of subject peoples.[20]

In much the same way, distributed authorship has been a feature of literary composition since archaic times. The story of Gilgamesh, for example, which contemporary critics often describe as the earliest extant literary masterpiece, evolved through a series of rewritings in the Sumero-Akkadian scribal curriculum over a period of roughly a thousand years.[21] The oldest stratum of the texts consists of five Sumerian poems celebrating Bilgameš, king of Uruk, which towards the end of the second millennium BCE circulated as independent compositions. Subsequently, an Akkadian redactor combined these poems into a cohesive narrative, now known as the Old Babylonian Version of the tale (eighteenth century BCE), which bore as its title the incipit *Šūtur eli šarrī* ['Surpassing all other kings']. Several centuries later, the Assyrian Sîn-lēqi-unninni reworked the older narrative into its definitive form, known today as the Standard Babylonian Version (c. 1300–1000 BCE), comprising twelve tablets and again titled according to its incipit: *Ša naqba īmuru* ['He who saw the abyss'].[22] In no way, however, can we consider Sîn-lēqi-unninni to be the 'author' of the poem, if what we mean by that is the Wordsworthian notion of a solitary thinker who produces poetry spontaneously out of a singular 'emotion recollected in tranquillity',[23] a notion of authorial creation which, as Jed Wyrick has shown, only began to emerge in the work of Augustine and Jerome, that is, over the course of the fifth century CE.[24] Instead, we need to speak here of 'collaborative meaning' or a 'poetics of consent', forged over centuries by a chain of mostly anonymous Mesopotamian scribes who, working synchronously as well as asynchronously, served as both receivers and producers of the text, another form of White's writing in the middle voice.[25] Samuel N. Kramer describes the multiple reworkings of the poem in several languages as follows:

> Of the various episodes comprising The Epic of Gilgamesh, several go back to Sumerian prototypes actually involving the hero Gilgamesh. Even in those episodes which lack Sumerian counterparts, most of the individual motifs reflect Sumerian mythic and epic sources. In no case, however, did the Babylonian poets slavishly copy the Sumerian material. They so modified its content and moulded its form, in accordance with their own temper and heritage, that only the bare nucleus of the Sumerian original remains recognizable. As for the plot structure of the epic as a whole – the forceful and fateful episodic drama of the restless, adventurous hero and his inevitable disillusionment – it is definitely a Babylonian, rather than a Sumerian, development and achievement.[26]

Despite this process of redaction, the Standard Babylonian Version effectively conceals the millennial chain of scribal production, attributing the narrative instead to Gilgamesh himself who, at the end of his adventures, as his crowning deed, memorialises his life in an inscription: 'He came a far road, was weary, found peace / and set all his labours on a tablet of stone.'[27] This scene of writing introduces reciprocally a scene of reading, in which the editorial 'I' introduces, for the first time in extant literature at least, a topos fated to have a long life in the poetry and prose of the Near East, Europe and America, a conceit that Edgar Allan Poe refers to slyly as the 'manuscript found in a bottle':[28]

> [See] the tablet box of cedar, [Release] its clasp of bronze!
> [Lift] the lid of its secret,
> [Pick] up the tablet of lapis lazuli and read out
> The travails of Gilgamesh, all that he went through. [I.24–8].[29]

This remarkable injunction apostrophises wayfarers who happen upon the box, exhorting them to open it, take out the tablet [*sic*] that it holds inside, and read what the poem claims to be the words of Gilgamesh himself.

Unexpectedly, moreover, the passage identifies the inscriptional medium not as clay, the usual impress for cuneiform texts, but as lapis lazuli, a metonym both for the implicit value of the tale and for the fixity of the text it bears as a now canonical classic.[30] Through this conceit, then, the poem not only conceals the labour of its own production under the sign of 'Gilgamesh', the protagonist who constitutes both the subject and the object of his quest.[31] Concomitantly, the cedar chest introduces, again for the first time in extant literature, what Paul de Man identifies as one of the oldest and most tenacious metaphors for reading, that is, '[the] model of literature as a kind of box that separates an inside from an outside, and the reader or critic as the person who opens the lid in order to release into the open what was secreted but inaccessible inside'.[32]

That this metapoetic conceit appears as early as the Standard Babylonian Version of Gilgamesh suggests that the figure of the cedar box, which effectively requires all future readers to 'lift the lid of its secret' [*niṣirtu(m)*, 'treasure, wealth, secret, hidden recess'] should they wish to gain access to Gilgamesh and the account of his heroic deeds, constitutes one of the enabling tropes of Levantine-Mediterranean literature. At the same time, moreover, this metaphor inaugurates the age of interpretation, where taking the tablet out of its container figures the hermeneutic search to 'open up the text' and reveal the meaning concealed therein.[33] Like the Lacanian self (*le Je*), however, which performs for the subject the psychic task of providing an illusory continuity and coherence to the otherwise dispersed and unrelated fragments of experience, the Standard Babylonian Version of the text presents itself, in staging both its scene of writing and its scene of reading, as complete, authoritative and immutable, fixed metaphorically in stone by the very protagonist whose exploits it recounts.[34]

If, as Joshua J. Mark contends, Gilgamesh constitutes 'the first epic hero in world literature', then distributed authorship is not an aberrant, belated or contemporary form of literary composition.[35] Rather, it is a writing practice that informs world literature from its inception. Had we started with the redactional history of Exodus or the *Iliad* the case would be no different. It comes as something of a surprise, then, that distributed authorship remains almost entirely absent both from theoretical discussions of world literature today, as well as from the numerous anthologies that have laid the groundwork for what has become a fast-growing academic field.[36] To address this issue, the discussion that follows falls into two related parts. The first attempts to outline – all too briefly, to be sure – the history and investments of world literature as discipline, while the second turns to a reassessment of the ancient and medieval lives of Aḥīqar as they might figure – but so far do not – within this critical terrain.

The age of world literature

The term 'world literature' is of relatively recent coinage, dating back no further than the first quarter of the nineteenth century. Karl Marx and Friedrich Engels refer pointedly to 'world literature' in the first part of their *Communist Manifesto* (1848), where it figures centrally in their description of capitalist accumulation and commodity exchange on a global scale:

> In place of the old wants, satisfied by the production of the country, we find new wants, requiring for their satisfaction the products of distant lands and climes. In place of the old local and national seclusion and self-sufficiency, we have intercourse in every direction, universal interdependence of nations. And as in material, so also in intellectual production. The intellectual creations of individual nations become common property. National one-sidedness and narrowmindedness become more and more impossible, and from the numerous national and local literatures, there arises a world literature.[37]

Whatever one may think of the *Manifesto*'s link between material and intellectual production, historically the term world literature comes into currency at precisely that moment when Europe was in the process of its most intensive colonial expansion, successfully incorporating virtually all remaining regions of the globe into the capitalist world-system.

However, market-driven colonial expansion inevitably brought Europeans into contact with peripheral and non-Western literary traditions. Simultaneously, moreover, technological advances in publishing and overland transport intensified the possibilities for cross-cultural transaction. For the most part, the traffic in writing went in only one direction. Just as Europeans imported 'raw material drawn from the remotest zones', so they also collected tens of thousands of Oriental, African and Mesoamerican manuscripts to fill the libraries of England, Germany and France, where – like the exotic species on display in the new botanical and zoological gardens that were springing up all over Europe – they served as metonyms for the expanse and impress of colonial power.[38] By contrast, the export of printed books from Europe to regions on the periphery of the modern world-system was minimal at best and, with the exception of the Christian Bible, there was next to no incentive for translation.

From its inception, then, 'world literature' has formed part and parcel of the cultural imaginary of the nineteenth-century European bourgeoisie, not least in its complicity with the larger imperialist designs of the western European nations and, somewhat later, the United States. From the mid-1990s, critics who are again mainly located in countries that make up the core of the modern world-system began to promote world literature as a curricular and programmatic enterprise. In part, this new world literature constitutes a populist response to the encumbrances of postcolonialism which, as Emily Apter observed, had since the 1970s come to serve as a 'code-language elected to speak to the issues of multiculturalism, canon realignment, global decentering, revisionist historiography, identity politics, and cultural hermeneutics'.[39] Curbing these political and ethical imperatives, world literature takes its bearings less from the international division of labour than from the ways in which literary artefacts have come to circulate as commodities across borders and around the globe. David Damrosch, director of Harvard's Institute for World Literature, describes the focus of the field as follows:

> The idea of world literature can usefully continue to mean a subset of the plenum of literature. I take world literature to encompass all literary works that circulate beyond their culture of origin, either in translation or in their original language. In its most expansive sense, world literature could include any work that has ever reached beyond its home base, [though] that work only has an *effective* life as world literature whenever, or wherever, it is actively present within a literary system beyond that of its original culture.[40]

What Damrosch envisions here is a process of *translatio ad infinitum*: a text – *any* text – becomes a piece of world literature when it is *received* into the space of another culture, a space defined by the host culture's national tradition and the present needs of its own writers and readers.[41] In this respect, Damrosch's vision of world literature as a type of perpetual *mouvance*, where Pali, Tibetan, Sogdian, Georgian, Arabic and Geèz can all be jettisoned along the way as the tale moves teleologically towards a Penguin paperback, has its closest affinities with the globalisation of the modern world-system as David Held describes it:

> Globalization can be on a continuum with the local, national and regional. At one end of the continuum lie social and economic relations and networks organized on a local and/or national basis; at the other end lie social and economic relations and networks that crystallize on the wider scale of regional and global interactions.[42]

Damrosch clearly intends to transform the organisation of human affairs 'by linking together and expanding human activity across regions and continents'. Once again, however, cultural capital tends to accrue in only one direction. In discussing the Epic of Gilgamesh, the story that Damrosch has to tell primarily concerns how three British agents – Austen Henry Layard, Hormuzd Rassam and George Smith, who unearthed the Standard Akkadian version of Gilgamesh at Quyunjuk in 1853 – smuggled the clay tablets out of the Ottoman Eyālet-i Mūṣul, transported them to London, and there began the work of translating them into English. What falls out of this account entirely, however, is that these scholars made no attempt to present Gilgamesh to either an Ottoman or an Iraqi audience, as if it were the patrimony of Britain or the world and not of Mesopotamia per se. Writing at the outbreak of the Iraq War, Damrosch describes world literature as 'a mode of reading: a form of *detached* engagement with worlds beyond our own place and time'. Indicatively, however, his narrative of how Europeans rescued Gilgamesh from Muslim negligence, made it available in English, and employed it in this form to validate the truth of the Bible, while it may shed light on nineteenth-century negotiations between Akkadian and Victorian cultures, simultaneously erases Islam, and Iraq in particular, from the global literary map in a way that dovetails uneasily with US military objectives.

The lives of Aḥīqar

The Life of Aḥīqar – arguably the earliest extant piece of novelistic prose – has survived longer than any other work of sapiential literature outside the Hebrew Bible, with a correspondingly extensive distribution throughout the Middle East, the Horn of Africa and the Balkan peninsula. Its earliest known version, written in Old Aramaic, dates to the late sixth century BCE, and it continues to be read in Neo-Aramaic among Assyrian communities today. Attested, then, across two and a half millennia in over twenty different languages – many of which have multiple recensions – the Life of Aḥīqar has proved one of the most popular stories that the Eastern Mediterranean world produced.

The composition is a fictionalised account of a distinguished Assyrian court scholar, comprised of what on linguistic grounds we know were originally two different compositions:[43] an introductory narrative reminiscent of the Joseph cycle in Genesis,[44] coupled with an eclectic set of apothegms closely related to such sapiential literature as Proverbs.[45] The tale, set in the court of Ēsarḥaddōn (681–669 BCE) in Ninwe,[46] recounts the vicissitudes of Aḥīqar, a 'wise and skilful scribe' from Yĕhud, according to Greek ancillary sources,[47] who, despite the Assyrian deportation of Israel's ten northern tribes (c. 720 BCE), 'became counsellor of all ʾAtūr and keeper of [Ēsarḥaddōn's] seal'; the king ordered that 'all the troops of ʾAtūr should rely on his decrees'. Powerful but childless, Aḥīqar grooms his clever nephew Nādin to become his successor, though once appointed to Ēsarḥaddōn's court, Nādin forges documents that accuse Aḥīqar of plotting to 'subvert the land against the king', most maleficently – in less lacunose Aramaic versions of the tale[48] – through false letters enjoining the Shah of Iran and the Pharaoh of Egypt to converge upon Ninwe under arms, in a totalising geographical phantasm from East and West.[49] The incriminating epistles adduced, Aḥīqar escapes forfeiting his head only through the beneficence of the executioner who, concealing the sage in a subterranean vault, produces the body of a decapitated slave instead.[50] Nonetheless, Nādin's political triumph proves short-lived: bereft of Aḥīqar's instructions, Ēsarḥaddōn regrets the precipitateness with which he had 'the father of all ʾAtūr' dispatched.[51] When Nādin's treason comes to light, Aḥīqar re-ascends from the pit, after which the king gratefully restores 'the master of good counsel' to his rightful office, where his first act is to throw the turncoat Nādin into prison. There Nādin passes his days, listening to royal scribes recite the adages that he refused to countenance in his career, in fact the very set of apothegms that follows seriatim directly after the tale: 'Choose the sayings you shall utter, then speak them to your brother to assist him. For the treachery of the mouth is more dangerous than the treachery of battle.'[52]

Despite its resilience, however, the Life of Aḥīqar has – outside the confines of Semitic philology – attracted next to no literary critical attention and, though clearly a piece of 'world literature', fails to appear in any of the supernumerary anthologies of that designation that clutter the marketplace today. This oversight, however, is not difficult to understand.

To begin with, texts such as the Life of Aḥīqar fail to affirm the geocultural investments of any of the literary critical turns that have developed since the nineteenth century within the coordinates of the modern world-system. Given, for example, the linguistic and geographical spread of the corpus, no modern nation could co-opt the Life of Aḥīqar to shore up its national literary history, just as the Eurocentric mission of comparative literature in the post-war period had little use for a set of texts composed outside western Europe in areas that had been peripheral to the modern world-system

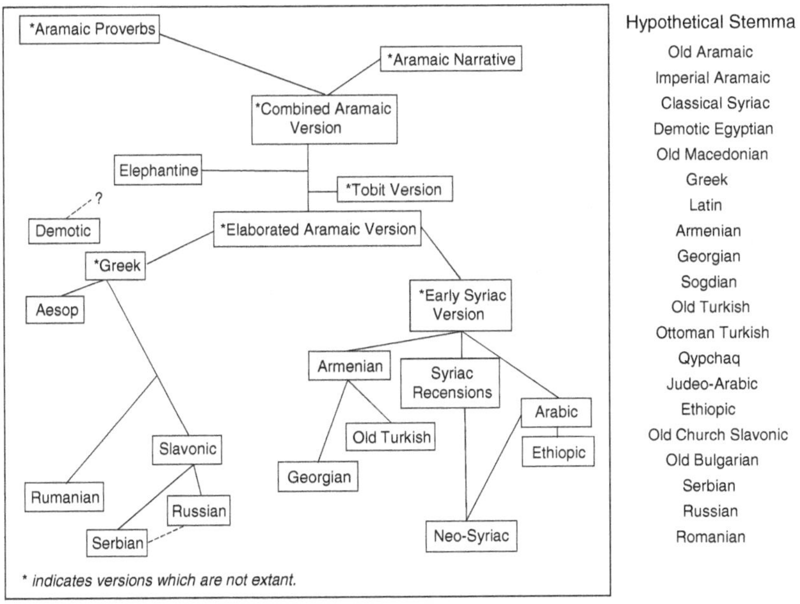

Figure 6.1 Manuscript distribution of the Life of Aḥīqar

for centuries. Similarly, the composition of the Life of Aḥīqar, in the vast majority of its versions, long predates the rise of European hegemony in the sixteenth century, so that the Georgian redaction, for example, a late antique composition that forms part of the Kartlvelian biblical canon, can in no way be construed within the modern world-system's global division of labour. Even Damrosch's programme for the study of how works of literature, in passing from one cultural space into another, become 'the locus of a negotiation between two different cultures',[53] though certainly promising in this context, would nonetheless presume that the thirteenth-century scribe who rendered a fifth-century Syriac version of Aḥīqar into Old Bulgarian knew enough about the anti-Chalcedonian community in Sasanian Iran from which his base text stems to meaningfully negotiate between Antiochene and Eastern Orthodox Christologies.[54] As Basil Lourié has shown, moreover, this mediation takes place largely at a linguistic level which requires, for appreciation, a deep knowledge of both South Slavic and East Syriac dialects, as well as of their orthographic peculiarities. Even if English translations of these two redactions did exist, there would be relatively little to be gained here in simply reading for the plot.

Let me suggest at this point that we turn to a different sort of historical contextualisation that will, I hope, shed a bit more light on the worlding of the Life of Aḥīqar, beginning with its oldest extant version, which survives among the Aramaic papyri produced in Egypt under the first Persian occupation (525–404 BCE). While Pharaonic Egypt developed its own indigenous tradition of court tales that harks back at least as far as the Middle Kingdom (c. 2040–1650 BCE),[55] it was not until Egypt became incorporated as a tributary holding within the rapidly expanding political economy of the Levantine-Mediterranean world-system[56] – a system consolidated under Achaemenid rule and extended through the tributary empires that followed in its wake – that novels with an international horizon began to circulate in Aramaic, Demotic, Greek, Hebrew, Middle Persian, Coptic, Latin and Arabic, each correlative with shifts in the culture of imperial administration. Redacted at the Jewish garrison on Abw (Elephantine Island),[57] along the south-westernmost margin of the Achaemenid domain, and copied over a Memphite customs account dated to 475 BCE, the Old Aramaic Aḥīqar takes as its geographical and historical horizon the compass of the Achaemenid empire of which the Jewish mercenaries in Egypt formed part.[58]

In contrast to the centrist policies circulating out of the Achaemenid satrapy of Yĕhud,[59] the Jewish colony on Abw effectively repudiated both the parochial nationalism of Exodus,[60] whose canonical redaction dates contemporaneously to the first half of the fifth century BCE,[61] as well as the ethnic separatism that the Book of Ezra–Nehemiah (c. 400 BCE) enjoined upon the exiles who had recently returned from Babylon to Jerusalem under the auspices of Cyrus (576–530 BCE):[62] '[The Levites] read to the people from the Book of Moses, and it was found written herein that no Ammonite or Moabite might ever enter the assembly of God ... When the people heard this teaching, they accordingly separated all the alien admixture from Israel' (Neh. 13:1-3). At Abw, by contrast, the Jewish community built its temples – one to Yāhu and one to Yā-hu's consort, the Queen of Heaven – directly beside the Egyptian temple dedicated to the ram-headed god Khnum, the patron deity of Abw.[63] Surviving documents, moreover, attest to considerable social interchange between the two communities, everything from commercial contracts and intermarriage to linguistic hybridisation and religious syncretism.[64] Thus, in a particularly well-preserved letter, the Aramaean Nabušah writes from northern Egypt to his sister Nanaiḥem in the town of Swn.t, just across the river from Abw: 'I blessed you by Ptah that he may let me behold your face in peace. Greetings, Bēytĕlnātan. Greetings to Šabbĕtai, son of Šūg. Greetings to Ša'il, son of Peṭeḥorṭais, and Ašah, son of Peṭekhnum. Greetings to the whole neighborhood!'[65] This multicultural onomastics finds its double in the palimpsest that underlies the Old Aramaic Aḥīqar, which records taxes levied on trans-imperial trade at Memphis, the satrapal seat of the Great King:

> On the 16th of Tybi they inspected for Egypt 1 ship of Somenes, son of Simonides, Ionian. One large ship it is, in accordance with its measurements. The oil which was found in it is oil, 50 jars. The tribute which was collected from it and made over to the house of the king [i.e., Xerxes]: gold, 10 staters of gold, 8 sheqels, 15 hallurs; silver, 10 karsh, 2 hallurs, 2 quarters.[66]

Crown agents, presumably from Yĕhud, imposed tariffs here on a Greek merchant transporting oil from the satrapy of Yaunā (Iōnia) to the satrapy of Mudrāya (Egypt), which they remitted, probably by way of the royal treasury at Memphis, to the household of the Great King at Susa in Elam.[67] Performed by day and month of the Egyptian calendar,[68] each entry weighs the tribute according to a mixture of Greek and Akkadian denominations,[69] thereby macaronically preserving local specificities,[70] at the same time that the registry sublates them within the totality of the non-homogenised, though clearly hierarchising, Achaemenid politico-economic space.[71]

Not only, then, do the customs account and the Life of Aḥīqar adumbrate the same geopolitical horizons; the tax records exemplify the basic sorts of economic transactions upon which the administrative, political and military organisation of the empire that the narrative imagines rests, where the ''Atūr' of the tale – by the mid-fifth century BCE – functions principally as a trope for the Achaemenid regime. That a provincial scribe, stationed on the outposts of the Achaemenid domain, should redact a tale about the meteoric rise of a fellow Aramaean who becomes not only master of his profession, but chief official at the court of Ēsarḥaddōn, speaks for itself as fantasmatic inspiration.[72] Above all, however, what the Life of Aḥīqar idealises is the potential for mobility – geographical, social and economic – within the Assyrian and Achaemenid tributary states. Under Ēsarḥaddōn, therefore, the scribal calling appears as a *carrière ouverte à tout talent*; unlike Mārĕdāeai in the closely related Hebrew Esther, Aḥīqar's enemies are not 'Amalekites' – the archetypal assailants who attempt to obstruct the Hebrew people in their pilgrimage from Egypt to Sinai[73] – but his own Aramaic kin. Assyrians of all classes, from executioner to king, prove Aḥīqar's greatest champions at court, in effect to emphasise that within the multi-ethnic arena of the empire – whether in Egypt, Aššūr or Elam – foreigners were as often as not allies, well-wishers and friends. So Aḥīqar questions in the adages:

> My own son spied out my house, what shall I say to strangers? He bore false witness against me; who, then, will declare me innocent? My poisoner came from my own house; before whom can I press my complaint?[74]

Lest the litigant avail himself, however, too hastily of imperial redress, Aḥīqar concomitantly stresses that 'A king's word is gentle, but keener and more cutting than a double-edged sword … His anger is swifter than lightning: look out for yourself!'[75] Here we see the importance of the Sayings to the romance as a whole: distilling the distinctive plotting of the narrative into a set of ideological propositions that appear, as Louis Althusser put it, 'to have no history in themselves',[76] they allow the tale to circulate throughout the empire in its entirety as a parable, ubiquitously valid irrespective of time, ethnicity or place.[77] Just as the triumph of the protagonist at the court of Ēsarḥaddōn vouches for the aptitude of Aḥīqar's adages as 'wisdom',[78] so the apothegms – which retain no more than superficial local references[79] – asymmetrically allow the narrative to exceed its function as a historical account of the splendours and miseries of an Assyrian imperial career.

The Life of Aḥīqar, Eduard Meyer observed in 1912, is 'the oldest book of world literature, internationally diffused through the most disparate tongues and diverse peoples'. What propels the worlding of this text, however, for which no two redactions are the same, has nothing to do with the global flow of cultural capital, but rather with the political and cultural dynamics of the tributary state, that is, the pre-capitalist political formation under which scribes produced all known versions of the work. Not only does the Abw-papyrus emplot the story of what Lawrence Wills calls the 'counselor in the court of the foreign king', redacted specifically for a displaced community within the multicultural conglomeration that constituted both the Assyrian and the Achaemenid states; the Life of Aḥīqar specifically thematises the confrontation that these empires afforded between the peoples, polities and cultures of Aram, Assyria, Iran, Egypt and Yĕhud, a confrontation played out in the linguistic tension between Eastern and Western Aramaic, as well as in the Akkadian loan-words that fill the tale. Like the empire that the novel represents, then, the Abw Life of Aḥīqar is nothing so much as a site for the cohabitation, condensation and displacement of ethnically specific speech genres, whose imbrication propels the reader from one culturally embedded literary formation to the next. The reception history of the narrative, as scribes recast it from one language and for one community after another, is thus nothing more than the historical realisation of the devices of culturo-linguistic crossing that are already thematised and enacted in the Abw-papyrus itself.

In conclusion, then, works of distributed authorship such as the Life of Aḥīqar are in no way marginal to world literature, if what we mean by that are works of ecumenical dissemination; rather, they constitute its core. As Richard Parkinson has pointed out, 'The modern reader is accustomed to reproductive transmission, as against a productive transmission by which texts are copied and recast in terms of their type and function.' For the most part, however, the increasingly numerous anthologies that claim to represent 'world literature' turn out to be little more than compilations of works that contemporary Euro-American readers consider to be other cultures' greatest literary achievements, thereby in effect retrojecting post-Gutenberg norms of reproducibility back on to what I have elsewhere called 'text networks', that is, corpora of literary works that proliferate cross-culturally through the productive transmission and transformation of the text.[80] Within this field, however, the Life of Aḥīqar constitutes something of an exemplary composition. In the first place, synchronically, the Life of Aḥīqar affords what Martin Heidegger called a 'world picture' (*Weltbild*) of its era. That is, the tale aims to represent the fundamental bases – political, economic, social, ideational – upon which its age, the age of tributary empires, established its fundamental constitution (*Wesensgrund*). And second, diachronically, the Life of Aḥīqar – unlike Gilgamesh which never passed beyond the confines of cuneiform culture – has over the course of the past two and a half millennia found its place in virtually every literary culture and lent itself to every form of writing system that flourished within the pre-capitalist Levantine-Mediterranean world-system, that is, effectively the better part of the Afro-Eurasian land mass west of the Zagros mountains. Historically, there can be no doubt that in terms of its vitality and geographical spread, the Life of Aḥīqar remains the more successful work.

Damrosch praises Gilgamesh for 'its profound psychological insight into the human fear of death', which he compares to the profundity of the Homeric epics – still, as they were for Goethe, the touchstone of literary excellence. By contrast, however, the Life of Aḥīqar declines to brood over mortality. Rather, like Petronius' 'Matron of Ephesus' or Shakespeare's *The Winter's Tale*, the story that the Life of Aḥīqar has to tell represents the triumph of life over death, a preoccupation which places it, in the terminology of Mikhail Bakhtin, among the earliest pieces of novelistic prose. My intention here is by no means to promote the Life of Aḥīqar as a 'better' representative of world literature than Gilgamesh. Nonetheless, the question with which I would like to conclude is why Gilgamesh appears in every anthology of world literature that I have seen, while texts such as Aḥīqar, the Alexander Romance, Barlaam and Ioasaph, Kalilah wa-Dimnah or Joseph and Aseneth find no place either in these anthologies or in the academic discipline of World Literature at all.

Notes

1 See Kristin Ross, 'The World Literature and Cultural Studies Program', *Critical Inquiry* 19 (1993): 666–76.

2 See https://ars.electronica.art/aeblog/en/?s=Ascott (accessed 14 August 2020).

3 Roy Ascott, 'Art and Telematics: Toward a Network Consciousness', in H. Grundmann (ed.), *Art + Telecommunication* (Vancouver: The Western Front, 1984), pp. 25–67, and Roy Ascott, 'Distance Makes the Art Grow Further: Distributed Authorship and Telematic Textuality in "La Plissure du Texte"', in A. Chandler and N. Neumark (eds), *At a Distance: Precursors to Art and Activism on the Internet* (Boston, MA: MIT Press, 2005), pp. 282–97.

4 Marie Chatel, 'New Media Precursor: Roy Ascott', *Digital Art Weekly*, 12 October 2018, https://arts-et-medias.net/en/articles/essays/new-media-precursor-roy-ascott (accessed 9 January 2022).

5 Roy Ascott, *La Plissure du Texte: A Planetary Fairy Tale* (1983). See also Ascott, 'Distance Makes the Art Grow Further'.

6 See J. L. Borges, *El jardín de senderos que se bifurcan* (Buenos Aires: Sur, 1941). See also Paul Delaney and George Landow, *Hypermedia and Literary Studies* (Cambridge, MA: MIT Press, 1991); Noah Wardrip-Fruin and Nick Montfort (eds), *The New Media Reader* (Cambridge, MA: MIT Press, 2003).

7 See Elza Adamowicz, *Surrealist Collage in Text and Image: Dissecting the Exquisite Corpse* (Cambridge: Cambridge University Press, 1998); and Kanta Kochhar-Lindgren et al., *The Exquisite Corpse: Chance and Collaboration in Surrealism's Parlor Game* (Lincoln, NE: University of Nebraska Press, 2009). For a recent example, see Apichatpong Weerasethakul's celebrated film *Dokfa nai meuman* [Eng.: *Mysterious Object at Noon*] (Thailand, 2000).

8 Roland Barthes, *Le plaisir du texte* (Paris: Seuil, 1973), pp. 100–1.

9 Axel Bruns, 'Distributed Creativity: Filesharing and Produsage', in S. Sonvil-la-Weiss (ed.), *Mashup Cultures* (Vienna: Ambra, 2010), pp. 24–37.

10 Axel Bruns, *Blogs, Wikipedia, Second Life and Beyond: From Production to Produsage* (New York: Peter Lang, 2008).

11 Axel Bruns, 'Towards Produsage: Futures for User-Led Content Production', in C. Ess et al. (eds), *Proceeding of the 5th International Conference on Cultural Attitudes towards Technology and Communication* (Perth, WA: Murdoch University, 2006), pp. 275–84; Axel Bruns and J.-H. Schmidt, 'Produsage: A Closer Look at Continuing Developments', *New Review of Hypermedia and Multimedia* 17 (2010): 3–7.

12 Hayden White, *The Fiction of Narrative: Essays on History, Literature, and Theory 1957–2007*, ed. R. Doran (Baltimore, MD: Johns Hopkins University Press, 2010), pp. 255–62.

13 See Anne Jamison et al., *Fic: Why Fanfiction is Taking over the World* (Dallas, TX: BenBella, 2014); Jonathan Gray et al. (eds), *Fandom: Identities and Communities in a Mediated World*, 2nd edn (New York: New York University Press, 2017); Kristina Busse, *Framing Fan Fiction: Literary and Social Practices in Fan Fiction Communities* (Iowa City, IA: University of Iowa Press, 2017); Ashton Spacey (ed.), *The Darker Side of Slash Fan Fiction: Essays on Power, Consent and the Body* (Jefferson, NC: McFarland, 2018).

14 A currently trending body of fanfic reworks James Ivory's and Luca Guadagnino's 2017 film *Chiamami col tuo nome/Call me by Your Name* (Sony Pictures Classics), whose unresolved ending has spawned multiple re-edits and music videos now available YouTube, TikTok and other websites, as well as sequels such as *Call Me by Your Name 2* in which Elio flies from Italy to the US to visit Oliver and his wife.

15 Sean Cubitt, 'From Internationalism to Transnations: Networked Art and Activism', in C. Ess et al. (eds), *Proceeding of the 5th International Conference on Cultural Attitudes towards Technology and Communication* (Perth, WA: Murdoch University, 2005), pp. 434–35.

16 Daniel Heller-Roazen (ed.), *The Arabian Nights*, trans. H. Haddawy (New York: W. W. Norton, 2010), p. viii. For an overview of the collection's metamorphoses, see Dwight F. Reynolds, '*A Thousand and One Nights*: A History of the Text and its Reception', in Roger Allen and D. S. Richards (eds), *The Cambridge History of Arabic Literature: The Post-Classical Period* (Cambridge: Cambridge University Press, 2006), pp. 270–91. For the European editions of the text and the nineteenth-century Arabic printings, see Muhsin Mahdi, *The Thousand and One Nights* (Leiden: Brill, 1995).

17 See Limor Shifman, *Memes in Digital Culture* (Boston, MA: MIT Press, 2013), which takes PSY's 'Gangnam Style' as its principal example (pp. 1– 8).

18 See Hayden White, *Tropics of Discourse: Essays in Cultural Criticism* (Baltimore, MD: Johns Hopkins University Press, 1986); E. J. Bryan,

Collaborative Meaning in Medieval Scribal Culture (Ann Arbor, MI: University of Michigan Press, 1999); Vincent Miller, *Understanding Digital Culture*, 2nd edn (London: Sage, 2020).

19 Henry P. Colburn, 'Globalization and the Study of the Achaemenid Persian Empire', in T. Hodos et al. (eds), *The Routledge Handbook of Archaeology and Globalization* (Abingdon: Routledge, 2017), pp. 871–84. See also Henry P. Colburn, 'Connectivity and Communications in the Achaemenid Empire', *Journal of the Economic and Social History of the Orient*, 56 (2013): 29–52.

20 See, inter alia, David Harvey, *The Condition of Postmodernity: An Enquiry into the Origins of Cultural Change* (Malden, MA: Blackwell, 1990); Fredric Jameson, *Postmodernism, or, The Cultural Logic of Late Capitalism* (Durham, NC: Duke University Press, 1992); David Holmes, *Virtual Globalization: Virtual Spaces/Tourist Spaces* (London: Routledge, 2001); W. E. Murray and J. Overton, *Geographies of Globalization*, 2nd edn (Abingdon: Routledge, 2015).

21 See, for example, David Damrosch, *The Buried Book: The Loss and Rediscovery of the Great Epic of Gilgamesh* (New York: Henry Holt, 2006). There is now a large bibliography on scribal culture in the ancient Near East and beyond. In this context, see particularly Karel van der Toorn, *Scribal Culture and the Making of the Hebrew Bible* (Cambridge, MA: Harvard University Press 2009); Sara J. Milstein, *Tracking the Master Scribe: Revision through Introduction in Biblical and Mesopotamian Literature* (Oxford: Oxford University Press, 2016); JiSeong James Kwon, *Scribal Culture and Intertextuality: Literary and Historical Relationships between Job and Deutero-Isaiah* (Tübingen: Mohr Siebeck 2016); Daisuke Shibata and Shigeo Yamata, *Cultures and Societies in the Middle Euphrates and Habur Areas in the Second Millennium BC – I: Scribal Education and Scribal Traditions* (Wiesbaden: Harrassowitz, 2016); Anneli Aejmelaeus et al. (eds), *From Scribal Error to Rewriting: How Ancient Texts Could and Could Not Be Changed* (Göttingen: Anechoic and Ruprecht, 2020); Molly Zahn, *Genres of Rewriting in Second Temple Judaism: Scribal Composition and Transmission* (Cambridge: Cambridge University Press, 2020).

22 Jeffrey Tigay, *The Evolution of the Gilgamesh Epic* (Philadelphia, PA: University of Pennsylvania Press, 1982); Andrew R. George (ed.), *The Babylonian Gilgamesh Epic: Introduction, Critical Edition and Cuneiform Texts*, 2 vols (Oxford: Oxford University Press, 2003).

23 William Wordsworth, *Lyrical Ballads, with Other Poems*, 2 vols, 2nd edn (London: T. N. Longman and O. Rees, 1800), vol. I, p. xxxiii. See further Jack Stillinger, *Multiple Authorship and the Myth of Solitary Genius* (New York: Oxford University Press, 1991).

24 Jed Wyrick, *The Ascension of Authorship: Attribution and Canon Formation in Jewish, Hellenistic, and Christian Traditions* (Cambridge, MA: Harvard University Press, 2004).
25 I take these phrases respectively from Bryan, *Collaborative Meaning in Medieval Scribal Culture*, and David F. Elmer, *The Poetics of Consent: Collective Decision Making and the Iliad* (Baltimore, MD: Johns Hopkins University Press, 2013).
26 Samuel N. Kramer, *History Begins at Sumer* (London: Thames and Hudson, 1961), p. 270.
27 Standard Babylonian Version I.9–10; translation: Andrew R. George, *The Epic of Gilgamesh: The Babylonian Epic Poem and Other Texts in Akkadian and Sumerian*, 3rd edn (London: Penguin, 2003), p. 1.
28 Edgar Allan Poe, 'Ms. Found in a Bottle', *Visitor*, 9 October 1833. Versions of this topos appear variously in the Demotic Egyptian tale *Setne Khamwas I*, Antonius Diogenes' *Wonders Beyond Thule*, Chretien de Troyes' *Cligès* and Nathaniel Hawthorne's *The Scarlet Letter*, among many other texts.
29 George, *The Epic of Gilgamesh*, p. 2.
30 See Sarah Searight, *Lapis Lazuli: In Pursuit of a Celestial Stone* (London: East & West Publishing, 2010).
31 Cf. Harold Bloom, *The Daemon Knows: Literary Greatness and the American Sublime* (New York: Spiegel and Grau, 2016), p. 34.
32 Paul De Man, *Allegories of Reading: Figural Language in Rousseau, Nietzsche, Rilke and Proust* (New Haven, CT: Yale University Press 1979), p. 8. See also Jacques Derrida, *De la grammatologie* (Paris: Minuit, 1967).
33 See Susan Sontag, *Against Interpretation and Other Essays* (New York: Farrar, Straus, and Giroux, 1966).
34 See Jacques Lacan, *Le Séminaire, Livre II: Le moi dans la théorie de Freud et dans la technique de la psychanalyse, 1954–1955*, ed. Jacques-Alain Miller (Paris: Éditions du Seuil, 1978).
35 See https://member.ancient.eu/gilgamesh/ (accessed 9 January 2022).
36 See, in particular, David Damrosch, *What is World Literature?* (Princeton, NJ: Princeton University Press, 2003), and Damrosch, *The Buried Book*.
37 www.marxists.org/archive/marx/works/1848/communist-manifesto/ch01.htm (accessed 8 February 2022).
38 Wilfrid Blunt, *The Ark in the Park: The Zoo in the Nineteenth Century* (London: Hamish Hamilton, 1976); Irus Braverman, *Zooland: The Institution of Captivity* (Stanford, CA: Stanford University Press, 2012).
39 Emily Apter, 'French Colonial Studies and Postcolonial Theory', *SubStance* 24 (1995): 169.
40 Damrosch, *What is World Literature?*, p. 4.

41 Ibid., p. 283.
42 D. Held, A. G. McGrew, D. Goldblatt and J. Perraton (eds), *Global Transformations: Politics, Economics, and Culture* (Stanford, CA: Stanford University Press, 1999).
43 For philological distinctions between the two parts of the composition, see Ingo Kottsieper, *Die Sprache der Ahiqarsprüche* (Berlin: De Gruyter, 1990).
44 Genesis 39–50; see, inter alia, Susan Niditch and Robert Doran, 'The Success Story of the Wise Courtier: A Formal Approach', *Journal of Biblical Literature* 96 (1977): 179–93.
45 See James Lindenberger, *The Aramaic Proverbs of Ahiqar* (Baltimore, MD: Johns Hopkins University Press, 1983); Jonas C. Greenfield, 'The Wisdom of Ahiqar', in J. Day et al. (eds), *Wisdom in Ancient Israel* (Cambridge: Cambridge University Press, 1998), pp. 43–54; M. Weigl, *Die aramäischen Achikar-Sprüche aus Elephantine und die alttestamentliche Weisheits- literature* (Berlin: De Gruyter, 2010).
46 Or perhaps Bābilim; Esarhaddon moved the Assyrian capital from Ninwe to Bābilim. Recensions vary as to which of these cities marks the locus for the action, though in terms of symbolic geography their significance remains the same; see Alison Salvesen, 'The Legacy of Babylon and Nineveh in Aramaic Sources', in S. Dallie (ed.), *The Legacy of Mesopotamia* (Oxford: Oxford University Press, 1968), pp. 139–61.
47 Tobit 1:21ff. See further Jonas Greenfield, 'Ahiqar in the Book of Tobit', in M. Carrez et al. (eds), *De la Torah au Messie* (Paris: Desclée, 1981), pp. 329–36; Lothar Ruppert, 'Zum Funktion der Achikar-Notizen im Buch Tobias', *Biblische Zeitschrift* NS 20 (1976): 232–7; Henri Cazelles, 'Le Personnage d'Achior dans le livre de Judith', *Recherche de science religieuse* 39 (1951): 125–37.
48 See F. Nau, *Histoire et Sagesse d'Ahiqar l'Assyrien* (Paris: Letouzey et Ané, 1909).
49 While Assyria never succeeded in absorbing Iran or Egypt into its empire, readers of the fifth century BCE would certainly have recognised Bābilim/Ninwe as centred within the Achaemenid domain, while Persia and Egypt represent its outer limits.
50 The Elephantine redaction breaks off at this point. For the reconstruction of the conclusion, see Lindenberger, *The Aramaic Proverbs of Ahiqar*.
51 Bezalal Porten and Ada Yardeni, *Textbook of Aramaic Documents from Ancient Egypt* (Jerusalem: Eisenbrauns, 1986–93), vol. III, p. 32.
52 Ibid., vol. III, p. 36.
53 Damrosch, *What is World Literature?*, p. 283.
54 See Basil Lourié, 'The Syriac *Ahiqar*, its Slavonic Version, and the Relics of the Three Youths in Babylon', *Slověne* 2 (2013): 64–117.

55 See Antonio Loprieno (ed.), *Ancient Egyptian Literature: History and Forms* (Leiden: Brill, 1996); Richard Parkinson, *Poetry and Culture in the Middle Kingdom: A Dark Side to Perfection* (London: Continuum, 2002); Stephen Quirke, *Egyptian Literature 1800 BC: Questions and Readings* (London: Golden House Publications, 2004).

56 On the ancient Levant and East Mediterranean as a cohesive world-system, see Samir Amin, 'The Ancient World Systems versus the Modern Capitalist World System', *Review* 14 (1991), 349–585; C. Chase-Dunn and T. Hall (eds), *Core/Periphery Relations in Precapitalist Worlds*, 2nd edn (Boulder, CO: Westview Press, 1991); Michael Rowlands et al. (eds), *Centre and Periphery in the Ancient World* (Cambridge: Cambridge University Press, 1987); Gil Stein, *Rethinking World-Systems: Diasporas, Colonies, and Interaction in Uruk Mesopotamia* (Tucson, AZ: University of Arizona Press, 1999); R. Denemark et al. (eds), *World System History* (London: Routledge, 2000); Immanuel Wallerstein, *World Systems Analysis: An Introduction* (Durham, NC: Duke University Press, 2004); Guillermo Algaze, *The Uruk World System*, 2nd edn (Chicago: University of Chicago Press, 2005); C. Chase-Dunn and E. Anderson, *The Historical Evolution of World-Systems* (New York: Palgrave, 2005).

57 See Bezalal Porten et al., *The Elephantine Papyri in English: Three Millennia of Cross-Cultural Continuity and Change* (Leiden: Brill, 1968); Joseph Modrzejewski, *Les Juifs d'Égypte de Ramesses II à Hadrien* (Paris: PUF, 1992); Bezalal Porten, *Archives from Elephantine: The Life of an Ancient Jewish Military Colony* (Berkeley, CA: University of California Press, 1996); Edward Bleiberg, *Jewish Life in Ancient Egypt: A Family Archive from the Nile Valley* (New York: Brooklyn Museum of Art, 2002); Albin van Hoonacker, *Une communauté judéo-araméenne à Éléphantine, en Égypte, aux 6e et 5e siècles av. J.-C.* (Toronto: University of Toronto, 2011 [1915]).

58 For Aramaic as the lingua franca of the period, see Jonas C. Greenfield, 'Aramaic in the Achaemenian Empire', in I. Gershevitch (ed.), *The Cambridge History of Iran* (Cambridge: Cambridge University Press, 1985), vol. II, pp. 698–713.

59 See Melody Knowles, *Centrality Practiced: Jerusalem in the Religious Practice of Yehud and the Diaspora in the Persian Period* (Atlanta, GA: Society of Biblical Literature, 2006).

60 So Barbara Johnson, *Moses and Multiculturalism* (Berkeley, CA: University of California Press, 2010), p. 1: '[Exodus is] the most nationalist … of all foundation narratives.' See further Lawrence Wills, *Not God's People: Insiders and Outsiders in the Biblical World* (Lanham, MD: Rowman and Littlefield, 2008), pp. 21–51.

61 For a good summary treatment, see William Propp, *Exodus 1–18* (New York: Doubleday, 1999), pp. 47–52. For the integrity of the book divorced from its later positioning within the Pentateuch, see E. Theodore Mullen, *Ethnic Myths and Pentateuchal Foundations* (Atlanta, GA: Scholars Press, 1997), pp. 163–6. On the Aleppo Codex, the earliest surviving manuscript of the book, see M. Goshen-Gottstein, 'The Aleppo Codex and the Rise of the Massoretic Bible Text', *The Biblical Archaeologist* 42 (1979): 145–63; Adrian Schenker, *The Earliest Text of the Hebrew Bible* (Atlanta, GA: Society of Biblical Literature, 2003).

62 See Wills, *Not God's People*, pp. 53–86.

63 See Porten et al., *The Elephantine Papyri*, pp. 105–99; Anke Joisten-Pruschke, *Das religiöse Leben der Juden von Elephantinien der Achämenidenzeit* (Wiesbaden: Harrassowitz, 2008).

64 For summation, see variously Porten et al., *The Elephantine Papyri*, pp. 173–9, 249–52; Porten, *Archives from Elephantine*, pp. 12–27; Takamitsu Muraoka and Bezalal Porten, *A Grammar of Egyptian Aramaic* (Leiden: Brill, 1998), pp. 378–80; Alejandro Botta, *Aramaic and Egyptian Legal Traditions at Elephantine* (New York: T. & T. Clark, 2009). Babylonians, Caspians, Khorazmians, Medes and Persians are also attested as members of the community (Porten et al., *The Elephantine Papyri*, p. 29).

65 Porten and Yardeni, *Textbook of Aramaic Documents*, vol. I, p. 10, condensed. On the Jewish onomastics, see Porten et al., *The Elephantine Papyri*, pp. 133–50.

66 Porten and Yardeni, *Textbook of Aramaic Documents*, vol. III, pp. 94ff., condensed. For the port in question, see vol. III, pp. xx–xxi.

67 Or at least this is one way to construe the geographical connections that the record lays out; that there are various scenarios, however, only foregrounds the complexity of the possible trans-imperial connections. For the satrapies of the Persian empire, see J. Junge, 'Satrapie und Natio', *Clio* 34 (1942): 1–55; A. Toynbee, 'The Administrative Geography of the Achaemenian Empire', in *A Study in History* (Oxford: Oxford University Press, 1954), vol. VII, pp. 580–689; W. Vogelgesang, *The Rise and Organization of the Achaemenid Empire* (Leiden: Brill, 1992).

68 For the Egyptian calendar, see Richard Parker, *The Calendars of Ancient Egypt* (Chicago: University of Chicago Press, 1950); Leo Depuydt, *Civil and Lunar Calendar in Ancient Egypt* (Leuven: Peeters, 1977).

69 See A. D. H. Bivar, 'Achaemenid Coins, Weights, and Measures', in I. Gershevitch (ed.), *The Cambridge History of Iran* (Cambridge: Cambridge University Press, 1985), vol. II, pp. 610–39.

70 On the non-Aramaic technical terms in the account, see A. Yardeni, 'Maritime Trade and Royal Accountancy in an Erased Customs Account

from 475 B.C.E. on the Aḥīqar Scroll from Elephantine', *Bulletin of the American Schools of Oriental Research* 293 (1994): 67–78.

71 For the economy of the Achaemenid empire, see Pierre Briant, *Lois, tributs et paysans* (Paris: Belles Lettres, 1982); Morris Silver, *Economic Structures of the Ancient Near East* (Totowa, NJ: Croom Helm, 1985); Christopher Tuplin, 'The Administration of the Achaemenid Empire', in I. Carradice (ed.), *Coinage and Administration in the Athenian and Persian Empires* (Oxford: Oxford University Press, 1987), pp. 109–66; Pierre Briant and C. Herrenschmidt (eds), *Le Tribut dans l'empire perse* (Paris: Peeters, 1989); Muhammad Dandamaev and Vladimir Lukonin, *The Culture and Social Institutions of Ancient Iran* (Cambridge: Cambridge University Press, 1989).

72 In the wake of Sennacherib's deportation of the Northern Israelite state in the generation immediately preceding Esarhaddon, it also becomes possible to read the Life of Aḥīqar as a type of nationalist allegory; cf. *mutatis mutandis*, Jameson, *Allegory and Ideology*, pp. 156–216.

73 See Exod. 17; Esth. 3:1; Mark Smith, *The Pilgrimage Pattern in Exodus* (Sheffield: Sheffield Academic Press, 1997).

74 Porten and Yardeni, *Textbook of Aramaic Documents*, vol. III, p. 42.

75 Ibid., vol. III, p. 36.

76 Louis Althusser, 'Ideology and Ideological State Apparatuses', in *Lenin and Philosophy, and Other Essays*, trans. B. Brewster (New York: Monthly Review Press, 1971), pp. 159–62.

77 For Aramaic as the lingua franca of the Persian empire, see R. Frye, 'Review of G. R. Driver's "Aramaic Documents of the Fifth Century B. C."', *Harvard Journal of Asiatic Studies* 18 (1955): 456–61; Klaus Beyer, *The Aramaic Language: Its Distribution and Subdivisions* (Göttingen: Vandenhoeck and Ruprecht, 1986).

78 See Weigl, *Die aramäischen Achikar-Sprüche aus Elephantine.*

79 Cf. the references to the deities Shamash and El – some scholars take these to be traces of an earlier Akkadian *Vorlage*, others as superficial references designed to link the apothegms to the Assyrian setting of the tale; see James Lindenberger, 'Ahiqar', in J. H. Charlesworth (ed.), *The Old Testament Pseudepigrapha* (New York: Doubleday, 1985), vol. II, pp. 479–507.

80 Daniel Selden, 'Text Networks', *Ancient Narrative* 8 (2010): 1–23.

Works cited

Adamowicz, Elza, *Surrealist Collage in Text and Image: Dissecting the Exquisite Corpse* (Cambridge: Cambridge University Press, 1998).

Aejmelaeus, Anneli, et al. (eds), *From Scribal Error to Rewriting: How Ancient Texts Could and Could Not Be Changed* (Göttingen: Anechoic and Ruprecht, 2020).

Algaze, Guillermo, *The Uruk World System* (Chicago: University of Chicago Press, 2005).

Althusser, Louis, 'Ideology and Ideological State Apparatuses', in *Lenin and Philosophy, and Other Essays*, trans. B. Brewster (New York: Monthly Review Press, 1971), pp. 159–62.

Amin, Samir, 'The Ancient World Systems versus the Modern Capitalist World System', *Review* 14 (1991): 349–585.

Apter, Emily, 'French Colonial Studies and Postcolonial Theory', *SubStance* 24 (1995): 169–80.

Ascott, Roy, 'Art and Telematics: Toward a Network Consciousness', in H. Grundmann (ed.), *Art + Telecommunication* (Vancouver: The Western Front, 1984), pp. 25–67.

— 'Distance Makes the Art Grow Further: Distributed Authorship and Telematic Textuality in "La Plissure du Texte"', in A. Chandler and N. Neumark (eds), *At a Distance: Precursors to Art and Activism on the Internet* (Boston, MA: MIT Press, 2005), pp. 282–97.

Barthes, Roland, *Le plaisir du texte* (Paris: Seuil, 1973).

Beyer, Klaus, *The Aramaic Language: Its Distribution and Subdivisions* (Göttingen: Vandenhoeck and Ruprecht, 1986).

Bivar, A. D. H., 'Achaemenid Coins, Weights, and Measures', in I. Gershevitch (ed.), *The Cambridge History of Iran* (Cambridge: Cambridge University Press, 1985), vol. II, pp. 610–39.

Bleiberg, Edward, *Jewish Life in Ancient Egypt: A Family Archive from the Nile Valley* (New York: Brooklyn Museum of Art, 2002).

Bloom, Harold, *The Daemon Knows: Literary Greatness and the American Sublime* (New York: Spiegel and Grau, 2016).

Blunt, Wilfrid J. W., *The Ark in the Park: The Zoo in the Nineteenth Century* (London: Hamish Hamilton, 1976).

Borges, Jorge. Luis, *El jardín de senderos que se bifurcan* (Buenos Aires: Sur, 1941).

Botta, Alejandro, *Aramaic and Egyptian Legal Traditions at Elephantine* (New York: T. & T. Clark, 2009).

Braverman, Irus, *Zooland: The Institution of Captivity* (Stanford, CA: Stanford University Press, 2012).

Briant, Pierre, *Lois, tributs et paysans* (Paris: Belles Lettres, 1982).

Briant, Pierre, and C. Herrenschmidt (eds), *Le Tribut dans l'empire perse* (Paris: Peeters, 1989).

Bruns, Axel, 'Towards Produsage: Futures for User-Led Content Production', in C. Ess et al. (eds), *Proceeding of the 5th International Conference on Cultural Attitudes towards Technology and Communication* (Perth, WA: Murdoch University, 2006), pp. 275–84.

— *Blogs, Wikipedia, Second Life and Beyond: From Production to Produsage* (New York: Peter Lang, 2008).

— 'Distributed Creativity: Filesharing and Produsage', in S. Sonvil-la-Weiss (ed.), *Mashup Cultures* (Vienna: Ambra, 2010), pp. 24–37.
Bruns, Axel, and J.-H. Schmidt, 'Produsage: A Closer Look at Continuing Developments', *New Review of Hypermedia and Multimedia* 17 (2010): 3–7.
Bryan, E. J., *Collaborative Meaning in Medieval Scribal Culture: The Otho La3amon* (Ann Arbor, MI: University of Michigan Press, 1999).
Busse, Kristina, *Framing Fan Fiction: Literary and Social Practices in Fan Fiction Communities* (Iowa City, IA: University of Iowa Press, 2017).
Cazelles, Henri, 'Le Personnage d'Achior dans le livre de Judith', *Recherche de science religieuse* 39 (1951): 125–37.
Chase-Dunn, C., and E. Anderson, *The Historical Evolution of World-Systems* (New York: Palgrave, 2005).
Chase-Dunn, C., and T. Hall (eds), *Core/Periphery Relations in Precapitalist Worlds*, 2nd edn (Boulder, CO: Westview Press, 1991).
Chatel, Marie, 'New Media Precursor: Roy Ascott', *Digital Art Weekly*, 12 October 2018, https://arts-et-medias.net/en/articles/essays/new-media-precursor-roy-ascott (accessed 9 January 2022).
Colburn, Henry P., 'Connectivity and Communications in the Achaemenid Empire', *Journal of the Economic and Social History of the Orient* 56 (2013): 29–52.
— 'Globalization and the Study of the Achaemenid Persian Empire', in T. Hodos et al. (eds), *The Routledge Handbook of Archaeology and Globalization* (Abingdon: Routledge, 2017), pp. 871–84.
Cubitt, Sean, 'From Internationalism to Transnations: Networked Art and Activism', in C. Ess et al. (eds). *Proceeding of the 5th International Conference on Cultural Attitudes towards Technology and Communication* (Perth, WA: Murdoch University, 2006), pp. 425–35.
Damrosch, David, *What is World Literature?* (Princeton, NJ: Princeton University Press, 2003).
— *The Buried Book: The Loss and Recovery of the Great Epic of Gilgamesh* (New York: Henry Holt, 2007).
Dandamaev, Muhammad, and Vladimir Lukonin, *The Culture and Social Institutions of Ancient Iran* (Cambridge: Cambridge University Press, 1989).
Delaney, Paul, and George Landow (eds), *Hypermedia and Literary Studies* (Cambridge, MA: MIT Press, 1991).
De Man, Paul, *Allegories of Reading: Figural Language in Rousseau, Nietzsche, Rilke and Proust* (New Haven, CT: Yale University Press, 1979).
Denemark, R. A., et al. (eds), *World System History* (London: Routledge, 2000).
Depuydt, Leo, *Civil and Lunar Calendar in Ancient Egypt* (Leuven: Peeters, 1977).
Derrida, Jacques, *De la grammatologie* (Paris: Minuit, 1967).
Elmer, David F., *The Poetics of Consent: Collective Decision Making and the Iliad* (Baltimore, MD: Johns Hopkins University Press, 2013).

Frye, Richard N., 'Review of G. R. Driver's "Aramaic Documents of the Fifth Century B. C."', *Harvard Journal of Asiatic Studies* 18 (1955): 456–61.
George, Andrew R.(trans.), *The Epic of Gilgamesh: The Babylonian Epic Poem and Other Texts in Akkadian and Sumerian* (London: Penguin, 2003).
— (ed.), *The Babylonian Gilgamesh Epic: Introduction, Critical Edition and Cuneiform Texts*, 2 vols (Oxford: Oxford University Press, 2003).
Goshen-Gottstein, M., 'The Aleppo Codex and the Rise of the Massoretic Bible Text', *The Biblical Archaeologist* 42 (1979): 145–63.
Gray, Jonathan, et al. (eds), *Fandom: Identities and Communities in a Mediated World*, 2nd edn (New York: New York University Press, 2017).
Greenfield, Jonas C., 'Ahiqar in the Book of Tobit', in M. Carrez et al. (eds), *De la Torah au Messie* (Paris: Desclée, 1981), pp. 329–36.
— 'Aramaic in the Achaemenian Empire', in I. Gershevitch (ed.), *The Cambridge History of Iran* (Cambridge: Cambridge University Press, 1985), vol. II, pp. 698–713.
— 'The Wisdom of Ahiqar', in J. Day et al. (eds), *Wisdom in Ancient Israel* (Cambridge: Cambridge University Press, 1998), pp. 43–54.
Harvey, David, *The Condition of Postmodernity: An Enquiry into the Origins of Cultural Change* (Malden, MA: Blackwell, 1990).
Held, D., A. G. McGrew, D. Goldblatt and J. Perraton (eds), *Global Transformations: Politics, Economics, and Culture* (Stanford, CA: Stanford University Press, 1999).
Heller-Roazen, Daniel (ed.), *The Arabian Nights*, trans. H. Haddawy (New York: W. W. Norton, 2010), p. viii.
Holmes, David (ed.), *Virtual Globalization: Virtual Spaces/Tourist Spaces* (London: Routledge, 2001).
Jameson, Fredric, *Postmodernism, or, The Cultural Logic of Late Capitalism* (Durham, NC: Duke University Press, 1992).
— *Allegory and Ideology* (London: Verso, 2019).
Jamison, Anne, *Fic: Why Fanfiction Is Taking Over the World* (Dallas, TX: Smart Pop, 2013).
Johnson, Barbara, *Moses and Multiculturalism* (Berkeley, CA: University of California Press, 2010).
Joisten-Pruschke, Anke, *Das religiöse Leben der Juden von Elephantinien der Achämenidenzeit* (Wiesbaden: Harrassowitz, 2008).
Junge, P. J., 'Satrapie und Natio', *Clio* 34 (1942): 1–55.
Knowles, Melody, *Centrality Practiced: Jerusalem in the Religious Practice of Yehud and the Diaspora in the Persian Period* (Atlanta, GA: Society of Biblical Literature, 2006).
Kochhar-Lindgren, Kanta, et al., *The Exquisite Corpse: Chance and Collaboration in Surrealism's Parlor Game* (Lincoln, NE: University of Nebraska Press, 2009).
Kottsieper, Ingo, *Die Sprache der Ahiqarsprüche* (Berlin: De Gruyter, 1990).
Kramer, Samuel N., *History Begins at Sumer* (London: Thames and Hudson, 1961).

Kwon, JiSeong James, *Scribal Culture and Intertextuality: Literary and Historical Relationships between Job and Deutero-Isaiah* (Tübingen: Mohr Siebeck, 2016).

Lacan, Jacques, *Le Séminaire. Livre II: Le moi dans la théorie de Freud et dans la technique de la psychanalyse, 1954–1955*, ed. Jacques-Alain Miller (Paris: Éditions du Seuil, 1978).

Lindenberger, James, *The Aramaic Proverbs of Ahiqar* (Baltimore, MD: Johns Hopkins University Press, 1983).

— 'Ahiqar', in J. H. Charlesworth (ed.), *The Old Testament Pseudepigrapha* (New York: Doubleday, 1985), vol. II, pp. 479–507.

Loprieno, Antonio (ed.), *Ancient Egyptian Literature: History and Forms* (Leiden: Brill, 1996).

Lourié, Basil, 'The Syriac *Ahiqar*, its Slavonic Version, and the Relics of the Three Youths in Babylon', *Slověne* 2 (2013): 64–117.

Mahdi, Muhsin, *The Thousand and One Nights* (Leiden: Brill, 1995).

Miller, Vincent, *Understanding Digital Culture*, 2nd edn (London: Sage, 2020).

Milstein, Sara J., *Tracking the Master Scribe: Revision through Introduction in Biblical and Mesopotamian Literature* (Oxford: Oxford University Press, 2016).

Modrzejewski, Joseph, *Les Juifs d'Égypte de Ramsès II à Hadrien* (Paris: PUF, 1992).

Mullen, E. Theodore, *Ethnic Myths and Pentateuchal Foundations* (Atlanta, GA: Scholars Press, 1997).

Muraoka, Takamitsu, and Bezalel Porten, *A Grammar of Egyptian Aramaic* (Leiden: Brill, 1998).

Murray, W. E., and J. Overton, *Geographies of Globalization* (Abingdon: Routledge, 2015).

Nau, F., *Histoire et Sagesse d'Ahiqar l'Assyrien* (Paris: Letouzey et Ané, 1909).

Niditch, Susan, and Robert Doran, 'The Success Story of the Wise Courtier: A Formal Approach', *Journal of Biblical Literature* 96 (1977): 179–93.

Parker, Richard, *The Calendars of Ancient Egypt* (Chicago: University of Chicago Press, 1950).

Parkinson, Richard, *Poetry and Culture in the Middle Kingdom: A Dark Side to Perfection* (London: Continuum, 2002).

Poe, Edgar Allan, 'Ms. Found in a Bottle', *Visitor*, 9 October 1833.

Porten, Bezalel, *Archives from Elephantine: The Life of an Ancient Jewish Military Colony* (Berkeley, CA: University of California Press, 1968).

Porten, Bezalal, and Ada Yardeni, *Textbook of Aramaic Documents from Ancient Egypt*, 4 vols (Jerusalem: Eisenbrauns, 1986–93).

Porten, Bezalal, et al., *The Elephantine Papyri in English: Three Millennia of Cross-Cultural Continuity and Change* (Leiden: Brill, 1996).

Posnett, H. M., *Comparative Literature* (New York: D. Appleton, 1886).

Propp, William, *Exodus 1–18* (New York: Doubleday, 1999).

Pugh, Sheenagh, *The Democratic Genre: Fan Fiction in a Literary Context* (Bridgend, Wales: Seren, 2005).

Quirke, Stephen, *Egyptian Literature 1800 BC: Questions and Readings* (London: Golden House Publications, 2004).
Reynolds, Dwight F., '*A Thousand and One Nights*: A History of the Text and its Reception', in Roger Allen and D. S. Richards (eds), *The Cambridge History of Arabic Literature: The Post-Classical Period* (Cambridge: Cambridge University Press, 2006), pp. 270–91.
Ross, Kristin, 'The World Literature and Cultural Studies Program', *Critical Inquiry* 19 (1993): 666–76.
Rowlands, Michael, et al. (eds), *Centre and Periphery in the Ancient World* (Cambridge: Cambridge University Press, 1987).
Ruppert, Lothar, 'Zum Funktion der Achikar-Notizen im Buch Tobias', *Biblische Zeitschrift* NS 20 (1976): 232–37.
Salvesen, Alison, 'The Legacy of Babylon and Nineveh in Aramaic Sources', in S. Dallie (ed.), *The Legacy of Mesopotamia* (Oxford: Oxford University Press, 1968), pp. 139–61.
Schenker, Adrian, *The Earliest Text of the Hebrew Bible* (Atlanta, GA: Society of Biblical Literature, 2003).
Searight, Sarah, *Lapis Lazuli: In Pursuit of a Celestial Stone* (London: East & West Publishing, 2010).
Selden, Daniel, 'Text Networks', *Ancient Narrative* 8 (2010): 1–23.
Shibata, Daisuke, and Shigeo Yamata, *Cultures and Societies in the Middle Euphrates and Habur Areas in the Second Millennium BC – I: Scribal Education and Scribal Traditions* (Wiesbaden: Harrassowitz, 2016).
Shifman, Limor, *Memes in Digital Culture* (Boston, MA: MIT Press, 2013).
Silver, Morris, *Economic Structures of the Ancient Near East* (Totowa, NJ: Croom Helm, 1985).
Smith, Mark, *The Pilgrimage Pattern in Exodus* (Sheffield: Sheffield Academic Press, 1997).
Sontag, Susan, *Against Interpretation and Other Essays* (New York: Farrar, Straus, and Giroux, 1966).
Spacey, Ashton (ed.), *The Darker Side of Slash Fan Fiction: Essays on Power, Consent and the Body* (Jefferson, NC: McFarland, 2018).
Stein, Gil, *Rethinking World-Systems: Diasporas, Colonies, and Interaction in Uruk Mesopotamia* (Tucson, AZ: University of Arizona Press, 1999).
Stillinger, Jack, *Multiple Authorship and the Myth of Solitary Genius* (New York: Oxford University Press, 1991).
Tigay, Jeffrey, *The Evolution of the Gilgamesh Epic* (Philadelphia, PA: University of Pennsylvania Press, 1982).
Toynbee, A., 'The Administrative Geography of the Achaemenian Empire', in *A Study in History* (Oxford: Oxford University Press, 1954), vol. VII, pp. 580–689.
Tuplin, Christopher, 'The Administration of the Achaemenid Empire', in I. Carradice (ed.), *Coinage and Administration in the Athenian and Persian Empires* (Oxford: Oxford University Press, 1987), pp. 109–66.
van der Toorn, Karel, *Scribal Culture and the Making of the Hebrew Bible* (Cambridge, MA: Harvard University Press, 2009).

van Hoonacker, Albin, *Une communauté judéo-araméenne à Éléphantine, en Égypte, aux 6e et 5e siècles av. J.-C.* (Toronto: University of Toronto Press, 2011 [1915]).

Vogelgesang, W., *The Rise and Organization of the Achaemenid Empire* (Leiden: Brill, 1992).

Wallerstein, Immanuel, *World Systems Analysis: An Introduction* (Durham, NC: Duke University Press, 2004).

Wardrip-Fruin, Noah, and Nick Montfort (eds), *The New Media Reader* (Cambridge, MA: MIT Press, 2003).

Weerasethakul, Apichatpong (dir.), *Dokfa nai meuman* [Eng.: *Mysterious Object at Noon*] (Thailand, 2000).

Weigl, M., *Die aramäischen Achikar-Sprüche aus Elephantine und die alttestamentliche Weisheitsliteratur* (Berlin: De Gruyter, 2010).

White, Hayden, *The Fiction of Narrative: Essays on History, Literature, and Theory 1957–2007*, ed. R. Doran (Baltimore, MD: Johns Hopkins University Press, 2010).

— *Tropics of Discourse: Essays in Cultural Criticism* (Baltimore, MD: Johns Hopkins University Press, 2010).

Wills, Lawrence, *Not God's People: Insiders and Outsiders in the Biblical World* (Lanham, MD: Rowman and Littlefield, 2008).

Wordsworth, William, *Lyrical Ballads, with Other Poems*, 2 vols, 2nd edn (London: T. N. Longman and O. Rees, 1800).

Wyrick, Jed, *The Ascension of Authorship: Attribution and Canon Formation in Jewish, Hellenistic, and Christian Traditions* (Cambridge, MA: Harvard University Press, 2004).

Yardeni, Ada, 'Maritime Trade and Royal Accountancy in an Erased Customs Account from 475 B.C.E. on the Aḥīqar Scroll from Elephantine', *Bulletin of the American Schools of Oriental Research* 293 (1994): 67–78.

Zahn, Molly M., *Genres of Rewriting in Second Temple Judaism: Scribal Composition and Transmission* (Cambridge: Cambridge University Press, 2020).

7

The Alexander Romance in the age of scribal reproduction: the aesthetics and precariousness of a popular text

Shamma Boyarin

The Alexander Romance, an episodic, largely fictional and embellished biography of Alexander the Great, was one of the most popular texts in the Middle Ages. Originally compiled in Alexandria in late antiquity, it was copied and read around the world in more than thirty languages by the end of the Middle Ages.[1] Though it is sometimes referred to as 'Pseudo-Callisthenes' (attributing authorship to Callisthenes, a Greek historian who accompanied Alexander on his travels), the text has no fixed version or authorship, and scribes and translators introduced various differences over its long period of transmission.[2] In its many different versions – which broadly span time, place and language – the Alexander Romance is a paradigmatic example of the popular text in the Middle Ages, often not valued in literary circles. Indeed, this was my experience when I chose to focus on the Romance for my doctoral dissertation. For two years, I had planned to write about the influence of Arabic literature on the Hebrew poetry and *belles-lettres* of medieval Spain. When composing my primary reading lists, however, I became interested in the Alexander Romance tradition in Hebrew and Arabic and switched my focus. I did not anticipate resistance from mentors, but, in retrospect, one reason for the resistance I did encounter was, clearly, my move from a corpus with well-established literary value to a popular, amorphous tradition that was considered of little importance from a literary or aesthetic perspective. Ultimately, in my doctoral work, I skirted the question of aesthetic quality altogether and argued for the importance of the Alexander Romance on other grounds. If we accept Robert Alter's distinction between literary approaches influenced by the New Historicism, which pay significant attention to questions of ideology, and approaches that pay more attention to style, I would say that my previous work focused on ideology.[3] In this chapter, instead, I consider style in the Alexander Romance, with specific attention to the Hebrew exemplars, and in this way argue for its literary and aesthetic merit. Alter suggests that one measure of a work's aesthetic merit is what can be called 'translatability' – that is to say, texts that are easy to translate do not have unique or particular literary merit. I argue that the Alexander Romance appears to be highly translatable, as is evidenced from the many versions of it in many languages, but this obscures aspects of it that are not translatable, and this has (wrongly) influenced our impression of its literary value.

Precariousness is the norm for the Alexander Romance in Hebrew. Even though several versions exist, each was translated into Hebrew from a different language of origin or by a different translator, and each is found only in one or two extant manuscripts (with one notable exception). There are two examples of translation from Arabic: these are in Paris, Biblioteque nationale de France, MS héb. 671.5, and New Haven, Beinecke Rare Book and Manuscript Library, MS Heb. supplement 103. While the sources of these two versions are very close, they represent two different translations into Hebrew – and, as I will discuss further below, there are significant stylistic differences between them. A translation from Greek into Hebrew is found only in Parma, Biblioteca I. B. de Rossi, MS. heb. 1087, while we have two closely related Hebrew versions whose source is unknown preserved in Modena, Biblioteca Estense, MS Liii, and Oxford, Bodleian Library, MS Heb. d. 11. A third version of a Hebrew Alexander Romance, similar to these two, was once seen in Damascus but is now lost. A translation from Latin or French used to exist in two manuscripts but now survives only in Paris, Bibliothèque nationale de France, MS héb. 750.3. The other, which I will also discuss further below, existed in a library in Turin but was destroyed in a fire, though parts of it were transcribed in the nineteenth century. The Alexander Romance, in other words, was a popular text for translation into Hebrew in the Middle Ages, and each translation opens a unique window into a specific context.

The notable exception is a Hebrew version that was interpolated into the *Yosippon*, a widely circulated medieval Hebrew adaptation of Josephus's writings. David Flusser showed that this Alexander Romance is a hybrid. First, a part of one version of the Hebrew Alexander Romance was copied into the *Yosippon*, and then, later, part of another version was added on to its beginning. The first addition came from a version of the Alexander Romance very similar to what is found in the I. B. de Rossi MS Heb. 1087 (translated from Greek), and a few extant copies of the *Yosippon* have just this one interpolation. However, this first addition does not tell the story of Nectanebus, the astrologer who had a role in the conception and birth of Alexander the Great, so a later scribe added material found in another Hebrew Alexander Romance. The second addition comes from a text very similar to the one now found in Beinecke MS Heb. supplement 103 (translated from Arabic). The resulting 'hybrid' is found in many copies of the *Yosippon*, including the first incunabulum.[4]

The Alexander Romance in Bibliothèque nationale MS héb. 750.3 and the version once found in a Turin library (translated from Latin or French) were very similar, but there were apparently some significant differences between them. The version from Turin contained an epigraph that is not found in the still extant Paris manuscript. Luckily, this was transcribed and published by Israel Levi before the manuscript's destruction. In the epigraph, Immanuel ben Jacob Bonfils, the fourteenth-century French translator of an Alexander Romance into Hebrew, explains his decision to translate the work thus:

אמר המעתיק בעל הכנפיים לא מהיותי חכם בעיניי וצחות לשון על שפתי השיאני לבבי
בהעתקת הספר הזה מלשון נוצרי אל לשון עברי כי בער אנכי מאיש ולא בינת אדם לי
אמנם נכסוף נכספתי בהעתקתו אחרי אשר ראיתי כתוב בספר הנוצרים ומצוייר בדמיונות
נאות ובצבעים שונים וכסף וזהב על רוב אהבתם אותו ורוב אנשים מאמינים את דבריו
ואינני מהם אף על-פי שכל דבר אפשר כי לפעמים אשיג בהם תועלת ונמצא העתקתו
ובניינו חזק ואל יאשימני קורא בו כי לא להתגדל בו העתקתיו כי אם למלאות חפצי
ולהפיק דעתי ואמרתי בשבתי עם אנשים נדיבים או עם עמי הארץ אספר להם מדברי
הספר הזה יערב אליהם ויהיו לפניהם כדבש למתוק אחלי ליוצר הכל להסיר שגגותי
ולמחול עונותי ולסלוח חטאי ויזכני לראות משיח צדקינו ובניין בית מקדשינו במהרה
בימינו אמן

'amar hama'tiq ba'al haknafayim lo meheyoti ḥakham be'einai vetzaḥot lashon 'al sefatay hish'ani levavi bha'ataqat hasefer hazeh milashon notzri 'el lashon 'ivri ki ba'ar 'anokhi me'ish velo binat 'adam li 'omnam nikhsof nikhsafti beha'taqato aḥarei asher ra'iti katuv besefer hanotzrim umetzuyar bedimyonot na'ot ubitzva'im shonim vekesef vezahav 'al rov 'ahavatam 'oto verov 'anashim ma'aminim 'et devarav ve'eineni mehem 'af 'al-pi shekol davar 'efshar ki lif'amim 'asig behem to'elet venimtza ha'ataqato vebinyano ḥazaq ve'al ya'ashimeni qore bo ki lo lehitgadel bo he'etaqtiv ki 'im lemal'ot ḥaftzi ulehafiq da'ati ve'amarti beshevti 'im 'anashim nedivim 'o 'im 'mei ha'aretz 'asaper lahem medivrei hasefer haze ye'erav 'aleihem veyihyu lefaneihem kedvash lematoq 'oḥli leyotzer hakol lehasir shgagotai velimḥol 'avonotai velislo'aḥ ḥaṭa'ai veyizkeni lir'ot meshi'aḥ tzidqenu ubinyan beit miqdashenu bimhera beyamenu 'amen

[The translator, author of *The Wings*,[5] said: 'Not because I see myself as wise or because of the eloquence of my lips has my heart seduced me to translate this book from the Christian tongue [i.e., either Latin or French] into Hebrew, for I am the most ignorant of men and lack wisdom. Nevertheless, I wished to translate it after I saw it written in the book of the Christians, illustrated with nice figures and different colours, including silver and gold, because of their great love for it [i.e., for the text]. Most people believe its words, though I am not one of them. Still everything is possible, and sometimes I find some benefit from them [the words]. Its translation and composition are sound. Let the reader not blame me, for I have not translated it to make myself great, but rather because of my own desire, and to carry out my wishes. But I said: "When I am sitting among the great or the simple, I will tell them of the words; it will be pleasing before them like sweet honey." My hope goes to the creator of all to remove my mistakes, forgive my sins, and pardon my transgressions, and may I merit seeing our righteous Messiah and the building of our Temple, soon in our days. Amen.'][6]

Bonfils observes that his translation of the Romance is 'sound' – in his judgement, it has stylistic merit – and this epigraph addresses many of the questions that are central to this volume of essays. Why is a certain text popular? How do we know it is popular? How do popular texts communicate value to their audience? Why do readers find them valuable?

Part of what prompted Bonfils to translate the Alexander Romance into Hebrew was his aesthetic response, albeit a visual rather than textual one: after he saw that Christians had made beautiful illuminated copies of this text, he wanted to translate it into Hebrew. Further, this visual artistic embellishment of the text was performed because, as he understands it, the Christians have a 'great love for' the Alexander Romance. These illuminations thus formed part of the aesthetic experience of the Hebrew Alexander Romance and of Bonfils's translation. While there is no surviving illuminated copy of the Hebrew Alexander Romance, it could be that Bonfils himself chose to feature such illustrations. The scribe of the later copy of the Bonfils manuscript (Bibliothèque nationale MS héb. 750.3) included descriptions of illustrations that were found in his exemplar, either in Bonfils's source or in his autograph. These descriptions (which may be copies of descriptive captions) are marked by slashes and dots, to distinguish them from the main narrative, and are often set slightly apart from the main text. For example, at the top of fol. 80r (Figure 7.1), the first page of the Alexander Romance in this codex, we find two such instances. The first says (close to the top of the page),

> צורת נאנטיניפו ושער ראשו וזקנו מגולחים ולבוש בגדי לבן
>
> tzurat ni'anṭinifu vesei'ar rosho uzekano megulaḥim velavush bigdei lavan
>
> [Image of Nectanebus with his hair and beard shaven, wearing white clothing]

And the second (in the middle of the page),

> צורת אנשי מצרים מתחננים לפני אלהיהם וצורת מצבת נאנטיניפו
>
> tzurat ʻanshei mitzrayim mitḥanenim lifnei ʻeloheihem vetzurat matzevat ni'anṭinifu
>
> [Image of the people of Egypt pleading before their gods, and an image of the statue of Nectanebus][7]

Such captions appear on most pages of this Alexander Romance but accompany none of the other texts in MS héb. 750.3.[8] At some point, the images had clearly become an important part of the transmission of this iteration of the Alexander Romance.

After the note on illuminations, the Bonfils epigraph goes on to discuss, more generally, why people value the Alexander Romance: 'most people believe its contents', says the translator. While it is beyond the scope of this chapter to fully parse what it means for people to 'believe' the contents of the Alexander Romance – do they believe it is an accurate account of Alexander's life? that the places described in it are real places? that all of its flamboyantly

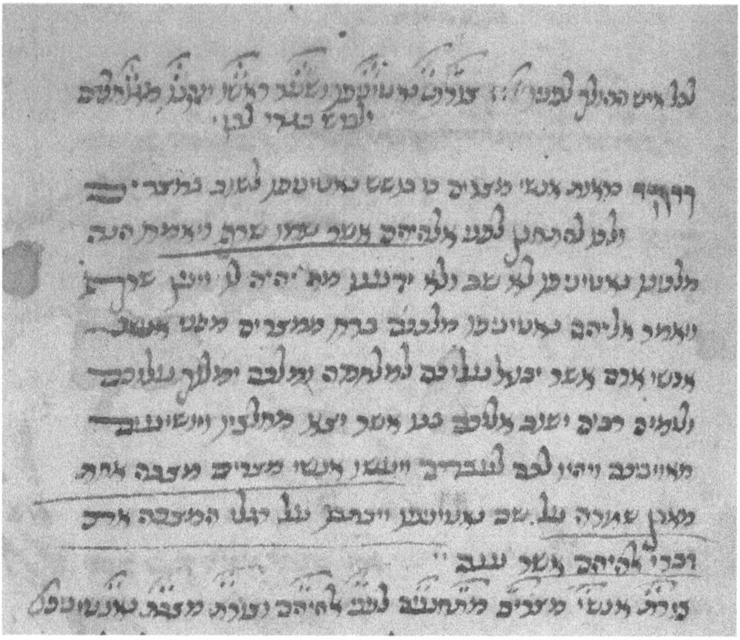

Figure 7.1 Bibliothèque nationale de France, MS héb. 750.3, fol. 80r, showing image descriptions marked by superscript dots and strokes. Reproduced by permission of the Bibliothèque nationale de France, Paris

legendary episodes are true? – Bonfils himself is not one of these people. He says that he does not believe the contents of the Romance, though he receives 'some benefit from them'. This suggests that, for this translator, part of the importance of the Alexander Romance is precisely the importance that other people attach to it. Put simply, he finds value in the fact that the text is popular.

Of course, not all decisions to translate the Alexander Romance into Hebrew are framed this way. Another manuscript, in fact, allows us to see that, at least in some cases, part of what was at stake was formal aesthetics: the colophon of the Hebrew Romance in Bodleian MS Heb. d. 11 connects the translation task, and the value of the source, to the complex legacy of Aristotelian knowledge and philosophy as transmitted through Arabic.[9] The Alexander Romance is perhaps like the modern novel, in that it is easily translatable. As Alter notes in his discussions of style, novels are 'urgently about a whole variety of things that are not made up of words', and so 'if the translator inevitably substitutes other words, and usually less adequate ones, than the novelist's', the work still manages to convey the sense of the original text.[10] From our perspective looking back, this also seems to be the case for the Alexander Romance – translated so many times and yet retaining the same essential narrative details and sensibilities.[11] In the many versions, across different languages and times and places, the same plot elements return and the central elements are stable, despite minor alterations.[12] This, I think, is part of what makes popular texts such as the Alexander Romance seem separate from those texts commonly considered masterpieces, such as, say, *Beowulf*. Although *Beowulf* has been translated many times, there is consensus that the style of the original Old English is not completely conveyable in translation. The same holds for other masterpieces, such as al-Ḥarīrī's *Maqāmāt*. Not all examples with a *unicum* surviving text fall into this translatable/untranslatable dichotomy, of course, and I would argue that, in instances where only one copy of a text survives, scholars retain an increased sense of its untranslatable essence, a feeling that the sole exemplar is its 'true' form.

But back to the Hebrew Alexander Romance. Alter proposes a partial list of the attributes of style that affect our experience of a work of fiction. This list includes 'sound (rhyme, alliteration, assonance and so forth), syntax, idiomatic usage and divergences from it, linguistic register (that is, level of diction), and the cultural and literary associations of language'.[13] With this in mind, let us consider a few examples in which translators of the Alexander Romance into Hebrew can be understood to be making stylistic decisions, not strictly required to convey the 'essence' of an original text.

For example, in Bibliothèque nationale MS héb. 671.5, in the episode in which the Egyptian king and astrologer Nectanebus scolds one of his spies for bringing him discouraging news, his words assume a poetic form:

ויאמר לו:
איש חלש ירא ורך הלבב
מבשר רעה וצופה קשה
סורה לך נטה הלאה
מה מאד נבער מדעת כל אשר ישלחך גדולה או קטנה

vayomer lo:
'ish ḥalash yare verakh halevav
Mevaser ra'ah vetzofe kasha
Sura lakh naṭe hal'ah
Ma me'od niv'ar mida'at 'asher yeshalḥekha gedola 'o qeṭana

[And He said to him: 'Weak, fearful and faint-hearted man,
Harbinger of evil and foreseer of difficulty
Turn away go away
How lacking of knowledge is he who sends you for anything great or small.'][14]

Nectanebus's speech is not typographically presented this way, either in the manuscript or in the modern print edition, but the two short clauses in the second line printed above ('harbinger of evil' and 'foreseer of difficulty') have a rhythm that suggests a poetic relationship between them. Further, four key words ('evil', 'difficulty', 'away' and 'small') rhyme in the Hebrew, a pattern that jumps out especially when reading aloud. The phrase ירא ורך הלבב ('fearful and faint-hearted'), moreover, is a biblicism, drawn from Deut. 20:8. It is appropriate for this context, because in Deuteronomy the phrase is used as part of a speech that a military commander is ordered to give to his solders before battle, asking those who are too scared to fight to leave. A reader of Hebrew would understand this as the implied context of Nectanebus's criticism of his subordinate.[15] The allusion heightens the hypocrisy or humour of the situation when, just a few lines later, we read that, once he realises that the battle will go against him, Nectanebus himself flees in the night, abandoning his subjects to be conquered.

While we cannot check the immediate source for this Hebrew version of the episode, for reasons that I will discuss shortly, we can compare it with another Hebrew Alexander Romance, that extant in Beinecke MS Heb. supplement 103, translated from a similar Arabic source text. This analogue also uses the biblicism present in Bibliothèque nationale MS héb. 671.5, starting Nectanebus's address with הוי איש חלש וירך הלבב ('oh, weak, fearful and faint-hearted man').[16] However, the rest of his speech does not correspond to the neatly rhyming lines we see above. The centrality of biblical Hebrew in medieval Jewish life was such that translators could not avoid echoing it either explicitly or indirectly, simply as part of the process of translating a text into Hebrew. But even echoes that are unavoidable create an aesthetic effect: they resonate with the Hebrew of the Bible. This kind of aesthetic effect is a prominent part of medieval Hebrew poetics, found both in liturgical poetry and the secular poetry of Spain. Both of these translators chose to echo Deut. 20:8 when presenting a speech about cowardice before battle, because the Bible was a shared intertext for any reader of Hebrew, and because making such allusions was part of the literary style.

In Beinecke MS Heb. supplement 103, another neat echo of biblical phrasing is the following statement about Nectanebus living in Macedonia anonymously: אמנם נקטנבור היה יושב מקדוניא לא נודע מי הוא ואיזה הוא ['At the same time Nectanebus was dwelling in Macedonia no one knew who and what he was'].[17] This phrase is a close parallel to Esth. 7:5, where King Ahasuerus asks Esther, מי הוא זה ואיזה הוא? ['Who is this and where is he?']. On one level, this allusion simply exemplifies the way translated texts are often made into a Hebrew text by echoing biblical phrases. On another level, it is possible that this echo points to a deeper resonance between Nectanebus and the subject of the king's question in Esther, that is, the evil Haman. Both Haman and Nectanebus serve as villainous advisors in the courts of Ahasuerus and Philipus, respectively. Further, in the Bible, just three verses after the one to which the Hebrew Alexander Romance refers, Ahasuerus accuses Haman of trying to seduce his queen, Esther – just as Nectanebus will seduce the queen in the Alexander Romance.

Perhaps because of Alexander's later exploits in Persia, Jewish translators might have seen the Book of Esther as a relevant reference. Or perhaps its themes – courtly intrigue, romance, sexuality – were understood to be compatible with the themes of the Alexander Romance. Yet another Hebrew Alexander Romance, the one found in Bodleian MS Heb. d. 11, uses a particularly high number of biblical phrases or paraphrases, and it also creates several resonances with Esther. Indeed, a whole episode, which has no parallel in any other Alexander Romance, closely follows an episode in Esther. When Alexander falls in love with a beautiful woman, he fights the king of the city where she lives in order to steal her away, and then he has a child by her and holds a feast in her honour. The translator describes this episode using phrases from Esther: ״עשה משתה לכל שריו ועבדיו וישם כתר בראש האשה ההיא וימליכיה ['he made a feast unto all his princes and his servants and placed a crown on the head of that woman and made her queen'].[18] The first part of this sentence is a direct quotation of Esth. 1:3, and the second part is slightly modified from Esth. 2:17. When a son is born to this woman, both Alexander's favourite horse and the woman die, and Alexander is inconsolable.[19] His advisors then devise a plan based on the plan recommended to King Ahasuerus after his first queen is executed in Esther 2. If part of literary style involves, as Alter says, 'the cultural and literary associations of language', then the creation of this episode, strongly invoking the story of Esther, is one aspect of style that we can confidently point to in this Hebrew Alexander Romance.

Part of the interest in works of literature that survive in a single copy, I wager, is the sense of precariousness and luck involved in their existence, a feeling that, but for this one survival, surely a survival that has value, we would lose knowledge, or a treasure would be lost. This notion can be connected to Walter Benjamin's idea about authenticity in relation to art, as expressed in his 'The Work of Art in the Age of Its Technological Reproducibility'. The original work of art, unlike its reproduction, has a certain element of 'authenticity' to it, formed by 'its unique existence in a particular place'.[20] Benjamin claims, further, that it is this unique existence – and nothing else – that bears the mark of the history to which the work has been subject.[21] Our scholarly elevation of medieval canons, often holding singular works of art at the level of masterpieces, and our devaluation of texts that appear to be 'bestsellers', surviving in dozens or hundreds of copies, stems from a similar (perhaps unconscious and undefined) idea about art.[22] On the one hand, the lone preserved example of a text has authenticity because, even if originally, as we often surmise, it may have existed in multiple versions and copies, it now bears the stamp of uniqueness. On the other hand, texts that have survived in many copies are akin to mass-reproduced works of art, which Benjamin described as having lost authenticity by failing to have a unique existence.

Unlike the technologically reproduced art that Benjamin discusses, however, medieval copies were made by hand, and there are thus no perfect reproductions. But somehow this makes them even *less* artistic: each difference, from version to version, whether accidental or by scribal design, serves to remind us moderns that we are not dealing with the original work of art. The scholarly history of tracing textual origins and textual corrections, to reconstruct an original, singular source, the unique work of art, attests to this devaluation. If such scholarship is no longer so widely practised, the reasons are intimately tied to what I am exploring here, though the impulse behind finding or reconstructing the lost 'original' colours our attitudes about the medieval canon nonetheless. The problem is most acute in the case of a popular text such as the Alexander Romance: tracing sources can never lead back to a singular origin, but only to other amorphous popular texts from which it was compiled.

In Benjamin's ideas about the work of art, the singular exemplar provides a chance opportunity to access 'authenticity', but the Alexander Romance tradition provides the exact opposite. We have so many versions in so many different languages that it is hard to see any one version as exceptional. In reality, however, each copy gives us a view of a unique place, and each is unique and as precarious as any text that survives in a single manuscript. The epigraph from Bonfils quoted above, for instance, found in only one manuscript, and that destroyed by fire, lives now only in Israel Levi's transcription.[23] Levi was able to compare it to the version of the Romance found in Bibliothéque nationale MS héb.750.3 and determine that both Romances were translated products of the same source, but the Paris manuscript is missing the first folio of the text; thus, we do not have any surviving version that contains the beginning of this Alexander Romance, nor the epigraph transcribed by Levi. The Paris manuscript is in fact a *unicum*, a sole surviving exemplar of one distinct way that the Alexander Romance tradition manifested in Hebrew literature. As I noted above, this is true of most of the versions of the Alexander Romance in Hebrew. We must consider this text both part of a literary tradition that was popular and can be found in many copies and also, in a particular instance, a rare and valuable surviving witness of a unique literary contribution.

These versions of the text (Bibliothéque nationale MS héb. 750.3 and the lost Turin manuscript) provide evidence of specific Hebrew or Jewish contexts for the Alexander Romance, while at the same time offering telling details about other, overlapping cultural and literary traditions. They point to an Arabic source and provide important information about the Alexander Romance tradition in Arabic: though Alexander Romances exist in Arabic, an Arabic text that is similar to these Hebrew manuscripts is not currently known to us. They raise questions about the transmission of the

Alexander Romance, since the translation of these Arabic texts into Hebrew most likely took place in al-Andalus, and further behind these versions is a Latin source, perhaps one step removed from the Arabic via Syriac. With these survivals, we can reconstruct a chain of transmission from Latin to Syriac (where?), from Syriac to Arabic (probably in the East), and from Arabic to Hebrew (in al-Andalus). While each step in this chain makes sense individually, and has analogues in other textual transmissions, the specific combination of all of these steps is intriguing, especially so if we consider the timeframe in which the Latin version of this branch of the Alexander Romance tradition was redacted for the translation into Hebrew. Tracing stemmata and relationships between Alexander Romances in this way is very different from analysis that seeks to establish a correct and singular source of a textual tradition. This process, by contrast, offers a window into a strand of cultural connections and interwoven communities, the kind only possible because of the popularity of the Alexander Romance. This kind of analysis promises to show how each individual example of the Romance carries its own authenticity.

I have outlined here only brief case studies, which should serve to complicate any picture of a neat binary between lone literary masterpieces and popular texts that seem to lack the same aesthetic qualities. While I have drawn on examples from the Hebrew branch of the Alexander Romance tradition, my own area of expertise, the same is possible for examples found in other languages, and working across languages will always create yet further possibilities. What if we could trace the descriptions found in the Bonfils version of the Romance to a group of Christian texts, if not to a particular manuscript he saw,[24] and what if that led to a more thorough understanding of the interactions between Jewish and Christian scholars in the fourteenth century? What if we looked for elements of style in those versions too, and considered how the Hebrew translator was working to transmit those elements? Or, more broadly, how might we expand this kind of reading to more examples of Alexander Romances, in various languages and with an expanded notion of the literary masterpiece? How might the relationship between works such as the *Song of Roland* and the Alexander Romance be transformed if we considered both as paradigmatic examples of medieval French literary style? What might it mean, indeed, for our contemporary sense of the literary to fully include popular texts? Both the kind of approach to reading Alexander Romances that I once undertook in my doctoral dissertation *and* the stylistic method I have sketched out here, for a full understanding of the place of the Alexander Romance in the medieval canon, can and should be integrated.

Notes

1 I know of no complete list of the languages into which the medieval Alexander Romance was translated, but there are versions in Greek, Latin, Persian, Pahlavi, Armenian, Syriac, Hebrew, Arabic, English, French, German, Dutch, Spanish, Serbian, Russian, Danish, Swedish, Bulgarian, Romanian and Polish. Further versions exist in various iterations within language groups, for example, in Byzantine Greek and Middle Greek, or in Old French and Anglo-Norman French.

2 Good, up-to-date overviews of the Alexander Romance tradition can be found in R. Stoneman, K. Erickson and I. Netton (eds), *Alexander Romance in Persia and the East* (Groningen: Barkhuis, 2012), and R. Stoneman, K. Nawotka and A. Wojciechowska (eds), *The Alexander Romance: History and Literature* (Groningen: Barkhuis, 2018).

3 R. Alter, *Pen of Iron: American Prose and the King James Bible* (Princeton, NJ: Princeton University Press, 2010), p. 21.

4 This paragraph summarises the discussion of the relationship between the various versions of the Hebrew Alexander Romance and the *Yosippon* found in D. Flusser (ed.), *The Josippon* [in Hebrew], vol. II (Jerusalem: Bialik Institute, 1980), pp. 216–51. For more on the Hebrew tradition, see also S. Boyarin, 'Hebrew Alexander Romances and Astrological Questions: Alexander, Aristotle, and the Medieval Jewish Audience', in M. Stock (ed.), *Alexander the Great in the Middle Ages: Transcultural Perspectives* (Toronto: University of Toronto Press, 2016), pp. 88–103.

5 *The Wings* most likely refers to *The Book of Six Wings*, a medieval Hebrew treatise on astronomy. Attribution to Immanuel ben Jacob Bonfils (d. c. 1377) is based on this identification.

6 The Hebrew text here is as transcribed in I. Levi, 'La traduction de l'Historia de Praeliis par Immanuel ben Jacob', *Revue des études juives* 6 (1882): 279. The translation is my own.

7 My transcriptions and translations. It is worth noting that the Hebrew word that I translate as 'image' has the same root as the word Bonfils uses for 'illustrated' in his epigraph. These types of images are clearly

the referent. It should also be noted that, in the various Hebrew versions of the Alexander Romance, Nectanebus's name is often garbled. Since it is clearly the same person in all instances, I render it consistently, to remove confusion for the modern reader. (It is not unthinkable, however, that a medieval reader or scribe reading various accounts of Alexander might have thought they were different people.)

8 More work on Bibliothèque nationale de France, MS héb. 750.3 will no doubt repay the effort. Examining the relationship between its various texts and the process by which they were brought together will surely teach us something new about the transmission and reception of the Alexander Romance in Hebrew, among other things.

9 For a detailed account of this colophon and its contexts, see Boyarin, 'Hebrew Alexander Romances and Astrological Questions'.

10 Alter, *Pen of Iron*, p. 25.

11 Nonetheless, as I have argued extensively elsewhere, the same episode might resonate significantly differently when transmitted to readers in different cultural contexts. See S. Boyarin, 'Diasporic Culture and the Makings of Alexander Romances', PhD dissertation, University of California, Berkeley, 2008.

12 For instance, the spelling of Nectanebus's name, mentioned above in note 7. But of course my generalisations are not quite true: there are versions of the Alexander Romance that do not include what some might consider 'central components' of his story, for example, details pertaining to Nectanebus and his role as the avatar or real father of Alexander. Similarly, many Alexander Romances do not include Alexander's visit to Jerusalem. Such differences may radically change the shape of the narrative and its cultural value. Here I am referring to broad tendencies.

13 Alter, *Pen of Iron*, p. 28.

14 W. J. van Bekkum (ed. and trans.), *A Hebrew Alexander Romance According to MS Heb.671.5 Paris, Bibliothèque nationale* (Groningen: Styx, 1994), p. 2. My translation here differs slightly from van Bekkum's in order to align better with a key biblical reference.

15 A medieval reader of Hebrew would easily recognise these biblical quotations and paraphrases and have their contexts readily to mind.

16 W. J. van Bekkum (ed. and trans.), *A Hebrew Alexander Romance According to MS London, Jews' College no. 145* (Leuven: Peeters, 1992), p. 36. The manuscript used for this edition has moved since Van Bekkum published: it is now New Haven, Beinecke Rare Book and Manuscript Library, MS Heb. supplement 103.

17 van Bekkum, *A Hebrew Alexander Romance According to MS London*, pp. 38–9.

18 R. Reich (ed. and trans.), *Tales of Alexander the Macedonian: A Medieval Hebrew Manuscript Text and Translation with a Literary and Historical Commentary* (New York: Ktav, 1972), p. 78.
19 This episode also alludes to Jacob's grief over hearing that Joseph is dead in Gen. 37:33–35, demonstrating interwoven biblicisms here.
20 W. Benjamin, 'The Work of Art in Age of Its Technological Reproducibility', in *The Work of Art in the Age of its Technological Reproducibility and Other Writings on Media*, ed. M. W. Jennings, B. Doherty and T. Y. Levin, trans. E. Jephcott, R. Livingstone, H. Eiland et al. (Cambridge, MA: Harvard University Press, 2008), p. 21.
21 Ibid.
22 In my view, this attitude to art, both on the part of Benjamin and more popularly, is influenced by Romantic ideals about the artist and his art – but exploring this idea is beyond the scope of this chapter.
23 It may be the case that Israel Levi published a full edition of the Turin Alexander Romance: there are references to this in older scholarship, but I have never been able to find it and have only encountered articles in which he published the epigraph.
24 As with many such things, traditional illumination 'cycles' were developed for the Alexander Romance. It is likely that the group of illustrations described by Bonfils in his viewing of versions contained in Christian books would have been shared by a number of illuminators.

Works cited

Manuscripts

Modena, Biblioteca Estense, MS Liii
New Haven, Beinecke Rare Book and Manuscript Library, MS Heb. supplement 103
Oxford, Bodleian Library, MS Heb. d. 11
Paris, Bibliotèque nationale de France, MS héb. 671.5
Paris, Bibliothèque nationale de France, MS héb. 750.3
Parma, Biblioteca I. B. de Rossi, MS. heb. 1087

Primary sources

A Hebrew Alexander Romance According to MS Heb.671.5 Paris, Bibliothèque nationale, ed. and trans. W. J. van Bekkum (Groningen: Styx, 1994).
A Hebrew Alexander Romance According to MS London, Jews' College no. 145, ed. and trans. W. J. van Bekkum (Leuven: Peeters, 1992).

Tales of Alexander the Macedonian: A Medieval Hebrew Manuscript Text and Translation with a Literary and Historical Commentary, ed. and trans. Rosalie Reich (New York: Ktav, 1972).

The Josippon [in Hebrew], ed. David Flusser (Jerusalem: Bialik Institute, 1980).

Secondary sources

Alter, Robert, *Pen of Iron: American Prose and the King James Bible* (Princeton, NJ: Princeton University Press, 2010).

Benjamin, Walter, 'The Work of Art in the Age of Its Technological Reproducibility', in *The Work of Art in the Age of its Technological Reproducibility and Other Writings on Media*, ed. M. W. Jennings, B. Doherty and T. Y. Levin, trans. E. Jephcott, R. Livingstone, H. Eiland et al. (Cambridge, MA: Harvard University Press, 2008), pp. 19–55.

Boyarin, Shamma, 'Diasporic Culture and the Makings of Alexander Romances', PhD dissertation, University of California, Berkeley, 2008.

— 'Hebrew Alexander Romances and Astrological Questions: Alexander, Aristotle, and the Medieval Jewish Audience', in Markus Stock (ed.), *Alexander the Great in the Middle Ages: Transcultural Perspectives* (Toronto: University of Toronto Press, 2016), pp. 88–103.

Levi, Israèl, 'La traduction de l'Historia de Praeliis par Immanuel ben Jacob', *Revue des études juives* 6 (1882): 279–80.

Stoneman, Richard, Kyle Erikson and Ian Netton (eds), *Alexander Romance in Persia and the East* (Groningen: Barkhuis, 2012).

Stoneman, Richard, Krzysztof Nawotka and Agnieszka Wojciechowska (eds), *The Alexander Romance: History and Literature* (Groningen: Barkhuis, 2018).

8

Wisdom literature and medieval bestsellers

Karla Mallette

What is wisdom? The *Oxford English Dictionary* defines the English word *wisdom* as 'Capacity of judging rightly in matters relating to life and conduct; soundness of judgement in the choice of means and ends; sometimes, less strictly, sound sense, esp. in practical affairs'.[1] It dates the earliest appearance of the word to the one-manuscript masterpiece typically identified as the point of origin of English literature, *Beowulf*. The word has clear ancestors – conceptual if not etymological – in words such as the Greek *sophía*, the Latin *sapientia* and the Arabic *ḥikma*. The category of 'wisdom literature', a loose generic title that characterises a large number of pre-modern literary works, includes books (sometimes fictional narratives) which pass on advice about living a virtuous and upright life. It typically refers first to ancient Mesopotamian and Egyptian works, the books of the Hebrew Bible and the ancient Greek literature that collect precepts to guide the good life, then to medieval works that follow in that tradition.

It is surprising, given the importance of 'wisdom' to ancient and medieval literature, that the word does not appear in a core work of medieval wisdom literature, the Book of Secundus.[2] This tradition – extant in Greek, Latin, Arabic, Syriac and Armenian – assembles definitions of words which, taken together, are the building blocks of wisdom. The various languages collate meanings for words such as *death* and *life*, *sun* and *moon*, *man* and *woman*. None of the languages, however, attempts to define *wisdom* – not even the wordy

Arabic version, which strays so far afield from the philosophical mainstream as to define terms such as 'flageolet' and 'fisherman'.[3]

A large portion of the works of imaginative literature that were popular in pre-modern letters but lost market share during the early modern period fall into the (admittedly vague) category of 'wisdom literature'. The narratives discussed in this chapter – the Book of Secundus, Kalilah and Dimnah, Barlaam and Josaphat and the Seven Sages of Rome[4] – have a short list of characteristics in common. They all circulated in numerous languages. Although core narrative elements remain the same, each work displays robust variation between languages and in transmission within languages. In some cases, a specific version of one of these works is associated with an individual author. The original Arabic version of Kalilah and Dimnah, for instance, was translated from the Pahlavi by Ibn al-Muqaffaʿ during the eighth century CE. This version does not survive, although it spawned numerous abridgements and imitations, and would provide a model for early Arabic prose composition.[5] Most of the works I discuss in this chapter, however, are anonymous. Each of the narrative traditions combines didactic material with fictional framing narratives that dramatise the importance of wisdom, often by pointing to death and ruin as the inevitable result of foolhardy or rash behaviour. In this sense, they distinguish themselves from the tales of Aesop, for instance, or from a work such as Petrarch's *De remediis utriusque fortunae* (discussed below). To a greater or lesser degree, each of the works involve elements of narrative embedding: a character in a fictional narrative relates tales (or, in the Book of Secundus, recites definitions) in response to a prompt in the framing narrative.

The works discussed here circulated widely, from late antique India to nineteenth-century Bulgaria, Serbia and Romania. All but Secundus have in common two stages in their long and eventful transmission histories: all were attested both in the Abbasid East and in late medieval Europe. We know about the Abbasid leg of their extensive travels because the bookseller Ibn al-Nadīm included them in his encyclopaedic catalogue of the books he had seen in tenth-century Baghdad.[6] Ibn al-Nadīm records divergent opinions about *Kalīlah wa-Dimnah* and *Sindbād al-Ḥakīm* (the source of the Seven Sages of Rome), variously attributed to Sanskrit or Pahlavi origins. In fact, scholars believe that Kalilah and Dimnah travelled from Sanskrit via Pahlavi into Arabic.[7] Previous versions of the

Sindbād/Seven Sages narrative are not extant, despite Ibn al-Nadīm's claim. Barlaam and Josaphat derives ultimately from Sanskrit tales about the Buddha, and related fragments are extant in Soghdian Buddhist and Manichean texts.[8] Thus, although the paths they follow between languages are not identical, all (with the exception of Secundus) worked their way – apparently from Sanskrit, Pahlavi, Turkic or another Central Asian language – into Arabic, thence to Persian, Greek, Armenian, Georgian, Syriac and other languages of Central and Western Asia, and finally into Latin and the vernaculars of western Europe. The three works generated a Hebrew version, translated from the Arabic, late in their transmission history, in al-Andalus (Muslim Spain). Kalilah and Dimnah, uniquely among the works on this list, remains current in the Islamic languages, although it is seldom read in the languages of the Christian West. Secundus seems to have emerged from the late antique Greek philosophical tradition. Extant versions in Greek, Syriac, Arabic and Armenian suggest that it circulated east of the Mediterranean, but it never crossed into the languages of western Europe.[9] Yet similarities between its framing narrative and the other works discussed in this chapter make it an intriguing point of comparison for the works with a more robust translation and transmission history.

Because the works discussed here exist in parallel traditions in multiple languages, and because their history stretches more than a millennium from the earliest attested to the latest versions, scholars often use genealogical strategies of analysis to discuss their entangled history. No analytical method can better account for them, it seems, than the arboreal ramifications of the genealogical tree. It is true that, if the scholar's ultimate goal is to prune variants in order to restore an authentic ur-text, then no method better serves the purpose. Yet, I will argue, this analytical strategy may obscure some of the most interesting dimensions of their complex transmission histories. In this chapter, I sketch a comparative reading of the narrative structures and transmission histories of the four works. My aim is to capture the irrational exuberance of these narrative traditions without overwhelming the reader with details. Given the abundance of the tradition, I cannot promise an exhaustive catalogue. Rather, my aim is to describe what did not survive the transition to modernity, as a foil to what did: why did certain articulations of 'wisdom' remain popular, while others faded away?

Given the sheer breadth of the transmission tradition – the number of languages in which these works appeared; their geographical reach, from the Indian subcontinent to Iceland and the Americas; and the period of their popularity, from late antiquity until (as we will see) the nineteenth century – variations between versions are inevitable. In some cases, the works were thoroughly transformed in transit between languages. Barlaam and Josaphat, for instance, started as a Buddhist work in the Indian subcontinent and Central Asia, and generated Muslim and Christian avatars as it travelled west.[10] The framing narrative of the Seven Sages of Rome remained largely identical in eastern and western versions; the embedded tales, however, had been almost entirely swapped for other tales by the time it reached the languages of western Europe. Kalilah and Dimnah – oddly, in this company – displayed a remarkable degree of narrative stability between late antiquity and the Middle Ages; the core narrative changed little from one language to the next. In almost every case, the extant versions of these narratives were anonymous. Perhaps their anonymity encouraged copyists and budding narrative artists of varying degrees of ambition and talent to make the tales their own. It also seems possible that some of these tales fed a luxuriant oral tradition. Indeed, the extant versions are probably the tip of an iceberg that scholars will never reconstruct. The paths that carried the narratives from one region and from one language to another must have included oral transmission alongside ephemeral written versions that have not survived.

The plots of these works typically test a young male protagonist, whom circumstances have placed at the centre of political, sexual or religious intrigue. The protagonist of Barlaam and Josaphat, the titular Josaphat, is an ascetic who faces a number of opponents: false teachers and his own father. They try to convince him to enjoy the pleasures of this life and return to orthodox religious practice; Josaphat instead converts each to his own true religion. The central figures in Kalilah and Dimnah are the eponymous anthropomorphised jackals, who serve as advisors to a foolish king. Dimnah – headstrong and rash – meddles in the king's affairs. Wise Kalilah counters the examples of both the king and Dimnah, modelling how a prudent man keeps his head when those around him are fools. The Seven Sages of Rome places a young man in a situation of sexual danger, and at the same time under a vow of silence. His father is the head of the state and a foolish man. His father's wife has accused him of attempting to rape her, and the young man's silence complicates his self-defence at the ensuing trial.[11] In the Book of Secundus, the protagonist, a young man named Secundus who had been sent away to study with philosophers as a boy, decides to test his widowed mother's virtue on his return. He has been gone for so long that she does not recognise him. When she agrees to sleep with him in exchange for payment, the young man reveals his identity. Horrified by the realisation that she was about to sleep with her own son, she kills herself; the young man, having seen the consequences of his actions, pledges never to speak again. The story is, in a sense, a variation on the Oedipal narrative, in which the son orchestrates the incestuous outrage, and anagnorisis comes to the mother rather than to him. Because the boy had been renowned for his learning before he fell silent, the emperor interests himself in Secundus's fate. The body of the book consists of notes that the young man writes out in response to the emperor's questions to him. In this case, the role of the older man who must be instructed or replaced by the protagonist is taken on by the emperor, the boy's tutor (who taught him that all women are weak and inherently sinful), and in a sense the boy himself, whose temptation of his mother backfires so spectacularly. The narrative dwells on his remorse for his actions.

Thus, in each of these works a young male hero who is a model of probity and self-control faces off against older men who serve as negative example, lacking in the virtues exemplified by the protagonist. Josaphat, Kalilah, the protagonist of the Seven Sages and Secundus each must keep their heads while those around them plot, vacillate or wait passively for the enlightenment that only the protagonist can provide. In most of the works, a feminine figure also provides conflict. The king's wife in the Seven Sages and the philosopher's mother in Secundus function as villains or fatally flawed figures, opposing the virtuous protagonist, and embedded material in both frame narratives underscores the misogynistic theme. In an embedded narrative in Barlaam and Josaphat, a woman appears to tempt the protagonist, only to be converted and redeemed. There are few women in Kalilah and Dimnah; the narrative is set in the homosocial world of the court. These works, that is, depict a world in which women are passive, not agents of their own fates – which helps to explain why they have faded from popularity today.

The 'wisdom' promised by the books appears in the form of embedded narratives or episodic events in the life of the protagonist. Of the four works under consideration, three use narrative embedding in a prominent way. In Kalilah and Dimnah, characters tell stories which serve to illustrate truths about the management of complex societies, and these form the bulk of the narrative. The story of the two eponymous jackals is but one of a sequence of framing narratives embedded within the main framing structure, in which a philosopher offers advice to a king in the form of didactic teaching tales. In the Seven Sages of Rome, a second wife of the protagonist's father has tried to seduce him. He resists her advances; after he spurns her, she accuses him of attempted rape. But the young man has taken a vow of silence, because he has seen in his horoscope that if he speaks, he will die. A series of embedded tales, told by the Seven Sages (the boy's tutors) and the wife, present a proxy trial before the father – a dithering and ineffectual king who holds ultimate power over the boy's fate. Embedded tales in the Seven Sages and Kalilah and Dimnah and the young man's responses to the emperor's questions in the Book of Secundus take up most of the book. The tale of Barlaam and Josaphat focuses on the deeds of the son (Josaphat) and the advice of his wise tutor (Barlaam), who must defend their virtuous lifestyle against the frivolous king and father and his nefarious religious advisors. Some embedded tales told to illustrate morals spice things up, but in this case, the exemplary life of the protagonist and his tutor's astute spiritual advice provide narrative focus.

In most of these narratives, a young man supersedes a father figure. Josaphat's father will ultimately embrace the ascetic life modelled by his son. The Emperor Hadrian will learn from the tutelage of the young philosopher Secundus. The Seven Sages of Rome ends with the son's rise – and, implicitly, the eclipse of the father's power. Because the son has taken a vow of silence, his tutors (and, in the western version, the queen who accused him of attempted rape) have taken turns telling stories that illustrate the son's innocence (or, in the queen's tales, his guilt). At the end of the narrative, the son regains his ability to speak, and tells a final story in self-defence. In this tale – essentially, a *mise en abîme* of the framing narrative – a young man prophesies his own rise to power, and that prophecy is fulfilled at the tale's end.[12] Sadly, both of the jackals who play starring roles in Kalilah and Dimnah fall victim to the political intrigues of the court; the narrative traces their rise and fall. In subsequent embedded narrative frames, after their demise, a philosopher continues his tutelage of a king. In this case, a subservient character – the jackals, who are ministers to a lion king; the philosopher, advisor to a king – advise a character in power, the king himself. But there is no generational dynamic to the narrative, and no formal succession of power from one character to another. With the exception of Kalilah and Dimnah, each of the narratives conveys a message of succession: a rising generation inherits the reins of power, and must push aside the generation of the fathers and take its place in the world.

The 'wisdom' embedded in the narratives treats a different theme in each work. Barlaam and Josaphat deals with religious and spiritual truths, related in the form of both homilies delivered by the two main characters and embedded tales. Kalilah and Dimnah collects teaching tales about managing complex social and political situations. The Seven Sages of Rome focuses on gender and relations between the sexes. The Book of Secundus takes the form of an analytical word list: a series of definitions of key terms from the fields of natural philosophy (the material world), spiritual and divine truths, and the social universe (including, inevitably, terms relating to gender). In response to each question – 'What is the universe?', 'What is God?', and so on – the text supplies a list of nouns and adjectives in apposition with the term defined. Because of the paratactic nature of the definitions, and because of the specialised vocabulary used in some of them, bizarre errors in translation inevitably occur.[13] Other divergences appear in the various languages, as each interpolates terminology that seems important. All the complete versions end with the ultimate question: 'What is death?' The form of the book sounds, and is, bizarre. It suggests that words construct or discover reality, as if they were the medieval equivalent of the molecular biologist's microscope or the astrophysicist's telescope. Its translation between languages adds another dimension of peculiarity to the picture, as definitions shift slightly in meaning, expand and contract, are added or pruned in parallel languages.

Of the four narratives examined here, the Seven Sages of Rome has a unique status, for two reasons in particular. First, although it is difficult to measure such things, the text probably circulated in more languages than any of the other texts under discussion. Scholars generally divide the Seven Sages narrative into an 'eastern version' and 'western version'. The two branches share a framing narrative but have different embedded narratives. Spin-offs of this tradition include a dizzying number of versions, often widely divergent in style and in narrative details, almost all anonymous, in poetry and in prose. Redactions of the eastern version survive in Arabic, Bulgarian, Greek, Hebrew, Persian, Romanian, Serbian, Spanish, Syriac and Turkish. The western version is extant in Armenian, Catalan, Celtic (both Scots Gaelic and Welsh), Danish, Dutch, English (including Midland, Northern, Scots and Southern English and a colonial American version), French (including numerous continuations of the core narrative), German, Hebrew, Hungarian, Icelandic, Italian, Latin, Lithuanian, Norwegian, Provençal, Slavic, Spanish, Swedish and Yiddish.[14] New versions continued to appear into the nineteenth century. Sofronij Vračanski's Bulgarian translation of a Greek version of the narrative was published in 1802; Romanian translations appeared in 1802 and 1834, and Serbian in 1809, 1848 and 1855.[15] Only Kalilah and Dimnah, still in print as a children's book in the Islamic languages, has more staying power than the Seven Sages.

Secondly, more than the other works discussed here, the Seven Sages of Rome gathers narratives spun to entertain while they instruct. Its central hero is a young man renowned for his wisdom, and the text claims to present truths about women and relations between men and women. But those truths are presented in the form of complex fictional narratives, not didactic tales or simple Aesopic fables. The presence of tales that entertain while they instruct may help to account for the ongoing popularity of the narrative into the nineteenth century.

Indeed, three of the four textual traditions discussed here successfully negotiated the transition into print, although the early modern print reception of these works has been little studied. Kalilah and Dimnah appeared in Spanish as *Exemplario contra los engaños, y peligros del mundo* (1515) and in Italian as *La Moral' filosophia del Doni* (1552). The Italian volume included a version of the Seven Sages of Rome, making it something of an omnibus of wisdom literature. A new translation from the Greek would be published in Italian as *Del governo de' regni* in 1583; it should be no surprise, given the tangled manuscript and publication history, that the transmission tradition of this version has been the topic of some scholarly debate.[16] Once the printing press reached the Arabophone world, Kalilah and Dimnah would regain its popularity in Arabic. Barlaam and Josaphat appeared in Latin in 1472–73 (the title is listed in modern catalogues as *Explicit Liber Barlaam et Iosaphat*) and in German as *Die Hystori Iosaphat vnd Barlaam* in 1475. It remained popular in printed versions in the languages of western Europe, and inspired stage plays in Spanish and French.[17] The Seven Sages of Rome would have continued popularity in the western European languages, under too many titles to track in a chapter of this length. It is not a work that we still read in the twenty-first century, and we do not teach it at universities today. But it did survive, and indeed win new readers, into the modern era. Bulgarian, Romanian and Serbian were relatively new languages of publication in the nineteenth century. The translation of the eastern version of the Seven Sages tradition into these languages was an important milestone in their evolution as modern national languages and as languages of literature during the print era. The Seven Sages may yet make another comeback; the movies or the emergent podcast industry may discover it and mine it for narrative material. If it has indeed faded for good this time, it may be because mainstream audiences have finally rejected its overtly misogynistic themes. The Book of Secundus alone, of the works considered in this chapter, did not survive the transition from manuscript to print (as far as I am aware).

Their claim to aggregate wisdom, each in a distinct field, alongside the entertainment value of the tales they include accounts for the appeal of these works during the pre-modern era. Why did they fade from popularity – quickly or gradually, as the case may be – during modernity? A comparison with works that were popular during pre-modernity and that lost none of their appeal during modernity may provide at least partial answers to that question. Giovanni Boccaccio's *Decameron*, for instance, circulated widely during Boccaccio's lifetime, and continues to be read in translation and in the original, for education and for pleasure.[18] The work shares a number of qualities with the Seven Sages of Rome. It, too, takes the form of a framed narrative. Boccaccio sets the scene during the plague of 1347. His framing narrative sends a group of young aristocrats off to the countryside to avoid the devastation of Florence;

there, they tell stories to pass the time. Like the Seven Sages, that is, the *Decameron* represents storytelling as a therapeutic exercise, which a community engages in together in order to address a social crisis. In the *Decameron*, however, the stories are told to entertain, not for the purpose of moral improvement. The *Decameron* differs from the Seven Sages too in that it is an authored work, not a big, baggy, messy tradition with ramifications and variations; there is a single correct version of it (an autograph manuscript survives).[19] Furthermore, the *Decameron* focuses on relations between the sexes and celebrates adulterous sex – but it is not overtly misogynistic. These facts, taken together, may help to account for its success. Of course, the chief reason for its ongoing popularity is Boccaccio's consummate skill as a storyteller. The *Decameron* is still hilarious, tragic, sexy and surprising, 600 years after its writing; this is part of the reason why we still read it (and teach it) today.

Dante's *Commedia* provides another example of a work that was read then and that we still read today. No one would call the *Commedia* 'wisdom literature', although it intersects with the works under discussion here in its effort to assemble truths about this life and the next. Like Barlaam and Josaphat, it has strong spiritual themes. Like Kalilah and Dimnah, it reflects upon the governance of states. Like Barlaam and Josaphat, the Book of Secundus and the Seven Sages of Rome, it features as its protagonist a man who must mature through understanding the limitations of a father figure: Virgil, who guides the pilgrim Dante through Hell and Purgatory. The *Commedia* was wildly successful then – although Dante lived near the close of the Middle Ages, more manuscripts of this work survive than of any other work in the western European languages besides the Bible – and still is today.[20] Its fortunes dimmed briefly during the eighteenth century, when a European public looked for wisdom beyond Dante's Catholic worldview. But the work rebounded during the nineteenth century, as readers came to appreciate Dante's consummate skill in characterisation and plotting. It continues to sell, and to inspire new translations, adaptations, movies, podcasts and video games, in the twenty-first century, and it remains a staple of undergraduate education in Europe and North America. In this case, the reason for the success of the work is evident: it is a work of sublime beauty, and even for non-Catholics or non-Christians, Dante's search for lasting truths resonates. It also, like the *Decameron*, is an authored text with few and minor manuscript variations.

Pre-modern audiences, like modern audiences, appreciated both the wisdom and wit embodied in these masterpieces. And both pre-modern readers and modern readers are moved by the magnificence of the *Commedia* and the *Decameron*: their consummate skill and artistry. It is instructive to note that the third Italian genius of the late Middle Ages, Petrarch, also produced a medieval bestseller and a modern masterpiece; but in his case, these were two different works. Petrarch's most popular work during the fourteenth and fifteenth centuries was *De remediis utriusque fortunae*, a Latin treatise of moral philosophy which has more in common with the wisdom literature discussed in this chapter than with the *Commedia* or the *Decameron*.[21] The collection of vernacular poetry written for Laura, most often read today – known as the *Canzoniere* or *Rerum vulgarium fragmenta* – circulated, but not widely before the Renaissance. Like the medieval masterpieces studied in other chapters in this volume, it spoke to later readers more compellingly than to Petrarch's contemporaries. The poems of romantic love – tormented, insistent, sublime and dejected by turns – had less interest for late medieval readers than the improving advice of *De remediis utriusque fortunae*. The poems, that is, are the outpouring of an eccentric, exceptional soul – like the *unicum* manuscripts that the Romantics embraced as expressions of a spirit both timeless and uniquely medieval in nature discussed in Part I of this volume.

The works that medieval audiences loved but modern readers do not, on the other hand, do not successfully balance 'wisdom' and narrative energy. The Book of Secundus, at the end of the day, is little more than a dreary misogynistic narrative followed by a word list. The ascetic message at the heart of Barlaam and Josaphat seems to have little future, at least for European and North American audiences. Kalilah and Dimnah possesses a certain narrative energy, as it pits tenacious ministers against thuggish monarchs. That dimension of the work was mined for a stage play by Kuwaiti playwright Sulayman al-Bassam; his play *Kalilah and Dimnah; or, the Mirror for Princes* was first performed at the Tokyo International Arts Festival in 2006 and had its UK premiere at the Pit Theatre in London on 10 May 2006. And the narrative remains popular in the Islamic languages, most often as a book for younger readers.

The Seven Sages of Rome – with its tale of a young man combating the vices of women and the lazy brutality of older men – seems to have a periodic appeal. The most recent iterations of that work appeared in the Balkans, two centuries ago. Since the tale has the ability to leapfrog continents and centuries, it may yet rebound; new versions may appear, in new languages. However, as scholars have recognised for years, the framing narrative of that work is indebted to the story of the prophet Joseph, as it is told in the Bible (Gen. 37:1–46:7) and the Qur'an (surah Yusuf).[22] It derives its narrative effectiveness as much from its scriptural sources as from its medieval sources. The framing narrative, that is, might make a fair claim to be one of the oldest stories in the world: about gender wars, and how a new generation tests itself against its elders. Packaged with the embedded narratives found in the eastern version (the Book of Sindbad the Wise) and the western version (the Seven Sages of Rome), it is indeed a unique work, which reflects on the (feminine and elderly masculine) opponents who pit themselves against a young man's propulsive energy and fate. If a writer of genius – such as Boccaccio or Dante, such as Niẓāmī (who wrote a Persian version of the Alexander Romance) or Ibn al-Muqaffaʿ (who brought Kalilah and Dimnah into Arabic) – had turned his hand to the work, it might still be read and studied today, like the *Decameron* and the *Commedia*. The misogynistic message, however, would not go down well with modern readers. Like Boccaccio's *Corbaccio*, a virulently misogynistic treatise, the Seven Sages seems excluded from modern bedside tables and nurseries by virtue of its message.

The transmission traditions I have sketched in this chapter are not generally analysed in parallel, because each narrative tradition displays complexities that comparative treatment flattens or erases. Yet when placed side by side, the traditions raise questions that might challenge literary historians to think differently about the works both individually and in aggregate. What was the audience for each of these works? Did the audiences overlap, or did each aim for a different market? In what format were these works most popular: poetry or prose, oral or written? Did the mode of delivery change across languages or was it stable? What does the manuscript history of the works tell us about their public, and how and why audiences consumed them? Do marginalia help to elucidate the morals that their readers took away from them? The early modern print reception of these works is virtually unstudied, yet three of the four narratives analysed here seem to have retained their popularity into the era of print. Who published these books? Who wrote the versions that were published? Who bought and read them?[23]

Genealogical analysis assumes that the oldest version of a text is the most valuable, and identifies deviations from the original text in order to remove them and restore an ur-text. This is a useful scholarly methodology for authored works that do not survive in an autograph manuscript, such as the *Commedia*, and it answers interesting questions about the transmission history of important works (not least scriptural texts). However, it ignores some of the most interesting questions about the transmission traditions I have discussed in this chapter. In order to characterise the complex patterns traced by works such as the Seven Sages of Rome, Barlaam and Josaphat, the Book of Secundus and Kalilah and Dimnah – as individual works, but also in aggregate, as a literary category – the scholar must be able to see the pattern created by a vast number of manuscripts and languages, narratives and variants. Is it possible to capture this kind of complexity in a single diagram? The arboreal designs favoured by scholars for tracing manuscript transmission do not capture complexity; they prune it, trimming divergence as the corruption of a more correct version, embodied in a previous manuscript generation. But the narrative traditions I have described here tell another story, on two levels at once. In this story, each new generation pushes aside the last, building on the foundation laid down by its elders or in previous iterations of the narrative. Each generation vows to get the story right this time. Rather than privileging earlier versions of the narratives, scholars might capture the complexity of these transmission traditions using scatter maps, for instance, in order to represent each new linguistic version or each specific narrative variant, from the Indian subcontinent to the Americas. Or we might create a GIF in order to track the historical movement of the narratives from region to region and/or from language to language. Such analytical strategies reward innovation, rather than identifying it as an invasive element to exclude from the tradition. To be sure, children are not always wiser than their parents. But – as these narratives teach – the future belongs to them; the most important story is always the one that the next generation will tell about their past.

Notes

1 *OED Online*, www.oed.com/view/Entry/229491 (accessed January 2020), s.v. 'wisdom'.

2 On the Book of Secundus, see B. E. Perry, *Secundus, the Silent Philosopher* (Ithaca, NY: American Philological Association and Cornell University Press, 1964), and Oliver Overwien, 'Secundus the Silent Philosopher', in Carolina Cupane and Bettina Krönung (eds), *Fictional Storytelling in the Medieval Eastern Mediterranean and Beyond* (Leiden: Brill, 2016), pp. 338–64.

3 Perry, *Secundus*, Arabic 40–1; English 146–7. On the verbosity of the Arabic version – which may be an accurate reflection of the Greek version translated by the Arabic – see Overwien, 'Secundus', p. 342.

4 In this chapter, I do not italicise the names of narrative traditions, as opposed to individual (authored or anonymous) works. The traditions I am discussing do not have a single, unified form to be designated by a single title. They also circulated under a vast number of titles; the names I have given them here represent the most common title used in Western scholarship on each of the traditions.

5 On Kalilah and Dimnah, see C. Brockelmann, 'Kalīla wa-Dimnah', in P. Bearman, T. Bianquis, C. E. Bosworth, E. van Donzel and W. P. Heinrichs (eds), *Encyclopaedia of Islam*, 2nd edn, BrillOnline Reference Works, 2012, https://referenceworks.brillonline.com/browse/encyclopaedia-of-islam-2 (accessed 8 February 2022); *Kalilah and Dimnah: An English Version of Bidpai's Fables Based upon Ancient Arabic and Spanish Manuscripts*, trans. Thomas Ballantine Irving (Newark, DE: Juan de la Cuesta, 1980); and Karla Mallette, 'The Secular Wisdom of Kalila and Dimna', in Christine Chism (ed.), *Wiley-Blackwell Companion to World Literature, 601–1450 CE* (Oxford: Wiley Blackwell, 2019) for an overview and further bibliography.

6 Ibn al-Nadīm, Muḥammad ibn Isḥāq, *Al-Fihrist*, ed. Sha'bān 'Abd al-'Azīz Khalīfah and Walīd Muḥammad 'Awzah, 2 vols (Cairo: al-'Arabī lil-Nashr wa-al-Tawzī', 1991), vol. I, pp. 610–12; *The Fihrist of al-Nadīm: A Tenth-Century Survey of Muslim Culture*, ed. and trans. Bayard Dodge (New York: Columbia University Press, 1970), pp. 715–17.

7 Kalilah and Dimnah derives ultimately from the *Panchatantra*, a Sanskrit work dating to c. 300 CE. A Pahlavi (Middle Persian) version is presumed to have existed, but is not extant; see Mallette, 'The Secular Wisdom of *Kalila and Dimna*', p. 4.

8 See D. M. Lang, 'Bilawhar wa-Yūdasaf', in P. Bearman, T. Bianquis, C. E. Bosworth, E. van Donzel and W. P. Heinrichs (eds), *Encyclopaedia of Islam*, 2nd edn, BrillOnline Reference Works, 2012, https://

referenceworks.brillonline.com/browse/encyclopaedia-of-islam-2 (accessed 8 February 2022).

9 The oldest extant manuscript witness is Syriac; see Overwien, 'Secundus', pp. 345–53. Scholars have seen al-Mas'ūdī's discussion of a silent philosopher from the age of the Emperor Hadrian as evidence that he knew an Arabic version of Secundus. Overwien argues convincingly that in fact al-Mas'ūdī referred to *vitae*, rather than to the text that we know from later extant versions. He points to works from the early eleventh century CE for the earliest Arabic cognate versions; see Overwien, 'Secundus', pp. 353–8.

10 On Barlaam and Josaphat, in addition to Lang, see Donald S. Lopez and Peggy McCracken, *In Search of the Christian Buddha: How an Asian Sage Became a Medieval Saint* (New York: W. W. Norton, 2014); *Hystoria Barlae et Iosaphat: Bibl. Nacional de Nápoles VIII. B.10*, ed. José Martínez Gázquez (Madrid: Consejo Superior de Investigaciones Científicas, 1997), for an edition of the oldest extant Latin version; Peggy McCracken, *Barlaam and Josaphat: A Christian Tale of the Buddha* (London: Penguin, 2014), for a translation of an Old French version of the tale; Daniel Gimaret, *Le Livre de Bilawhar et Būdāsf selon la version arabe Ismaélienne* (Geneva: Droz, 1971), for a translation of the oldest extant Arabic version; *Kitāb Bilawhar wa-Būdhāsaf*, ed. Daniel Gimaret (Beirut: Dār al-Mashriq, 1972), for an edition of the Arabic version; and Marion Uhlig, *Le Princes des clercs: Barlaam et Josaphat ou l'art du recueil* (Geneva: Droz, 2018), for an interesting recent account of the tradition.

11 In part because of the number and diversity of medieval versions in the languages of western Europe, the bibliography on the Seven Sages of Rome is truly bottomless. Since the nineteenth century, when scholars still believed that they could understand the full sweep of a transmission tradition like this, few have attempted a synoptic overview; for the culmination of the nineteenth-century scholarship, see Killis Campbell, 'A Study of the Romance of the Seven Sages with Special Reference to the Middle English Versions', *PMLA* 14 (1899): 1–107. Scholars divide the tradition into two branches, an 'eastern version' and a 'western version'. The 'eastern version' is older, yet has been much less studied. Among other differences, the titles of works in the eastern version tend to derive from the name of the central character: Sindbad the Wise in the Arabic, Syntipas in the Greek, Sendebar in the Hebrew, and so on. B. E. Perry, 'The Origin of the Book of Sindbad', *Fabula* 3 (1959): 1–94, attempts an overview encompassing both eastern and western versions, in order to determine the origins of the eastern version. The complexity of the work (and the scholarship) is compounded by the

fact that the frame tale draws on the story of Yusuf and Zulaykha related in the Qur'an (see Gayane Karen Merguerian and Afsaneh Najmabadi, 'Zulaykha and Yusuf: Whose "Best Story"?', *International Journal of Middle East Studies* 29 [1997]: 485–508) and is entangled with both the frame tale of the *1001 Nights* and an embedded tale in that tradition (see ibid. and Karla Mallette, 'Reading Backward: The *1001 Nights* and Philological Practice', in Suzanne Akbari and Karla Mallette (eds), *A Sea of Languages: Literature and Culture in the Pre-Modern Mediterranean* [Toronto: University of Toronto Press, 2013], pp. 100–16). In recent years, the bibliography maintained by Hans Runte has aggregated scholarship on the tradition across languages. That website is no longer maintained, although it is currently archived. It is a snapshot of scholarly responses to a tradition so diverse and so rich that, like the torments of Tantalus, it both tempts scholars and defies any effort to master it. I will reference the archived website in this chapter where it remains the authoritative source.

12 Both the temptation of the protagonist and the protagonist's prophecy of his rise to power reflect the tale's similarity to, and presumed origins in, scriptural tales about Joseph.

13 For examples, see Perry, *Secundus*, pp. 34–6.

14 The Seven Sages Society, The Book of Sindbad and the Seven Sages: Versions, https://dalspace.library.dal.ca/handle/10222/49107 (accessed January 2022).

15 Hans R. Runte, portal, Society of the Seven Sages, 2014, https://dalspace.library.dal.ca/handle/10222/49107 (accessed March 2020).

16 For discussion, see John-Theophanes Papademetriou, 'The Sources and the Character of *Del governo de' regni*', *Transactions and Proceedings of the American Philological Association* 92 (1961): 422–39.

17 For the stage plays, see Peggy McCracken, 'Translations and Travels of a Pious Prince: *Barlaam and Josaphat* and the Text Network', in Wiebke Denecke (ed.), *Wiley-Blackwell Companion to World Literature, Third Millennium BCE–600 CE* (Oxford: Wiley Blackwell, 2019), p. 2, https://www.onlinelibrary.wiley.com/doi/10.1002/9781118635193.ctwl0048 (accessed March 2020).

18 Sixty manuscripts of the *Decameron* copied during the fourteenth and fifteenth centuries survive; see Marco Cursi, *Il Decameron: Scritture, Scriventi, Lettori. Storia di un Testo* (Rome: Viella, 2007), pp. 14–15, 161–238 (for a detailed manuscript catalogue). This is all the more impressive considering that Boccaccio died only in 1375.

19 The most authoritative autograph manuscript is Berlin, Staatsbibliothek Preussischer Kulturbesitz, Hamilton 90 (B); see Guyda Armstrong,

Rhiannon Daniels and Stephen J. Miller (eds), *The Cambridge Companion to Boccaccio* (Cambridge: Cambridge University Press, 2015), p. xviii.

20 Eight hundred manuscripts of the *Commedia* survive; 600 of those are complete manuscripts of all three canticles (*Inferno*, *Purgatorio* and *Paradiso*). See Prue Shaw, 'Transmission History', in Zygmunt G. Barański and Simon A. Gilson (eds), *The Cambridge Companion to Dante's 'Commedia'* (Cambridge: Cambridge University Press, 2019), p. 229.

21 On *De remediis*, see Timothy Kircher, 'On the Two Faces of Fortune', in Armando Maggi and Victoria Kirkham (eds), *Petrarch: A Critical Guide to the Complete Works* (Chicago: University of Chicago Press, 2009), pp. 245–53.

22 See Merguerian and Najmabadi, 'Zulaykha and Yusuf'.

23 For a consideration of one of these narratives – the Seven Sages of Rome, versified by an anonymous author and published in Italy as *Erasto* in 1542, with frequent reprints – see Karla Mallette, 'St Elmo's Fire: Fortune and Fortune Telling in Mediterranean Literature', in Mario Mignone (ed.), *The Idea of the Mediterranean* (Stony Brook NY: Forum Italicum, 2017), pp. 114–32.

Works cited

Primary sources

Barlaam and Josaphat: *A Christian Tale of the Buddha*, trans. Peggy McCracken (London: Penguin, 2014).

Al-Bassam, Sulayman, *Kalilah Wa Dimnah, Or, The Mirror for Princes* (London: Oberon Books, 2006).

Boccaccio, Giovanni, *Decameron. Tutte le opere di Giovanni Boccaccio*, ed. Vittore Branca, vol. IV (Milan: Mondadori, 1964).

— *The Decameron*, trans. G. H. McWilliam, 2nd edn (New York: Penguin, 1995).

Dante Alighieri, *La Commedia secondo l'antica vulgata*, ed. Giorgio Petrocchi, 2nd edn, 4 vols (Florence: Le Lettere, 1994).

— *The Divine Comedy*, trans. John D. Sinclair, 3 vols (Oxford: Oxford University Press, 1981).

Del governo de' regni: Sotto morali esempi di animali ragionanti tra loro, ed. Domenico Mammarelli (Bologna: Commissione per i testi di lingua, 1968).

Exemplario contra los engaños, y peligros del mundo (Zaragoza: Jorge Coci, 1515).

Die Hystori Iosaphat vnd Barlaam (Augsburg: G. Zainer, 1475).

Liber Barlaam et Iosaphat (Speyer, Germany: [Printer of Gesta Christi], 1472–73).

Hystoria Barlae et Iosaphat: Bibl. Nacional de Nápoles VIII. B.10, ed. José Martínez Gázquez (Madrid: Consejo Superior de Investigaciones Científicas, 1997).

Ibn al-Nadīm, Muḥammad ibn Isḥāq, *Al-Fihrist*, ed. Sha'bān 'Abd al-'Azīz Khalīfah and Walīd Muḥammad 'Awzah, 2 vols (Cairo: al-'Arabī lil-Nashr wa-al-Tawzī', 1991).

— *The Fihrist of al-Nadīm: A Tenth-Century Survey of Muslim Culture*, ed. and trans. Bayard Dodge (New York: Columbia University Press, 1970).

Kalilah and Dimnah: An English Version of Bidpai's Fables Based upon Ancient Arabic and Spanish Manuscripts, trans. Thomas Ballantine Irving (Newark, DE: Juan de la Cuesta, 1980).

Kitāb Bilawhar wa-Būdhāsaf, ed. Daniel Gimaret (Beirut: Dār al-Mashriq, 1972).

Le Livre de Bilawhar et Būdāsf selon la version arabe Ismaélienne, ed. Daniel Gimaret (Geneva: Droz, 1971).

La Moral' filosophia del Doni (Venice: Marcolini, 1552).

Petrarch, Francesco, *Il canzoniere*, ed. Marco Santagata (Milan: Mondadori, 2004).

— *The Canzoniere, or Rerum Vulgarium Fragmenta*, trans. Mark Musa (Bloomington, IN: Indiana University Press, 1996).

— *Petrarch's Remedies for Fortune Fair and Foul*, trans. Conrad H. Rawski (Bloomington, IN: Indiana University Press, 1991).

— *Les remèdes aux deux fortunes*, trans. Christophe Carraud (Grenoble: Millon, 2002).

Secondary sources

Armstrong, Guyda, Rhiannon Daniels and Stephen J. Miller (eds), *The Cambridge Companion to Boccaccio* (Cambridge: Cambridge University Press, 2015).

Brockelmann, C., 'Kalīla wa-Dimna', in P. Bearman, T. Bianquis, C. E. Bosworth, E. van Donzel and W. P. Heinrichs (eds), *Encyclopaedia of Islam*, 2nd edn, BrillOnline Reference Works, 2012, https://referenceworks.brillonline.com/browse/encyclopaedia-of-islam-2 (accessed 8 February 2022).

Campbell, Killis, 'A Study of the Romance of the Seven Sages with Special Reference to the Middle English Versions', *PMLA* 14 (1899): 1–107.

Cursi, Marco, *Il Decameron: Scritture, Scriventi, Lettori. Storia di un Testo* (Rome: Viella, 2007).

Kircher, Timothy, 'On the Two Faces of Fortune', in Armando Maggi and Victoria Kirkham (eds), *Petrarch: A Critical Guide to the Complete Works* (Chicago: University of Chicago Press, 2009), pp. 245–53.

Lang, D. M., 'Bilawhar Wa-Yūdāsaf', in P. Bearman, T. Bianquis, C. E. Bosworth, E. van Donzel and W. P. Heinrichs (eds), *Encyclopaedia of Islam*, 2nd edn,

BrillOnline Reference Works, 2012, https://referenceworks.brillonline.com/browse/encyclopaedia-of-islam-2 (accessed 8 February 2022).

Lopez, Donald S., and Peggy McCracken, *In Search of the Christian Buddha: How an Asian Sage Became a Medieval Saint* (New York: W. W. Norton, 2014).

Mallette, Karla, 'Reading Backward: The *1001 Nights* and Philological Practice', in Suzanne Akbari and Karla Mallette (eds), *A Sea of Languages: Literature and Culture in the Pre-Modern Mediterranean* (Toronto: University of Toronto Press, 2013), pp. 100–16.

— 'St Elmo's Fire: Fortune and Fortune Telling in Mediterranean Literature', in Mario Mignone (ed.), *The Idea of the Mediterranean* (Stony Brook, NY: Forum Italicum, 2017), pp. 114–32.

— 'The Secular Wisdom of *Kalila and Dimna*', in Christine Chism (ed.), *Wiley-Blackwell Companion to World Literature, 601–1450 CE* (Oxford: Wiley Blackwell, 2019), www.onlinelibrary.wiley.com/doi/10.1002/9781118635193.ctwl0098 (accessed March 2020).

McCracken, Peggy, 'Translations and Travels of a Pious Prince: *Barlaam and Josaphat* and the Text Network', in Wiebke Denecke (ed.), *Wiley-Blackwell Companion to World Literature, Third Millennium BCE–600 CE* (Oxford: Wiley Blackwell, 2019), www.onlinelibrary.wiley.com/doi/10.1002/9781118635193.ctwl0048 (accessed March 2020).

Merguerian, Gayane Karen, and Afsaneh Najmabadi, 'Zulaykha and Yusuf: Whose "Best Story"?', *International Journal of Middle East Studies* 29 (1997): 485–508.

Overwien, Oliver, 'Secundus the Silent Philosopher in the Ancient and Eastern Tradition', in Carolina Cupane and Bettina Krönung (eds), *Fictional Storytelling in the Medieval Eastern Mediterranean and Beyond* (Leiden: Brill, 2016), pp. 338–64.

Papademetriou, John-Theophanes, 'The Sources and the Character of *Del governo de' regni*', *Transactions and Proceedings of the American Philological Association* 92 (1961): 422–39.

Perry, B. E., 'The Origin of the Book of Sindbad', *Fabula* 3 (1959): 1–94.

— *Secundus, the Silent Philosopher* (Ithaca, NY: American Philological Association and Cornell University Press, 1964).

Runte, Hans R., portal, Society of the Seven Sages, 2014, https://dalspace.library.dal.ca/handle/10222/49107 (accessed March 2020).

Shaw, Prue, 'Transmission History', in Zygmunt G. Barański and Simon A. Gilson (eds), *The Cambridge Companion to Dante's 'Commedia'* (Cambridge: Cambridge University Press, 2019), pp. 229–44.

Uhlig, Marion, *Le Prince des clercs: Barlaam et Josaphat ou l'art du recueil* (Geneva: Droz, 2018).

9

Lost worlds: encyclopaedism and riddles in the tale of Tawaddud/Theodor

Christine Chism

This chapter focuses on an Arabic story of a scholarly slave girl, trained as a court singer and savant in Baghdad, who saves her master and proves her command of all the branches of knowledge by winning a question-and-answer contest with all the scholars that the Abbasid caliph, Hārūn al-Rashīd, can throw at her.[1] Her name in Arabic texts is Tawaddud, which connotes a range of loving attachments: showing and winning love or friendship, currying favour, ingratiating by flattery, attracting and captivating. The heroine therefore embodies forms of seduction, social climbing, devotion and rapture, which is apt because her story's appeals to its various adaptors seem equally compelling and various. Although some versions of the story may date to as early as the eighth century, the setting of the best-known Arabic versions is ninth-century Baghdad; Claudine Gerresch, however, associates its panoply of learning with Ayyubid Egypt.[2] The story's earliest extant Arabic version is a thirteenth-century manuscript in the Real Academia de Historia's Pascual de Gayangos collection, Ms. LXXI, in Madrid, though another mid-thirteenth-century Arabic version found in Granada is described by José Vasquez Ruiz.[3] In Arabic it circulated both as an independent manuscript and within the frame tale collections of *Alf Layla wa-Layla*, where it turns up in the nineteenth-century Calcutta II edition as 'The Tale of Abū'l Ḥusn and his Slave Girl, Tawaddud'. In Iberia it was de-Islamised, aligned with European wisdom traditions, and translated multiple times into Castilian, and when printing began it circulated even more widely: Rivera and Rogers compare various Spanish versions in their diplomatic edition.[4] Margaret Parker traces its trajectories in Spain, where it was expanded into an adventurous family romance by Lope de Vega.[5] It travelled from Spain and Portugal to the Americas, where abridged versions were translated into Mayan and appear in three Mayan community books, amid calendrical and medical lore and astronomical planting schedules.[6] It also resounded into nineteenth-century Brazilian *cordel* narratives.[7] As Damiana L. Eugenio shows, the story was also shipped by colonists to the Philippines, where it was expanded into a two-part romance and translated into Tagalog and other languages, intimating anti-colonial resistance along the way.[8] Within Islamicate cultures, the story circulated into and out of Persian,[9] and thanks to the world-literary spread of *The Thousand and One Nights* I do not doubt that there are also South Asian versions waiting to be discovered. I first encountered its Arabic version as a solitary manuscript of unknown provenance, though probably post-eighteenth century, in the Caro-Minasian collection at UCLA special collections, where it did not even name its characters until the ending colophon, where the name Tawaddud appeared. In sum, the global spread and adaptability of this narrative is extraordinary, signalling that it was not simply a medieval bestseller, but was translated, transculturated and reimagined until the nineteenth century in many widespread global cultures.

My argument about the Arabic version of the story of Tawaddud is twofold. First, the tale's initial appeal lay in its encyclopaedic capacity for making knowledge into worlds through heterogeneous assemblages. Second, it draws readers into its worlding through an interplay of two oppositional modes, encyclopaedic exposition and riddling, which offer audiences different forms of engagement. In the tale's Arabic versions, the two modes operate like a good cop/bad cop routine in which Tawaddud can play by turns a superlatively obedient and forthcoming slave, and a terrifying and enigmatic master. This interplay of exposition and riddling seems to have struck a global chord that resonated long beyond the medieval period.

However, modern editors and translators have not been as susceptible to its charms. Edward William Lane omitted the tale from his English translation of *The Thousand and One Nights* because it was both extremely technical, requiring 'a volume of commentary ... [and would be] extremely tiresome to most readers of the present work'.[10] It is hard to swallow someone else's cultural world. The adjective 'tedious' seems to have stuck. Robert Irwin classed Tawaddud with Nuzhat al-Zaman as partners in the crime of boredom 'in a world of tedious slave girls'.[11] Richard Burton commented that Lane's assessment was 'Quite true', but he defended the tale as 'valuable to Oriental Students who are beginning their studies, as an excellent compendium of doctrine and practice according to the Shafi' school',[12] and fenced it gleefully with an armature of explanatory notes. It seems too didactic or abstruse (jurisprudential, astrological and exegetical minutiae abound) even for recent editors; it is sometimes omitted from Arabic editions of *The Thousand and One Nights*, even when they otherwise follow Calcutta II closely.[13]

So what accounts for the narrative's nineteenth- and twentieth-century eclipse? In addition to its technical content, the tale's history of global dissemination may have discouraged uptake within nationally and linguistically organised disciplinary fields. Stories that promiscuously cross language barriers, regional boundaries and confessional cultures have often fallen into scholarly oblivion because tracing their dissemination requires so much expertise. However, recently a number of travelling tales have come to the attention of critics interested in crossing the national and linguistic boundaries established by nineteenth-century European medievalists. Scholars from many disciplines are collaborating, sharing expertise through productive confederations such as Mediterranean Studies, Indian Ocean Studies, Silk Road Studies, trans-Saharan Studies and Global Medievalism. As a result, some of the most enduring and peripatetic medieval bestsellers are attracting new attention.

The remarkable spread of the story of Tawaddud attests to its appeal to pre-nineteenth-century readers. Here I want to focus on an Arabic version of the story to try to parse what made it so appealing to so many people. For all its dubious compilation and late provenance, I am going to use the version extant in the Calcutta II edition of *The Thousand and One Nights*, because it has recently been translated by Malcolm C. Lyons and Ursula Lyons in a three-volume edition, and is therefore easily teachable.[14] I will also refer to one of the Mayan variants, in the Chilam Balam of Kaua, because it shows how deftly the narrative can be appropriated through strategies of deliberate transcultural adaptation and educative syncretism.[15]

The story is simple: a rich Baghdadi merchant prays for a son and is granted one, beautiful as the dawn. In life he gives the son everything he needs and, when he dies, he leaves the son a good endowment. The son, Abū al-Ḥusn, however, listens to profligate friends and becomes profligate himself, wasting his entire inheritance with the exception of a remarkable *qayna* (a well-educated female slave), Tawaddud.[16] When he calls her and tells her that he must sell her, she has a counter-proposal: that he offer her to the caliph, Hārūn al-Rashīd himself, for no less than 10,000 dinars. When the caliph asks why Tawaddud is worth so much, Abū al-Ḥusn should say that she will prove her worth by debating with all the great scholars of the land. Abū al-Ḥusn follows her plan, and Harūn al-Rashīd is intrigued. Scholars are called, including a famous Mu'tazilite theologian and rhetorician, Ibrahīm al-Naẓẓām, who is put in charge of operations. The date of the contest arrives. After introducing herself and giving a formidable curriculum vitae, Tawaddud dictates the structure of the exchanges: all the experts may examine her in a variety of subjects, and if she is able to answer all of their questions, she may pose several of her own to them. If they cannot answer, they must strip off their robes and present them to her, and if she cannot answer them, she will do the same.

The rest of the story comprises the scripts – from question-and-answer to next question – of this public, courtly, high-stakes examination contest, ending with a rhetorical examination by al-Naẓẓām consisting mostly of riddles. Tawaddud answers every question and collects a heap of robes, adroitly avoiding the entrapments of her interlocutors and keenly diverting the court, a pleasure that culminates when she caps her performance by enchanting them with her singing and dancing (a performance that was probably added late in the nineteenth century). When offered a reward, Tawaddud asks only to be returned to her master, but Harūn al-Rashīd endows both of them with a princely sum and makes Abū al-Ḥusn a court companion for life.

This story is among the longest in *The Thousand and One Nights*, because the exam scripts are reported so thoroughly. Tawaddud is grilled on Islamic ritual law, the Qur'an and its traditions, anatomy and medicine (including humoral theory and health regimes for best digestion and intercourse), astronomy (from the twenty-eight stations of the moon to calendrical astrology), philosophies of time and space, and rhetoric, including traditional lore, aphorisms and literary riddles. Lest we think this is simply an impossible curriculum, we may compare Tawaddud's accomplishments to those of another extraordinary (perhaps tactically hyperbolised) *qiyān*, described in the *Dakhīra* of Ibn Bassām (1058–1147), and purchased by Hudhayl ibn Razīn of Sahla, whose skills included grammatically correct singing and poetry, medicine, natural history, human anatomy, making weapons, and fighting with swords, spears and sharpened daggers.[17]

Since a *qayna*'s value rose with her accomplishments, Ibn Bassām reports that the slave merchant who sold this 3,000-dinar paragon to Hudhayl boasted that he had effectively trained other slaves in 'logic, philosophy, geometry, music ... the astrolabe, astronomy, astrology, grammar, prosody, literature and calligraphy' as well as Qur'anic exegesis.[18] The character of Tawaddud similarly assembles a level of expertise that at once indexes and hyperbolises into legend a cultural fantasy: the ultimate *qayna*. At the same time, she remains rooted in the pragmatics of female slavery as a profitable court industry.[19] Answering all the exam questions is key to an even larger prize: to prove herself worthy of the 10,000 dinars she names as her price and to incite even more generosity from the caliph.

To gain that prize Tawaddud proves her mastery not only of all the areas of art and science in which she is tested, but of the medium of the examination itself: she has to turn examination swotting into engaging narrative plotting. To keep readers awake, Tawaddud's examinations oscillate between two contrasting interrogatory modes: encyclopaedism and riddles. Together these modes make and unmake a system of culturally valued knowledge, and in so doing they perform 'worldings' in Gayatri Spivak's sense and then render those worlds strange and marvellous.[20] Encyclopaedism organises knowledge for easy uptake, and its organisation strategies are crucial to the worldings it performs. Encyclopaedism is more interested in organising answers than it is in asking questions. By contrast, riddles artfully camouflage knowledge; they are more invested in defamiliarising the world through artful acts of estrangement than in pinning down answers about it.

Tawaddud's examiners alternate these tactics. The terms of the knowledge contest are that Tawaddud will answer any scholar's questions for as long as he has any to ask, and then she may ask one or two of her own. If the master cannot answer, he must yield to her his robes of scholarship, shamefully stripping in public before the court. The high stakes of the contest are clear. Thus, once Tawaddud shows that she has mastered encyclopaedic knowledge, the increasingly desperate examiners change tack to throw her off by sudden turns of subject and trick questions. The final examiner, Ibrahīm al-Naẓẓām himself, asks only riddles – in as hostile a fashion as possible; he is the last and highest-stakes examiner, and his reputation is on the line. Tawaddud outmanoeuvres them all, and turns the tables on them with her own riddles, minutiae and aphorisms.

This chapter argues that the heady mixture of encyclopaedism and enigma is what appealed to pre-modern audiences, that wheeling between familiar systems of knowledge and their playful detournement helps account for the tale's early popularity and wide dissemination. Like *The Thousand and One Nights* itself, the story's frame heightens narrative stakes by pitting a woman against authoritative men, a slave against masters. However, within that frame it is the flavour of knowledge itself – by turns systematic and nimble – that provides the entertainment. The chapter also suggests that it is this very mixture that discouraged post-medieval audiences from the tales, since we like our encyclopaedias nicely bound in peer-reviewed volumes or sequestered in an internet database of public testing and review, as free as possible from figurative or ambiguous language. Literary riddles, by contrast, sprout from figurative and ambiguous language. A mixture of encyclopaedism and enigma strikes at our already shivering boundaries between fact and fiction, data and literature, truth and tales, risking both the authority of fact and the autonomy of fiction in ways that many post-nineteenth-century readers find distasteful.

This chapter falls into three sections: 1) encyclopaedism as a form of world making, 2) the perlocutionary force of the riddles with which Tawaddud turns the tables on her examiners, and 3) the productivity of riddling in the last examination with al-Naẓẓām. The conclusion reconsiders how riddling and encyclopaedism work in tandem. I make use of both Deleuzian assemblage theory and folklore and literary analysis of riddles across these sections.

Encyclopaedism and the making of worlds

I will follow the lead of recent work on pre-modern encyclopaedic texts by treating encyclopaedic writing less as a genre than an adaptable mode of systematising knowledge for a range of cultural uses.[21] Tawaddud does not recite an encyclopaedia, nor is she staking an anachronistic claim to the formal structures of modern encyclopaedias. However, like many other pre-modern gatherings of knowledge, her exam scripts snapshot the kinds of knowledge that other court scribes were composing as courtly *adab* encyclopaedic compilations. The editors of the *Encyclopedia of the Arabian Nights*, Ulrich Marzolph and Richard van Leewen, distinguish Tawaddud's tale from the popular, oral narratives that surround it in *Alf Layla wa Layla*, classing it closer to *adab* as a sententious mix of formal rhetoric, cultural literacies, basic science and *phronesis*.[22] To a reader immersed in the suspenseful narratives that surround it, it can come like a narrative slap in the face – all exposition, no action.[23] Its drama inheres instead in the breathless, momentary pause between question and answer, question and answer for twenty-five nights of Shahrazād's life.

Education in *adab* was specific to court cultures (Tawaddud's chosen forum in the tale) and the bureaucracies they generated. *Adab* included knowledge of culturally specific religious law, poetry and history, parts of all the sciences (philosophy, astronomy, mathematics and medicine), and finally manners, etiquette, witty conversation and diplomacy (and the various cultures/geographies with which it liaises). Tawaddud's list of accomplishments hews closely to an *adab* curriculum: she claims mastery of grammar, poetry, jurisprudence, Islamic ritual law, Qur'anic interpretation, Qur'anic *tafsīr*, *hadīth* and the *isnāds* that anchor them, ancient legends, mathematics, geometry, philosophy, medicine, rhetoric and exposition, music, flute playing and lute playing, dancing and singing. These last qualities were added to the late and European-produced version in Calcutta II, probably to re-feminise and re-exoticise Tawaddud after the dauntingly technical curriculum vitae.

Tawaddud's examination thus assembles a wide range of expertise into an encyclopaedic Islamic *Weltanshauung*. Such encyclopaedic gestures appeal to historians, because they so fiercely condense for transcultural portage the brain-map of a resonant cultural time-space, a chronotope. Thus, we have late editors such as Richard Burton, who sought such portals to various historically situated Oriental pasts: for him, Tawaddud was appealing as 'an excellent compendium of doctrine and practice according to the Shafi' school'.[24]

Tawaddud's encyclopaedism is both highly portable and cumulative. Although I do not do this work here, a study of various manuscripts might chart its assemblage and adaptation procedures, as it bears controversies from the early Abbasid court of its diegesis to the Ayyubid and Mamluk and Andalusian societies of its ongoing consumption, and beyond to other venues where it will shed Islamic features and acquire Christian ones or Mayan ones or Philippine ones, by processes of gnomic addition, reduction and adaptation. Thinking about this tale as an invitation to encyclopaedic assemblage (and reassemblage) can account for its pre-modern popularity, its global spread.

Assemblages that constellate unlike things create worlds that shed, reamalgamate and shift centres of gravity. Tawaddud's examinations liaise between bodies of ritual practice and legal study, exegesis and scriptural memorisation, anatomy and wellness practices, celestial/calendrical conjunctions and philosophy. Tawuddud's answers lay bare the customary practices of Islamic ritual law, but link to them the division of the Qur'an into Meccan and Medinan revelations, and the veins and bones of the human body, its digestive frailties, its sexual practices. Bodies in the motions of ritual law, temperate eating, tithing, fasting and sex cohabit with the textual body of the Qur'an, its histories of revelation, enriched by *hadith* transmissions through chains of trustworthy and untrustworthy authority. When astronomy is added to the assemblage, the human and textual bodies begin to resonate with even larger celestial bodies. Bodies are caught in a webwork of planetary forces that urge them historically and medically, exerting influences without suborning free will. A 1540 edition of a Spanish version of the narrative, found in Madrid BN R-10.688, visualises this conventional interpenetration of bodies by heavens by having the heroine draw a diagram of the human body marked with zodiacal influences, which the manuscript includes.[25] Through these assemblages, as the pile of surrendered robes of scholarship grows higher in front of her, Tawaddud maps her knowledge into a territory that becomes common and navigable to her courtly audience, and to many of the subsequent readers who adapted and reassembled this text.

This kind of territorialisation[26] seductively encapsulates a time-space of cultural production, inviting entry. The text conveys narrative worlds, and I think this is one of the most powerful pre-modern appeals of Tawaddud's story. That encyclopaedic texts make worlds is so much a truism that two recent important works on pre-modern encyclopaedism weave world and book into their titles.[27] Elias Muhanna vividly describes his experience of reading classical Islamic encyclopaedic works as similar to that of opening a surreal window or a distorting mirror into another world:

> The world that appears ... is not a plain reflection of ... quotidian reality but rather a medieval imaginary of warped dimensions, a dreamworld inhabited by real and fantastical creatures, living and long-dead monarchs, the sights and sounds of fourteenth-century Cairo alongside scenes from once-glorious Baghdad during its golden age.[28]

This description radiates the excitement of mixture: historical periods miscegenating, geographical spaces collapsing, the everyday and the epic interpenetrating. The heterogeneity of such assemblages is both disorienting and intoxicating.

In a similar way, Tawaddud's examination acquires a world-creating force that is intensely interactive, gaining power over readers through its collapse of historical order and juxtapositions of unlike things into a cultural brain-map. Her answers – similarly articulated and coherent, similarly bland – convey both the everydayness and the abstruseness of dissimilar systems of knowledge. The fullness of her answers has a powerful effect on her interlocutors, whose own worlds of comfortable expertise are invaded by the wit of a *qayna*.

For this is not simply an encyclopaedic text. Its knowledge is produced under pressure, through an audacious challenge to all the scholars of the realm. The frame story in which a slave speaks knowledge to power condenses the information she assembles into a challenge to social hierarchies. That this challenge does not end in social upheaval and punishment rests on two forms of containment. First, Tawaddud targets not the caliph nor his powerful courtiers but a number of scholars, judges and *ʿulama* hastily assembled for his amusement. This is a much safer target, because in Sunni Islamic societies scholars often had an uneasy relationship with state power. To see a *qayna* flout a conscripted *ʿālim* in a court setting reminds us that the imported scholars are more alien and vulnerable in the sultan's courtly reception hall than the accomplished slave girl. The caliph laughs in delight as the scholars divest themselves of their robes and pile them higher before the demure challenger.

Second, Tawaddud does not merely inform but also questions, turning the tables on her interrogators, when they have exhausted themselves on her expertise. And when Tawaddud asks questions she shifts modes, from encyclopaedic exposition to riddles. As a result, the contest shifts from centralising knowledge to something more, a performance of power veering on the pleasurable display of wit and wisdom. This second mode of performing knowledge has a different power structure and a different way of encountering knowledge: not by assemblage but by synthesis and dissimulation; a question is contrived to lead the audience as far from the answer as possible. While Tawaddud's riddles lay bare the hostilities of the competition between her and her examiners, their artfulness and playfulness aims not at political upheaval but tactical and cognitive detournement. The riddles enable Tawaddud to better her situation in the face of attack, but at the same time they startle and incite wonder in onlookers.

In fact, by using riddles and trick questions as her best offensive weapon, Tawaddud is actually doing what the most famous and praised historical Baghdadi *qiyān* were praised for: using their wits to rebuke and deliver a stinging lesson to the men around them in order to preserve their own reputation and value. In contrast to the *qiyān* of al-Andalus, the *qiyān* of the Near East became famous for their witty snubs. Dwight Reynolds argues that this capacity publicly to turn the tables on the men who challenge their skill or attack their morals is a theme in Eastern *qiyān* anecdotes, taken from al-Iṣbahānī's *Kitāb al-aghānī* (a generally appreciative depiction), al-Jāḥiẓ's *Risālat al-qiyān* (a hostile one), al-Washsha's *Kitāb al-Muwashshā* and others: 'The most famous *qiyān* had a reputation for being able to best the men who listened to them not only in the spontaneous composition of poetry and music, but also in banter, wordplay, and witty comebacks.'[29] These comebacks were opportunities for enhancing reputation, and a *qayna* could be both elevated and crude in her responses, depending on the method of attack.

The contradictions of a *qayna*'s existence excited talk and interest because they appear to break so many social norms while negotiating the boundaries of elite appreciation. *The Thousand and One Nights* is full of alluring slave girls who incite love, communicate wisdom, entrap men, free them and teach new ways of speaking about the world. Thus, even as Tawaddud joins hands with her historical *qiyān* sisters, she also functions within an elite literary world propagated (at least in *The Thousand and One Nights*) for appreciative popular consumption. Her riddles remain entertainment – though not without a hint of sting. Later transmigrated versions of the tale of Teodor in the Mayan community books and the Philippine metrical romances expand the potential of the slave's riddles for bespeaking resistance to enslavement and talking back to colonialising powers who presume too much.[30]

So, if Tawaddud's riddles do not promise emancipation, what do they do? How do they complicate the encyclopaedic assemblage of knowledge that her exam scripts lay out for us? In the next section I will argue that they focus on four mutually consequential gestures: 1) they defamiliarise the world and make it wonderful, 2) they induce appreciation of the ongoing mysteries of God's creation, 3) their intensity cultivates a responsive attention to language and builds a community of readers/learners among the audience, and 4) in all these ways they transmute knowledge into culturally transportable forms of wisdom.

Riddles, defamiliarisation and the phenomenology of play

Riddling, both popular and literary, exemplifies yet again a mode of cultural production that was immensely popular and widespread in pre-modern periods, and that has faded in modern and contemporary ones.[31] Riddle contests span pre-modern world cultures and have spawned an immense ethnographic, linguistic and literary corpus of study.[32] The riddle contests of Tawaddud's narrative actually travel much more easily than its encyclopaedic sections: not as replication of the same riddles, but as cultural translations that adapt the indigenous riddle cultures of new audiences. Castilian, Mayan and Filipino versions of the narrative often reduce or jettison the encyclopaedic examinations and capitalise on the riddle contests. As each culture translates Tawaddud/Teodor's narrative, it activates its own long-standing riddle traditions: such riddle traditions are attested in all of the narrative's translational destinations: Arabic, Persian, Iberian, Mayan and Filipino.

Scholars agree that a riddle consists of two parts, a question and an answer, but popular riddles take so many different forms in so many languages that they cannot be fitted into a culturally universal field theory of riddling. They are grouped into popular and literary riddles depending on their media of performance. Popular riddles, like other knowledge systems, are culturally embedded and are best studied *in situ*. In a study of Finnish popular riddles, Annikki Kaivola-Bregenhøj points out that riddles conscript and exploit the common material cultures of their users.[33] Sociolinguistically, then, these ties to common material cultures suggest that even as popular riddles work as an intensely engaging form of entertainment, they also enculturate their audiences. Like encyclopaedic assemblages, they invite participation in a particular world, educating and training participants. Children who play riddle games learn their worlds by occupying different roles and experimenting with many voices.[34] Readers of the Old English Exeter Book riddles have argued that such interactive pedagogies extend to adults, teaching them ways to become more responsive to the wonders of their worlds.[35]

Riddle games can instantiate the mores of a culture, but they can also induce questioning of those mores through modes of estrangement and critique.[36] Their agonistic and competitive structure may bespeak hostilities between rival social agents, but their sustained modes of non-violent engagement can also modulate interpersonal aggressions and humiliations into more culturally acceptable forms.[37] Tawaddud's riddles take a number of different forms, some drawing from popular traditions and even proverbs. Several of her riddles, however, are elaborately literary and artistic (such as the one she directs at the doctor discussed below).[38] Literary riddles come to life through elaborate metaphors deliberately made heterogeneous and misleading, by multiple analogies, by distracting blocks that lead audiences up metaphorical blind alleys, and by an aura of mystery that sits at odds with the frequently everyday objects being described.[39] To create a literary riddle, start with the answer and then generate a metaphorical series of figures that estranges it as much as possible. Arabic literary riddles have a long and illustrious history, enlivening *ḥadīth*, showing up in legal disputes[40] and taking their most elaborate forms in the intricate *maqāmāt* narratives of Badī' az-Zamān al-Hamadhānī (969–1007), and his even more uncannily numinous successor in the genre, Al-Ḥarīrī of Basra (1054–1122).[41]

The main term for them in Arabic is *lughz* (pl. *alghāz*), which might be derived from the feinting action of a small animal escaping from its prey (like the wily fox in *Sir Gawain and the Green Knight*). However, they are also referred to by many different words, including *mu'ammā*, which means 'blinded' or obscured. These terms underscore Arabic literary riddles as essentially dissimulating; they aim to conceal. Senderovich suggests that there can even be a double concealment: a mundane answer that is given or guessed, and an esoteric one that persists; the euphemism implicit in sexual riddles preserves this doubleness.[42]

In Tawaddud's narrative, riddles are available to everyone, Tawaddud and her examiners alike. Their emergence signals rhetorical desperation or the need to turn the tables by shifting tactics. Hostile examiners use other means than riddles to manoeuvre Tawaddud into silence: the doctor tries to embarrass her by asking her about sexual intercourse, and al-Naẓẓām tries to entrap her by asking which was the better man, Ali or al-Abbas (in front of the Abbasid caliph!), and her diplomatic answer (each had his own excellence) brings Harun al-Rashid to his feet, exclaiming, 'By the Lord of the Ka'ba, that was well done, Tawaddud.'[43] The astronomer even asks her an impossible question: 'Will it rain this month?', and her response is shocking: 'Bring me a sword that I can cut off his head for he is an atheist!' [*tu'ṭīnī sayfan aḍrib bi-hi 'unqahu li-annahu zindiq* تعطيني سيفا أضرب به عنقه لأنه زنديق] because such knowledge belongs to God alone, at which everyone laughs. However, riddles represent the biggest guns that can be levied in this contest of wits. Ibrahīm al-Naẓẓām signals the high-stakes nature of Tawaddud's final examination by asking *only* riddles in dazzling, rapid-fire succession. I will talk about two series of riddles that have different narrative results: first, the ones Tawaddud asks at the end of each examination that silence and defeat her examiners, and second, the exchanges with her ultimate examiner, Ibrahīm al-Naẓẓām, which meld both encyclopaedism and riddling by giving us a veritable encyclopaedia of riddles.

Within the first series of exams, riddles emerge as a kind of rhetorical nuclear bomb, which Tawaddud uses to turn the tables and demolish interlocutors whom she has already exhausted by her encyclopaedic fecundity. Her riddles exert perlocutionary force, shifting the hierarchy of examination. A master-scholar interrogator cloaked in knowledge and a *jāriya* neophyte with everything to prove become instead, through riddles, a *jāriya* guardian of mysteries who refuses admittance to wisdom to a blinded master-scholar, whose own occupational mysteries are stripped away along with his court robes.

I would like to look at just three of the riddles that Tawaddud asks at these table-turning moments. They range between several of the riddle types discussed by folklorists: false riddles, alphabetical puns and true riddles. Tawaddud's first riddle is a false riddle. False riddles are riddles that do not encode their answers: they are almost impossible to guess unless one can read the riddler's mind or recent experience. Samson's biblical riddle is a good example of a false riddle: 'Out of the eater came something to eat; out of the strong came something sweet' – to which the answer is a honeycomb in a lion's carcass that Samson had just encountered on a journey. These false riddles are unfair but fascinating because they make the world stranger than we can ever know.

Tawaddud asks this false riddle to the second *faqīh*, who actually deserves it. In the course of quizzing her on belief and its opposite, he has badgered her with insanely vague riddles such as 'Tell me about something, about half of something, and about nothing' [*fa-akhbirīnī ʿan shayʾ wa-ʿan niṣf shayʾ wa-ʿan lā shayʾ* فأخبريني عن شيء وعن نصف شيء وعن لا شيء] (apparently, a Muslim, a hypocritical Muslim and an unbeliever). Tawaddud gets her own back by asking the following question about the ultimate precept:

> Tell me, what is the injunction of injunctions, the injunction that initiates all the others, the injunction needed by all the others, the injunction that embraces all others, the custom of the Prophet that is found in every injunction, and the custom of the Prophet that completes every injunction?
>
> *fa-akhbirnī ʿan farḍ al-farḍ wa-ʿan farḍ fī ibtidāʾ kull farḍ wa-ʿan farḍ yuḥtāju ilayhi kull farḍ wa-ʿan sunna dākhila fī al-farḍ wa-ʿan sunna yatimmu bi-hā al-farḍ*
>
> فأخبرني عن فرض الفرض وعن فرض في ابتداء كل فرض وعن فرض
> يحتاج إليه كل فرض وعن سنة داخلة في الفرض وعن سنة يتم بها الفرض

To this riddle, Tawaddud's answer synthesises and assembles knowledge, faith and purity into a unique assemblage of Islamic belief and ritual practice. Everything in it is true, but perhaps only Tawaddud would organise it that way. How could the *faqīh* guess these answers: 1) the knowledge of the Almighty God, 2) the confession of faith (*shahāda*), 3) ritual ablution, 4) cleansing of impurity, 5) the wiping between fingers and toes and combing of thick beards, and 5) circumcision. In this injunction series, the riddle becomes an excuse to probe and connect a range of thematically linked but disparate ordinary behaviours and ritual practices. The answer reveals their practical heterogeneity, while the riddle itself at once synthesises them, hyperbolises them and makes them mysterious and wonderful. The *faqīh*, reduced to silence, removes his robe and flees.

Tawaddud's second table-turning riddle shows the use of a block: a distraction deliberately placed into the riddle to muddle the hearer. Here too, she adapts her riddle to mimic the strategies of her questioner, the Qur'an reciter, who has veered between the doggedly systematic and the whiplashingly haphazard, asking her everything from the order of Qur'anic revelations to a list of all the winged creatures that are mentioned in the Qur'an. Tawaddud caricatures his emphasis on minutiae. She leads up to an alphabetical pun by asking several straightforward but data-crunching alphabetical questions

> Which Qur'anic verse contains twenty-three instances of the letter *kāf*, which has sixteen *mīms*, which has a hundred and forty *ʿayns*, and which portion of the Qur'an does not contain the formula covering the sublimity of God?
>
> *mā taqūlu fī āya fīhā thalātha wa-ʿishrūn kāfan wa-āya fīhā sitta ʿashara mīman wa-āya fīhā miʾa wa-arbaʿūn ʿaynan wa-ḥizb laysa fīhi jalāla*
>
> ما تقول في آية فيها ثلاثة وعشرون كافاً وآية فيها ستة عشر ميماً وآية فيها مائة وأربعون عيناً وحزب ليس فيه جلالة؟

Here the riddle is buried in the straightforward questions and actually turns on a pun. Tawaddud names the verses with the 23 *kafs* and the 16 *mims*. But 140 *ʿayns*? In a single verse? She says:

> The 140 *ʿayns* are found in *Sūrat al-Aʿrāf* in God's words: 'Moses chose seventy men from his people to go at the appointed time' – for each man had two eyes ['*aynān*].
>
> *wa innā al-āya allatī fīhā miʾa wa-arbaʿūn ʿaynan fī Sūrat al-Aʿrāf wa-hiya qawluhu taʿālā wa-ikhtāra Mūsā qawmahu sabʿīn rajulan li-mīqātinā li-kull rajul 'aynān.*
>
> وإن الآية التي فيها مائة وأربعون عيناً في سورة الأعراف وهي قوله تعالى: (واختار موسى قومه سبعين رجلًا ميقاتنا) لكل رجل عينان.

This second riddle shows not only knowledge but wit. By fencing two straightforward letter questions with a pun on the letter *ʿayn*, Tawaddud shows her capacity to collapse the letters of holy scripture into the historical world they describe in a way that synthesises unlike things into new unities. She also provides entertainment and wakes up her audience in the midst of letter-counting Qur'anic minutiae.

Upping the ante, Tawaddud's third table-turning riddle is her first true riddle: a riddle that provides clues to its answer and blocks to distract from them in equal proportions. It is also her first literary riddle, based on a series of elaborate metaphors. She asks it of the doctor, who had previously tried to embarrass her by asking about sexual intercourse. Her riddle also stages a kind of intercourse, but one that unseats the doctor's emphasis on pleasure. Instead it opens to the larger worlds of outer show and reputation that both the slave girl and the doctor negotiate.

> What do you have to say about something that is as round as the earth and whose spine and whose resting place are hidden from sight? It is of little value; it has a narrow chest and a fetter around its throat, although it is not a runaway slave; it is in chains, although it is not a thief; it has been stabbed, but not in battle, and wounded, but not in fight. It eats away time as it passes and it drinks water in abundance. At times, it is beaten for no fault, and made to serve, although it has no competence. After being scattered it is collected together; it is humble but not because it wants to flatter, and pregnant, although it has no child in its womb. It leans over, but does not rest on its side. It becomes dirty and then cleans itself; it endures heat and is changed; it copulates without a penis; it wrestles without anyone being wary of it; it gives rest and seeks rest; it is bitten but does not cry out; it is more generous than a boon companion but further removed than summer heat. It leaves its wife at night and embraces her by day; and it lives in the outer parts of the dwellings of the noble.

This riddle compares its object to the circuit of the earth advisedly, for it has an earth-encompassing force. It renders strange and wonderful an everyday world of habit, utility, appetite, humility, sex, slavery, love, fear and aristocratic outer show. The answer is a button, which penetrates and wrestles with its buttonhole, is fettered by its buttonhole and chained by its thread, drinks when it is washed and eats time as it is worn down through use. It suffers the everyday violence of its piercings though which its threads pass and endures the wrestling of its fastenings under daily use. Most of all, it is a connector and stabiliser of outer garments, bringing parts of a robe together by day and letting them part at night. It brings peace and security to the public parts of clothing and thus implicates the outer dwellings – facades – of nobles. The soon-to-be-disrobed doctor might have been warned that his outer garment is about to come off, unnaturally in daylight, and he will lose the reputation and stability that his mastery provides.

Further, if riddles generate cognitive worlds from the humblest common objects in the material cultures of their societies, we can see ultimately how the button and buttonhole riddle implicates the buttoned-together performances – the improvised assemblages – that comprise Tawaddud's examinations themselves and the Abbasid court of their audiences. Like the humble button she renders wonderful, Tawaddud's riddle comments upon the thought-worlds of her audience, their everyday connections, violences, appetites and facades. The button riddle implicates all of Tawaddud's masters, whether endowers or exploiters, from the doctor, to the caliph, to her own improvident Abū l-Ḥusn, who has hung his fortune on Tawaddud's plot. In this way, it provides a meta-commentary on the narrative itself as a connector of language games both constative and performative, which will persist and become mysterious in the last stage of the contest, where riddles are the only language spoken.

The final contest: an encyclopaedia of riddles

The last examination, between Tawaddud and Ibrahīm al-Nazzām, showcases a riddle's capacity for both estrangement and uncanny mutability. At its conclusion, then, the tale that created worlds from encyclopaedic assemblages of unlike things turns and splinters those worlds by shifting perspectives. It puts worlds into motion to draw attention to the contrivances through which language constitutes worlds, rendering language itself wonderful, and the worlds even more mysterious. The contest signals its own totalising aims from the onset. Having overborne all the other opponents, Tawaddud wants one who can speak on every art and science at once [*kull fann wa-ʿilm*]. Al-Naẓẓām, the famous Mu'tazilite philosophical theologian, rises at once, bristling with arrogance. He begins by warning Tawaddud that this final contest will not be like the others; that he intends to make a shameful defeat resound through the centuries. This is a prediction that is truer than he knows, but not in the way he anticipates.

The first questions al-Naẓẓām asks suggest the power of rhetoric to create worlds by beginning with creation itself: that of the world by God, of Islam (fathered by Muhammad), of Muhammad's father (Abraham) and finally the creation of Tawaddud herself. Her sombre answer draws attention to the speed and circularity of mortal existence: she quotes the following poem:

> I was created from the earth and became a person, eloquent in question and answer.
> Then I returned to the earth and was buried there, as if I had never left the earth at all.[44]

khuliqtu min al-turāb fa-ṣirtu shakṣan   faṣīḥan fī al-su ʾāl wa-fī al-jawāb
wa-ʿudtu ilā al-turāb fa-ṣirtu fīhi   ka-annī mā bariḥtu min al-turāb

خلقت من التراب فصرت شخصا فصيحا في السؤال وفي الجواب
وعدت إلى التراب فصرت فيه كأني ما برحت من التراب

The sombre repetition of *turāb* (earth or dust) and its assonance with *jawāb* (answer) connects the earthly materials of which humanity is made with humanity's highest cognitive accomplishments: Tawaddud's ability to speak the world in question and answer. This poem circumscribes the arrogant competition in which she and al-Naẓẓām are engaging by recognising its connection with mortality. Questions and answers – from encyclopaedic assemblage to riddles – do not only make worlds, but they are of the earth. If life ever escapes from dust, it never leaves dust far behind.

These intimations of mortality are then ratified by riddles that dwell upon mutability. Al-Nazzam then gives Tawaddud a series of questions on sudden Qur'anic transformations: from death to life (Moses' rod); a male who births a female (Adam and Eve) and a female who births a male (Mary and Jesus); along with four miraculous fires that eat and drink in different ways. At the end of this series of questions, the world has become more wonderful than it was before, in some of the senses that Caroline Walker Bynum discusses when she draws attention to how pre-modern wonder arrests attention, decentres singular perspectives and opens to cognitively productive hybridities.[45]

Al-Naẓẓām builds to a whirlwind climax: fifteen wisdom riddles about the joys and sorrows of human social life, followed by one about a composite monster dwelling in the wilderness. Al-Naẓẓām asks these riddles without pausing for answers, leaving us in suspension between question and answer while piling on more questions, something that happens nowhere else in the text. However, Tawaddud remembers them all and answers them cumulatively: what is sweeter than honey? (dutiful children), sharper than a sword? (the tongue), swifter than poison? (the evil eye), the pleasure of an hour? (sex), three days' happiness? (a woman's depilatory! – oh, the life of a *qayna*), the pleasantest day? (a day of business profit), a week's happiness? (marriage – ouch), a liar's undeniable due? (death), the prison of the tomb? (a bad son).

Moments of cogent analogy to Tawaddud's character and situation appear at the end of the list. The answer to 'What is the heart's delight?' can be both an obedient wife and also eating meat: the riddle suggests the consumability of women. Even closer to home is 'What tricks the soul?' (a disobedient slave) and 'What is the death of life?' (poverty, fear of which provoked Tawaddud's master to sell her in the first place). The disease that cannot be cured is an evil character, and finally, the disgrace that cannot be effaced is a disobedient daughter. Are these character aspersions targeting Tawaddud? Is al-Naẓẓām manipulating Tawaddud into speaking self-incriminating cultural truisms? Al-Naẓẓām ends the series with a riddle about an asocial monster that lives in the wilderness, hates humankind and contains the natures of seven powerful creatures. Tawaddud interprets this as a locust: horse's head, bull's neck, eagle's wings, camel's feet, snake's tale, scorpion's belly and gazelle's horns. This creature is not only multitudinous but also contains multitudes within it. It gestures once more to the processes of heterogeneous assemblage that link and organise all the forms of knowledge in this tale.

Al-Naẓẓām's series generates riddles from deconstructed proverbs. It seems to be one of the most appealing portions of the narrative, persisting verbatim in many of its translations. For instance, the version that appears in the Mayan community book of Kaua condenses or elides most of the content of the examinations while retaining three proverbial riddles from this series:

> 'What is stronger than steel?' 'He who tells the truth without lies contaminating it.' 'What is sweeter than honey?' 'This is a good child.' 'What moves more swiftly than anything else?' 'That is a man's thought. Now it is here, now it is in Spain, or at the end of the world.'[46]

These riddles, re-leveraged in a post-conquest context, resonate both backwards, with the Castilian and Arabic source texts, and forwards, to the politics of knowledge under Spanish colonial *reducción* (enculturation) in Maya communities.[47] The riddle comparing the good child to honey syncretises the Arabic original with traditional Mayan riddling rituals, such as the Suiua riddle test, which dramatised the interregnal continuities of right ways of thinking, proving new rulers fit to rule (good children).[48] The riddle about the swiftness of thought introduces Spain into the Maya text, where it does not exist in either of the sources, analogising Spain to the end of the world, and thus linking highly bridgeable cultural distances with the apocalypse – the end of the Maya world that came with the Spanish conquests.[49] That cultural intelligibility can effect domination, syncretisation and resistance alike recognises the subtleties of colonialism transformation: the domination of the distant coloniser as well as the agency of the syncretising colonised. The Maya uptake of the gnomic riddles thus suggests that gnomic riddles are both 1) culturally specific repositories of wisdom and 2) opportunities for recognition (and leveraging) of cross-cultural structural commonalities to do critical social work for both oppressor and oppressed. Because they invite readers to negotiate cultural traditions by testing for mutually agreeable truths, gnomic riddles also index changes in literary taste between pre- and post-nineteenth-century audiences. They are another feature of medieval bestsellers that seems to have a limited shelf-life for modern readers.

Conclusion

Al-Naẓẓām's examination urges a different take on knowledge than the encyclopaedic exams that preceded it. It hints at the ongoing mysteries of the world and suggests that riddles don't exhaust mystery when they are answered. With so many defamiliarising tactics and perspectives available, language that names and resolves can exist apart from the world, generating itself, spawning more language, more narratives, more worlds. Patricia Dailey argues that riddles, like naming, draw attention to their own arbitrariness, leaving intact the mystery of what is actually out there, beyond the slapping down of a single resolution.[50] The inclusion of Tawaddud's narrative in the omnivorous story vortex that is *The Thousand and One Nights* suggests that this narrative fecundity amounts to a way of survival, productive literary displacement and the re-enchantment of a disenchanted world. Even Tawaddud's sombre little poem, which takes us from dust to riddler to dust again, suggests that question and answer are not only the only form of life she has, but are a way of communicating new forms of life for her readers. This is a final pre-modern appeal of Tawaddud's narrative, and translations of her tale will continue to generate culture in the cut and thrust of question and answer in global cultures across the centuries.

Where encyclopaedias wear their ordering systems as transparently as possible to render access easy, riddles draw our attention to the contrivance of all ordering systems through the extremity of their artifice and perspectival play, turning cognitive habits into tricks by enticing with 'blocks' and thus slipping the moorings of our reflexes for organising the world. Thus, linking encyclopaedic assemblages of knowledge to riddles is a powerful pedagogical combination: absorptive and participatory, deductive and inductive, familiarising and estranging, monologic and dialogic. The alternation of modes is also a political dynamic, in which the submission of a slave can suddenly turn into the *coup de grâce* of a master. I think these political dynamics are one reason why colonialist indoctrinations through the tale were seized upon and redeployed as anti-colonial resistance in the Mayan and Tagalog versions. The power dynamics between the slave and the scholars wake up the inequities between the coloniser and the colonised, and leaping into Tawaddud's shoes they can rewrite her story, using the master's tools to dismantle the master's house.

This text and its vast network of transmigrations suffered an eclipse in the nineteenth and early twentieth centuries, I would argue, because Western academic categories rendered it illegible and exotic. It does not fit into the nationalised philological departments that remain the basis of our own academic institutions, and even comparatists generally confine themselves to one part of its translation networks. In its indigenous-language versions it also fades because it preserves a story introduced by colonial powers, too easily associated with European indoctrination. It is harder to see the evidence of active syncretism and even resistance on the part of indigenous writers among the Mayan, Brazilian and Philippine adaptors. Processes of decolonisation also often privilege the recovery of authentic pre-colonial traditions. A syncretised medieval European or Mediterranean tale can never satisfy those desires. In Arabic collections of *The Thousand and One Nights* it is also sometimes difficult to find Tawaddud's narrative. A recent Beirut version that otherwise follows Burton's order discards it, along with the didactic short tales on the Angel of Death that surround it, I suspect because they seem too sententious. *The Thousand and One Nights* has been marketed as popular and entertaining rather than wise, and to see the drama within the didacticism one must look closely. I suspect that a twenty-first-century Tawaddud is re-emerging because all of these tactical disciplinary divisions are being questioned. We increasingly collaborate between disciplinary fields, note the negotiations through which transculturation occurs, and question the habit of sequestering the academic and the popular. In current more associative epistemological spaces, the shifting assemblages and insurgent riddles of Tawaddud can be seen as interventions that do fascinating work in ways we may have forgotten.

Notes

1 I am grateful for the astute editing of Dwight Reynolds and Heather Blurton, for Azeem Malik's care and assistance with Arabic transliterations, and to Karla Mallette and the Michigan Medieval Seminar who generously offered feedback on versions of this chapter. All infelicities are despite and not because of their help.

2 Claudine Gerresch, 'Un Récit des Mille et une Nuits: Tawaddud. Petite encyclopédie de l'Islam médiéval', *Bulletin de l'Institut fondamental de l'Afrique noire* 35 (1973): 57–175.

3 José Vasquez Ruiz, 'Una versión en árabe granadino del, "Cuento de la Doncella Teodor"', *Prohemic* 2 (1971): 331–65.

4 Isidro J. Rivera and Donna M. Rogers, *Historia de la donzella Teodor: Edition and Study* (Binghamton, NY: Global Publications/CEMERS, 2000).
5 Margaret R. Parker, *The Story of a Story Across Culture: The Case of the Doncella Teodor* (Woodbridge: Tamesis, 1996).
6 I am indebted to Paula Karger's ongoing research in this area; see also Gordon Brotherston, *The Book of the Fourth World: Reading the Native Americas Through Their Literature* (Cambridge: Cambridge University Press, 1993).
7 Parker, *The Story of a Story*, pp. 124–6.
8 Damiana L. Eugenio, *Awit and Corrido: Philippine Metrical Romances* (Quezon City: University of the Philippines Press, 1987), pp. 130–5. I am indebted to Stephanie Matabang's ongoing research in this area.
9 Rosemary Stanfield-Johnson, 'From *One Thousand and One Nights* to Safavid Iran: A Persian *Tawaddud*', *Der Islam* 94.1 (2017): 158–91.
10 Edward William Lane (ed. and trans.), *The Thousand and One Nights*, ed. Edward Stanley Poole, vol. II (London: Routledge, Warne, and Routledge, 1865), p. 572
11 Robert Irwin, 'Political Thought in the "Thousand and One Nights"', *Marvels and Tales* 18.2 (2007): 249.
12 Richard Francis Burton, *The Thousand Nights and A Night* (London: Burton Club, 1885–88), vol. V, p. 189, n. 1.
13 See, for example, *Alf Layla wa Layla*, intro. Afif Nayef Hatoum (Beirut: Dar Sader, 1999).
14 Malcolm C. Lyons with Ursula Lyons (trans.), *One Thousand and One Nights* (London: Penguin, 2010), vol. II, pp. 275–321. Arabic text is William Hay Macnaghten, *Alf Layla*, vol. II (London: W. Thacker, Wm. H. Allen, 1839). See Dwight Reynolds, '*A Thousand and One Nights*: A History of the Text and its Reception', in Roger Allen and D. S. Richards (eds), *The Cambridge History of Arabic Literature: The Post-Classical Period* (Cambridge: Cambridge University Press, 2008), pp. 270–91.
15 Amy Hirons, 'Yokol Cab: Mayan Translation of Astrological Texts and Images in the Book of Chilam Balam of Kaua', *Ethnohistory* 62.3 (2015): 525–52.
16 *Qiyān* singers and poets offer a view into the intersectionality of slavery, race, gender and political power, about which more later. Recent useful studies include Matthew S. Gordon and Kathryn A. Hain (eds), *Concubines and Courtesans: Women and Slavery in Islamic History* (Oxford: Oxford University Press, 2017); and Fuad Matthew Caswell, *The Slave Girls of Baghdad: The Qiyan in the Early Abbasid Era* (London: I. B. Tauris, 2011).

17 Ibn Bassām, *al-Dhakhīra*, vol. III, pp. 70–1, cited and translated in Dwight Reynolds, 'The *Qiyān* of al-Andalus', in Matthew S. Gordon and Kathryn A. Hain (eds), *Concubines and Courtesans: Women and Slavery in Islamic History* (Oxford: Oxford University Press, 2017), p. 114.
18 Reynolds, 'The *Qiyān*', p. 115.
19 For *qiyān* social mobility and precarity, see Matthew S. Gordon, 'Abbasid Courtesans and the Question of Social Mobility', in Gordon and Hain (eds), *Concubines and Courtesans*, pp. 27–51; and Pernilla Myrne, 'A *Jariya*'s Prospects in Abbasid Baghdad', in Gordon and Hain (eds), *Concubines and Courtesans*, pp. 52–74.
20 Spivak appropriates and politicises Heidegger's idea of the 'worlding of a world' from *Being and Time* in 'Three Women's Texts and a Critique of Imperialism', *Critical Inquiry* 12.1 (1985): 235–61.
21 Jason König and Greg Woolf (eds), *Encyclopaedism from Antiquity to the Renaissance* (Cambridge: Cambridge University Press, 2013), pp. 1–21; Mary Franklin-Brown, *Reading the World: Encyclopedic Writing in the Scholastic Age* (Chicago: University of Chicago Press, 2012), pp. 1–11; and Elias Muhanna, *The World in a Book: al-Nuwayri and the Islamic Encyclopedic Tradition* (Princeton, NJ: Princeton University Press, 2018), pp. 11–13.
22 Ulrich Marzolph and Richard van Leeuwen, *Arabian Nights Encyclopedia* (Santa Barbara, CA: ABC-CLIO, 2004), p. 409
23 In this it is a little like Chaucer's Tale of Melibee, which can function by turns as an encyclopaedia of proverbs, a snail's-pace family fight, and a sermon against war and for patience. Any one of those narrative threads might be interesting in itself, and yet somehow their assemblage poses a challenge for modern readers.
24 Burton, *The Thousand Nights and A Night*, vol. V, p. 189, n. 1.
25 Parker, *Story of a Story*, p. 67.
26 On assemblage as a form of territorialisation, see Gilles Deleuze and Félix Guattari, *A Thousand Plateaus: Capitalism and Schizophrenia*, trans. Brian Massumi (Minneapolis, MN: University of Minnesota Press, 1987), pp. 3–24.
27 Muhanna, *The World in a Book*; Franklin-Brown, *Reading the World.*
28 Shihab al-Din al-Nuywayri, *The Ultimate Ambition in the Arts of Erudition*, ed. Elias Muhanna (New York: Penguin, 2016), pp. xii-xiii.
29 Reynolds, 'The *Qiyān*', p. 103.
30 Brotherston, *The Book of the Fourth World*, pp. 320–6.
31 See Annikki Kaivola-Bregenhø, *Riddles: Perspectives on the Use, Function, and Change in a Folklore Genre*, trans. Susan Sinisalo (Helsinki: Finnish Literature Society, 2001), p. 16.

32 Most helpful for a study of literary language in riddles are W. J. Pepicello and Thomas A. Green, *The Language of Riddles: New Perspectives* (Columbus, OH: Ohio State University Press, 1984), and Savely Senderovich, *The Riddle of the Riddle: A Study of the Folk Riddle's Figurative Nature* (London: Kegan Paul, 2005).
33 Kaivola-Bregenhøj, *Riddles*, p. 14.
34 John Holmes McDowell, *Children's Riddling* (Bloomington, IN: Indiana University Press, 1979), pp. 221–42.
35 Patricia Dailey, 'Riddles, Wonder and Responsiveness in Anglo-Saxon Literature', in Clare A. Lees (ed.), *The Cambridge History of Early Medieval English Literature* (Cambridge: Cambridge University Press, 2013), pp. 451–72.
36 Senderovich, *Riddle of the Riddle*, pp. 65–9; Charles Francis Potter, 'Riddles', in Maria Leach (ed.), *Standard Dictionary of Folkore, Mythology and Legend II* (New York: Funk and Wagnall, 1950), pp. 938–44.
37 Thomas Rhys William, 'The Form and Function of Tambunan Dusun Riddles', *The Journal of American Folklore* 76 (1963): 75–110.
38 For a regional linguistic analysis of Arabic literary riddles, see Charles T. Scott, *Persian and Arabic Riddles: A Language-Centered Approach to Genre Definition* (Bloomington, IN: Indiana University Press, 1965). A more structuralist approach to common gestures in Arabic popular riddles is Michael L Chyet, '"A Thing the Size of Your Palm": A Preliminary Study of Arabic Riddle Structure', *Arabica* 35.3 (1988), 267–92.
39 Pepicello and Green, *Language of Riddles*, pp. 91–122.
40 Matthew L. Keegan, 'Levity Makes the Law: Islamic Legal Riddles', *Islamic Law and Society* 27 (2020): 214–39.
41 Michael Cooperson, *Impostures* (New York: New York University Press, 2020).
42 Senderovich, *Riddle of the Riddle*, pp. 59–64.
43 Lyons and Lyons (trans.), *One Thousand and One Nights*, vol. II, p. 317.
44 The translation of the last hemistich is mine.
45 Caroline Walker Bynum, 'Wonder', *The American Historical Review* 102.1 (1997): 1–26.
46 Victoria Bricker and Helga-Maria Mirram, *An Encounter of Two Worlds: The Chilam Balam of Kaua* (New Orleans, LA: Tulane University Middle American Research Institute Publications, 2002), p. 233.
47 William F. Hanks, *Converting Words: Maya in the Age of the Cross* (Berkeley, CA: University of California Press, 2010); Hirons, 'Yokol Cab'.

48 Gordon Brotherston, 'Tawaddud and Maya Wit: A Story from the Arabian Nights Adapted to the Community Books of the Yucatan', *Indiana* 7 (1982): 131–41.
49 Ibid., 139.
50 Dailey, 'Riddles, Wonder and Responsiveness', p. 464.

Works cited

Bricker, Victoria, and Helga-Maria Mirram, *An Encounter of Two Worlds: The Chilam Balam of Kaua* (New Orleans, LA: Tulane University Middle American Research Institute Publications, 2002).

Brotherston, Gordon, 'Tawaddud and Maya Wit: A Story from the Arabian Nights Adapted to the Community Books of the Yucatan', *Indiana* 7 (1982): 131–41.

— *The Book of the Fourth World: Reading the Native Americas Through Their Literature* (Cambridge: Cambridge University Press, 1993).

Burton, Richard Francis, *The Thousand Nights and A Night*, vol. V (London: Burton Club, 1885–88).

Bynum, Caroline Walker, 'Wonder', *The American Historical Review* 102.1 (1997): 1–26.

Caswell, Fuad Matthew, *The Slave Girls of Baghdad: The Qiyan in the Early Abbasid Era* (London: I. B. Tauris, 2011).

Chyet, Michael L., '"A Thing the Size of Your Palm": A Preliminary Study of Arabic Riddle Structure', *Arabica* 35.3 (1988): 267–92.

Cooperson, Michael, *Impostures* (New York: New York University Press, 2020).

Dailey, Patricia, 'Riddles, Wonder and Responsiveness in Anglo-Saxon Literature', in Clare A. Lees (ed.), *The Cambridge History of Early Medieval English Literature* (Cambridge: Cambridge University Press, 2013), pp. 451–72.

Deleuze, Gilles, and Félix Guattari, *A Thousand Plateaus: Capitalism and Schizophrenia*, trans. Brian Massumi (Minneapolis, MN: University of Minnesota Press, 1987).

Eugenio, Damiana L., *Awit and Corrido: Philippine Metrical Romances* (Quezon City: University of the Philippines Press, 1987), pp. 130–5.

Franklin-Brown, Mary, *Reading the World: Encyclopedic Writing in the Scholastic Age* (Chicago: University of Chicago Press, 2012).

Gerresch, Claudine, 'Un Récit des Mille et une Nuits: Tawaddud. Petite encyclopédie de l'Islam médiéval', *Bulletin de l'Institut fondamental de l'Afrique noire* 35 (1973): 57–175.

Gordon, Matthew S., 'Abbasid Courtesans and the Question of Social Mobility', in Matthew S. Gordon and Kathryn A. Hain (eds), *Concubines and Courtesans: Women and Slavery in Islamic History* (Oxford: Oxford University Press, 2017), pp. 27–51.

Gordon, Matthew S., and Kathryn A. Hain (eds), *Concubines and Courtesans: Women and Slavery in Islamic History* (Oxford: Oxford University Press, 2017).

Hanks, William F., *Converting Words: Maya in the Age of the Cross* (Berkeley, CA: University of California Press, 2010).

Heath, Peter, 'Knowledge', in Maria Rosa Menocal, Raymond P. Scheindlin and Michael Sells (eds), *The Cambridge History of Arabic Literature: The Literature of al-Andalus* (Cambridge: Cambridge University Press, 2012), pp. 96–125.

Hirons, Amy J., 'Yokol Cab: Mayan Translation of Astrological Texts and Images in the Book of Chilam Balam of Kaua', *Ethnohistory* 62.3 (2015): 525–52.

Irwin, Robert, 'Political Thought in the "Thousand and One Nights"', *Marvels and Tales* 18.2 (2007): 246–57.

Kaivola-Bregenhø, Annikki, *Riddles: Perspectives on the Use, Function, and Change in a Folklore Genre*, trans. Susan Sinisalo (Helsinki: Finnish Literature Society, 2001).

Keegan, Matthew L., 'Levity Makes the Law: Islamic Legal Riddles', *Islamic Law and Society* 27 (2020): 214–39.

Könic, Jason, and Greg Woolf (eds), *Encyclopaedism from Antiquity to the Renaissance* (Cambridge: Cambridge University Press, 2013).

Lane, Edward William (ed. and trans.), *The Thousand and One Nights*, ed. Edward Stanley Poole, vol. II (London: Routledge, Warne and Routledge, 1865).

Lyons, Malcolm C., with Ursula Lyons (ed. and trans.), *One Thousand and One Nights*, vol. II (London: Penguin, 2010).

Macnaghten, William Hay (ed.), *Alf Layla*, vol. II (London: W. Thacker, Wm. H. Allen, 1839).

Marzolph, Ulrich, and Richard van Leeuwen, *Arabian Nights Encyclopedia* (Santa Barbara, CA: ABC-CLIO, 2004).

McDowell, John Holmes, *Children's Riddling* (Bloomington, IN: Indiana University Press, 1979).

Muhanna, Elias, *The World in a Book: Al-Nuwayri and the Islamic Encyclopedic Tradition* (Princeton, NJ: Princeton University Press, 2018).

Myrne, Pernilla, 'A *Jariya*'s Prospects in Abbasid Baghdad', in Matthew S. Gordon and Kathryn A. Hain (eds), *Concubines and Courtesans: Women and Slavery in Islamic History* (Oxford: Oxford University Press, 2017), pp. 52–74.

al-Nuywayri, Shihab al-Din, *The Ultimate Ambition in the Arts of Erudition*, ed. Elias Muhanna (New York: Penguin, 2016).

Parker, Margaret R., *The Story of a Story Across Culture: The Case of the Doncella Teodor* (Woodbridge: Tamesis, 1996).

Pepicello, W. J., and Thomas A. Green, *The Language of Riddles: New Perspectives* (Columbus, OH: Ohio State University Press, 1984).

Potter, Charles Francis, 'Riddles', in Maria Leach (ed.), *Standard Dictionary of Folkore, Mythology and Legend II* (New York: Funk and Wagnall, 1950), pp. 938–44.

Reynolds, Dwight, '*A Thousand and One Nights*: A History of the Text and its Reception', in Roger Allen and D. S. Richards (eds), *The Cambridge History of Arabic Literature: The Post-Classical Period* (Cambridge: Cambridge University Press, 2008), pp. 270–91.
— 'The *Qiyān* of al-Andalus', in Matthew S. Gordon and Kathryn A. Hain (eds), *Concubines and Courtesans: Women and Slavery in Islamic History* (Oxford: Oxford University Press, 2017), 100–23.
Rivera, Isidro J., and Donna M. Rogers, *Historia de la donzella Teodor: Edition and Study* (Binghamton, NY: Global Publications/CEMERS, 2000).
Ruiz, José Vasquez, 'Una versión en árabe granadino del, "Cuento de la Doncella Teodor"', *Prohemic* 2 (1971): 331–65.
Scott, Charles T., *Persian and Arabic Riddles: A Language-Centered Approach to Genre Definition* (Bloomington, IN: Indiana University Press, 1965).
Senderovich, Savely, *The Riddle of the Riddle: A Study of the Folk Riddle's Figurative Nature* (London: Kegan Paul, 2005).
Spivak, Gayatri Chakravorty, 'Three Women's Texts and a Critique of Imperialism', *Critical Inquiry* 12.1 (1985): 235–61.
Stanfield-Johnson, Rosemary, 'From *One Thousand and One Nights* to Safavid Iran: A Persian *Tawaddud*', *Der Islam* 94.1 (2017): 158–91.
William, Thomas Rhys, 'The Form and Function of Tambunan Dusun Riddles', *The Journal of American Folklore* 76 (1963): 75–110.

Index

Abbasid dynasty 216, 234, 241
Abū Bakr, Muḥammad b. Aḥmad b. 87
Abw (Elephantine Island) 180–1
Achaemenid Empire 171–2, 180–3, 189n.49
adab (refined courtly knowledge) 84, 87, 240
Adam and Eve 125–7
adīb (man of letters) 25
Aeneid 144
aesthetic qualities 9, 16, 199–200, 202–3, 206–7, 210
African-American studies 56, 62
Ahasuerus, King 207–8
Aḥmad al-Manṣūr 27
Aizenberg, Edna 117, 131–2n.26
al-Andalus 94, 210, 217
Aldhelm of Malmesbury, *Carmen de virginitate* 50
Alexander Romance
  aesthetic merits of 199–200
  authenticity and 209
  believability of 203–4
  Hebrew translations of 200–3
  illuminations in *204*
  popularity of 3–4, 15–16
  style of 205–8, 212n.12
  transmission history of 210–11
  see also romances
Alexander the Great 3, 16, 199
Alf Layla wa-Layla 234, 240
  see also Thousand and One Nights, The
Alfonsi, Petrus (Pedro Alfonso) 122
  Dialogi contra Judeos 115
  Disciplina clericalis 115
Alfonso VI, King of Castile and León 114, 118, 120, 125
Alfonso X, King of Castile 121–2
  Cantigas de Nuestra Señora 123, 134–5n.50
  Estoria de España 121
Alfonso XI, King of León 120
Alighieri, Dante 16
  Divina Commedia 224–7, 231n.20
  Inferno 126
Alter, Robert 200, 205, 208
Althusser, Louis 183
American University in Beirut (AUB) 31–3, 36
Andalusian texts 94–6
Andreas 51
Anglo-Saxon Chronicle 61

Anglo-Saxons 53, 55, 58–9
Angoulême cathedral 143
anonymous authors 8, 173, 199, 216, 218
  see also distributed authorship (Ascott)
anti-Judaism 14, 114–20, 123–7, 131–2n.26
Antolínez, Martín (el Cid's vassal) 115–16, 119, 123, 125
apothegms 178–9, 183, 192n.79
Apter, Emily 176
Aquinas, Thomas 124, 135n.52
Arabic Language Association 36
Arabic literature
  Alexander Romance and 199–200, 206, 209
  canon formation and 10
  Derenbourg and 23–4
  Hitti and 34–7
  Kalilah and Dimnah and 223
  in Leiden University Library 96–7
  manuscript notes in 100–1n.14
  The Neck-Ring of the Dove and 79–80
  popularity of texts in 4–6
  riddles in 245–9
  scholarship and 1–2
  Tawaddud/Teodor tales and 234–5
  wisdom literature and 216–17
Aramaic 172, 178, 180–3, 190n.58
Aristotelian ideals 9, 204
art 143, 156, 208–9, 213n.22
  see also telematic art
Arthur, King 3
Ascott, Roy, *La Plissure du Texte* 169–70
assemblages 235, 239, 241–4, 250–1, 254, 257n.23, 257n.26
Assyria 178, 182–3, 189n.49
astronomy 240–1
Atlanta University 56
authorship 216, 224–5, 227, 228n.4
  see also anonymous authors; distributed authorship (Ascott)
avarice 122–6
Ayyubid dynasty 26, 234, 241

Babinski, Paul 104–5n.40
badīʿ movement 25
Baghdad 234, 237
Bakhtin, Mikhail 184
Baldwin, James 65
Barlaam and Josaphat 6, 15–16, 216–21, 223–5, 227
Bar-sur-Aube, Bertrand de, *Girart de Vienne* 144
Barthes, Roland, *The Pleasure of the Text* 169–70
al-Bārūdī, Murād Bey 32, 43n.30
al-Bassām, Sulayman, *Kalilah and Dimnah; or, the Mirror for Princes* 225
Bayezid II 95
Bede 49–50
Bede's Death Song 13, 49–51
Bédier, Joseph 15
  Légendes épiques 145
Beinecke Rare Book and Manuscript Library, MS Heb. supplement 103 200–1, 206–7
Belgium 29
ben Jacob, Nissim 115
Benjamin, Walter 7, 213n.22
  'The Work of Art in the Age of Its Technological Reproducibility' 208–9
Beowulf
  American women and 56–7
  as children's literature 60
  history of 13–14
  Millay and 60–1
  modern canon and 3–4
  modern readings of 62–6
  as national epic 8

in nineteenth century 58–9
popularity of 50–1
Tolkien and 52–5
translatability of 205
wisdom literature and 215
Bernard of Clairvaux 126
bestsellers *see* popular texts
Bibles moralisées 123, 127, 134n.47
Biblioteca Estense, MS Liii 200
Biblioteca I. B. de Rossi, MS. heb. 1087 200
Bibliotheca Arabica 81, 101n.15
Bibliothèque nationale 95
MS héb. 671.5 200–1, 205–6
MS héb. 750.3 200–4, *204*, 209, 212n.8
Black Americans 56, 58–9, 69n.34
Blackmore, Josiah, *Queer Iberia* 152
Boccaccio, Giovanni 16
Corbaccio 226
Decameron 223–6, 230–1nn.18–19
Bodel, Jehan 144
Bodleian Library 140
MS Heb. d. 11, 200, 204, 207–8
Bonaventure 123–4
Bonfils, Immanuel ben Jacob 201–4, 209–10, 211n.5, 213n.24
Book of Contemplation (Usāma ibn Munqidh)
canon formation and 4, 13
Derenbourg and 24, 27–30
history of 25–7, 37–9, 40–1n.9, 45n.60
Munro and Hitti and 30–7
Book of Secundus, the 15–16, 215–17, 219–21, 223–5, 227, 228n.3, 229n.9
Booth, Marilyn 9
Bordeaux, France 155
Boyarin, Shamma 7, 16
Brawley, Benjamin Griffith 70n.39
A New Survey of English Literature 56
Breton, André, *Cadavre exquis* 169–70
Brooks, A. Russell 56
Brown, Anna Robertson
'The Battle with the Water-Sprite' 57
'The Passing of Scyld' 57
Bruns, Axel 170
Brut 2–3
Bryher 61
Beowulf 54
Buchanan, Peter 61
Buddhist literature 217–18
Burton, Richard 236, 240
Bynum, Caroline Walker 252

Cairo, Egypt 83–5, 89
Callisthenes 199
Cannon, Christopher 17n.4
capitalism 172, 175, 183
Carnegie family 28
Caro-Minasian collection 235
Carroll, Lewis, *Through the Looking Glass* 53
Castaño, Javier 118–21, 132n.33
castles 13, 32
Catholic Church 118–21, 124–7
Celebī, Kātib 26, 93, 107–8nn.64–5
Kashf al-ẓunūn 97
Cerquiglini, Bernard 140, 145
Chanson de Guillaume 144
Chanson de Roland, Alexander Romance and 210
Chanson de Roland, La
background and plot of 140–2
canonisation of 145–50
chansons de geste and 7
literary history and 143–4
as masterpiece 12–13
as modern bestseller 150–3, 159n.24
as national epic 8

as object biography 154–7
popularity of 14–15
chansons de geste 7, 15, 143–4, 146–7, 159n.21
Charlemagne 141–2, 148–50, 154–5, 159n.22
Chatel, Marie 169
Chaucer, Geoffrey 3, 17n.4
Chilam Balam of Kaua 236, 253
children's literature 3, 59–60
see also fairy tales
Chism, Christine 7, 16
chivalric imagery 28–9
Chobham, Thomas of 124–5
Chrétien de Troyes romances 141
Christ 114–15, 117–23, 125, 129n.11
Christians 116, 118–22, 125–6, 128, 147–52, 202–3, 210
Cid, El
anti-Judaism and 115–19
Christ and 129n.11
Jews and 127–8
thirty pieces of silver and 121
usury and 125–6
Cobb, Paul 7, 13, 45n.60
Cohen, Jeffrey Jerome, 'On Saracen Enjoyment' 152
coincidentia oppositorum (confrontation of meaningful opposites) 126–7
Colburn, Henry 171–2
Cole, Teju 54, 62–4
Open City 62–3
Collegiate Gothic style 28
colonialism 175–7, 253–5
see also imperialism; postcolonialism
colophons 82, 95, 102n.16, 114, 204
Columbia University 33, 35, 38
Columbia University Press 33, 36–7
Comestor, Petrus, *Historia Scholastica* 121
commoners 90, 104n.35
connectivity 171–2, 191n.67
Constantinople 79–80, 82, 94
see also Istanbul
Conybeare, John Josias, *Illustrations of Anglo-Saxon Poetry* 52
copyists *see* scribes
cordel narratives 235
counter-canon 7
see also modern canon
Crichton, Michael, *Eaters of the Dead* 54
Critical Race studies 150–3, 157
criticism *see* literary scholarship
Crusades 13, 24–5, 28–33, 121
Cubitt, Sean 171
cultural contexts
Alexander Romance and 209, 212n.11
encyclopaedism and 240–2
Life of Aḥiqār and 180–3
riddles and 244–5, 253
Tawaddud/Teodor tales and 235–6
translated texts and 9
world literature and 176–7
curricula 2–3, 8, 55, 79, 140, 150, 176, 224
Cuthbert 50
cybernetics 169
Cyrus the Great 181

Dailey, Patricia 254
Damascus, Syria 25, 28–9
Damrosch, David 176–7, 180, 184
Dante *see* Alighieri, Dante
D'Aulnoy, Madame 4
defamiliarisation 238, 244, 254
Deleuze, Gilles 239
Del governo de' regni see Kalilah and Dimnah
De Man, Paul 174
Derbes, Ann 126
Derenbourg, Hartwig
discovery of *Book of Contemplation* and 13, 23–4, 40n.1

history of *Book of Contemplation* and 38
Hitti and 34–5
Munro and 30–2
translation of *Book of Contemplation* and 27–30
ʿUmāra and 41n.12
Usāma ibn Munqidh and 39
Deuteronomy, Book of 206–7
al-Dhahabī 26
Díaz de Vivar, Rodrigo 113, 129–30n.12
see also Cid, El
didacticism 16, 216, 222–5, 236, 255
Diego, Bishop 118
distributed authorship (Ascott) 15–16, 169–70, 172–4, 179–80, 183–4
Dockray-Miller Mary 55, 57, 68–9nn.31–3
Donoghue, Daniel 50
Duggan, Joseph 143, 146
Durendal (Roland's sword) 149, 154–5, 161n.34, 162n.40

Egypt 89, 180–2
embedded narratives 218–21, 222, 226
encyclopaedism
knowledge and 238–9
riddles and 245–6, 254
worlding and 235, 239–44, 250–1
Engels, Friedrich, *Communist Manifesto* 175
entertainment 16, 222–5, 239, 243–9
Epic of Gilgamesh 172–4, 177, 184–5
epic poems 8, 15, 51, 113–14, 144–5, 174
see also chansons de geste; poetry
Epistola de obitu Bedae (Letter on the Death of Bede) 50
Esarhaddon 178, 182–3, 189n.46
Escorial Library 4, 13, 23–4, 26–7, 35, 38
Esther, Book of 207–8
Esther, Queen 207–8
estrangement 245–7, 250
Eugenio, Damiana L. 235
Europe 1–4, 10, 12, 15, 175–6, 216–18
Evans, Austin P. 33
Exemplario contra los engaños, y peligros del mundo. see Kalilah and Dimnah
Exodus, Book of 181, 191n.61

fairy tales 4–5, 169
see also children's literature
fanfiction 170–1, 186n.14
father figures 218–21, 224
Fatimid dynasty 26
Fazienda de ultramar 121–2
Fernando I, King of Spain 118
Fernando III, King of Spain 118
Fiske, Christabel 61
Fisk University 56
Flusser, David 201
framing narratives 216–18, 220, 222–4, 226, 234, 239, 242
France 14–15, 29, 140–1, 143–5
Franco-Prussian War 145
Franks 30–1, 140–2, 148–50

Galland, Antoine 4–5, 80
Gardner, John, *Grendel* 54, 65
Garrett, Robert 32
Garrett Collection (Princeton University) 32
Gautier, Léon 145
Geisel, Theodor (Dr. Seuss) 60
gender relations 221, 224, 226
genealogical analysis 217, 227
Genesis, Book of 121–2, 124–6, 178, 226
Gerli, Michael 113
Gerresch, Claudine 234
Giles, Ryan 7, 14

Gilman, Sander 125
Giotto di Bondone
Last Judgment 136n.67
Visitation of Mary and Elizabeth 126
globalisation 171–2, 177
Godfrey of Viterbo 133n.43
Pantheon / *Liber universalis* 122
Gospel of John 122
Gospel of Luke 125
Gospel of Matthew 121–2
Gottheil, Richard 33
Gower, John 3, 17n.4
grammatical errors 87, 89–90
Gratian, *Decretum* 124
Grousset, René, *Histoire des Croisades et du royaume franc de Jérusalem* 28
Gullah 56
Gwinn, Mary, 'The Ballad of Hart Hall' 57

ḥadīth (prophetic traditions) 92, 95, 107n.57, 241, 245
Hadrian, Emperor 220
Ḥājjī Khalīfa *see* Celebī, Kātib
Hall, Stuart 54, 62
Hallam, Arthur Henry 58
al-Hamadhānī 5, 245
Haman (biblical villain) 207
handwriting 84, 86, 90–1
al-Ḥarīrī 245
Maqāmāt 5–6, 85, 205
Harvard University 56, 62, 176
Headley, Maria Dahvana, *The Mere Wife* 54
Heaney, Seamus 63–4
Hebrew 115, 199–208, 210, 217
Heidegger, Martin 184
Held, David 177
Heller-Roazen, Daniel 171
Heng, Geraldine, *The Invention of Race in the European Middle Ages* 153
Hess, Steven 113–14
Hickes, George, *Thesaurus* 51
Historia Hierosolymitana 121
historical chronicles 144, 155
Historically Black Colleges and Universities (HBCUs) 55–6, 68–9n.31
Hitti, Philip 31–9, 45–6n.62
al-Hoda newspaper 35, 44n.47
Hollywood 54
Holsinger, Bruce, 'The Color of Salvation' 151
Holthausen, F. 61
Howard University 56, 69n.34
Hutcheson, Gregory, *Queer Iberia* 152
hybrid texts 201
Hystoria de Juda 122

Iberia 115–16, 118–20, 152
see also Spain
Ibn al-Muqaffaʿ 216, 226
Ibn al-Nadīm 11, 216–17
Ibn al-Sammān, ʿAlī b. Ḥājj Abū Bakr 88–90, 96
Ibn al-Walīd 25
Ibn ʿAsākir 25
Ibn Bassām, *Dakhīra* 238
Ibn Ḥazm
al-Muḥallā 95
manuscript creation and 82–3
The Neck-Ring of the Dove and 4, 13–14, 79, 99
popularity of 94–6, 100n.11
Risāla fī faḍl al-Andalus 96
Ibn Qayyim al-Jawzīya 100n.11
Ibn Taghrī Birdī, *al-Nujūm al-zāhira* 89
Ibn Ṭufayl, *Ḥayy Ibn Yaqẓān* 80
Ibn Zamrak 4
Ifranj (medieval term for Europeans) 13, 24
ijāza (certificate of authority) 11
Iliad 144, 174
illuminations 202–3, 211–12n.7
imperialism 10, 113, 172, 175–7, 180–2, 191n.67
see also colonialism

International Congress on Medieval Studies 63
Iran 189n.49
Irwin, Robert 236
al-Isbahānī, *Kitāb al-aghānī* 243
al-Iṣfahānī, ʿImād al-Dīn 25
Islamic scholars 96, 234, 237–43
Islamic world 15, 94, 162n.40, 177, 235
  see also Middle East; Muslims
Istanbul 91–2, 95–6
  see also Constantinople

al-Jāḥiẓ, *Risālat al-qiyān* 243
Jaillant, Lise 60
Jerusalem 86–7, 120–1
Jews
  Achaemenid Empire and 180–1
  Alexander Romance and 210
  Judas Iscariot and 127
  in *Poema de mio Cid* 114–17
  thirty pieces of silver and 118–23
  usury and 124–6
Jones, Chris 52, 57–9, 70n.48
Joseph (prophet) 121–2, 226
Josephus 201
Judas Iscariot 116, 118–19, 121–2, 126–7, 136n.67

Kaivola-Bregenhøj, Annikki 245
Kalamazoo, Michigan 63
Kalilah and Dimnah 15–16, 79, 216–27, 228n.7
Kay, Sarah 144
Kelmscott Press 59
Kemble, John Mitchell 52, 57–8
Kerkering, John D. 58–9
Khalidi Library 86
Khayat, Paul 36
Khayat Publishing 36–7
Kim, Dorothy 53–4
Kinoshita, Sharon 7, 14
Kitāb al-Iʿtibār see Book of Contemplation (Usāma ibn Munqidh)

knowledge
  encyclopaedism and 240–2
  riddles and 243–8, 253–4
  worldings and 238–9
Kramer, Samuel N. 173
Kratchkowsky, Ignace 98, 108n.69

Labīd 26
Lacarra, María Eugenia 113–14
La Moral' filosophia del Doni see Kalilah and Dimnah
Lane, Edward William 235–6
Lane-Poole, Stanley, *Saladin and the Fall of the Kingdom of Jerusalem* 31
Langland, William 3, 17n.4
Lanier, Sidney 57–9
Latin legends 116
Lavezzo, Kathy 54
Lawrence, T. E. 28
Layard, Austen Henry 177
Lebanon 31–2
Leeuwen, Richard van, *Encyclopedia of the Arabian Nights* 240
Legatum Warnerianum 80, 97, 107–8n.64
Le Goff, Jacques 124, 135n.56
Leiden University Library 80, 85–6, 90–1, 94–5, 97, 104n.37, 104–5n.40
Letter of Alexander to Aristotle 4
Levantine-Mediterranean world-system 180, 184, 190n.56
Levi, Israel 201, 209, 213n.23
Lévi-Provençal, Évariste 4
Liber monstrorum 51
Liber Sancti Jacobi 155, 161–2nn.38–9
Liebrenz, Boris 7, 14, 108n.66
lieu de mémoire 140, 150, 154
Life of Aḥiqār
  cultural context of 181–2
  distributed authorship and 15–16, 179–80

popularity of 177–8
world literature and 183–5
linotype printing 35–6, 44nn.49–50
Lipton, Sara 123, 127
literacy 10–11, 146
literary culture
Beowulf and 57
Chanson de Roland and 14–15
Life of Aḥiqār and 184
in medieval western Europe 12
in Middle East 10–12
non-Western traditions and 175–7
riddles and 245–6, 249–50
literary history
Beowulf and 62–3
Chanson de Roland and 143
formation of canon and 16–17
imperialism and 10
Life of Aḥiqār and 179–81
textual differences and 171
in United States 55–6
wisdom literature and 226–7
literary scholarship
Alexander Romance and 199–200
Arabic literature and 4–6, 11–12
Beowulf and 52–7, 66
canon formation and 6–8, 13
Chanson de Roland and 150
European literature and 3–4
Life of Aḥiqār and 179
literary history and 16–17
of *The Neck-Ring of the Dove* 79–81, 98–9
Poema de mio Cid and 113–14
of popular texts and 1–3
reading and 173–4
Usāma ibn Munqidh and 29–30
Longfellow, Henry Wadsworth 57, 62
López, Macario Sánchez 35
López González, Luis 118, 121
Lourié, Basil 180
love 14, 79, 92, 94–6, 225
Lydgate, John 56
Lyons, Malcolm C. 236
Lyons, Ursula 236

Macmillan Company 37
Madrid, Spain 23–4, 29
Mallette, Karla 7, 16
Malory, Thomas, *Morte d'Arthur* 28
Mamluk era 82, 86, 94, 241
manuscript notes 81, 83–94, 99, 100–1nn.12–14, 102–3n.26, 105n.41
manuscripts
Chanson de Roland and 143
colonialism and 175–7
copies of medieval English literature and 50
creation of *The Neck-Ring of the Dove* and 82–3
Derenbourg and 23–4
Hebrew translations of Alexander Romance and 200–6, *204*, 209
in Leiden University Library 90–1, 95, 104n.37, 104–5n.40
MS Leiden Or. 927 and 80–1
survival of 3–4
wisdom literature and 226
manuscript stemma 7, 80, 100nn.8–9, 145, *179*, 210
maqāmāt genre 5–6, 245
al-Maqqarī, *Nafḥ al-ṭīb* 96
Mardam Bey, Khalīl 36
Mark, Joshua J. 174
Marrakesh, Morocco 26–7
Marshall, Henrietta Elizabeth, *Stories of Beowulf* 60
Marx, Karl, *Communist Manifesto* 175
Marxism 54
Marzolph, Ulrich, *Encyclopedia of the Arabian Nights* 240
Marzouki, Samir 151

masterpieces 1–2, 16, 224–5
materialism 38–9
materiality 82–3
Mayans 235–6, 244, 253–5
McGrady, Donald 117
medievalism 52, 56, 60
  see also romantic medievalism
medieval literature 1–4, 6–10, 50, 56
  see also Old English literature
Mediterranean 15
memory 14, 62–4, 147–8, 159n.23
Memphis, Egypt 181–2
Menéndez Pidal, Ramón 14, 113–15, 117, 127–8, 128n.7, 130–1nn.21–2
Mergenthaler Printing Company 35–6, 44–5nn.48–50
Mevlevī dervishes 91
Meyere, Eduard 183
Michel, Francisque 145
Middle Ages 2–4, 8, 10–11, 25–6, 115–19
Middle East 10–12, 31, 81
  see also Islamic world
middle voice 170, 173
Millay, Edna St Vincent, *The King's Henchman* 60–1, 72nn.73–4
misogyny 16, 219–20, 223–6
Modena cathedral 143
modern canon
  Beowulf and 51–5
  Book of Contemplation and 38–9
  Chanson de Roland and 140, 145–50
  formation of 7–10, 16–17
  medieval popularity of texts and 1–4, 6
  nineteenth and twentieth century scholarship and 13
  Poema de mio Cid and 113
  as recent phenomenon 60
  wisdom literature and 16, 223–4
  world literature and 176
  see also counter-canon
Mokarzel, Salloum 35–6, 44n.47
Momma, Haruko 52
money 93, 118–22, 123–7, 134n.49, 135n.56
moneylenders 114, 116–19, 121–8, 131n.23, 134–5n.50, 135n.54
  see also usury
Morris, William 57, 59, 71n.62
Morrison, Toni 54, 65–6
  'Grendel and his Mother' 65
MS Berlin Petermann II 594 95, 100n.11
MS Leiden Or. 927 *see Neck-Ring of the Dove, The*
MS Paris, BnF Arabe 3414 91
Muhanna, Elias 242
Mūlay Zaydān 26
multiculturalism 176, 181–3
Munro, Dana Carleton 30–3, 42n.23, 43n.35
Murad IV 92
Muslims 24, 29–30, 120–1, 151–3, 247–9
  see also Islamic world
mutuality of making (Cubitt) 171

al-Nahāwandī, Sharaf al-Dīn Muḥammad b. ʿUthmān b. Abī Bakr 83–7, 101n.13
narrative networks 15, 51, 184, 216–18, 236, 254–5
  see also networks
narrative structure 16
narrative traditions 16, 216–22, 225–7
nationalism (and national literature)
  Beowulf and 53–4, 60
  canon formation and 6–8
  Chanson de Roland and 140, 145, 150, 157, 159–60n.25
  Derenbourg and 41–2n.18
  distributed authorship and 15

Life of Aḥiqār and 179–80, 192n.72
Menéndez Pidal and 113–14
modern canon and 7–8
Poema de mio Cid and 113–14, 127–8
al-Nawājī, *Ḥalbat al-Kumayt* 90, 96, 104n.39
al-Naẓẓām, Ibrahīm (Tawaddud's examiner) 237, 239, 246, 250–3
Neck-Ring of the Dove, The
creation of manuscript and 82–3
history in East of 83–94
manuscript notes in 101n.13
modern canon and 4, 13–14
popularity of 79–81
scarcity of 94–6
transmission history of 98–9
Warner and 96–8
Nectanebus (astrologer) 205–7, 211–12n.7, 212n.12
networks 171–2
see also narrative networks
New Historicism 200
New Philology 59
New York City Metropolitan Opera 60–1
Nibelungenlied 144
Nykl, A. R. 84, 101n.13

O'Berski, Mark 61
O'Camb, Brian 51
Odyssey 144
Oedipal narrative 122, 219
Old English 51–3, 55–8, 64, 205
Old English literature 13–14, 49–54, 61, 69n.33, 70n.39
see also medieval literature
Old French 56, 143
oliphants 142, 154–6, 161n.35, 161–2nn.39–40, 162n.47
oral tradition 12, 50, 113–14, 129n.9, 145–8, 218
Orientalism 31–2, 41–2n.18, 140, 153
orphan texts *see* unica manuscripts
orthographic errors 89–90
Orton, Peter 50
Ottoman Empire 89, 91–4
Oxford University 55, 60–2

pagans 147–51, 160n.26
Pahlavi 216–17
Paris, BnF Arabe 3939 85
Parker, Margaret 235
Parkinson, Richard 184
Parry-Lord thesis 146
participatory poiesis 170–1
Paton, David 32
Pelayo, Bishop 118–19
Penguin Classics 37
Pennsylvania History of the Crusades 31
Perrault, Charles 4–5
Persia 92, 207
Petrarch
Canzoniere or *Rerum vulgarium fragmenta* 225
De remediis utriusque fortunae 216, 225
Pétrof, Dmitrii Konstantinovich 14, 80, 97–8, 108n.69
Philip II, King of Spain 23–4
Philippines 235, 244, 254–5
philology 30, 41–2n.18, 52, 56, 58, 97–8, 113–14, 145, 189n.43, 254–5
photostatic reproductions 35, 44nn.43–4
Pick, Lucy 118–20
Piers Plowman 54, 62
Plato, *Timaeus* 141
Poe, Edgar Allan 173
Poema de mio Cid
anti-Judaism in 130n.21
modern canon and 13–14
as national epic 8, 113–14, 127–8
thirty pieces of silver and 122–3

treatment of Jews in 114–19
usury and 124–7
see also Vivar codex
Poet Lore journal 57, 70n.40
poetry
Beowulf and 52–3, 57, 60–6
manuscript notes and 102–3n.26
manuscript notes in *The Neck-Ring of the Dove* and 85, 88–90, 94
medieval Hebrew and 206–7
in Middle East 84
The Neck-Ring of the Dove and 95–6
Petrarch and 225
Usāma ibn Munqidh and 25–6
see also epic poems
politics 120, 170, 176, 182–4, 221
popular texts
Alexander Romance and 16, 199, 202–5, 210–11
Arabic literature and 4–6
authenticity and 208–9
Bede's Death Song and 49–50
Beowulf and 51–5
Chanson de Roland and 143, 150–3, 159n.24
as counter-canon 7
European literature and 3–4
Life of Aḥiqār and 177–8, 184
in medieval Middle East 11–12
in medieval western Europe 12
The Neck-Ring of the Dove and 79–81, 94
reception and 15
scholarship and 1–3
translation and 9
wisdom literature and 223–6
postcolonialism 150–3, 176
see also colonialism
poststructuralism 54
Prick of Conscience, The 2, 6
Princeton Oriental Texts 36
Princeton University 30, 31–3
Princeton University Press 36
printing press 12, 223
produsage (Brun) 170
Propp, Vladimir, *Morphology of the Folktale* 169

qiyān (well-educated enslaved women) 237–9, 243–4, 256n.16
Qur'ān 35, 95, 226, 240–1, 248, 251–2
Queensland University of Technology 170

race 53, 59, 73n.90, 117, 132n.27
Rachel and Vidas *see* moneylenders
racism 55–6, 58–60, 62–3, 69n.33, 132n.27, 150–3
see also white supremacy
Ramírez del Río, José 115
Rare Book and Manuscript Library (Columbia University) 35
Rassam, Hormuzd 177
reading 11, 173–4
Real Academia de Historia 234
reality 221
reception history 25–6, 39, 183, 222, 225–7
'Records of Civilization' (Columbia University Press) 33, 38
redactions 173–4, 180–3, 191n.61, 222
Reeves, Roger, 'Grendel' 65
Reiske, Johann Jacob 97–8
religious violence 120, 151
Remein, Daniel 7, 13
reproduction
of art 208–9
of money 124–5, 128, 135nn.55–6
Resnick, Seymour 117–18
Reynolds, Dwight 243
rhetoric 246–52

riddles
defamiliarisation and 244–50
encyclopaedism and 243–4
Tawaddud's examination and 237–9
worlding and 235, 250–3
al-Riṣāṣ, ʿAlāʾ al-Dīn ʿAlī b. 85–7
Rivera, Isidro J. 235
Rockefeller family 28
Rogers, Donna M. 235
romances 3, 144–5
see also Alexander Romance
Roman de Roncevaux 140, 143, 145
romantic medievalism 28–9, 41–2n.18, 225
see also medievalism
Rosen, Victory 98, 108n.69
rubrication 82–3
Ruiz, José Vasquez 234

Ṣabūḥī efendī 91
sacred fisc 118–22, 127, 132n.33
Ṣafad, Palestine 83–5, 86
al-Ṣafadī, Khalīl Ibn Aybak 84, 89
Safi, Morocco 27
Ṣafī al-Dīn, Shaykh 91
sagas *see* epic poems
Sainte Foy de Conques 143, 158n.6
Saint Seurin de Bordeaux 155
al-Sakhāwī, Muḥammad b. ʿAbd al-Raḥmān 86
Saladin 25, 28–9, 38–9, 41n.16, 42n.20
Salvador Miguel, Nicasio 118
al-Sāmarrāʾī, Qāsim 24
sand-filled chest deception 114–17
Sandona, Mark 126
Sanhedrin 118, 123, 126
San Lorenzo Monastery 23–4
San Pedro de Cardeña monastery 115, 119
Sanskrit 216–17
Santiago de Compostela 155, 158n.6
sapiential literature *see* wisdom literature
Saracens 140–2, 146, 151–5, 160n.26
Saragossa, Spain 140–1
Scandanavian literature 51
Schichler, Robert L. 60
scholarship *see* Islamic scholars; literary scholarship
Schulman, Jana 55
Scott, Sir Walter 29
Ivanhoe 52
scribes 82–7, 95, 173–4, 181–3, 187n.21, 199–201, 218
see also copyists
Scrovegni, Enrico 126
Scrovegni, Reginaldo 126
Scrovegni chapel 126
Scyldings (medieval Danish dynasty) 51
secretarial arts 92
Secundus *see* Book of Secundus, The
Selden, Daniel 3, 7–8, 15–16
Semitic literature 32–3
Senderovich, Savely 246
Setton, Kenneth 31
Seuss, Dr *see* Geisel, Theodor (Dr Seuss)
Seven Sages of Rome 6, 15–16, 216–24, 226–7, 229–30n.11, 231n.23
sexuality 152, 224, 246, 249
Seybold, Christian Friedrich 98, 108n.69
Shafi' school 236, 240
Shankar, Naren 65
Shayzar, Syria 25, 32, 39, 43n.29
Sindbād al-Ḥakīm 216–17
single manuscript exemplars *see* unica manuscripts
Sîn-lēqi-unninni 172
Sir Gawain and the Green Knight 4, 12
Skeat, W. W. 63
Smith, Colin 117
Smith, George 177
Sobre la secta mahometana 121

social systems 90, 171, 177, 181, 184, 242
Song of Roland. *see Chanson de Roland, La*
Southern, Robert, *The Making of the Middle Ages* 144
Spain 27, 113–14, 141–2, 235, 253
see also Iberia
Spelman College 56
Spitzer, Leo 117, 130–1n.22
Spivak, Gayatri 238, 257n.20
Staatsbibliothek München 95
Staatsbibliothek zu Berlin 95
Star Trek: Voyager 64–5, 73n.90
Stein, Robert 144, 146, 157
Strong, Archibald 53
style 82–3, 200, 205–8, 210–11
Sufis 91–2
Sünnetçioğlu, Evren 104–5n.40
sūq al-warrāqīn (bookseller marketplace) 11
Swedish–Geatish wars 51
Sweet, Henry, *Anglo-Saxon Reader* 61, 72n.73
Syria 24–5, 31–2
Syriac 180, 210, 217
Syrian-American Press 35
Syrian World, The magazine 36

'Tale of Abū'l Ḥusn and his Slave Girl, Tawaddud The' 234
taste 2–3, 6, 9–10, 51, 95–6
Tawaddud/Teodor tales
assemblages and 257n.23
encyclopaedism in 235–6, 239–44
examination of Tawaddud and 237–9
popularity of 15–16
riddles in 244–50
Tawaddud's final contest 250–3
transmission history of 234–5
wonder in 254–5
Ṭawq al-ḥamāma see Neck-Ring of the Dove, The
tax 181–2
see also sacred fisc
telematic art 169–70
see also art
Tennyson, Alfred Lord 70n.48
'Battle of Brunanburh' 57
In Memoriam A. H. H. 58
'Sonnet to J. M. K(emble)' 58
territorialisation 241–2
thirty pieces of silver 116–23, 127, 133–4n.44
Thomas, Clara *The Adventures of Beowulf* 59–60
Thorkelín, Grímur Jónsson 54
Thousand and One Nights, The
Calcutta II edition 234–6, 240
canon formation and 4–6
distributed authorship and 171
qiyān in 243–4
Tawaddud/Teodor tales and 237–9, 254–5
Ṭiflī, Aḥmad 90–3, 104–5n.40
Tillman, Nathaniel 56
Titus, Emperor of Rome 118, 121
Tolkien, J. R. R. 14, 52–7, 62, 66, 68n.25
Beowulf and the Critics 53–4
'*Beowulf*: The Monsters and the Critics' 52–3, 68n.18
translation
of Alexander Romance 16, 199–206, 209–10, 211n.1
of Arabic texts 12
of *Beowulf* 56–7, 59
of *Book of Contemplation* 27–8, 34–5, 37
of Book of Secundus 221
of *Chanson de Roland* 150
Life of Aḥiqār and 180
of *The Neck-Ring of the Dove* 79, 97–8, 108n.66
popular texts and 2–3
of Seven Sages of Rome 222–3
The Thousand and One Nights and 4–5

wisdom literature and 216–18
world literature and 176–7
transmission histories
of Alexander Romance 199, 209–10
Beowulf and 62
canon formation and 9
Chanson de Roland and 14, 143
Life of Aḥiqār and 183–4
of *The Neck-Ring of the Dove* 79–81, 83–95
The Neck-Ring of the Dove as unicum manuscript 98–9
of *The Neck-Ring of the Dove* in Leiden and 96–8
of Seven Sages of Rome 222, 229–30n.11
of Tawaddud/Teodor tales 254–5
of Tawaddud/Teodor tales and 234–6
of wisdom literature 216–18, 223, 226–7
Trethewey, Natasha 54
Domestic Work 64
Turner, Lorenzo Dow 62
Africanisms in the Gullah Dialect 56
Turner, Sharon, *The History of the Manners, Landed Property, Government, Laws, Poetry, Literature, Religion, and Language, of the Anglo-Saxons* 52

unica manuscripts
(un)translatability of 205
of Arabic texts 12, 108n.70
authenticity and 208–9
as authoritative texts 7–8
Beowulf and 54, 66
canon formation and 6–8
Chanson de Roland and 140, 142
as masterpieces 13–14
The Neck-Ring of the Dove and 79–81, 94–5, 98–9
Poema de mio Cid and 114–15, 127
popularity of 1–4
The Thousand and One Nights and 5
United States 30, 31, 55–8
University of Chicago 56
University of Minnesota 32
University of Pennsylvania 30, 31
al-ʿUrḍī, Abū l-Wafā 93, 96–7
Usāma ibn Munqidh
Book of Contemplation and 4, 13, 25–6
Dīwān 25
history of *Book of Contemplation* and 37–9
Hitti and 45–6n.62
Kitāb al-Badīʿ 27
modern canon and 29–35
reputation of 40n.7
writing of *Book of Contemplation* 24–7
usury 116, 123–7, 135nn.55–6
see also moneylenders

Vallvé, Manuel 60
van Koningsveld P. S. 84, 102n.16
Vassar College 61
Venjeance Nostre Seigneur, La 121
Vernon, Matthew X. 55–6
Vindicta Salvatoris 120–2, 133n.43
Virgil 224
Virgin Mary 126
Vitry, Jacques de 126, 136n.64
Vivar codex 114–16, 129n.9
see also Poema de mio Cid
Voragine, Jacobus de 123
Legenda aurea 121–2, 134n.45
Vračanski, Sofronij 222

Wanley, Humphrey 51
al-Wardī, Zayn al-Dīn ʿUmar b. 89

Warner, Levinus 79–82, 91–3, 95–7, 99, 100n.10, 107–8n.64
al-Washsha, *Kitāb al-Muwashshā* 243
Weaver, Erica 7, 13
White, Hayden 170, 173
White, James 96
Whitelock, Dorothy 55
white supremacy 54–5, 64–5, 69n.33
  see also racism
Wilhelm II, Kaiser of Germany 28
William and Annie S. Paton Foundation 32–3
Wills, Lawrence 183
Wisconsin History of the Crusades *see* Pennsylvania History of the Crusades
wisdom literature
  genealogical analysis of 227
  Life of Aḥiqār and 178–9, 182–3
  masterpieces and 224–5
  narrative traditions of 218–1
  Tawaddud/Teodor tales and 234
  translation of 222–3
  transmission histories of 215–18
wisdom literature, popularity of 15–16, 225–6
wit 242–3
Witkam, Jan Just 84, 108n.66
women
  Beowulf and 55–7
  chansons de geste and 144–5
  misogyny and 16
  in wisdom literature 219–20, 222
  women's colleges and 55, 68–9n.31
wonder 243–5, 249–54
Woolf, Virginia 55
worlding 181–3, 235, 238–45, 250, 254
world literature 7, 15–16, 169, 174–7, 179, 183–5
World War I 28–9
Wulfstan Cantor, *Narratio metrica* 13, 50
Wyatt, A. J. 59
Wyrick, Jed 173

Yoruba 64
Yosippon 200–1, 211n.4

Ẓāhirism 95, 107n.55
Zangid dynasty 26
Zechariah, Book of 121

EU authorised representative for GPSR:
Easy Access System Europe, Mustamäe tee 50,
10621 Tallinn, Estonia
gpsr.requests@easproject.com

www.ingramcontent.com/pod-product-compliance
Lightning Source LLC
Chambersburg PA
CBHW051604230426
43668CB00013B/1979